Africa's Development Dynamics 2018

GROWTH, JOBS AND INEQUALITIES

The opinions expressed and arguments employed herein do not necessarily reflect the official views of the African Union Commission; of the OECD, its Development Centre or their member countries.

This document, as well as any data and any map included herein, are without prejudice to the status of or sovereignty over any territory, to the delimitation of international frontiers and boundaries and to the name of any territory, city or area.

Please cite this publication as:
AUC/OECD (2018), *Africa's Development Dynamics 2018: Growth, Jobs and Inequalities*, AUC, Addis Ababa/OECD Publishing, Paris.
https://doi.org/10.1787/9789264302501-en

ISBN 978-92-64-30249-5 (print)
ISBN 978-92-64-30250-1 (PDF)

African Union Commission
ISBN 978-92-95104-14-3 (print)
ISBN 978-92-95104-15-0 (PDF)

Photo credits: Cover design by Aida Buendia (OECD Development Centre) on the basis of images from Smilewithme, Taparong Siri, Sidhe, baldyrgan/Shutterstock.com

Corrigenda to OECD publications may be found on line at: *www.oecd.org/about/publishing/corrigenda.htm*.

Foreword

This new annual report, *Africa's Development Dynamics*, analyses the continent's development policies. It presents a fresh narrative on Africa's development, assessing the economic, social and institutional performance in light of targets of the African Union's Agenda 2063. This first edition examines the relations between growth, employment and inequalities in Africa and draws strategic policy implications.

Africa's Development Dynamics 2018 is the product of a collaborative approach. It results from a unique, broad partnership between the African Union's Commission for Economic Affairs and the OECD Development Centre. A team of academic researchers, economists, statisticians, and other experts from Africa and diverse world regions contributed to this edition.

The report contains eight chapters. The first offers an overview of Africa's development dynamics and its integration into the global economy. The second chapter introduces five key trends shaping the continent's current and future development dynamics. Chapters 3 to 7 focus on Africa's five regions as defined by the Abuja Treaty. They provide detailed analyses of growth, employment and inequalities and offer tailored policy recommendations for each region. The final chapter wraps up the analysis by recommending ten policy actions that can help Africa achieve its development targets.

The statistical annex, published online, contains the latest economic, social and institutional indicators across African countries for which data is comparable. This compilation of policy-relevant data can inform decision makers, advisors, business analysts, private sector actors, journalists, non-governmental organisations and engaged citizens around the globe interested in measuring African countries' development trajectories.

Editorial

This first edition of the African Union Commission's Annual Economic Report, produced with the OECD Development Centre, plays a part in furthering the project to integrate and transform Africa as set out by the adoption of Agenda 2063 in January 2015 and of the Continental Free Trade Area in March 2018. These pan-African initiatives are milestones along the path towards a united, integrated, peaceful and prosperous Africa that can participate fully in international governance.

The aim of this new report is to illuminate this path in the context of globalisation. By analysing the economic development of Africa using an African analytic grid, it will contribute to the definition and implementation of innovative policies that are adapted to the specific characteristics of each economy and that further the African Union's priorities. Each year, the report will address a strategic theme for the realisation of Agenda 2063, specifying its vision at the national, regional and continental levels. The comparative analysis of Regional Economic Communities (RECs) in Southern, Central, East, North and West Africa also will be enhanced with local and national examples. In addition to encouraging open dialogue between African decision makers, the report will document best practices, identify grey areas and assess the need for comparable data and statistics to better evaluate policies.

Africa's Development Dynamics is the first report of its kind by the AU Commission at the initiative of its Department of Economic Affairs. Conceived and developed by African experts, supported by the OECD, it aims to fuel debate between members of the Union, citizens, business people and researchers. It also undertakes to bring an African contribution to fair and sustainable models of development, and to play a part in the development of a new kind of international co-operation more focused on mutual learning and the co-construction of public policy necessary for the preservation of our shared resources. It is to this end that the African Union Commission requested that the OECD Development Centre (of which nine member states are equally AU members) extend its partnership to the production of this report.

This year's theme "Growth, Jobs and Inequalities" is central to Agenda 2063: the goal of a prosperous African population requires strong, sustainable and inclusive growth that creates decent jobs and reinforces social cohesion by curbing inequality. Although Africa has the second highest rate of gross domestic product (GDP) growth in the world – it should reach 3.7% in 2018 – this remains below the goal fixed by African leaders of 7% annual growth over a long period. In addition, while extreme poverty has declined, it still affects 35% of Africans, or 395 million people. Lastly, the multiple inequalities of access to economic and social opportunities, particularly for women and the young, are such that they hinder the effectiveness of public policy and social cohesion.

In confronting these challenges, Africa possesses several assets including: a young and entrepreneurial population, territories that are transforming quickly with growing regions and rapid urbanisation, considerable natural resources, dynamic economies, rich ecosystems and a supportive diaspora. If, too often, policy has not managed to harness these resources effectively, then new strategic approaches are necessary.

This report takes up the challenge by proposing ten key actions to guide development strategies and accompanies them with specific recommendations for the five regions. These ten actions focus on: sustainable *economic* development by stimulating domestic investment, diversifying exports, deepening rural-urban linkages and promoting green growth; inclusive *social* development, through education provision aligned with labour market needs and effective and universal social protection; and lastly, stronger *institutions* via real regional integration, better mobilisation of domestic resources and ongoing improvement of political and economic governance.

Realising the African Union's vision will require strong, innovative partnerships that draw on lessons from the past. To this end, the AU Commission has committed with the OECD to supporting the efforts of both its members and the RECs to develop, promote and introduce better policies for better lives in order to improve the well-being of the population, and the prosperity of the African continent.

Moussa Faki Mahamat
Chairperson
African Union Commission

Angel Gurría
Secretary-General
Organisation for Economic Co-operation and Development

Acknowledgements

The annual economic report *Africa's Development Dynamics 2018: Growth, Jobs and Inequalities* was jointly prepared by the African Union Commission and the Development Centre of the Organisation for Economic Co-operation and Development (OECD). It is published under the aegis of H.E. Moussa Faki Mahamat, Chairperson of the African Union Commission, and H.E. Angel Gurría, Secretary-General of the OECD. It was guided by H.E. Victor Harison, Commissioner for Economic Affairs of the African Union, and Mario Pezzini, Director of the Development Centre and Special Advisor to the OECD Secretary-General on Development. The report was initiated by René N'Guettia Kouassi, Director of Economic Affairs of the African Union Commission, who supervised its writing with Federico Bonaglia, Deputy-Director of the OECD Development Centre.

The team of the African Union Commission was led by René N'Guettia Kouassi, Director of Economic Affairs, with Ligane Massamba Sène, Economist, Economic Policy and Research Division. The members of the team included Désiré Avom (University of Dschang), Jude Eggoh (University of Angers), Kouadio Clément Kouakou (Université Félix Houphouët-Boigny), Joweria Teera Mayanja and Ibrahim Mukisa (Makerere University), Chrispin Mphuka (University of Zambia) and Mohamed Ben Omar Ndiaye (Cheikh Anta Diop University of Dakar). The team at the OECD Development Centre, led by Arthur Minsat, Head of Unit for Africa, with Bakary Traoré, Economist, included Rodrigo Deiana, Sébastien Markley, Thắng Nguyễn-Quốc as well as Hamsa Hefny, Clémence Pougué Biyong, Yosra Elchinnawy and Semhar Haile, helped by contributions by Jason Gagnon, Michael Stemmer, Manuel Toselli and Carine Viac. The report also benefited from valuable data by Vijaya Ramachandran (CGDEV) and Astrit Sulstarova (UNCTAD).

The report benefited from comments received from the Scientific Committee put in place by the African Union and from consultations with the ambassadors of member countries of the Development Centre. The chapters were improved by the comments of Joël Boutroue, Bert Brys, Stéphane Buydens, Claire Charbit, Amal Chevreau, Koen De Backer, Juan De Laiglesia, Peter Green, Mohamed Hammouch, Michelle Harding, Philipp Heinrigs, Alin Horj, Ryan Jacildo, James Karanja, Alexandre Kolev, Przemyslaw Kowalski, Frans Lammersen, Willi Leibfritz, Giorgia Maffini, Sam Mealy, Angel Melguizo, Guannan Miao, Kaori Miyamoto, Alexander Pick, Annalisa Primi, Jan Rieländer, Varsha Singh, Laura Stefanelli, Kensuke Tanaka, Kurt Van Dender, Yingyin Wu (OECD) and José Pineda (University of British Columbia). Djeinaba Kane, Kokobe George and Julia Peppino gave valuable support co-ordinating the work.

The involvement of the editing, translation and proofreading team was crucial to producing the report on time. It was edited by Sabine Cessou and Jill Gaston and translated by Franck Manara, Catherine Nallet-Lugaz and Eleanor O'Keeffe. Delphine Grandrieux supervised production with Aida Buendía, Irit Perry and PYKHA, who were responsible for page layout. Aida Buendía created the graphic design and the cover.

The OECD Development Centre is grateful to Germany (BMZ/GIZ), Italy (Ministry of Foreign Affairs and International Co-operation) and Portugal (Camões – Instituto da Cooperação e da Língua, I.P.) for their additional support to this first edition.

Table of contents

Figures

Tables

Boxes

Abbreviations and acronyms

AfDB	African Development Bank
AGOA	African Growth and Opportunity Act
ANSD	Agence Nationale de Statistique et de la Démographie (National Agency for Statistics and Demographics)
ATAF	African Tax Administration Forum
AU	African Union
AUC	African Union Commission
BEAC	Banque des états de l'Afrique centrale (Bank of Central African States)
BEPS	Base Erosion and Profit Shifting
CAADP	Comprehensive Africa Agriculture Development Programme
CEMAC	Communauté Économique et Monétaire des États de l'Afrique Centrale (Economic and Monetary Community of Central Africa)
CEPED	Centre Population et Développement (Development and Population Center)
CEQ	Commitment To Equity
CFTA	Continental Free Trade Area
CICOS	Commission Internationale du Bassin Congo-Oubangui-Sangha (International Commission of The Congo-Oubangui-Sangha Basin)
CIPR	Center for Inter-American Policy and Research
COMESA	Common Market for Eastern and Southern Africa
DAC	Development Assistance Committee
DFI	Development finance institutions
DRC	Democratic Republic of Congo
EAC	East African Community
EAPP	East African Power Pool
ECCAS	Economic Community of Central African States
ECOWAS	Economic Community of West African States
EPA	Export promotion agency
ESW	Electronic Single Windows
EU	European Union
FDI	Foreign direct investment
FIP	Finance and Investment Protocol
FTA	Free trade agreement
GDP	Gross Domestic Product
GGDC	Groningen Growth and Development Centre
GVCs	Global value chains
HDI	Human development index
HIPC	Heavily Indebted Poor Countries
ICA	Infrastructure Consortium for Africa
ICGLR	International Conference of the Great Lakes Region
ICRW	International Center for Research on Women
ICT	Information and Communications Technology
ICTSD	International Centre for Trade and Sustainable Development
IFFs	Illicit Financial Flows
IIAG	Ibrahim Index of African Governance
ILO	International Labour Organization
IMF	International Monetary Fund
INDH	Initiative Nationale pour le Développement Humain (National Initiative For Human Development)

IPA	Investment promotion agency
IPAP	Industrial Policy Action Plans
ITC	International Trade Centre
ITU	International Telecommunication Union
KODI	Kenya Open Data Initiative
MDB	Multilateral Development Banks
NCTTCA	Northern Corridor Transit and Transport Coordination Authority
NEET	Not in Education, Employment or Training
NEPAD	New Partnership for Africa's Development
ODA	Official Development Assistance
OECD	Organisation for Economic Co-operation and Development
ONS	National Office of Statistics
OPHI	Oxford Poverty & Human Development Initiative
PAI	Plan d'accélération industrielle (Improving industrialisation plan)
PPP	Purchasing Power Parity
PPP	Public Private Partnership
R&D	Research and development
REC	Regional Economic Communitiy
RIGA	Rural Income Generating Activities
SACU	Southern Africa Customs Union
SADC	Southern African Development Community
SCT	Single Customs Territory
SDG	Sustainable Development Goal
SHaSA	Strategy for the Harmonisation of Statistics in Africa
SIGI	Social Institutions and Gender Inequality index
SME	Small and Medium-sized Entreprise
SWAC	Sahel and West Africa Club
TEVET	Technical, Entrepreneurial and Vocational Education and Training
TFP	Total factor productivity
TNC	The Nature Conservancy
UNCOMTRADE	United Nations Commodity Trade
UNCTAD	United Nations Conference on Trade and Development
UNDESA	United Nations Department for Economic and Social Affairs
UNDP	United Nations Development Programme
UNECA	United Nations Economic Commission for Africa
UNEP	United Nations Environment Programme
UNESCO	United Nations Educational, Scientific and Cultural Organisation
UNHCR	United Nations High Commission for Refugees
UNICEF	United Nations Children's Fund
UNIDO	United Nations Industrial Development Organization
VAR	Vector Auto Regressive
VAT	Value added tax
WAEMU	West African Economic And Monetary Union
WBG	World Bank Group
WEMZ	West African Monetary Zone
WTO	World Trade Organization

Executive summary

Africa's Development Dynamics 2018 shows that despite the continent's strong growth, quality jobs remain scarce and inequalities high. Africa's economy grew 4.7% per year between 2000 and 2017, making it the world's second fastest growing region. However, to achieve the aspirations of the African Union's Agenda 2063, new development strategies are necessary for at least five reasons:

1. **Growth remains volatile, despite accumulating much capital and acquiring new trade partners.** Some governments may no longer be able to sustain current levels of public investment.
2. **Recent growth has not translated into higher well-being.** In Africa, gross domestic product per capita is less correlated with well-being indicators than is the world average.
3. **Quality jobs remain scarce.** If current trends persist, the share of vulnerable employment in Africa will remain at 66% until 2022 – far from the Agenda 2063 target of 41% by 2023. Today, 282 million workers are vulnerably employed.
4. **Reducing inequalities is essential for lowering poverty.** Were Africa's Gini coefficient equal to that of developing Asia, its 1990-2016 level of growth would have lifted an additional 130 million people out of poverty.
5. **Structural transformation may be hard to sustain without improving productivity growth.** African firms lag behind the global productivity frontier in many labour-absorbing sectors. Firms need to boost their productivity to sustain long-term growth.

Regional and global markets offer several avenues for new and stronger growth patterns. Deepening regional integration and regional value chains can provide sizable opportunities for diversifying exports. Currently, intermediate goods account for less than 15% of Africa's trade. Also, regional demand for goods is rising, and the technology to produce them is increasingly accessible. Demand for food products alone is expected to triple by 2030. Governments can help African firms catch up with global productivity by building stronger industrial linkages and developing local capacity. Innovative policies can help channel financial inflows to unlock private investment.

Five megatrends are shaping Africa's integration into the global economy. Each brings opportunities and risks and has important policy implications. First, global wealth is shifting with emerging countries producing more than half of the global output. New partnerships with Africa are increasing. Second, the new production revolution offers additional markets and different production methods but also creates obstacles for African producers. Third, the continent's population boom could create a "demographic dividend" if local economies can supply enough jobs and basic services to meet the growing demand. Fourth, rapid urbanisation is changing economic structures and posing new challenges. Fifth, many African countries need "green growth" strategies to adapt to climate change.

The dynamics of growth, employment and inequalities vary across Africa's regions. East Africa has benefited from higher and more resilient economic growth than the other regions thanks to a more diversified economy. While underemployment and vulnerable employment characterise the majority of African labour markets, some Northern and Southern African countries also face high structural unemployment. In Central Africa, net job creation has been negative in the formal sector since 2015. Poverty has fallen: in East and West Africa, extreme poverty rates fell by 23 and 12 percentage points respectively between 1990 and 2013. Southern Africa is the most unequal region, hosting six of the world's top ten unequal countries in terms of income.

The continent's development agenda calls for context-specific, multifaceted and holistic development strategies. This report recommends ten policy actions to meet the development targets of Agenda 2063. Actors at all levels can contribute. The recommendations rest on three pillars: sustainable economic development, social development and institutional development. The report tailors actions for each region in several main policy areas, as summarised in the table below. This can serve as a tool for policy dialogue and reform for African decision makers.

Main policy areas for African regions

Region	Main policy areas
Central Africa	• Deepen regional co-operation on fiscal, monetary and trade policies, to promote regional value chains and enhance private sector competitiveness. • Encourage the local processing of raw materials by ensuring local businesses have access to electricity, basic services, qualified labour and equipment. Target support for women and youth. • Facilitate national and regional infrastructure investments, especially in electricity and transportation. Foster a stable business environment to attract long-term investment. • Strengthen tax collection, redistributive policies and social protection systems to ensure that rents from the extractive sector better benefit the population.
East Africa	• Continue the reform agenda to improve the business climate. Stimulate investment through structural and institutional measures such as simplifying business regulations and liberalising imports of capital and intermediate goods. • Boost agricultural productivity and support high-potential firms in the industrial and services sectors in order to accelerate economic transformation. • Reduce poverty by enhancing social protection programmes and by investing in education and skills development.
North Africa	• Invest in strategic sectors that create quality jobs for the youth and engage further in intra-African trade. • Link lead firms with local small- and medium-sized enterprises to help the enterprises meet standards, and improve co-operation between local governments and the private sector. • Promote workplace flexibility to encourage female participation. Align education with labour market needs to ensure youth employment.
Southern Africa	• Implement the Southern African Development Community's Industrialization Strategy and Roadmap 2015-2063 by facilitating investments in domestic technological and industrial capabilities and by encouraging intra-regional trade. • Invest in skills training programmes together with the private sector, notably among high-potential local entrepreneurs. • Expand and integrate labour market policies and social assistance programmes into social protection systems. Continue poverty reduction efforts, especially in rural areas.
West Africa	• Develop the domestic private sector by supporting business clusters, including informal ones, by improving regulatory frameworks and tax systems to attract investment. • Strengthen rural-urban linkages through intermediary cities, better domestic and cross-border infrastructure and corridors, and agribusiness activities. • Invest in universal education and professional skills development that match labour market demand.

Overview: Harnessing Africa's development dynamics to realise Agenda 2063

Africa's Development Dynamics 2018 examines policies to foster inclusive growth, create jobs and reduce inequalities. These policies, in turn, aim to achieve Agenda 2063's aspirations of "a prosperous Africa based on inclusive growth and sustainable development" and meet the objectives of its First Ten Year Implementation Plan 2013-2023. The dynamics of growth, jobs and inequalities also depend on Africa's integration into the global economy and on megatrends affecting the continent. The five regional chapters of the report demonstrate important differences in the dynamics of growth, jobs and inequalities between Southern, Central, East, North and West Africa, and propose specific policies for each region. The report provides African decision makers with an up-to-date tool for policy dialogue and reform at national, regional economic community and pan-African levels.

Achieving Agenda 2063 requires changing Africa's growth dynamics

The African continent has experienced strong growth since 2000, leading to a "rising Africa" narrative. Between 2000 and 2016, Africa enjoyed higher growth rates (4.6%) than Latin America and the Caribbean (LAC) (2.8%), though not as high as developing Asia (7.2%). Africa's recent growth benefited from high commodity prices, improved macroeconomic management, debt relief, and growth diversification strategies in some countries. Many African countries have invested strongly in public infrastructure. Countries have also diversified their trade partnerships, in particular with the People's Republic of China (hereafter "China"), India and other emerging partners. However, quality jobs remain scarce and inequality high.

To achieve the aspirations of Africa's Agenda 2063, new growth dynamics are necessary for at least five reasons:

1. **Growth remains volatile, despite a strong process of capital accumulation and new trade partners.** Having fallen in 2016, real gross domestic product (GDP) growth is projected to bounce back to 4% per year between 2018 and 2020. Individual trajectories from 1970 to 2016 reveal that growth spells tend to be shorter in African and Latin American countries than elsewhere. Sustaining growth over a long period is challenging for most African economies, especially for the continent's resource-rich countries. As prices for commodities dropped sharply between 2012 and 2016 (a decline of 58% for fuel and almost 37% for metals and minerals), growth in these countries was reduced to 1.5% in 2016. In a less favourable macroeconomic environment, several African governments may not be able to sustain current levels of public investment. Only three African countries are projected to meet Agenda 2063's annual growth target of 7% during 2016-20 (Table 1).
2. **Recent growth has not translated into higher well-being.** Outcomes related to dimensions of well-being, such as quality of education, health status and housing conditions, have a much weaker association with GDP per capita in Africa than the world average. Results are similar for several dimensions of subjective well-being, including satisfaction with standards of living and with health coverage availability. Dimensions related to public governance – satisfaction with educational systems and perceived corruption – are also sources of concern. Improving well-being outcomes by 2023 is necessary to achieve Goal 1 of the African Union's Agenda 2063 Ten Year Implementation Plan.
3. **The continent needs to generate more quality jobs for its large labour force, particularly for women and youth.** Growth has not created enough decent jobs. If trends persist, the share of vulnerable employment in Africa is projected to remain

at 66% in 2022 – far from meeting the target of 41% by 2023 set by Agenda 2063. Today, 282 million workers are vulnerably employed and 30% of workers remained poor despite working. Women and youth are particularly vulnerable in the labour force. Only 12% of Africa's working-age women were in waged employment in 2016, compared to 22% in Asia and 33% in LAC. About 42% of Africa's working youth live on less than USD 1.90 a day (at purchasing power parity).

4. **Further alleviating poverty requires reducing income inequality.** If Africa lowered its Gini coefficient from 41 to 35 (the level of developing Asia), each percentage point of GDP growth would reduce its poverty headcount by an additional 0.5 percentage points a year. Such a decrease in inequality would reduce the number of poor people by 130 million. Progress in reducing extreme poverty is too slow. Between 2009-16, 36% of the African population (about 400 million people) lived on USD 1.90 a day or less, compared to 49% in the 1990s. To fight poverty more rapidly, growth must become more inclusive and inequalities must be reduced.
5. **If business continues as usual, structural transformation may be hard to sustain.** Since 2000, structural transformation has boosted labour productivity in Africa by 0.4 percentage points a year as labour has moved from less productive activities to more productive ones. This is essential for ensuring long-term growth. However, this process is reaching limits as Africa's labour is moving into sectors where relative productivity levels are declining. Among 13 African countries, the share of wholesale and retail trade, restaurants and hotels in total employment almost doubled in two decades, from 11.4% in 1990 to 20.1% in 2010. Labour productivity in Africa is also falling behind Asia's level. Keeping the progress of structural transformation requires strategic policy actions to boost productivity and create productive jobs that can quickly absorb a large number of unskilled workers. Compared to other global competitors, African firms lag behind the productivity frontier in many labour-absorbing sectors, such as agro-processing, construction, logistical services and light manufacturing.

Table 1. **Growth rates for African countries, other developing countries and high-income countries, 2000-20**

		Number of countries in each growth category			
		2000-05	2006-10	2011-15	2016-20 (p)
African countries	Growth above 7%	9	9	6	3
	Growth of 0-7%	38	41	43	48
	Negative growth	5	2	3	3
Other developing countries	Growth above 7%	15	14	10	6
	Growth of 0-7%	63	64	65	73
	Negative growth	2	4	6	2
High-income countries	Growth above 7%	6	1	1	0
	Growth of 0-7%	46	43	43	51
	Negative growth	0	8	8	1

Note: (p) projections.
Source: Authors' calculations based on IMF (2018), *World Economic Outlook* (database).

Regional and global markets offer Africa new opportunities, if governments adapt their development strategies

To take advantage of the many opportunities regional and global markets offer for growth, jobs and equality, African governments need to adapt their strategies to the new economic reality. Technological change, global value chains, and evolving trade and investment agreements are reshaping opportunities for integration into regional and global markets.

The challenge for most African countries is better rather than more integration into the global economy. Imports and exports of goods and services represented about 50%

of Africa's GDP in 2015-16, which is similar to Asia and higher than in the LAC region (44%). However, most of Africa's exports are unprocessed commodities. Upgrading the quality of existing products, expanding export products and improving access to capital goods and inputs can provide ways to sustain growth, increase job quality and reduce inequality. Diversification can be achieved by tapping regional value chains and better targeting emerging markets.

Deepening regional integration can help. In this process of regional integration, the new continental free trade area (CFTA) – initially signed by 44 member states of the African Union – offers an important stepping-stone for policy action. Fully liberalising trade in goods could boost Africa's GDP by 1% and total employment by 1.2%. Intra-African trade could grow by 33% and Africa's total trade deficit could be halved.

Africa's regional markets are increasingly favourable to growth for several reasons:

- **The contribution of private consumption to economic growth has increased progressively and reached 3.5 percentage points of GDP annually over 2009-16.** This is comparable to the level in China and other developing Asian countries (Figure 1). The rapid urban growth of African economies, a better educated population and higher purchasing power of Africa's emerging middle class are underpinning this growing private consumption. The middle class, defined as those spending between USD 5 and USD 20 a day, increased from 108 million people in 1990 to 247 million by 2013.
- **Africa's regional demand is growing and shifting towards more processed goods.** Sub-Saharan Africa's food market is expected to triple to reach USD 1 trillion by 2030. Demand for processed food is growing fast, more than 1.5 times faster than the global average between 2005 and 2015.
- **Africa's business opportunities are now attracting international investors.** The potential of domestic and regional markets attracted 53.4% of new foreign direct investment (FDI) projects to Africa in 2013-17. This share is similar to Asia's level (55.7%) and ten percentage points higher than LAC's (44.8%).
- **Simplified administrative procedures and reduced start-up and operational costs have made the business environment more attractive**: 29.5% of foreign investors cite this improvement among the main motivations to invest in Africa, compared to 12% in 2003-07.

Figure 1. **Decomposition of growth by expenditure in Africa, Asia and LAC, 1990-2016**

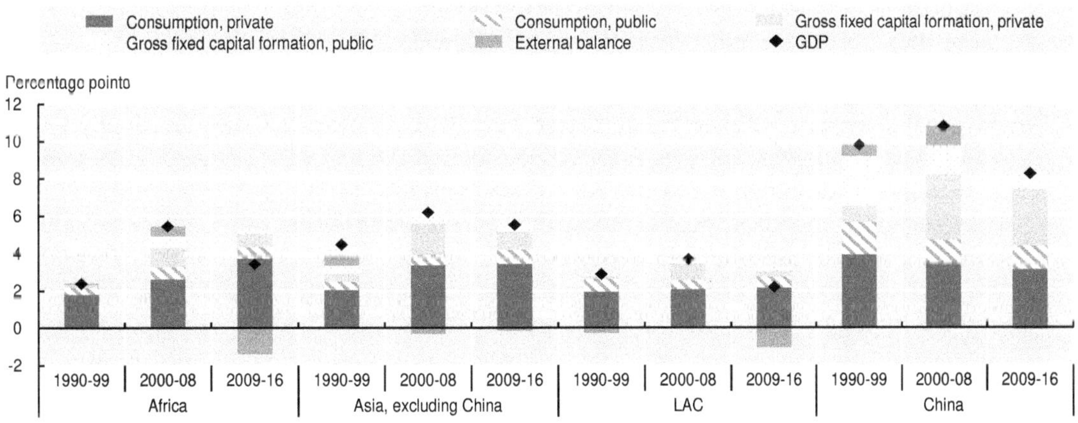

Note: Data include 52 African countries, 34 developing Asian countries and 23 developing LAC countries. Contribution to growth by change in inventory is close to zero (±0.01 percentage points) and is thus suppressed from the figure.

Source: Authors' calculations based on World Bank (2017a), *World Development Indicators* (database) and IMF (2018), *World Economic Outlook* (database).

StatLink http://dx.doi.org/10.1787/888933782696

This rising regional market brings great growth opportunities for local companies that can upgrade their products. Local entrepreneurs, and small and medium-sized enterprises (SMEs) enjoy relative advantage owing to their proximity to, and their knowledge of, the home market. However, African firms must catch up with global productivity or lose their home markets to global competitors. Africa's labour productivity has been falling behind that of Asia in many sectors such as agriculture, transports, financial activities, construction and manufacturing.

African firms need a new set of policies to increase productivity and take advantage of new business opportunities. Ongoing doing-business reforms and fiscal holidays are not sufficient to address this productivity gap. They have not led to a significant increase in private investment. Special economic zones (SEZs) can attract lead firms and create a few thousand manufacturing jobs; but too often SEZs have become enclaves with limited productivity and with few linkages to the local economy and to local jobs. According to a survey of 91 SEZs in 20 sub-Saharan countries, SEZs account for approximately 1 million jobs, or 0.2% of national employment.

Bridging the productivity gap also depends on capacity building and complementary policies. Strategies to increase productivity include improving management capabilities and technical skills, promoting financing opportunities, decreasing inequalities in labour markets, giving more opportunities for firms to formalise, and improving transparency and governance. Developing stronger industrial linkages among firms, including through clusters and suppliers' development programmes, will play an essential role.

Local economies can attract more long-term and productive investment if policies can better mobilise domestic resources and external financial inflows.

- **Domestic financial markets and resources mobilisation, as well as government expenditure, must become more efficient in the following ways:**
  - Improving financial intermediation to help mobilise domestic savings in support of productive investment. On average in Africa, domestic savings represented USD 422 billion annually over 2009-16, which is 20% of the continent's GDP.
  - Improving tax policies, the collection of non-tax revenues, and enhancing the effectiveness of public spending. According to the most recent data, the African continent mobilised USD 312 billion in tax revenues or about 1.7 times more than the USD 185 billion in external financial inflows in 2016 (Table 2).
  - Combating illicit financial outflows, which amount to USD 50 billion annually.
- **External financial inflows must better benefit diversification and productivity, and create more jobs.** Inflows into Africa reached 8.8% of GDP between 2009 and 2016, significantly higher than in Asia (3.8%) and LAC (5.2%). But 36% of total FDI between 2003 and 2014 went into extracting resources, while remittances largely went into consumption goods. Fostering stronger linkages between FDI firms and the local economy is crucial to create more jobs and better transfer knowledge and technology. Finally, official development assistance (ODA) can de-risk private investment and encourage SMEs to comply with international standards. Between 2012 and 2015, such development finance helped mobilise USD 81 billion of private investment.

Table 2. **Foreign and domestic financial flows and tax revenues to Africa (current USD, billion), 2010-16**

			2010	2011	2012	2013	2014	2015	2016 (p)
Foreign	Private	Inward foreign direct investment	46	45	55	62	64	49	59
		Portfolio investments	28	26	42	32	31	20	13
		Remittances	53	60	64	64	68	65	62
	Public	Official development assistance	47	52	52	57	54	51	50
Total foreign flows			**175**	**182**	**214**	**215**	**217**	**185**	**185**
Domestic tax revenues			**332**	**407**	**421**	**418**	**412**	**343**	**312**

Sources: Authors' calculations based on IMF (2018), *World Economic Outlook* (database), OECD-DAC (2017), *International Development Statistics* (database) and World Bank (2017a), *World Development Indicators* (database).

Development strategies must also consider five megatrends affecting Africa's integration into the global economy

Development strategies must also consider megatrends that are shaping Africa's development dynamics and integration into the global economy. Each of these megatrends brings large opportunities and risks, from which African countries can draw important policy implications (Chapter 2).

1. **"Shifting wealth"**, or the stronger role of emerging countries in the global economy, offers Africa the opportunity to trade with more partners, diversify its export basket and upgrade in global value chains, as well as attract new investments, development finance, technology and innovation. For example, China committed USD 118 billion, or 34% of its total development finance, to Africa during 2000-14. Shifting wealth also brings the opportunity to attract labour-intensive manufacturing activities to Africa. To realise that potential, African economies must become more competitive than other emerging economies. African countries may also have to boost their engagement with global partners.
2. The **new production revolution** brought about by technological change and digitalisation allows African firms to access new markets, produce at lower cost and tap new equity markets. At the same time, it allows African governments to deliver basic services more efficiently and transparently. For instance, Africa already counts over 277 million registered mobile money accounts, more than all other developing regions put together. However, robotisation brings big risks for Africa's industrialisation. In Ethiopia, 85% of jobs are in sectors susceptible to automation.
3. The continent's demographic growth could bring a **"demographic dividend"** if the local economies can supply enough jobs and basic services to meet the growing demand. Between 2015 and 2050, Africa's working age population (defined as 15-64 year-olds) will increase by 902 million people, about 69% of the total increase across the world. Africa's demographic dividend could contribute 10-15% of gross GDP volume growth by 2030. However, the formal economy must create millions of additional jobs: on average between today and 2030, 29 million additional young people turn 16 years old every year. Access to quality education must also improve, particularly for girls. Many African youth lack the technical and managerial skills to succeed in the labour market. Only 10.5% of secondary students are enrolled in vocational programmes, and these are often underfunded.
4. With the **urban transition** ongoing, most Africans are projected to live in urban areas by 2035. Urbanisation brings big opportunities, such as a rising domestic market for both labour and consumption. It can also catalyse productivity gains and innovation in the economy. However, by the beginning of this century, about 62% of sub-Saharan Africa's urban population lived in informal settlements. In

several countries, unplanned urbanisation could lead to tripling the population living in informal settlements by 2050.

5. **Climate change** is a big risk for 27 African countries out of 33 globally, although Africa contributes less than 4% to global greenhouse gas emissions. "Green growth" strategies can enable Africa to develop new economic activities, create new jobs and save on future adaptation cost. African countries can tap the potential of renewable energy, with its costs decreasing rapidly. That of solar energy declined by 80% between 2008 and 2015. Half of sub-Saharan Africa's growth in electricity generation is likely to come from renewable energy by 2040.

Ten policy actions are strategic at the continental level

The continent's development agenda calls for context-specific, multifaceted and holistic development strategies. In response, this report proposes ten policy actions to address growth, job creation and inequalities in Africa. The recommendations rest on three pillars: sustainable economic development, social development and institutional development. These actions aim to meet development targets of the African Union's Agenda 2063 (see Table 3) and the Sustainable Development Goals (SDGs), as well as to tackle the risks and opportunities brought by the megatrends. Actors at all levels can contribute to this agenda: pan-African institutions; regional communities; national, subnational and local governments; the local private sector; African citizens; and international partners. Generating quality data is key to monitor, evaluate and adjust policies to meet Africa's aspirations.

Table 3. **Ten policy actions to meet the targets of Agenda 2063 and related SDGs**

Policy action	Proposed measures	Agenda 2063 goals	Sustainable Development Goals
Action 1: Encourage investment for domestic private sector development	• Making investment easier for domestic firms • Ensuring consistency between FDI promotion strategies and capacity of local private sector • Leveraging domestic savings and remittances to increase domestic investment • Increasing the efficiency of public investment	**Goal 4.** Transformed economies and jobs **Goal 12.** Capable institutions and transformative leadership in place at all levels **Goal 20.** Africa takes full responsibility for financing its development	SDG 8, 9, 12, 17
Action 2: Help the private sector to diversify production and exports	• Designing export strategies that are consistent with the country's potential • Facilitating imports of intermediate and capital goods • Empowering export promotion agencies to support diversification	**Goal 4.** Transformed economies and jobs **Goal 5.** Modern agriculture for increased productivity and production	SDG 8, 9, 17
Action 3: Strengthen linkages between rural and urban economies	• Reforming land ownership and management • Upgrading urban infrastructure and services • Strengthening rural-urban linkages through sustainable intermediary cities	**Goal 1.** High standard of living, quality of life and well-being for all **Goal 10.** World-class infrastructure crisscrosses Africa	SDG 1, 8, 10, 11
Action 4: Foster green growth	• Promoting the circular economy • Greening existing economic activities	**Goal 5.** Modern agriculture for increased productivity and production **Goal 6.** Blue/ocean economy **Goal 7.** Environmentally sustainable and climate-resilient economies and communities	SDG 7, 13, 14, 15
Action 5: Expand education while improving the quality of education and skills	• Pushing for universal access to education, especially for girls • Promoting specialised education in strategic sectors • Improving technical and vocational education and training • Bringing education institutions closer to the job market and private firms	**Goal 2.** Well-educated citizens and skills revolution underpinned by science, technology and innovation **Goal 17.** Full gender equality in all spheres of life **Goal 18.** Engaged and empowered youth and children	SDG 4, 5, 12

Table 3. **Ten policy actions to meet the targets of Agenda 2063 and related SDGs** *(cont.)*

Policy action	Proposed measures	Agenda 2063 goals	Sustainable Development Goals
Action 6: Increase the coverage of social protection systems, including labour and health	• Establishing social protection floors • Financing social protection systems sustainably	**Goal 1.** High standard of living, quality of life and well-being for all **Goal 3.** Healthy and well-nourished citizens	SDG 1, 3, 10
Action 7: Boost Africa's engagement with its global partners	• Strengthening global co-operation • Improving existing African partnerships and co-operation	**Goal 19.** Africa as a major partner in global affairs and peaceful co-existence **Goal 20.** Africa takes full responsibility for financing its development	SDG 10, 17
Action 8: Deepen regional integration	• Improving coordination and governance of regional economic communities (RECs) and rationalising memberships • Facilitating trade in goods • Deepening regional integration to include free movement of people, capital and services	**Goal 4.** Transformed economies and job creation **Goal 8.** United Africa (federal or confederate) **Goal 9.** Key continental financial and monetary institutions established and functional **Goal 10.** World-class infrastructure crisscrosses Africa	SDG 9, 10, 11, 17
Action 9: Mobilise domestic resources	• Designing tax systems that broaden the tax base and incentivise compliance • Investing in more efficient and effective tax administrations • Co-operating at international level to improve tax systems	**Goal 20.** Africa takes full responsibility for financing its development	SDG 8, 17
Action 10: Enhance economic and political governance	• Increasing accountability and transparency of policy-making processes and redistributive policies • Promoting good corporate governance • Investing continually in upgrading institutional capacity • Ensuring reforms are implemented at the appropriate level of government	**Goal 8.** United Africa (federal or confederate) **Goal 11.** Democratic values and practices, universal principles of human rights, justice and the rule of law entrenched **Goal 12.** Capable institutions and transformative leadership in place at all levels	SDG 8, 16, 17

Development strategies must be actionable at the regional level

Apart from the continental agenda, strategies must also be actionable at the regional level and consider the diversity of Africa's regions and national economies. Deeper regional integration is necessary to generate economies of scale and ensure greater efficiency in African markets. Across the five regions defined in the Abuja Treaty, Africa's RECs are playing an essential role in co-ordinating implementation of the continent's action plan for growth, jobs and reducing inequalities.

In Southern Africa

Since 2000, Southern Africa has registered steady economic growth, but it is now decelerating. Real GDP grew at 5.2% annually between 2000 and 2008 before slowing to 2.6% between 2009 and 2016. The volatility in commodity prices and in investment in the extractive sector strongly affected performance. Manufacturing value added in the region dropped from 18.2% of GDP to 12.6% of GDP between 2000 and 2015. This trend of "premature deindustrialisation" is a big challenge to inclusive growth and the achievement of Agenda 2063.

Employment remains a major challenge in Southern Africa, especially for the additional 1.1 million young people who enter the labour force every year. The region is home to six of the world's top ten unequal countries, despite progressive fiscal systems and redistributive policies in countries such as South Africa and Zambia (Figure 2). Extreme poverty headcount remained at 35.6% in 2013, down from 43.8% in 1990. Gender inequality remains a significant impediment to inclusive growth and well-being, although Southern Africa performs better than other African regions.

Figure 2. **Gini coefficients and difference in income share in Southern African countries**

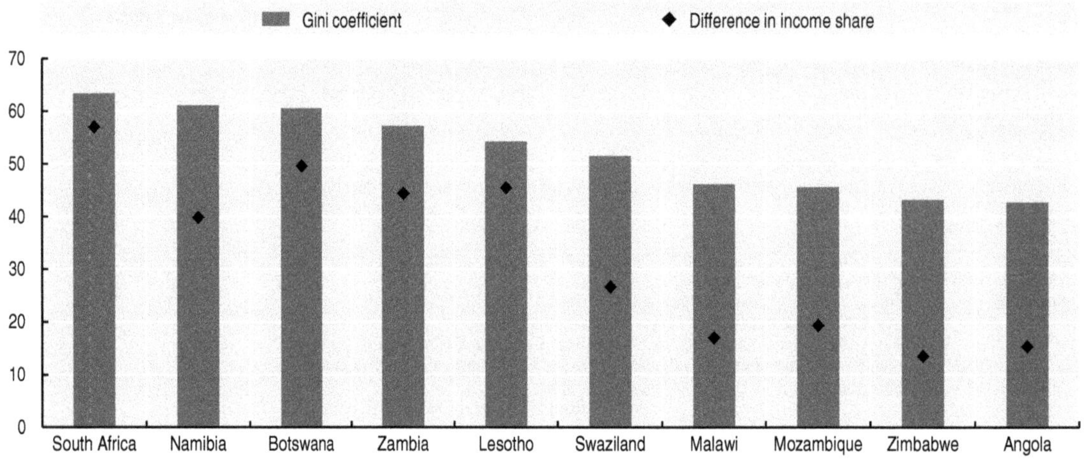

Note: The difference between the top and bottom group refers to the ratio between the income shares held by the richest 10% to the income held by the poorest 10% in the national income distribution. The latest available data are shown for each country.

Source: Authors' calculations based on World Bank (2017b), *PovcalNet* (database).

StatLink http://dx.doi.org/10.1787/888933783190

To ensure that growth successfully reduces inequality and unemployment, governments in Southern Africa could take the following priority actions:

- Advancing implementation of the Southern African Development Community Industrialization Strategy and Roadmap 2015-2063. Such progress entails facilitating investments in developing domestic technological and industrial capabilities, encouraging intra-regional trade and identifying opportunities for job-rich industrialisation.
- Encouraging different types of local entrepreneurship and investing in skills training programmes together with the private sector. This would increase workers' employability, especially for youths and women.
- Expanding and integrating the social protection systems, and continuing poverty reduction efforts, especially in rural areas. The entrenched nature of inequality and unemployment calls for combining labour market policies and social assistance programmes.

In Central Africa

Central Africa has grown strongly at 5.6% on average since 2000, but the region could not transform this wealth into resilient and sustainable development. Central African economies remain highly resource-dependent. Unprocessed goods (mostly hydrocarbons, copper and timber) account for 84% of the region's exports, the highest share among the five African regions (Figure 3). Growth depends on commodity prices. This volatility can deter long-term investment, which poses a challenge for bridging the gap in access to infrastructure and electricity.

Since 2015, formal job creation has decoupled from economic activity. The unequal distribution of natural resources has created spatial inequalities and considerable wealth disparities between countries and between economic sectors. This has added to the stagnation of income inequality with the Gini coefficient in Central Africa remaining at 42 on average since 2000, higher than the other African regions.

Figure 3. **Trade composition in Central Africa, 2016**

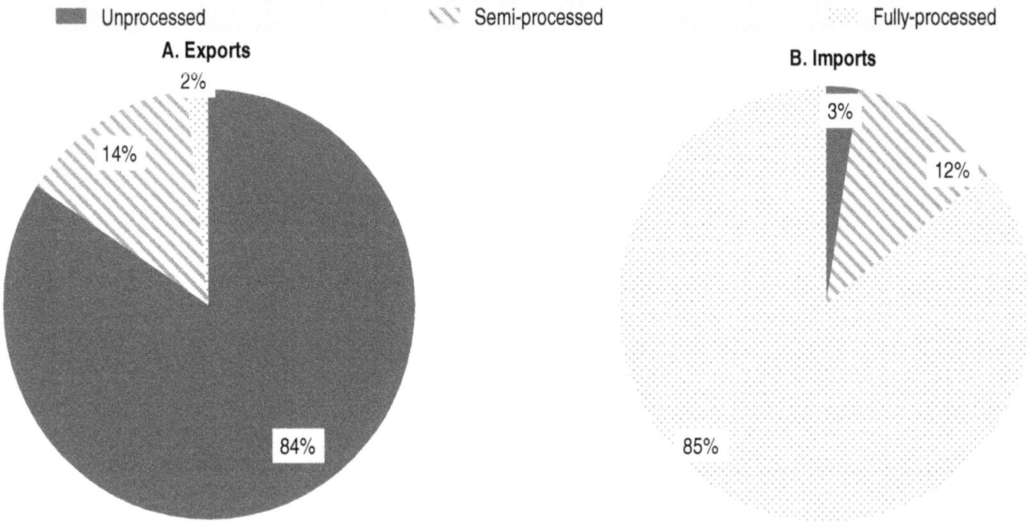

Source: Authors' calculations based on United Nations Statistics Division (2017), UNCOMTRADE database (2017).
StatLink http://dx.doi.org/10.1787/888933783285

Governments may explore multiple policies to improve social and economic resilience, create jobs and support sustainable and inclusive growth, including the following:

- Deepening regional co-operation on fiscal, monetary and trade policies, to promote regional value chains and enhance private sector competitiveness. Facilitating national and regional investments in transportation, electricity and telecommunication infrastructures is crucial to implement the commitments to regional integration.
- Ensuring local businesses have access to electricity, basic services, qualified labour and imported equipment, to encourage the local processing of raw materials. Targeted policies are also needed to encourage women and youth participation in the labour force and to reduce their vulnerability.
- Strengthening tax collection, redistributive policies and social protection systems to ensure that rents from the extractive sector better benefit the population. This requires improving statistical systems to ensure that data are available, reliable and used effectively to inform policies.

In East Africa

East Africa has benefited from higher and more resilient economic growth compared to other regions due to its more diversified economic profile. Since 1990, annual growth rates in the region have exceeded 4%. This growth has been driven by the services sector, now representing almost 60% of GDP (Figure 4). However, this expansion derives from mostly informal and non-tradable services. A large agriculture and export-led growth model that focuses on a narrow set of products (e.g. coffee, tea and minerals) makes the region vulnerable to commodity price fluctuations and currency depreciations.

Figure 4. **Average sector value added as a percentage of GDP in East Africa, 1991-2016**

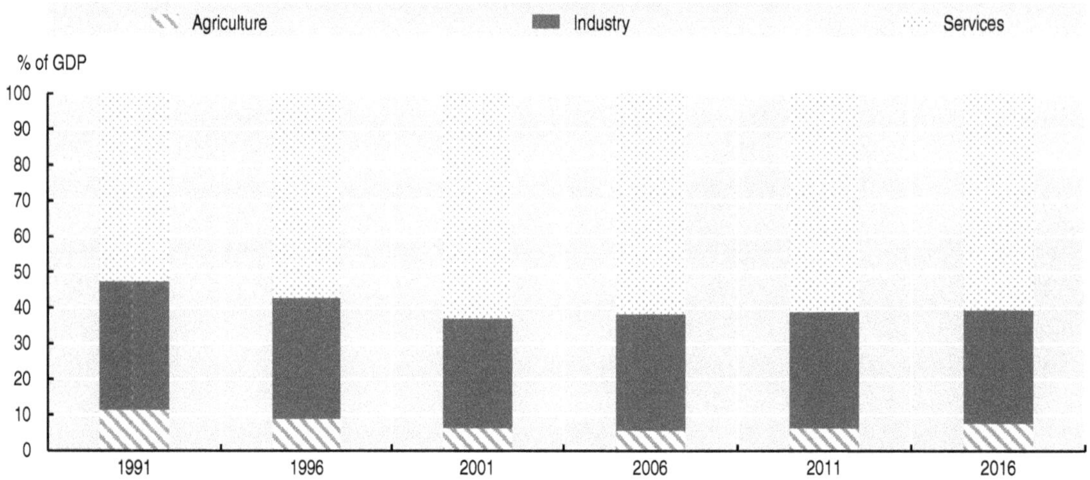

Source: Authors' calculations based on World Bank (2017a), *World Development Indicators* (database).
StatLink http://dx.doi.org/10.1787/888933783703

Nevertheless, growth from recent years has not translated into rapid structural transformation and job creation. With 35% of the population still in extreme poverty, growth has not reduced poverty and income inequality significantly. On the contrary, income inequality is on an upward trend, with only four countries having a Gini coefficient below 40. The overall gender gap in employment has decreased only slightly, with the male-to-female employment ratio falling from 1.41 in 1991 to 1.39 in 2017. Most women work in the informal sector (e.g. from 50% in Uganda to 80% in Kenya and Rwanda).

GDP growth increasingly results from private consumption, which presents both an opportunity to tap a growing domestic market, but also a risk of worsening trade balances through demand of imported goods. East African governments may emphasise the following economic and social policies:

- Improving the policy and regulatory framework and the overall business environment is crucial to foster diversification and more sustainable growth. Policy makers can stimulate productive investment in the economy through structural and institutional measures such as simplifying business regulations and removing import tariffs on capital and intermediate goods. Boosting agricultural productivity and supporting high-potential firms in the industrial and services sectors will help the region accelerate its economic transformation.
- Several countries are addressing poverty by enhancing social protection programmes and by investing in education and skills development, which are sorely needed. Such investments will have to increase significantly for these programmes to support more inclusive development.

In North Africa

Despite growth volatility, governments in North Africa have been able to reduce poverty and inequality of opportunity. Growth averaged 2.6% between 2010 and 2015 (compared with 4% between 1995 and 2009). This lower growth is mainly due to the volatility of oil prices, slow European demand after the 2008 global financial crisis, the carry-over effects of the Arab Spring and ongoing conflicts. Productivity gains are insufficient, showing a lack of innovation in the economies (Figure 5).

Figure 5. **Total factor productivity growth by country in North Africa, 1990-2015**

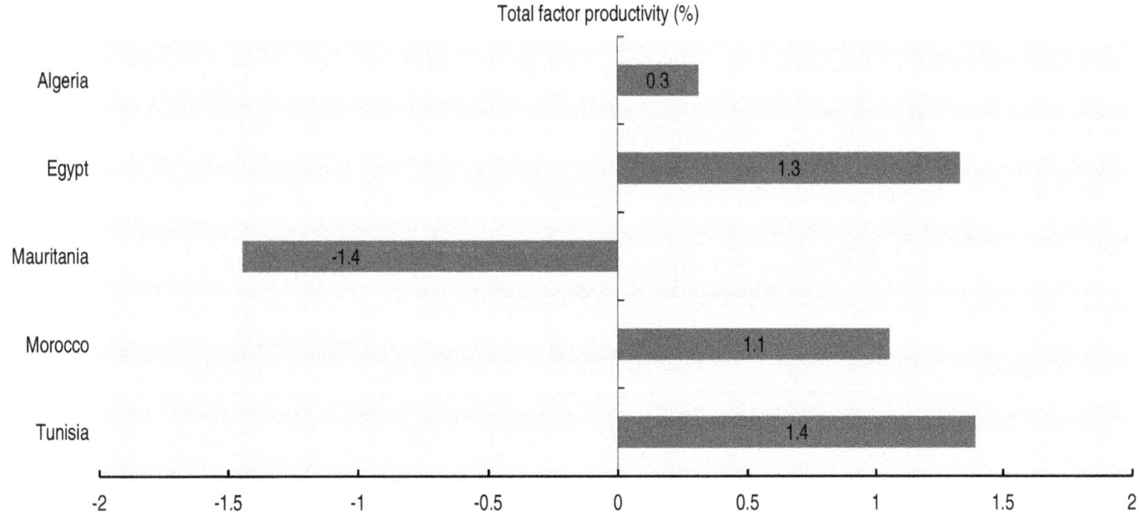

Source: Authors' calculations based on World Bank (2017a), *World Development Indicators* (database).
StatLink http://dx.doi.org/10.1787/888933783931

Inequalities and poverty have also decreased significantly thanks to improved access to basic services and social protection programmes. However, income inequality persists, as the richest 20% earn 7.5 times more than the poorest 20%, and part of the population remains vulnerable to poverty.

Labour participation rates remain low in North Africa (40.9% from 1990 to 2015). Youth and women are the most disfavoured in the labour market. The main challenge in youth unemployment is the lack of high skilled jobs for the increasingly educated population. Youth unemployment (age 15-24) is 28.8%, double the world average. Only 16.6% of young women are employed or seeking employment, compared with 46.8% of young men. Around one-quarter of these young workers live in poverty. About 26% of young people between the ages of 15 and 24 are not in education, employment or training (NEET), the second highest rate globally.

To overcome these challenges, policies will need to improve and strengthen political stability and institutional accountability, accelerate the structural transformation of economies, and target job creation for women and youth via structural policy levers. The following actions are recommended:

- Shifting economies towards strategic sectors that create added value and employment for young and qualified workers. Developing the manufacturing sector and focusing on exporting goods and services to the rest of Africa could help achieve that objective.
- Promoting flexibility in the workplace to encourage female participation, support female entrepreneurs and align education with labour market needs to ensure higher youth employment.

In West Africa

Between 2000 and 2014, West Africa has experienced one of the continent's strongest growth rates at above 5%. Yet it is uneven as Nigeria, Ghana and Côte d'Ivoire represent 85% of regional GDP. High informality, increasing inequalities and poverty also undermine growth resilience.

West Africa's demographic growth, growing regional demand and emerging middle class are big opportunities for development, but call for the creation of millions of jobs in the formal economy. Economic growth is mainly driven by the exploitation of raw materials and the agricultural sector, activities that do not offer enough job opportunities for youth. As a result, youth and women, who are also excluded from the formal job market, resort to informal sector activities, which represent between 68% and 90% of jobs (Table 4). Lack of formal jobs is becoming a major challenge, as those aged 15-24 years will represent 20% of the population by 2035 (117 million).

Table 4. **Informal sector share of non-agricultural employment by gender in West Africa**

Country	Year	Informal sector share (%)	Gender share (%)	
			Women	Men
Benin	2011	94.5	97.7	90.2
Côte d'Ivoire	2016	87.7	93.8	82.4
Gambia	2012	68.2	77.6	62.0
Ghana	2015	83.2	88.3	75.9
Liberia	2010	77.6	86.3	68.8
Mali	2015	92.1	96.9	87.9
Niger	2011	86.4	95.2	76.4
Senegal	2015	90.4	93.5	88.2

Source: Authors' calculations based on ILO (2017) *ILOStat* database.

Even though access to basic services has improved, the distribution of income remains unequal. Due to rapid population growth, the number of people living in extreme poverty grew from 98.9 million (55.4%) in 1990 to 144.4 million (43.8%) in 2013. Inequalities remain high, with a Gini coefficient of 0.39 in 2014, and this is higher in several countries. The human development index (HDI) is one of the lowest of the continent, at 0.47. Social security remains insufficient and half of West African countries display strong gender inequality.

To generate sustainable and inclusive growth, developing strategies need to rely on three main axes:

- Developing the domestic private sector by supporting business clusters, improving regulatory frameworks and tax systems to attract investment, and promoting economic diversification.
- Strengthening rural-urban linkages by improving the capacity of intermediary cities, improving domestic and cross-border infrastructure and corridors, and promoting agribusiness activities.
- Investing further in universal education, particularly of girls, while improving the quality of education and of professional skills development to match labour market demand.

References

ILO (2017), *ILOSTAT* (database), www.ilo.org/ilostat/ (accessed 1 March 2018).

IMF (2018), *World Economic Outlook, April 2018* (database), www.imf.org/external/pubs/ft/weo/2018/01/weodata/index.aspx (accessed 20 April 2018).

OECD-DAC (2017), *International Development Statistics* (database), www.oecd.org/dac/stats/idsonline.htm (accessed 15 February 2018).

UN Statistics Division (2017), *UN COMTRADE* (database), http://wits.worldbank.org/wits/ (accessed 1 February 2018).

World Bank (2017a), *World Development Indicators* (database), http://wdi.worldbank.org (accessed 15 February 2018).

World Bank (2017b), *PovcalNet* (database), http://iresearch.worldbank.org/PovcalNet/povOnDemand.aspx (accessed 20 April 2018).

Chapter 1

Africa's integration into the global economy

This chapter analyses the overall development trajectory in Africa and its position in the global economy since 1990. It first addresses the determinants, components and dynamics of growth in gross domestic product and their impact on job creation and inequality. The analysis then proposes five reasons why Africa needs better growth patterns in light of its Agenda 2063 development targets. The second part of the chapter looks at growth avenues that regional and global markets present to African economies. The chapter presents the policy challenges to boost domestic competitiveness, further develop domestic markets and unlock investments.

IN BRIEF

Between 2000 and 2016, Africa experienced strong economic growth rates (averaging 4.6% annually), higher than Latin America and the Caribbean (2.8%) yet lower than developing Asia (7.2%). These resulted from high commodity prices, improved macroeconomic management and strategies to diversify growth. Many countries have invested strongly in public infrastructure; some have also diversified their trade partnerships, in particular with China, India and other emerging partners.

Despite this, Africa would benefit from improving its economic growth patterns for several reasons:

- African countries need to strengthen the drivers of **long-term growth**. Growth has been highly volatile, and only three African countries are forecasted to meet Agenda 2063's growth target of 7% a year during the 2016-20 period.
- Growth has not created enough jobs, and quality jobs remain scarce. If current trends persist, the share of **vulnerable employment** in Africa is projected to remain at 66% in 2022, far above the target of 41% by 2023.
- Africa's recent growth has not improved **well-being** as much as has growth in the rest of the world.
- Reducing **inequality** is essential to make growth more inclusive and resilient. If Africa lowered its current Gini coefficient to that of developing Asia, growth between 1990 and 2016 could have potentially reduced the number of poor people by an additional 130 million.

Both global and regional markets offer new avenues for better growth. Export diversification can help Africa benefit more from **integration into the global economy**. Deepening regional integration, particularly increasing intra-African trade in intermediate goods, can also help. **Domestic demand in Africa** offers new opportunities for local companies, such as entrepreneurs and small and medium-sized enterprises. African governments can do more to help them catch up with global productivity, especially through building industrial linkages and developing local capacity. To mobilise more financial resources for countries' development, African governments can improve tax policies and revenue collection, enhance the effectiveness of public spending and promote better financial intermediation to channel savings towards investment in local economies.

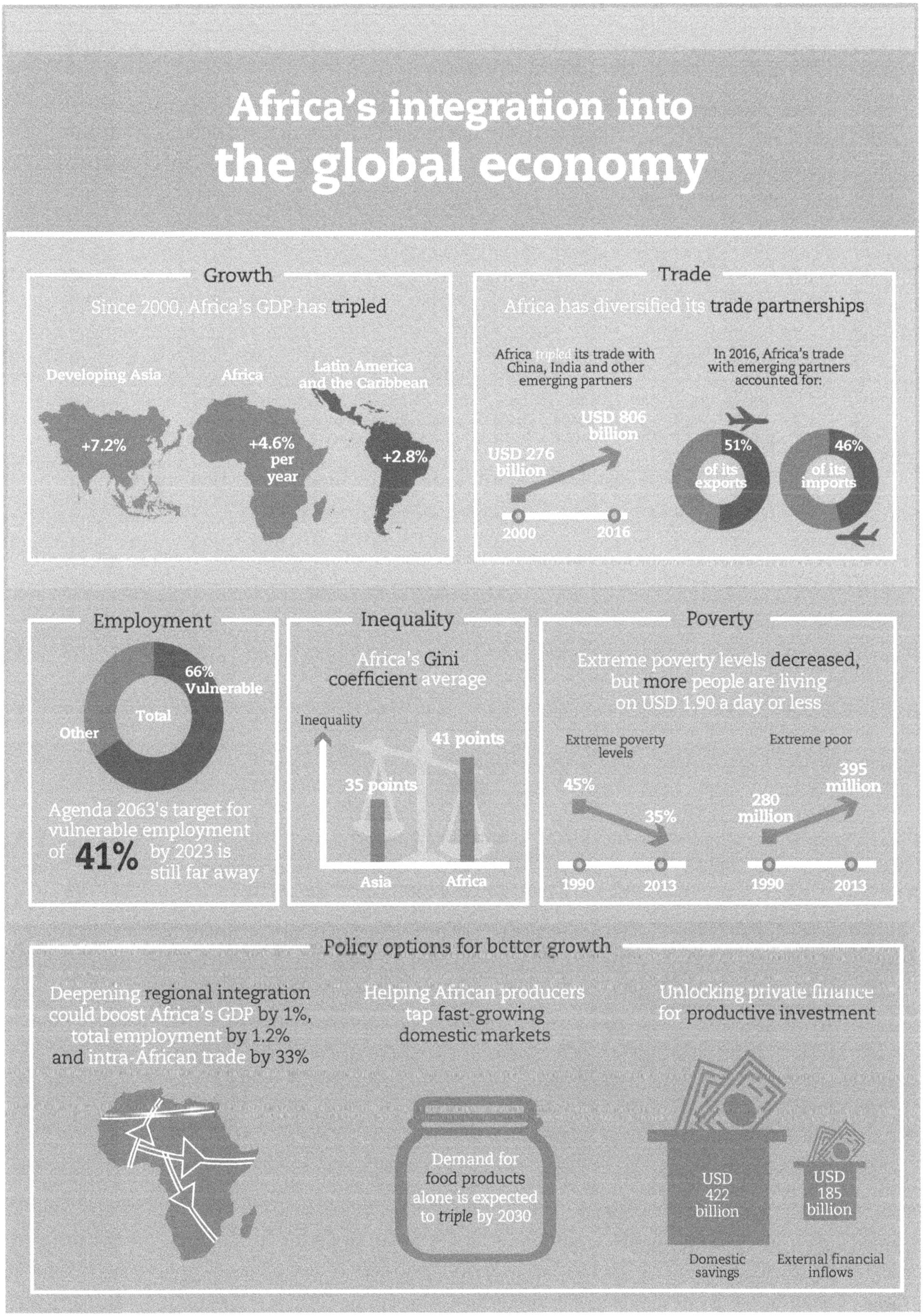
Africa's integration into the global economy
Growth
Since 2000, Africa's GDP has tripled
Developing Asia
Africa
Latin America and the Caribbean
+7.2%
+4.6% per year
+2.8%
Trade
Africa has diversified its trade partnerships
Africa tripled its trade with China, India and other emerging partners
USD 276 billion
USD 806 billion
2000
2016
In 2016, Africa's trade with emerging partners accounted for:
51% of its exports
46% of its imports
Employment
66% Vulnerable
Total
Other
Agenda 2063's target for vulnerable employment of 41% by 2023 is still far away
Inequality
Africa's Gini coefficient average
Inequality
35 points
41 points
Asia
Africa
Poverty
Extreme poverty levels decreased, but more people are living on USD 1.90 a day or less
Extreme poverty levels
45%
35%
1990
2013
Extreme poor
280 million
395 million
1990
2013
Policy options for better growth
Deepening regional integration could boost Africa's GDP by 1%, total employment by 1.2% and intra-African trade by 33%
Helping African producers tap fast-growing domestic markets
Demand for food products alone is expected to triple by 2030
Unlocking private finance for productive investment
USD 422 billion
USD 185 billion
Domestic savings
External financial inflows

Basic indicators: Africa in the global economy

Table 1.1. **Basic indicators for Africa, Asia and LAC, 2017**

	Africa	Asia	LAC
Population (thousands)	1 202	4 011	620
Land area (thousands of km²)	30 143	25 071	20 412
Population density (pop./km²)	39.9	160.0	30.4
GDP, PPP (USD billion)	6 377	45 114	9 783
GDP per capita, PPP (USD)	5 305	11 246	15 785

Source: Authors' calculations based on data from UNDESA (2017), *World Population Prospects: The 2017 Revision* (database), World Bank (2017a), *World Development Indicators* (database), and IMF (2018), *World Economic Outlook* (database).

Table 1.2. **Foreign and domestic financial flows and tax revenues to Africa (current USD, billion), 2010-16**

			2010	2011	2012	2013	2014	2015	2016
Foreign	Private	Inward foreign direct investment	46	45	55	62	64	49	59
		Portfolio investments	28	26	42	32	31	20	13
		Remittances	53	60	64	64	68	65	62
	Public	Official development assistance (net total, all donors)	47	52	52	57	54	51	50
Total foreign flows			**175**	**182**	**214**	**215**	**217**	**185**	**185**
Domestic tax revenues			**332**	**407**	**421**	**418**	**412**	**343**	**312**

Sources: Authors' calculations based on IMF (2018), *World Economic Outlook* (database), OECD-DAC (2017), International Development Statistics (database), and World Bank (2017a), *World Development Indicators* (database).

Figure 1.1. **Real economic growth in Africa, Asia and LAC, 1990-2018**

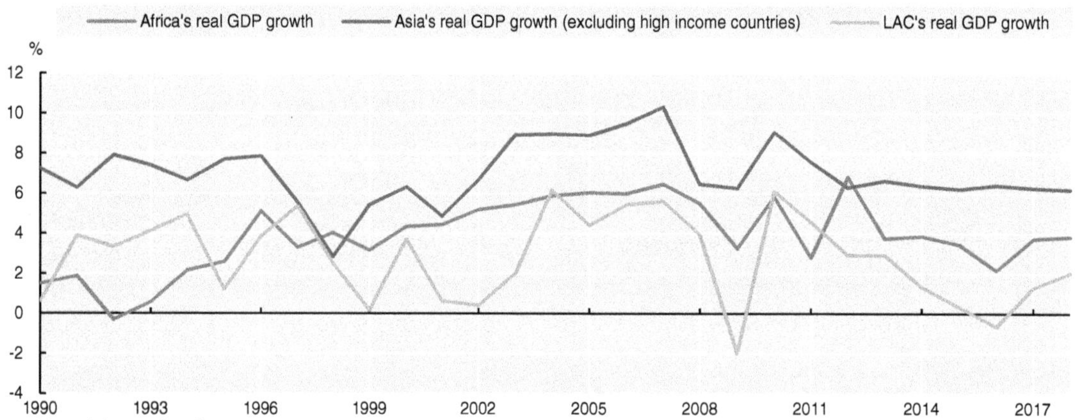

Note: (p) = projections.

Source: Authors' calculations based on IMF (2018), *World Economic Outlook Database.*

StatLink http://dx.doi.org/10.1787/888933782411

Figure 1.2. **Trade composition in Africa, 2016**

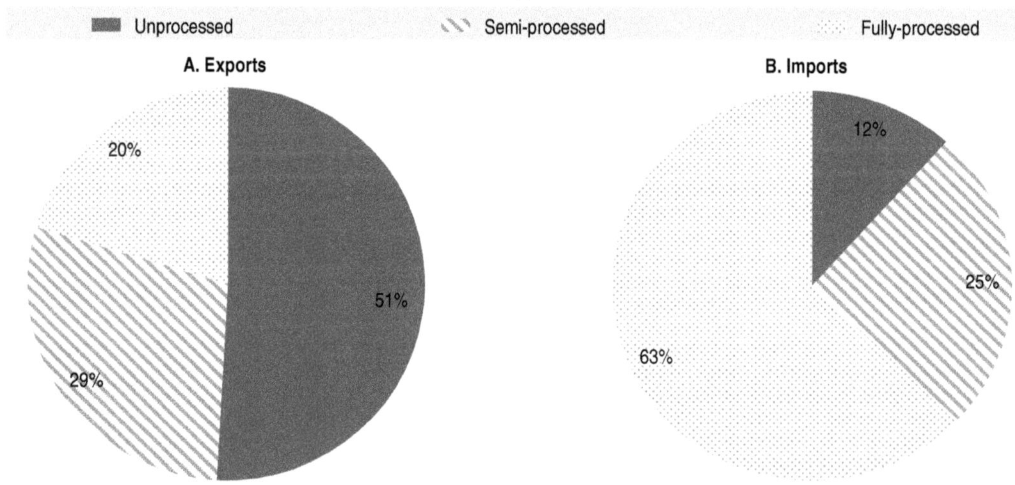

Source: Authors' calculations based on United Nations Statistics Division (2017), *UNCOMTRADE* (database).

StatLink http://dx.doi.org/10.1787/888933782430

Five reasons why Africa needs better growth patterns

Growth remains volatile, despite a strong process of capital accumulation and new trade partners

The African continent has experienced strong growth since 2000, leading to a so-called "rising Africa". From a historical perspective, Africa's growth performance has much improved compared to the 1990s when its per capita growth was negative. Between 2000 and 2008, Africa's growth rebounded at about 5.5% and per capita growth at 3.1%. This aggregate performance is better than that of LAC at 3.6% but lower than Asia's average of 8.0% for the same period. The number of African countries with GDP growth rates above their population growth also substantially increased. This growth performance benefited from favourable commodity prices, improved macroeconomic management and debt-relief, but also from growth diversification strategies in some countries (see Box 1.2).

Many African countries have invested strongly in public infrastructure, leading to a process of capital accumulation across the continent. Whereas capital stock in Africa grew roughly by only 2.5% in the early 1990s,[1] capital accumulation quickly accelerated in the early 2000s and reached 6.6% in 2009, a level similar to Asia's capital expansion (Figure 1.3, Panel A). The capital ratio per worker in Africa has increased steadily and attained a similar growth rate to LAC, even after adjusting for Africa's rapid labour expansion. This acceleration reflects the low starting point in many African countries. The average gross fixed capital formation was 22% of GDP for the whole continent (Figure 1.3, Panel B). For 16 African countries, it was over 30% of GDP. While private sector accounts for the majority of investment, public investment also amounted to 7% of GDP per year. During this period, many African governments invested in projects to fill the large infrastructure gap and boost aggregate demands in relation to the global economic crisis.

Figure 1.3. **Capital growth in Africa, Asia and LAC, 1992-2016, and gross fixed capital formation in Africa, 2009-16**

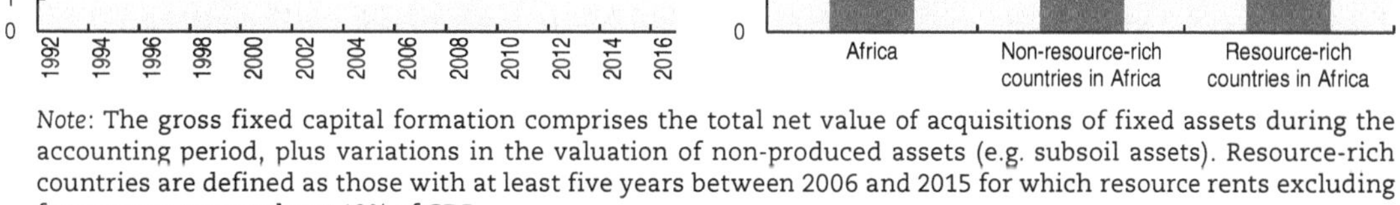

Note: The gross fixed capital formation comprises the total net value of acquisitions of fixed assets during the accounting period, plus variations in the valuation of non-produced assets (e.g. subsoil assets). Resource-rich countries are defined as those with at least five years between 2006 and 2015 for which resource rents excluding forest rents were at least 10% of GDP.

Sources: Panel A: Authors' calculations based on data from The Conference Board (2017), *Total Economy* (database), Panel B: World Bank (2017a), *World Development Indicators* (database); IMF (2018), *World Economic Outlook* (database).

StatLink http://dx.doi.org/10.1787/888933782449

Countries have also diversified their trade partnerships. Between 2000 and 2016, Africa tripled its trade with the rest of the world, from USD 276 billion to USD 806 billion. Trade flows with emerging partners like China and India expanded significantly (Figure 1.4). As a result, Africa's trade shifted from traditional to emerging trade partners. This holds both for African exports and imports. Trade with emerging economies accounted for 51%

of Africa's exports and 46% of Africa's imports in 2016. Nevertheless, expanding trade relations has not diversified the continent's export basket.

Figure 1.4. **Distribution of Africa's trade, 2000-16**

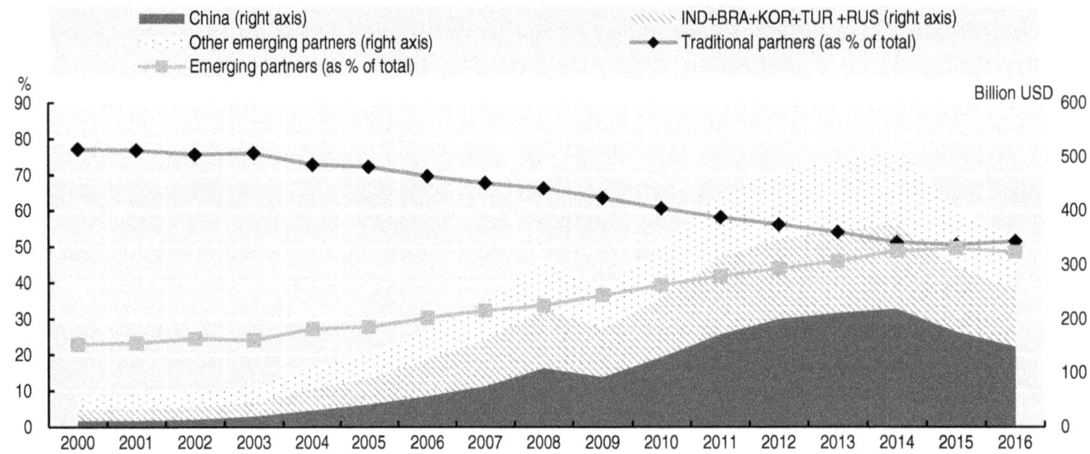

Note: India (IND), Brazil (BRA), Korea (KOR), Turkey (TUR), and Russia (RUS). Trade is the sum of Africa's exports and imports. Africa's emerging partners are those defined by OECD et al. (2011).

Source: Authors' calculations based on UN Statistics Division (2017), *UN COMTRADE* (database).

StatLink http://dx.doi.org/10.1787/888933782468

Sustaining growth over a long period is challenging for most African economies. Individual growth trajectories from 1970 to the mid-2000s reveal that growth spells tend to be shorter in African and Latin American countries than elsewhere (see Berg, Ostry and Zettelmeyer, 2012, for details). Recent data shows that growth volatility remains widespread:

- Africa's growth experienced a dip in 2008/09. In net-importing countries, a sharp increase in oil and food prices seriously affected household purchasing power and countries' current account balances, demonstrating Africa's vulnerability to external commodity shocks.
- Africa's growth experienced a second low point in 2010 largely related to the Arab Spring. This revealed, among other things, that prior growth did not create enough jobs and was not inclusive.
- In 2016, the continent's GDP growth dropped temporarily as unfavourable commodity prices again hit many large economies that are based on natural resources. GDP growth is expected to recover slowly and reach 2.8% in 2018, in part due to Africa's resilient domestic demand and a recovery in oil prices.

The volatility of growth varies widely across countries, depending on the structures of their exports and production. The standard deviation of annual growth between 2000 and 2017 is significantly higher for resource-rich African countries, at 9.0 points, than for non-resource-rich African countries (3.2 points), developing Asian countries (4.1 points) and developing LAC countries (2.6 points). This comparison between resource-rich and non-resource-rich countries is instructive:

- The resource-rich countries have enjoyed stronger terms of trade and have average growth since 2000 at more than 6% a year due to high commodity prices, especially for fuel (petroleum, natural gas and coal) and metals (Figure 1.5, Panel A). However, the high concentration of export earnings from only few natural resources has led to unstable government revenues. It has deterred governments from committing to long-term public investment and from sustaining social spending. As commodities prices dropped sharply between 2012 and 2016 (57% for fuel and almost a third for metals and minerals), domestic revenues in resource-rich countries decreased by 44%. The slump in commodity prices reduced the continent's growth to 2.2% in 2016.

- By contrast, non-resource-rich countries have registered more stable growth at about 4% a year since 2000. Between 2000 and 2015, the services sector contributed about 3 percentage points a year to annual GDP growth, compared to 1.1 percentage points for industry and 0.6 percentage points for agriculture (Figure 1.5, Panel B). A number of countries, such as Ethiopia, Kenya and Rwanda, have successfully boosted growth through public investment (mostly in large infrastructure projects) and buoyant services. In addition, net oil importers have benefited from lower fuel prices in recent years, hence reducing their import bills. The second half of this chapter will elaborate on the drivers of growth across African countries.

Figure 1.5. **Sectors driving the annual growth in Africa: Resource-rich versus non-resource-rich countries, 1990-2016**

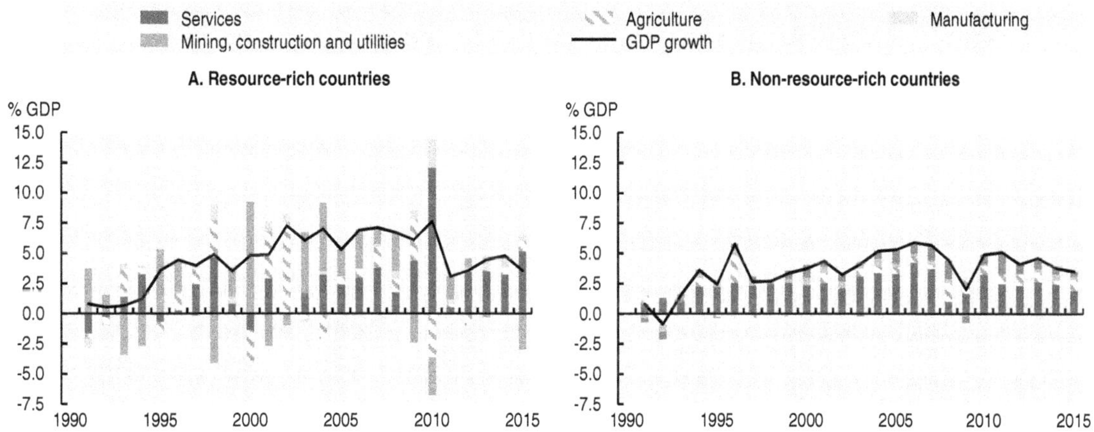

Note: Resource-rich countries are defined as those with at least five years between 2006 and 2015 during which resource rents excluding forest rents were at least 10% of GDP. For the resource-rich countries, the peak in the contribution of services in 2010 is in part due to the "rebasing" effect of Nigeria's GDP. The rebasing happened in 2015, but the GDP series of country was readjusted back to 2010.

Source: Authors' calculations based on IMF (2018), *World Economic Outlook* (database).

StatLink http://dx.doi.org/10.1787/888933782487

Under a business-as-usual scenario, Africa is unlikely to meet the targets set in the first ten-year implementation plan of the African Union's Agenda 2063. In the first half of the plan (2013-17), Africa's real GDP grew at 3.4% a year. For the next five-year period (2018-22), Africa's real GDP growth is projected at 3.9%. Africa is lagging behind its 7% a year target by more than 3 percentage points annually. Achieving high growth rates has proven difficult for all countries worldwide since the 2009 global crisis (Table 1.3).

Table 1.3. **Growth rates for African countries, other developing countries and high-income countries, 2000-20**

		Number of countries in each growth category			
		2000-05	2006-10	2011-15	2016-20 (p)
African countries	Growth above 7%	9	9	6	3
	Growth of 0-7%	38	41	43	48
	Negative growth	5	2	3	3
Other developing countries	Growth above 7%	15	14	10	6
	Growth of 0-7%	63	64	65	73
	Negative growth	2	4	6	2
High-income countries	Growth above 7%	6	1	1	0
	Growth of 0-7%	46	43	43	51
	Negative growth	0	8	8	1

Note: (p) : projections.
Source: Authors' calculations based on IMF (2018), *World Economic Outlook* (database).

African countries need to strengthen the drivers of long-term growth. The contribution of labour to growth has not increased much over time, and total factor productivity (TFP) gains have remained small and volatile. Despite the process of strong capital accumulation between 2009 and 2016, Africa experienced virtually no growth in TFP (Figure 1.6). This situation is better than in LAC, where TFP growth was negative during the same period. But Africa lags behind Asia, where TFP contributed 1 percentage point to annual growth. Slow TFP growth is a source of concern as long-term growth depends on sustained improvement in productivity. The vulnerability of African economies to external shocks and climatic conditions such as droughts is one of the main factors explaining the volatility of TFP. In agriculture-based economies, for example, higher agricultural commodity prices, rather than agricultural productivity growth, have been the driving force for TFP gains (IMF, 2016a).

Figure 1.6. **Contribution of total factor productivity, labour, and capital to GDP growth in Africa, Asia and LAC, 1990-2016**

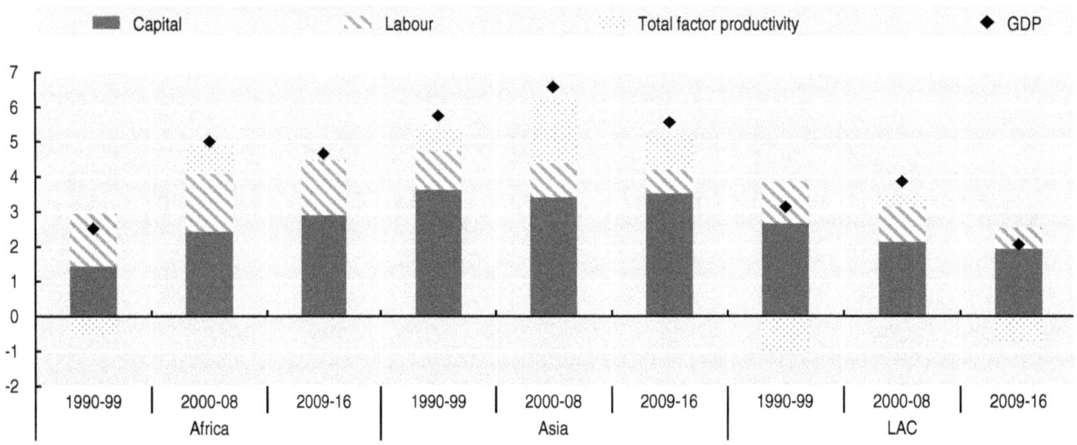

Note: TFP stands for total factor productivity, measured as the variation in GDP not explained by the contribution of labour and capital to GDP.

Source: Authors' calculations based on data from The Conference Board (2017), *Total Economy* (database).

StatLink http://dx.doi.org/10.1787/888933782506

While public investments can help jump-start growth, sustaining it over a long period depends on a set of country-specific policy factors. The literature suggests that a number of factors can sustain growth (e.g. Berg, Ostry and Zettelmeyer, 2012). Prolonging growth episodes depends on the stability of macroeconomic environments (such as inflation rates), higher financial development (proxied by the ratio of private credit to GDP) and more equal income distribution. Political competition and the strength of policy-making institutions also help countries enjoy longer growth spells. Countries' capacity to manage external shocks – such as changes in interest rates and in the terms of trade – plays a crucial role in increasing the probability of growth episodes, while decreasing the probability of growth reversals. Many African countries have improved their macroeconomic management, their regulatory frameworks and the quality of public institutions. However, further steps are needed to reduce vulnerability and to achieve stronger and less volatile growth that translates into higher levels of well-being.

Recent GDP growth has not increased well-being

Despite Africa's strong growth performance since 2000, the correlation between the continent's GDP per capita and well-being indicators appears weaker than the world average. In Africa, like in the rest of the world, gross national income per capita and gross secondary school enrolment rates correlate relatively strongly with GDP per capita. However, outcomes related to other dimensions of well-being, such as years of schooling, health status and housing conditions, have a much weaker association with GDP per capita in Africa than the world average (Table 1.4). Results are similar for several dimensions of subjective well-being, including satisfaction with standards of living and with health coverage availability. Dimensions related to public governance – satisfaction with educational systems and perceived corruption – are also sources of concern. Compared to other countries with similar levels of income per capita, many African countries seem less able to transform resource flows into positive outcomes for the well-being of their citizens.

It is possible that, in a number of African countries, policies have not been effective enough in improving well-being. This may be the case where indicators of well-being weakly correlate with GDP per capita (Box 1.1). Resource-rich countries lag behind non-resource-rich countries in a number of well-being dimensions (Christiansen, Schindler and Tressel, 2013: 9-10). One hypothesis is that the dependence on resources makes their growth too volatile and less conducive to an increase in well-being.

Box 1.1. The correlation between GDP per capita and selected well-being indicators in Africa and the world

Development is often considered synonymous with economic growth, and yet GDP growth is only one indicator of development among many. Human development fails when aggregate increases in productivity and material wealth do not produce meaningful gains in the overall well-being of a country's population. Economic growth is only a means to an end: the sustainable and equitable improvement of people's lives. Going beyond macroeconomic metrics and monitoring well-being across the many different areas that matter for citizens are necessary to comprehensively assess the quality of life within a country.

The OECD measures well-being in non-OECD countries by looking at well-being outcomes in two broad areas: material conditions and quality of life (see Boarini, Kolev and McGregor, 2014). Material conditions encompass various consumption possibilities, work, housing conditions and infrastructure. Quality of life comprises health status, education and skills, social connections, empowerment and participation, vulnerability and life evaluations, and feelings and meaning – which are the main aspects of subjective well-being.

Table 1.4. Correlation between well-being indicators and GDP per capita in Africa and the world

	Correlation			Correlation	
Variables	All countries	Africa (average)	Variables	All countries	Africa (average)
Gross national income per capita	0.9969	0.9966	Having someone to count on in an emergency	0.4825	0.2951
Vulnerable employment	0.7860	0.7212	Satisfaction with water quality	0.4586	0.1961
Education and skills: gross enrolment ratio (secondary school)	0.7504	0.7932	Satisfaction with roads	0.4376	0.3033
Expected years of schooling	0.7085	0.4876	Lack of money for shelter	0.4209	0.3213
Access to improved sanitation	0.7139	0.4763	Having no health problem	0.4008	0.2196
Child mortality ratio	0.6861	0.4138	Satisfaction with standard of living	0.3916	0.2502
Life satisfaction	0.6707	0.4871	Satisfaction with health coverage availability	0.3621	0.1092
Life expectancy	0.6689	0.2186	Dissatisfaction with household income	0.2750	0.3614
Lack of money for food	0.6361	0.3574	Change in forest land cover	0.2432	0.0826
Adult literacy	0.6256	0.4234	Satisfaction with educational system	0.2395	0.0525
Maternal mortality ratio	0.6038	0.4139	Sense of safety when walking alone at night	0.1424	0.0005
Health coverage	0.5851	0.3207	Perceived widespread corruption	0.1193	0.0484
Perceived Corruption Index	0.5522	0.148			

Note: The correlation between variables is calculated using the R square.

Source: Authors' calculations based on World Bank (2017a), *World Development Indicators* (database), and Gallup (2017), *Gallup World Poll*.

The continent needs to generate more quality jobs for its large labour force

Quality jobs remain scarce across the continent. Relatively high growth since 2000 has not created enough quality jobs, and the share of vulnerable employment remains stubbornly high. According to International Labour Organization data, 34% of Africa's workers had wage-paying jobs or were employers in 2017, and 66% were in vulnerable employment as own-account or family workers (Figure 1.7). While the unemployment rate stood at only 7.2% of the labour force in 2017, 30% of the workers remained poor despite working.

The continent also has one of the highest rates of informality outside the agricultural sector. The rates range from 34% of employed people in South Africa to 90.6% in Benin (ILO, 2018). The income level for informal workers is often highly vulnerable to various economic shocks, and the social protection system covers few informal workers.

Figure 1.7. **Employment status for Africans, 1990-2022, and the 2023 targets of Agenda 2063**

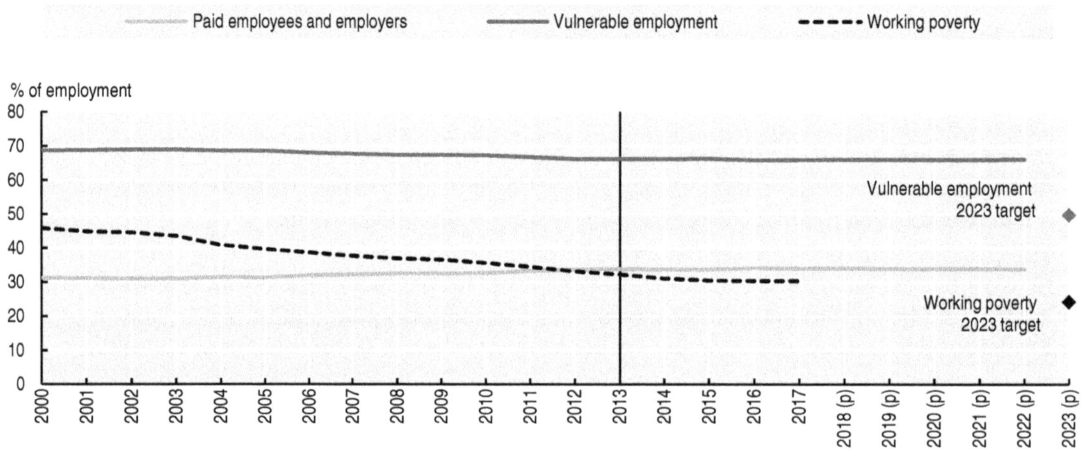

Note: (p) : projections.
Source: Authors' calculations based on the ILO (2017), *ILOSTAT*.
StatLink http://dx.doi.org/10.1787/888933782525

If current trends continue, Africa will not meet the quality employment targets set out in the first ten-year implementation plan of Agenda 2063.

- The most challenging target relates to vulnerable employment. The share of vulnerable employment has fallen by only 2 percent points since 2000, and is projected to persist at 66% in 2022 (Figure 1.7). If this trend continues, Africa would not make any progress on its target of reducing the vulnerable employment rate by 25 percentage points, from 66% in 2013 to 41% in 2023.
- The share of workers living on less than USD 1.90 (purchasing power parity [PPP]) a day decreased from 46% in 2000 to 30% in 2017. However, such progress may not suffice to meet the 2023 target of reducing the share of the working poor to 24%. If the working poverty rate follows the average trend between 2000 and 2017 and declines by 0.91 percentage points a year, working poverty will decrease to 25%.

Despite general progress, workplace disparities between men and women continue to worsen in many countries. African countries have made much progress in increasing educational attainment for women since 2000. However, only 12% of Africa's working age women were on wage-paying employment in 2016 (Figure 1.8). Other developing countries have much better rates: 22% in Asia and 33% in LAC. In 2016, 75% of Africa's female workers remained in vulnerable employment, and almost 35% were working poor

(ILO, 2018). Inequalities are also found in relation to females' participation in the labour force, in entrepreneurship opportunities and in access to economic assets (UNDP, 2016). The gender pay gap in the non-agricultural sector stands at 30% (UNDP, 2017: 4).

Figure 1.8. **Waged employees as a percentage of the working-age population in Africa, Asia and LAC, 2000 and 2016**

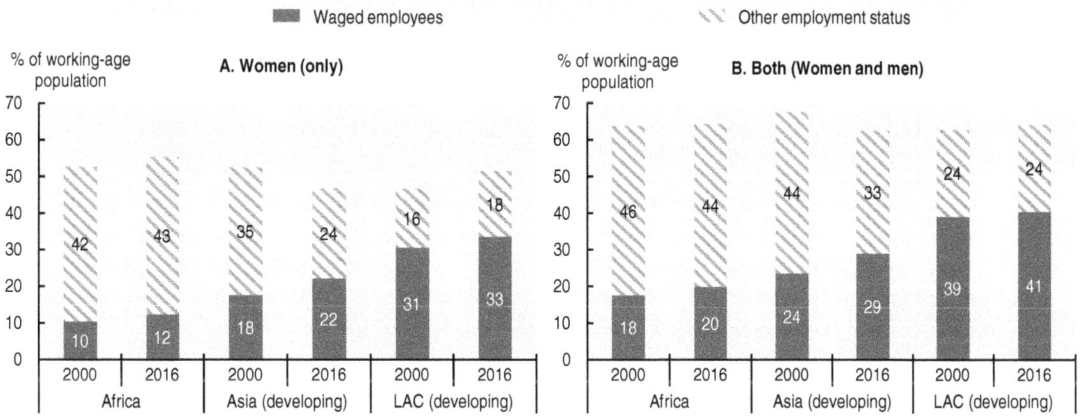

Source: Authors' calculations based on the ILO (2017), *ILOSTAT* (KILM database).
StatLink http://dx.doi.org/10.1787/888933782544

Young people suffer from underemployment and a lack of wage-paying jobs. About 42% of the working youth live on less than USD 1.90 a day (PPP). In low-income African countries, only 17% of the working youth (7% of all youth) are full-time employees (AfDB/OECD/UNDP/UNECA, 2012). The lack of wage-paying jobs is challenging for governments, as the majority of African countries face extremely rapid demographic and urban growth. Middle-income countries in Africa face a similar dearth of quality jobs, as many young people remain out of the labour market. In North Africa for example, 26.1% of young people between the ages of 15 and 24 are not in education, employment or training (NEET), the second highest rate globally (ILO, 2018). In that region, youth make up more than 34% of the total unemployed population while representing only about 15% of the labour force. In South Africa, the share of youth in NEET has stayed consistently high, at over 30%, every year for which data is available since 2012.

Further alleviating poverty requires reducing income inequality

All in all, the continent has made good progress in fighting extreme poverty since 2000. Africa's share of the population living on USD 1.90 a day or less declined from an average of 49% in the 1990s to 36% in the 2009-16 period.

- Six countries – Algeria, Egypt, Mauritius, Morocco, Seychelles and Tunisia – have almost eliminated extreme poverty (Figure 1.9). In Morocco, for example, the national initiative for human development (INDH), launched in 2005, has successfully helped vulnerable groups by encouraging income-generating activities and social protection measures such as health coverage. By end 2015, about 8.5 million people belonging to the poor or the most vulnerable households in Morocco had access to free or partly-free health care in public hospitals through the RAMED insurance launched in 2008 (see OECD, 2017a: 163). The government also provides a 24-month exemption of social security contributions for the long-term unemployed who take part in the Idmaj training programme.
- In six other countries – Burkina Faso, Chad, Guinea, Liberia, Niger and Tanzania – the annual pace of poverty reduction since 2000 was similar to China's between 1996 and 2013.

- Overall, non-resource-rich countries in Africa have been notably successful in reducing poverty rates, from 57% to 37%. However, most of these countries have benefited from debt relief programmes which may no longer be available in the future (see note for Figure 1.9).

Many African governments need to further reduce poverty for four reasons:

1. Although the proportion of poor people has decreased, their absolute number has increased due to rapid population growth in the poorest segments of society. The number of people living on less than USD 1.90 a day increased by 105 million between 1990 and 2013, from 280 million to 395 million. Resource-rich countries accounted for 65% of this increase (68 million people).
2. About half the countries (27) still have poverty rates above 25%. Resource-rich African countries have managed to decrease poverty rates by only 5 percentage points, from 41 % to 36 % despite strong growth since 2000. This is disappointing, because resource-rich countries in other world regions such as Asia and LAC have been much more successful at reducing poverty. In LAC, for example, the poverty headcount ratio fell from 14% to 5% between 1990 and 2013.
3. Debt relief from the Heavily Indebted Poor Countries (HIPC)[2] and multilateral debt relief initiatives helped 30 African countries increase their social spending between 1998 and 2012. As they are completing the HIPC programmes, the countries will need to find new approaches for financing poverty reduction programmes.
4. About 45% of the population earn USD 1.90-5.50 a day and remain poor or vulnerable to falling back into poverty. Further efforts to boost their income and social protection are essential to move this group firmly out of poverty.

Figure 1.9. **Poverty reduction in 42 African countries, Brazil, China, India, Indonesia and Viet Nam**

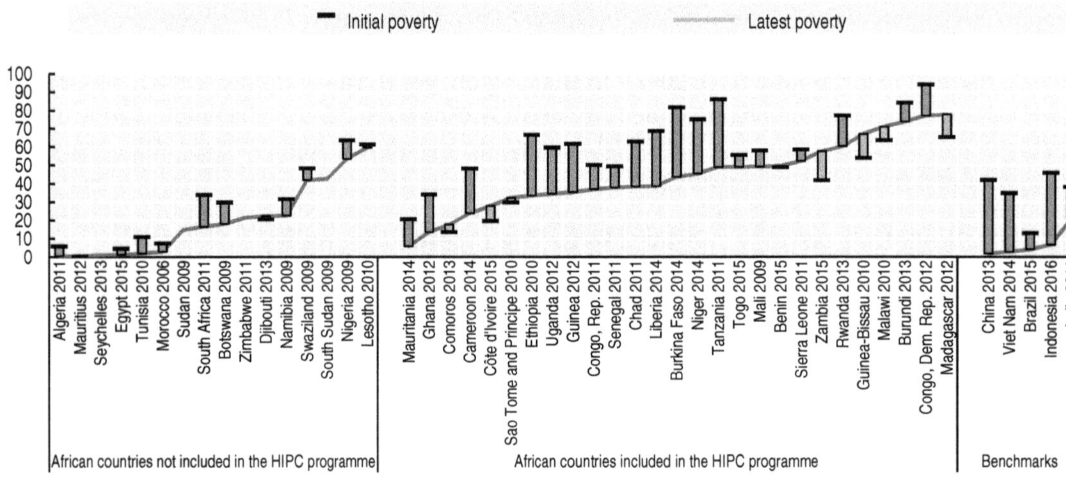

Note: Heavily Indebted Poor Countries (HIPC). The year indicates the latest survey year for calculating the poverty rate.

Source: World Bank (2017b), *PovcalNet* (database).

StatLink http://dx.doi.org/10.1787/888933782563

Reducing income inequality can help reduce poverty faster. The unweighted Gini coefficient[3] for Africa averages 41 points, which is higher than Asia's unweighted average of 35 points. Several econometric analyses show that reducing income inequalities in Africa would enable growth to reduce much more poverty (see Christiansen, Schindler and Tressel, 2013: 13; Thorbecke and Ouyang, 2017: Table 3). Our estimations based on the PovcalNet database (World Bank, 2017) show that lowering Africa's current Gini level to Asia's average

(35 points) would decrease its poverty headcount by about 2 percentage points for each percentage point of GDP growth. This compares to the actual decrease of 1.5 percentage points observed between 1990 and 2016. Such a decrease of inequality would reduce the number of poor people by 130 million, from 394 million in 2016 to 264 million.

Several African governments have managed to reduce inequality by using fiscal policies and reforms, however lower growth prospects in the short term may put budgetary pressure on these programmes. South Africa in particular has developed a progressive tax and social protection system that reduced its Gini coefficient from 77 to 60. South Africa has the highest reduction in Gini coefficients among a sample of 29 developing countries in the Commitment to Equity Database (Figure 1.10). Other African countries in the sample, namely Ethiopia, Ghana, Tanzania, Tunisia and Uganda, have also succeeded to reduce their Gini coefficients, though to a lesser extent. The decline in the number of conflicts has also helped to reduce inequality.

However, a high concentration of land and of physical and human capital (often due to historical legacies) limits the impact of redistributive policies. In many countries, weak governance of taxation and low social spending contribute to a limited redistributive capacity of the state, to biased public policies that favour politically-connected regions, and to ethnic and gender inequalities (UNDP, 2017).

Figure 1.10. **Gini coefficients of market and final income in selected countries**

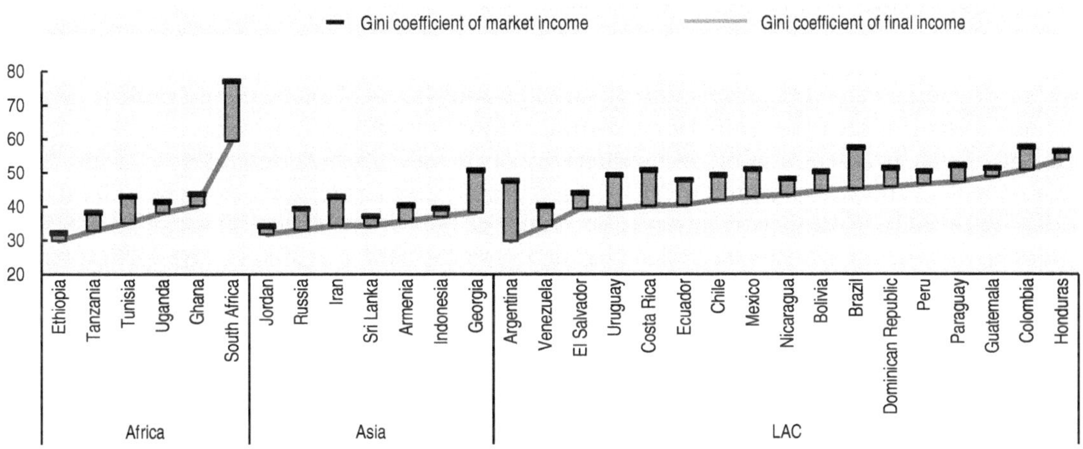

Source: CEQ Institute (2018), *Commitment to Equity Institute Data Center on Fiscal Redistribution.*[4]
StatLink http://dx.doi.org/10.1787/888933782582

If business continues as usual, structural transformation may be hard to sustain

Since 2000, Africa has experienced positive structural transformation as labour has moved from less productive activities to more productive ones. In a sample of 13 African countries where data is available, the sectoral shift of labour contributed 0.5 percentage points per year to labour productivity growth between 2000 and 2010, the same contribution as in Asia (Figure 1.11). Services like wholesale and retail trade, restaurants, and hotels absorbed the most surplus agricultural workers. Their share in total employment almost doubled in two decades, reaching 20.1% in 2010, up from 11.4% in 1990. An increase in natural resource rents and remittances boosted the demand for domestic consumption of non-tradable goods and services. In addition, opening up to private investment and competition helped expand activities with higher productivity levels such as telecommunications and banking services. As a result, overall labour productivity in Africa increased by 2.5% a year between 2000 and 2010, compared to 1% one decade earlier.[5]

Figure 1.11. **Decomposition of labour productivity growth in 31 developing countries in Africa, Asia and LAC, 1990-2010**

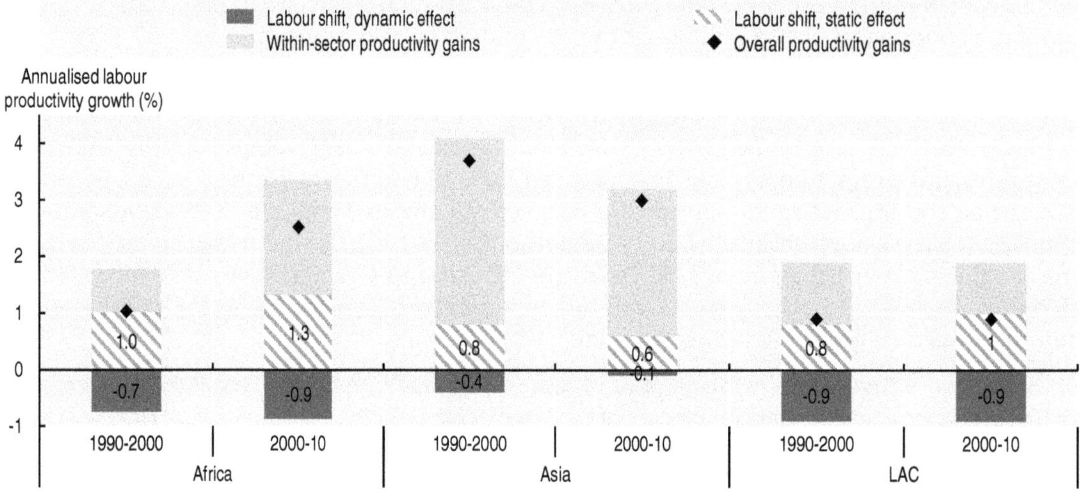

Note: African countries include Botswana, Egypt, Ethiopia, Ghana, Kenya, Malawi, Mauritius, Morocco, Nigeria, Senegal, South Africa, Tanzania and Zambia. Asia includes 11 countries, and LAC includes 9 countries. The overall effect of the sectoral shift of labour is the sum of static and dynamic effects.

Source: Authors' calculations based on De Vries et al. (2015), *GGDC 10-Sector Database*.

StatLink http://dx.doi.org/10.1787/888933782601

However, this process is reaching its limits as Africa's labour is moving into activities where productivity levels are declining. As more and more workers move into sectors experiencing declining productivity, the overall productivity gains from labour reallocation diminish over time. The decline in productivity of the labour-absorbing sectors reduced annual labour productivity growth by 0.9 percentage points annually between 2000 and 2010 (Figure 1.11). With the exception of South Africa (where the effect is negligible), this effect is observed in all other 12 African countries where data is available. The variations are significant, ranging from -0.6 percentage points in Nigeria to -2.2 percentage points in Botswana. Such "dynamic losses" during a structural transformation resemble those experienced by LAC, but not by Asia (De Vries, Timmer and de Vries, 2015).

African firms' productivity tends to lag behind that of their global competitors in many sectors. The Africa-to-Asia ratio of labour productivity has decreased since 2000 (Figure 1.12). This has been obvious in agriculture, as well as in market services such as transports, financial activities, construction and manufacturing. The next section will use firm-level data on 11 manufacturing activities to explain the factors contributing to this negative TFP differential for African firms.

In terms of the employment outlook, service-led development is a challenging opportunity for most African countries due to higher skill requirements. The services sector plays an increasingly important role in Africa's development. Recently, legal, financial and business services have been increasingly traded across African countries. If this trend continues, more services may become tradable and even expand to foreign markets thanks to new technologies, improved infrastructure and lower barriers to trade. However, most of the new generation of tradable services require high skill levels, which may not yet be accessible to the majority of Africa's labour force. Skill requirements are even greater in services than in many segments of manufacturing. Today the services sector as a whole absorbs a significant share of entrepreneurs and wage employment, but its productivity levels are low and employment is often vulnerable or informal. Many service firms in African countries need support to comply with the quality and other standards required to gain access to exports markets (ECA, 2017).

Figure 1.12. **Africa/Asia ratios of labour productivity in services, construction and manufacturing, 1990-2010**

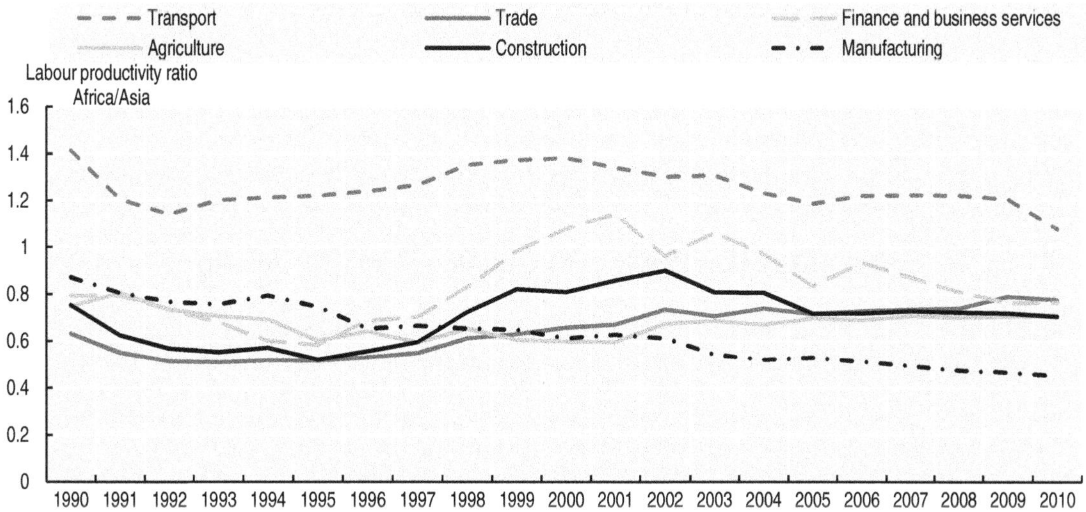

Note: African countries include Botswana, Egypt, Ethiopia, Ghana, Kenya, Malawi, Mauritius, Morocco, Nigeria, Senegal, South Africa, Tanzania and Zambia. Asia includes 11 countries.

Source: Authors' calculations based on De Vries et al. (2015), *GGDC 10-Sector Database*.

StatLink http://dx.doi.org/10.1787/888933782620

Regional and global markets offer Africa opportunies for growth but require new policies

This section analyses new growth avenues that regional and global markets present to African economies. To take advantage of the many opportunities they offer, African governments need to adapt their strategies to a new economic reality. Technological change, global value chains, and evolving trade and investment agreements are reshaping opportunities for integration into regional and global markets. Governments will need to be innovative in mobilising domestic savings and external financial inflows.

Better integration into global economy can increase growth, employment and equality

The continent can build on its current level of global integration to achieve better growth, employment and equality. This chapter's first section highlighted that Africa's growth is high but volatile and does not translate into sufficient development outcomes. The present section shows that upgrading the quality of existing products, expanding exports products and improving access to capital goods and inputs can provide ways to sustain growth, increase job quality and reduce inequality. In this process, intra-African trade will be an important lever for policy action.

The challenge for most African countries is not to further integrate into the global economy but how to integrate in a better way. Africa is already open to international trade and connected to global value chains (GVCs). Imports and exports of goods and services represented about 50% of Africa's GDP in 2015-16, which is similar to Asia, and higher than in the LAC region (44%). Integration into GVCs is also higher in Africa than in LAC and South Asia. GVC participation have increased since the 1990s (AfDB/OECD/UNDP, 2014).

Diversifying exports can increase and sustain economic growth. The majority of Africa's exports are unprocessed commodities (Figure 1.2). More diversified export baskets are associated with higher economic growth rates (Figure 1.13). Introducing new products to export markets strongly correlates with cumulative long-term growth of GDP per capita (Klinger and Lederman, 2004; Rieländer and Traoré, 2016). More diverse product baskets lead to more stable export earnings over the longer run, reducing macroeconomic uncertainty and encouraging more investment in the economy (Ghosh and Ostry, 1994; Bleaney and Greenaway, 2001). Moreover, developing the capabilities to export more sophisticated products tends to help countries recover from stagnation periods and to prolong growth spells (Hausmann, Pritchett and Rodrik, 2005; Berg, Ostry and Zettelmeyer, 2012). Upgrading to more sophisticated export products builds countries' capacity to move to other export baskets, leading to higher growth in the context of adverse shocks.

Figure 1.13. **Export discoveries and long-term GDP growth**

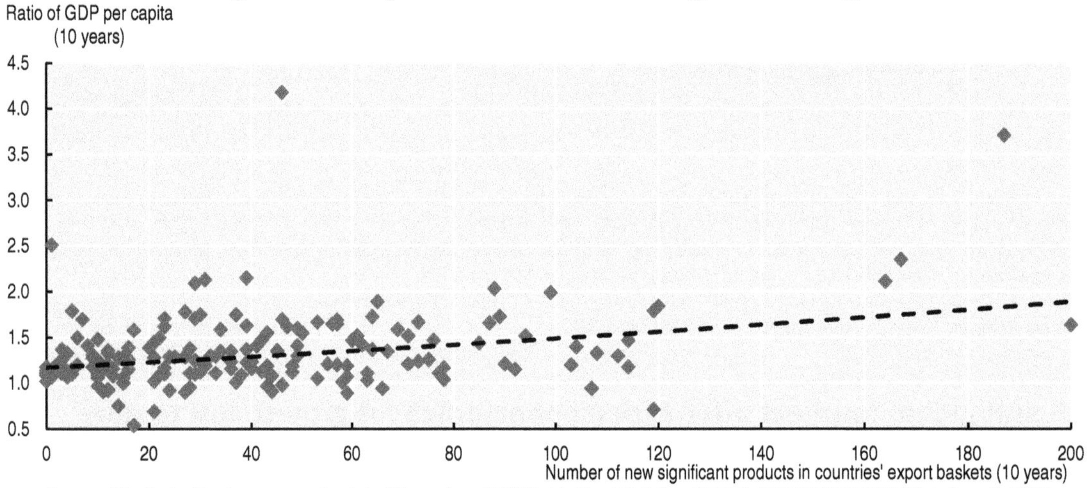

Source: Trade indicators are calculated based on UN Statistics Division (2017), *UN COMTRADE* (database). GDP per capita figures are calculated based on World Bank (2017a), *World Development Indicators* (database).

StatLink http://dx.doi.org/10.1787/888933782639

Concentrating exports on few products also influences inequality outcomes and job quality across the continent. Improving a country's ability to produce and export more complex goods is likely to help it generate and distribute more wealth across society. Currently, the majority of African countries export few fully-processed products, as shown by their positions in Figure 1.14, Panel A. Diversifying into products with larger spill-overs and a strong influence on other sectors can help create formal jobs and encourage local informal firms to formalise. Figure 1.14, Panel B shows the negative correlations between export complexity and the share of vulnerable employment. In contrast, concentrating exports on few products can lead to spatial inequalities, especially where the export industries are concentrated in a specific place, as is the case of mining.

Facilitating access to imports of high quality – both capital and intermediate inputs – can help diversify Africa's exports. Africa has steadily increased its imports of capital and intermediate goods, from 7% of GDP in 1990-99 to 9% in 2009-14 (Figure 1.15, Panel A). However, many firms, especially SMEs, face difficulties in getting import licenses, according to firm-level surveys. A systematic review of tariffs in the East African Economic Community also shows that many intermediate goods are misclassified and face higher tariffs than final consumption goods. High quality inputs enable domestic firms to increase productivity and the quality and variety of the end products (Lopez Gonzalez, 2016).[6] Moreover, importing and exporting activities create numerous synergies at the firm level. Facilitating local firms' access to lower-priced imported inputs can decrease their fixed costs of exporting, thus encouraging them to export (Pierola, Fernandes and Farole, 2017).

Figure 1.14. Export diversification, income inequality and job quality in African countries

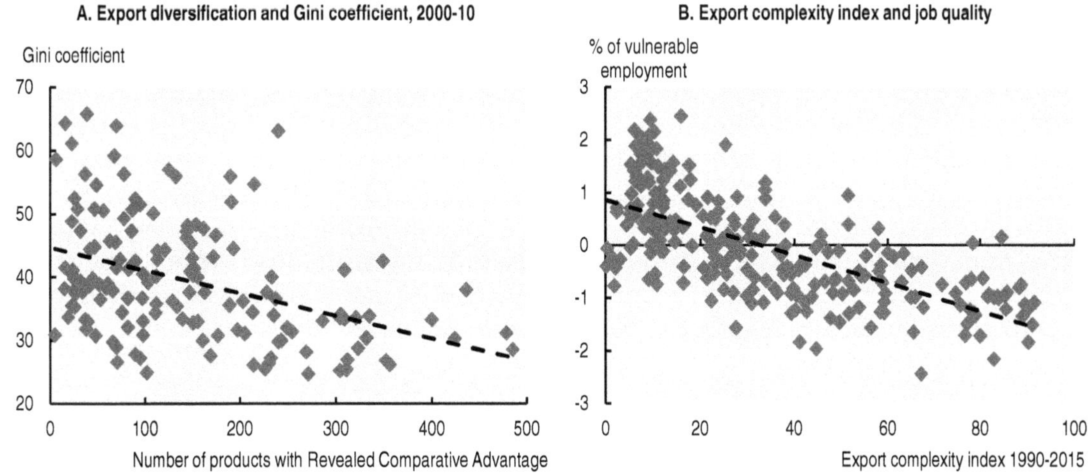

Note: A higher Gini coefficient suggests a higher level of income inequality within the country.

Source: Export diversification is calculated based on UN Statistics Division (2017), *UN COMTRADE* (database). The export complexity index is from Atlas of Economic Complexity (2017). Gini coefficients are from World Bank (2017b), *PovcalNet* (database).

StatLink http://dx.doi.org/10.1787/888933782658

Figure 1.15. Trade in intermediate and capital goods within and outside selected world regions, 2014

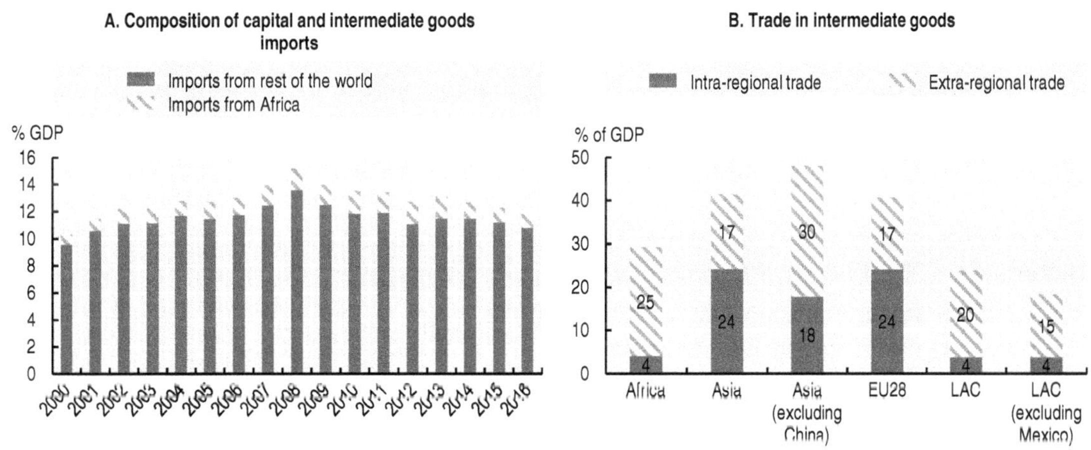

Note: Trade in intermediate goods is defined as total trade (i.e. the sum of gross exports and gross imports) in the sectors classified as primary and processed food and beverages destined mainly for industry, other industrial supplies, fuels and lubricants other than processed motor spirits, and parts and accessories for capital goods and transport equipment. The sectors previously mentioned are drawn from the classification by Broad Economic Categories.

Source: Authors' calculations based on UN Statistics Division (2017), *UN COMTRADE* (database).

StatLink http://dx.doi.org/10.1787/888933782677

Regional value chains and emerging markets offer sizable opportunities for small exporters as standards are lower and growth rates higher. In the case of Africa, intra-regional trade in intermediate goods stands at only 4.1% of GDP compared to 24.2% in Asia and 16.6% in the European Union (Figure 1.15, Panel B). Data for 152 countries over 15 years confirm that access to intermediate inputs from regional and global markets have positive impacts on countries' export competitiveness, exports sophistication and domestic value addition (Kowalski et al., 2015). Improving trade facilitation measures such as logistics and customs performance, intellectual property protection policies, trade infrastructure and the electricity supply significantly contribute to developing regional value chains.

Having a regional integration agreement does not automatically lead to strong trade flows or to establishing regional value chains (IMF, 2016b). Three of the regional economic communities in Africa provide interesting insight in this respect. Cross-border exchanges within the East African Community are found to be five times larger than average trade flows within Africa, while in the West African Economic and Monetary Union, they are about three times larger (see Chapters 5 and 7). At the same time, the Economic Community of Central African States region continues to exhibit low levels of integration, with only 1.3% of total trade being intra-regional. This is mainly due to limited complementarity between countries' trade profiles and underdeveloped trading infrastructure (Avom and Mignamissi, 2017; see also Chapter 4).

The new continental free trade area (CFTA) offers a stepping-stone for Africa's regional economic communities (RECs) to boost regional integration. On 21 March 2018 in Kigali, Rwanda, the head of 44 African countries signed the CFTA, one of the world's largest free trade areas. The CFTA aims to achieve four main objectives:

- create a single continental market for goods and services, with free movement of business people and investments, and thus accelerate the establishment of the Continental Customs Union and the African Customs Union
- expand intra-African trade through better harmonisation and co-ordination of trade liberalisation and facilitation regimes and instruments across RECs and Africa in general
- resolve the challenges of multiple and overlapping memberships and expedite the regional and continental integration processes
- enhance competitiveness at the industry and enterprise levels by exploiting opportunities for scale production, continental market access and better reallocation of resources.

African countries should consider four types of economic upgrading, depending on their current production structure and export performance, as well as the nature of the value chains (OECD, 2013a; Kaplinsky and Morris, 2002):

- **Functional upgrading** entails expanding the range of activities that a country already performs within a specific value chain. If the initial link to a global value chain is in production only, for example in cutting, sewing and trimming shirts, functional upgrading could entail developing upstream activities such as the sourcing of textiles.
- **Product upgrading** refers to the production of more sophisticated products, such as going from whole pineapples to freshly cut ones.
- In **chain upgrading**, the skills acquired are used to enter a new value chain, for example moving to textile production based on the knowledge and skills gathered in the apparel value chain.
- Finally, **process upgrading** refers to increasing productivity in a given stage of a value chain through local innovation (OECD/WTO, 2013; Morris and Barnes, 2009).

Strategies to tap the African and global markets must tailor to the local conditions. Since 2000, some African countries have successfully implemented export-led growth strategies but without creating enough jobs. Box 1.2 proposes several examples to show different paths that African governments have pursued so far.

Box 1.2. **Selected examples of African governments' global integration strategies**

The four African countries below illustrate various global integration strategies, according to their respective strengths and weaknesses.

In **Ethiopia**, the government's Industrial Development Strategy aims to promote exports in labour-intensive sectors such as textiles and garments, leather, sugar, flowers and cement. The government has set up a number of special economic zones to attract foreign investors into these sectors and has linked local producers' associations to the world market. Massive public-led infrastructure investments have taken place in the energy, transport, communications, agriculture and social sectors, albeit their initial levels were low (Moller and Wacker, 2017). Investors in strategic sectors benefit from generous fiscal incentives, reduced import duties for capital goods and raw materials necessary for production, and preferential access to land and concessionary funding. The strategy also includes transport arrangements by the state-owned Ethiopian Airlines.

Morocco has attracted FDI into new export activities to take advantage of its geographical proximity to European Union markets, existing trade agreements and political stability. The strategic plans Emerging Morocco 2005-09, followed by the National Pact for Industrial Emergence 2009-2015, focused on seven specific export-oriented activities – known as the seven World Crafts of Morocco: the aeronautics, automotive, electrical equipment, agro-processing, textile and leather sectors and off-shoring activities. The country is performing well in the automotive, electrical equipment, and aeronautics industries and in service related off-shoring activities (e.g. business process outsourcing). The automotive industry became the country's biggest export sector in 2014, and reached USD 5.3 billion in 2015. However, traditional export sectors, such as apparel and textiles, have been losing jobs due to declining competitiveness (El Mokri, 2016; OECD, 2017a).

Senegal has successfully begun diversifying its exports through an agricultural value-chain approach. Active government support for selected agricultural chains, such as rice, onions, groundnuts and fruits, has helped the country improve food security and diversify its export basket. Since 2010, Senegal has significantly boosted its exports of horticultural products, mostly to European markets. However, government support has mostly focused on the production side. Post-production segments of the value chain, such as processing, storage and marketing, face important binding constraints, especially in the rice sector.

Senegal's trade openness (total imports and exports of goods and services) was about 75% of GDP between 2011 and 2015. Remittance inflows were at about 10% of GDP annually, boosting growth. Yet, between 2007 and 2009, the economy proved vulnerable to the exogenous shocks of the energy, food and financial crises.

South Africa has been successful in upgrading into global value chains. In addition to functioning as an assembly hub for the automotive industry, South Africa has become a global supplier of components (seats and catalytic converters), capitalising on locally available skills and intermediate products. To further diversify the economy, since 2007, the Industrial Policy Action Plans (IPAP) prioritise sectors that are medium to high value added and labour-intensive such as agro-processing, vehicles, textiles and green energy.

On top of promoting trade and attracting FDI, the IPAP provide incentives and co-ordinate actions to strengthen skills and industrial and scientific capabilities (Zalk, 2012). These policies have enhanced co-operation and discussion among government ministries, the national development bank, private-sector stakeholders, civil society and universities (Baloy, 2012). Moreover, South Africa's lead companies in the telecommunication, banking and mining sectors are also making direct investments in other African countries to exploit the regional markets. For example, Africa's biggest retail chain, Shoprite of South Africa, now has more than 260 supermarkets in 16 African countries.

Despite the government's effort to support young entrepreneurs, the share of people aged 15-24 not in employment, education or training remains consistently high. It has been over 30% every year since 2012 – in 2016, over 3 million youth (OECD, 2017b: 131).

Expanding domestic markets hold great promise for local companies if they can upgrade their products

Africa's regional demand is increasingly favourable to growth for several reasons:

1. The contribution of private consumption to GDP growth has increased progressively and reached 3.7 percentage points annually over the period 2009-16 (Figure 1.16). This is comparable to the level in China and other developing Asian countries.
2. Africa's business opportunities are now attracting international investors interested in more than the continent's endowment in natural resources. The potential of domestic and regional markets attracted 53.4% of new FDI projects to Africa in 2013-17 (fDi markets, 2017). This share is similar to Asia's level (55.7%) and almost ten percentage points higher than LAC's (44.8%).
3. Recent progress in reducing both administrative procedures and the costs of starting and running a company have made the business environment more attractive: 29.5% of foreign investors cite this improvement among the main motivations to invest in Africa, compared to 12% in 2003-07.

Figure 1.16. **Decomposition of growth by expenditure in Africa, Asia and LAC, 1990-2016**

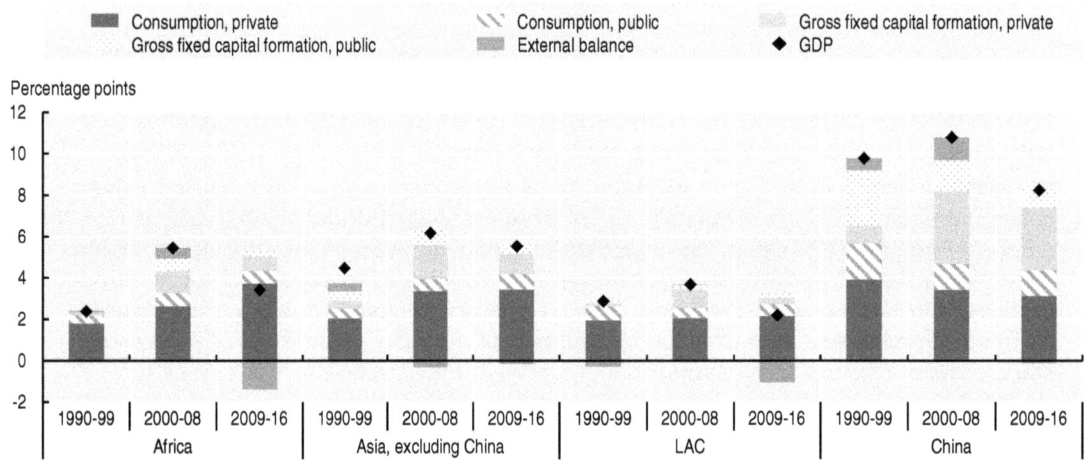

Note: Data include 52 African countries, 34 developing Asian countries and 23 developing LAC countries. Contribution to growth by change in inventory is close to zero (±0.01 percentage points) and is thus suppressed from the figure.

Source: Authors' calculations based on World Bank (2017a), *World Development Indicators* (database), and IMF (2018), *World Economic Outlook* (database).

StatLink http://dx.doi.org/10.1787/888933782696

Demand is shifting towards more processed goods. The rapid urban growth of African economies and a higher purchasing power of Africa's emerging middle class are underpinning the growth of private consumption. The middle class, defined as those spending between USD 5 and USD 20 a day, increased from 108 million people in 1990 to 247 million by 2013. Both food and non-food markets, excluding oil products, are more dynamic than the global averages. This change in the demand is driven by Africa's urbanisation and demographic growth, and Chapter 2 will discuss these two processes further.

Food markets are rising over the continent and should triple by 2030 (Byerlee et al., 2013). The diet preferences are changing from staples to higher-value processed foods (see Bricas, Tchamda and Thirion, 2014; Reardon et al., 2018). COMTRADE data shows that demand for processed food is growing fast, more than 1.5 times faster than the global average between 2005 and 2015. The two most dynamic food imports over that period were meat products (+323% in value in ten years) and beverages (+306%, excluding coffee and cocoa preparations).

Some non-food products are also particularly fast-growing (Figure 1.17). These patterns are common to all Africa's five regions.[7]

Figure 1.17. **Africa's top 15 non-food imports, 2013-15**

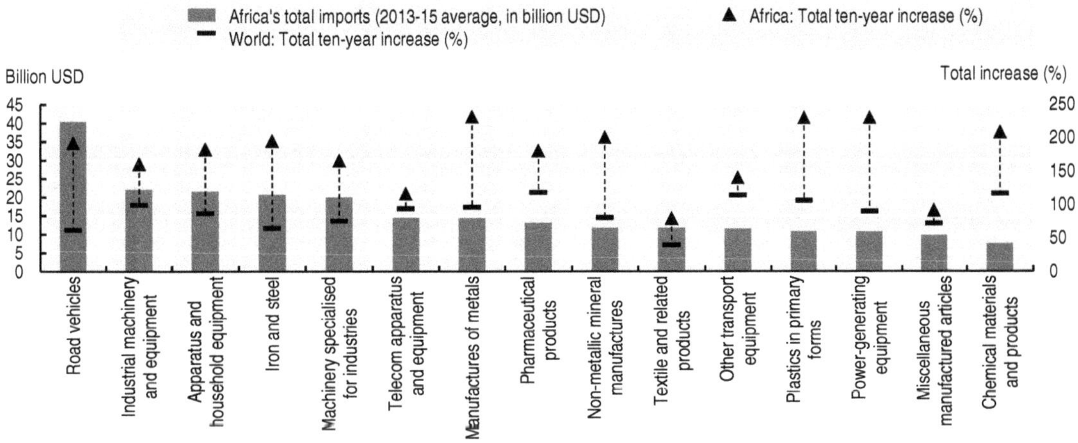

Note: Excluding oil products. Using the two-digit product codes in the Standard International Trade Classification, revision 3 classification. The right axis shows the total increase of the values over a ten-year period.

Source: Authors' calculations based on UN Statistics Division (2017), *UN COMTRADE* (database).

StatLink http://dx.doi.org/10.1787/888933782715

The level of complexity of Africa's import products has decreased over time, both for consumption goods and other imported products (Figure 1.18). The complexity level of consumption goods imported to Africa has decreased by half, from 0.8 to 0.4 between 1998 and 2016 (Figure 1.18, Panel A). The lower complexity level suggests that the production technology for those products is becoming more widespread, allowing more countries to supply them. Lower fixed costs allow African firms to vary their products.

Figure 1.18. **Level of complexity of imports into Africa, Asia and LAC, 1998-2016**

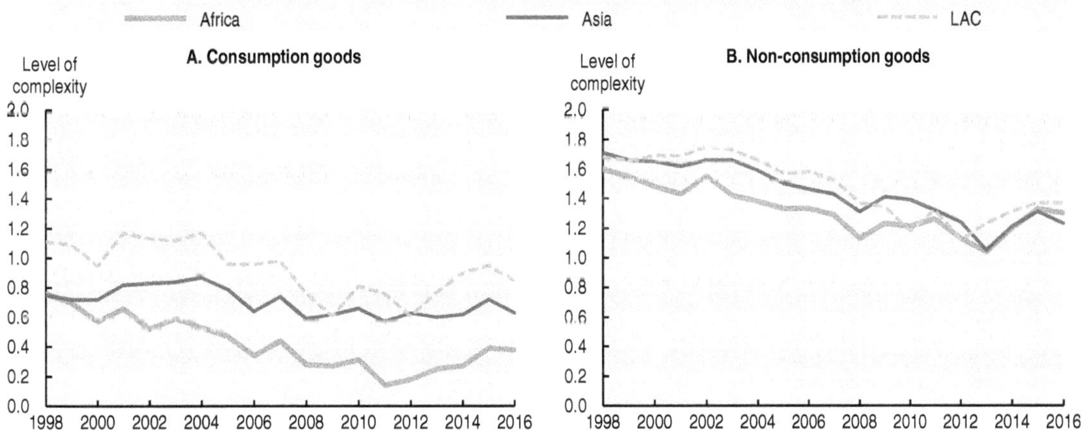

Note: Excluding oil products. The types of goods are defined by Broad Economic Categories classifications for consumption goods (categories 1, 5 and 6) and non-consumption goods (categories 3, 4 and 7). The complexity index of each product, a measure of the relative knowledge intensity in producing the product, is calculated for each year using Hausmann and Hidalgo's methodology (2011).

Source: Authors' calculations based on UN Statistics Division (2017), *UN COMTRADE* (database).

StatLink http://dx.doi.org/10.1787/888933782734

Local firms must upgrade their technology and production processes if they are to meet the new domestic demand. For instance, improving production processes and products technology, adding desirable features, quality labelling and certification are necessary to compete on global markets (Porter, 1990). Cross-country analysis shows a positive correlation between improvements in firm-level efficiency and countries' comparative advantage in exports of semi- and processed-goods (Figure 1.19). Microeconomic studies show that households with higher incomes look for higher quality products and standards. In Western Africa, rising incomes are associated with a lower propensity for households to consume informal sector goods, as well as a lower propensity to use informal distribution channels (Böhme and Thiele, 2012).

Figure 1.19. **Total factor productivity for manufacturing firms in African countries and other developing countries**

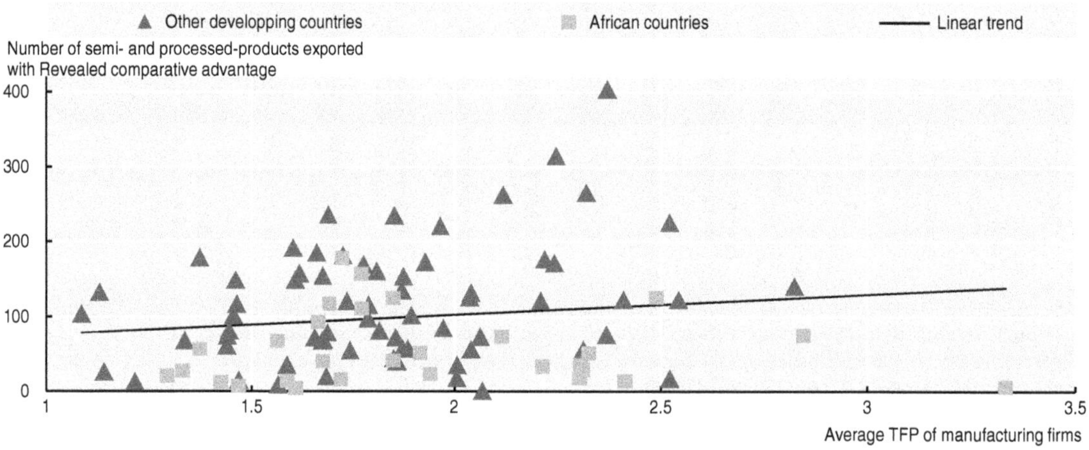

Source: TFP calculations for manufacturing firms based on Nguyen and Véganzonès-Varoudakis (2017) using Enterprise Surveys (2017), *World Bank Enterprise Surveys*. The number of products with revealed comparative advantages is calculated based on UN Statistics Division (2017), *UN COMTRADE* (database).

StatLink http://dx.doi.org/10.1787/888933782753

African firms largely lag behind the global technology frontier in most fast-growing sectors. This finding is drawn from a panel of 7 000 enterprises from the World Bank Enterprise Surveys over the period 2006-15 in 70 developing countries and 11 manufacturing industries (Nguyen and Véganzonès-Varoudakis, 2017). In Nigeria, for example, average levels of TFP in manufacturing stand at only 53% of the top 10% most productive firms in developing countries. Nigeria's non-metal manufacturing and food sectors are far below the global production frontier, reaching only 27% and 38% of the highest performers respectively.

Some interesting exceptions stand out, notably in Morocco and South Africa. Firms in Morocco perform well in several sectors, such as food, leather and metal products. Firms in South Africa appear to be among the best performers in Africa's developing countries in eight manufacturing sectors. The country's TFP level averages 91% of the frontier performance in the food sector and up to 100% in non-metal manufacturing, wood furniture and machinery (see Table 2 in Nguyen and Véganzonès-Varoudakis, 2017).

New policies can help domestic firms reach the productivity frontier and tap business opportunities

Stronger policies in favour of firms' productivity are required for two main reasons. First, despite the promise of Africa's rising markets, private investment has not yet responded. The contribution of private investment to Africa's growth has significantly lagged behind Asia's level, despite business-friendly reforms (Figure 1.20). In Asia (excluding China), private investment contributed 1.3 percentage points to GDP growth per year between 2009 and 2016. This is more than double the contribution of private investment to growth in

Africa (0.6 percentage points). African entrepreneurs tend to prefer engaging in activities with a relative quick turnover that do not require long-term investment. The largest share (55%) of entrepreneurs work in retail trade, hotels and restaurants (AfDB/OECD/UNDP, 2017). Second, helping African firms reach the global productivity frontier will require additional policy support, beyond the usual business reforms that reduce start-up costs.

Figure 1.20. **Contribution of private gross fixed capital formation to GDP growth in Africa, Asia and LAC, 1990-2016**

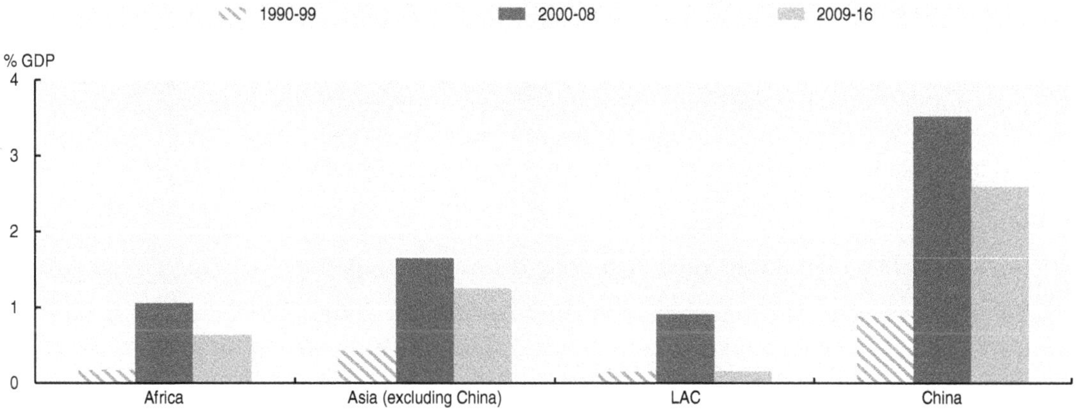

Note: Data include 52 African countries, 34 developing Asian countries and 23 developing LAC countries.

Source: Authors' calculations based on World Bank (2017a), *World Development Indicators* (database), and IMF (2018), *World Economic Outlook* (database).

StatLink http://dx.doi.org/10.1787/888933782772

Even after controlling for factors such as the business environment, most African firms are less productive than those elsewhere. Constraints in the business environment, such as the cost and lack of credit to the private sector, corruption and regulatory uncertainties, and infrastructure bottlenecks, do not fully explain this. After controlling for these factors, the results show that the majority of African firms remain far below the average TFP of the top 10% most productive manufacturing firms in developing countries (Figure 1.21).

Figure 1.21. **Distance of African firms to top 10% of total factor productivity for manufacturing in developing countries**

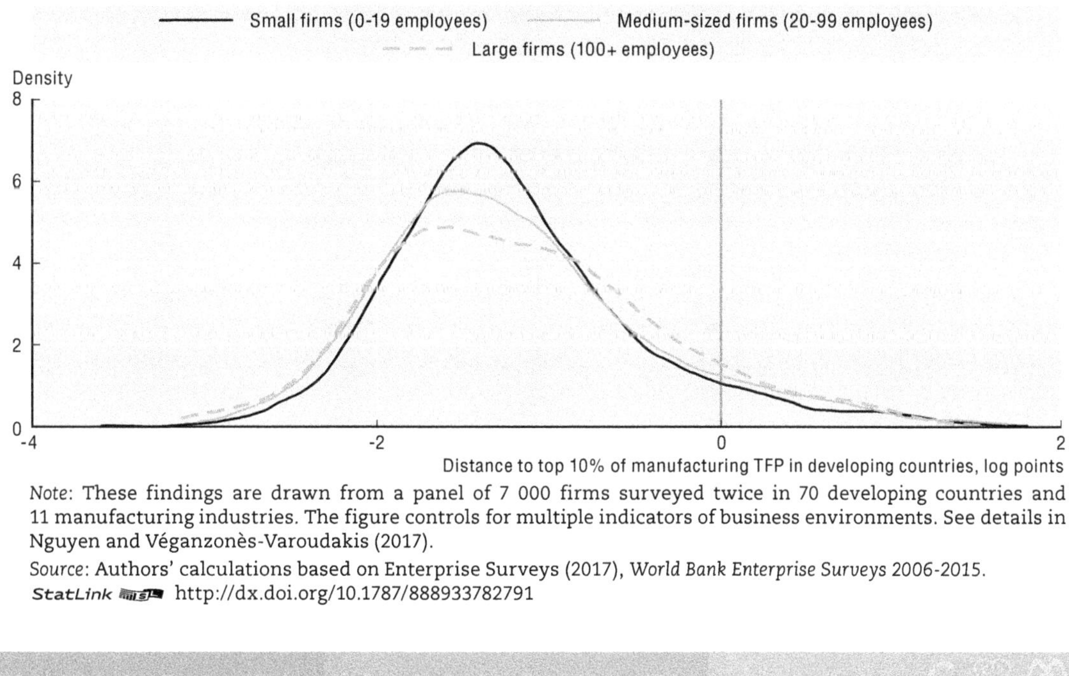

Note: These findings are drawn from a panel of 7 000 firms surveyed twice in 70 developing countries and 11 manufacturing industries. The figure controls for multiple indicators of business environments. See details in Nguyen and Véganzonès-Varoudakis (2017).

Source: Authors' calculations based on Enterprise Surveys (2017), *World Bank Enterprise Surveys 2006-2015*.

StatLink http://dx.doi.org/10.1787/888933782791

A number of firm-level factors also contribute to this poor performance, including these two:

1. Management quality of African firms is lower. Bloom, Sadun and Van Reenen (2017) show that, while management capabilities explain a third of variations in TFP across manufacturing firms, management quality is the lowest among the six African countries in their sample.
2. Informality limits productivity growth. Africa's micro-enterprises and SMEs in the manufacturing sector face high opportunity costs to move out of informality, which prevents them from investing and upgrading (Rodrik, 2017: 12). Limited access to good marketing networks, to quality labelling and certification, and to reliable demand make it difficult for informal firms to invest profits in innovation or in improving their products. Even the most productive informal firms face significant constraints. For example, in Ethiopia's manufacturing sector, the largest informal firm has a median capital stock of 16 425 birr (about USD 600) and earns a marginal return to capital of only 1%; whereas a formal firm with comparable capital stock earns at least 16.5% (see Table 4 in Siba, 2015).

To reap the benefits from investing in special economic zones, African policy makers will need policies that include firms serving local markets. Many promising small businesses can benefit from the spill-over effects from business clusters to scale up, upgrade and compete in the production networks. Recently, several African countries such as Ethiopia and Morocco have identified SEZs to attract lead firms and create manufacturing jobs.

However, SEZs alone cannot provide enough jobs and productivity spill-overs for at least four reasons:

1. Lead firms in SEZs often demand skills and quality levels that African firms and labour pools cannot provide. Therefore, attracting global FDI firms in SEZs can create isolated growth enclaves that lack sufficient production linkages or technology spill-overs to the local economy.
2. The export focus of these SEZs tends to exclude a number of domestic firms that need to operate in local markets. In certain cases, policies offering fiscal exemptions can prevent firms in SEZs from producing for local markets.
3. SEZs will not create enough jobs for the incoming youth bulge in Africa. According to a survey of 91 SEZs in 20 sub-Saharan countries, SEZs account for approximately 1 million jobs, or 0.2% of national employment (Kingombe and Te Velde, 2013).
4. With few exceptions, such as Ethiopia, most African countries do not have the wage structure to compete on labour costs (see Megatrend 1, Chapter 2).

Sound policies can help domestic savings and external financial inflows unlock private investment

Mobilising domestic resources – especially domestic savings – is necessary to foster investment in activities that can increase productivity and create jobs. Domestic savings are the most important and well-distributed resource across developing countries. On average in Africa, they represented USD 422 billion annually over the period 2009-16, which is 20% of the continent's GDP. This is higher than tax revenues over the same period (Figure 1.22). The top ten largest African economies had private savings rates ranging from 49% of GDP in Angola to 9% in Sudan. Yet lower commodity prices and slower economic growth may limit public revenue and spending in the short and medium terms. Improving financial intermediation can help mobilise domestic resources to support productive investment (see Chapter 8).

Figure 1.22. **Gross private savings and general government taxes, as share of GDP in Africa, Asia and LAC, 2009-16**

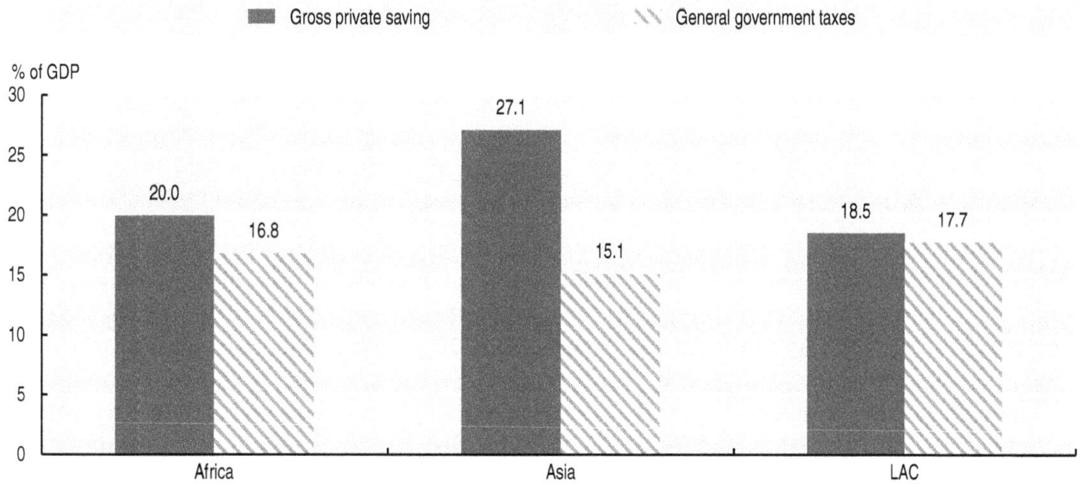

Note: Data include 42 African countries, 33 Asian countries and 20 LAC countries.
Source: Authors' calculations based on IMF (2018), *World Economic Outlook* (database).
StatLink http://dx.doi.org/10.1787/888933782810

Since 2015, lower natural resource rents and lower economic growth have reduced public revenues in many resource-rich countries, limiting public investment. Countries such as Angola and Nigeria are consolidating their fiscal balance, mostly by cutting capital investment. Public debt is rising is many countries and has already reached 100% of GDP in some (Figure 1.23). The number of low-income countries in debt distress or facing a high risk of it increased from 7 in 2013 to 12 in 2016, and almost all African countries with credit ratings have been downgraded below investment grade (IMF, 2017). This increases the exposure of countries' budgets to external shocks such as the availability of liquidity on international markets and interest rate levels. Maintaining growth momentum and capital accumulation may therefore require mobilising sources other than government debt.

Figure 1.23. **Gross government debt versus public gross fixed capital formation in Africa, Brazil, China and India, 2009-16**

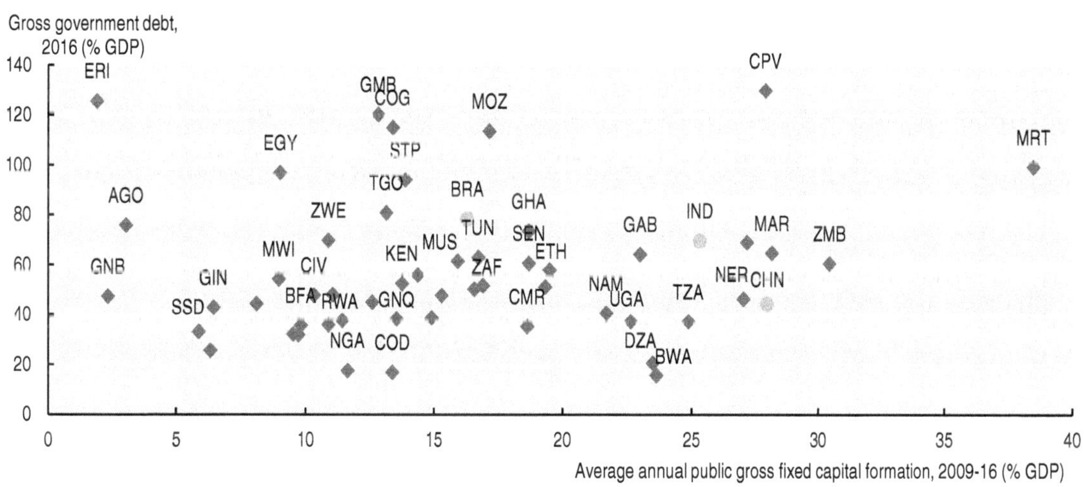

Note: Data include only 52 African countries because of the limited availability.
Source: Authors' calculations based on World Bank (2017a), *World Development Indicators* (database), and IMF (2018), *World Economic Outlook* (database).
StatLink http://dx.doi.org/10.1787/888933782829

Africa will need to encourage private investment in productive activities. The public sector already invests more than 20% of GDP annually between 2009 and 2016 in 12 out of 52 African countries where data is available. In another 27 countries, annual public investment was between 10 and 20% of GDP on average in the same period. Investment solely based on public spending can hardly be sustained in the medium and long terms. Private investment stood at only 15% of GDP on average between 2009 and 2016, significantly lower than developing Asia's average of 24% and LAC's average of 17%. In resource-rich African countries, private investment accounted for only 13% of GDP, compared to 18% in non-resource-rich African countries (Figure 1.3, Panel B).

Governments need to combat illicit financial flows (IFFs). IFFs deprive countries of resources that could be used at least partially for redistribution, for financing public goods and for fostering private investments in local businesses. Illicit financial outflows from Africa amount to USD 50 billion annually (AUC/ECA, 2017). This amount is similar to the official development assistance that Africa receives (see Table 1.2). IFFs have five major sources: bribes, tax evasion, criminal enterprise earnings, corporate profit shifting and currency regulation evasion (see Reuter, 2017). The channels for moving illicit funds are many, including trade misinvoicing and money leakages from the balance of payments (Global Financial Integrity, 2015).

Africa needs to improve the overall efficiency of public investment in order to boost productivity. Weak governance of public investments can lead to financial mismanagement and insufficient maintenance (IMF, 2016b) or to low appropriability of investment projects. For example, due to the lack of skills and support services to adapt the imported machineries and technologies to the Africa's context, agricultural productivity growth in Africa is roughly half the average rate of developing countries (Ninn-Prat, 2015). Infrastructural bottlenecks also reduce the capital utilisation rates. For example, electricity outages prevent workers from working multiple shifts and delay production cycles.

Financial inflows can play an important role in sustaining productive investment, in particular in landlocked or non-resource-rich countries. Total financial inflows (remittances, FDI, portfolio inflows and net ODA) into Africa reached 8.8% of GDP between 2009 and 2016. This level is significantly higher than the average for Asia (3.8%) and LAC (5.2%) (Figure 1.24). In absolute amounts, total inflows into Africa increased from USD 103 billion in 2005 to USD 185 billion in 2016. Between 2009 and 2016, financial inflows into Africa relied much more on remittances and ODA than they did in other continents; remittances and ODA amounted to 2.8% and 2.4% of Africa's GDP respectively. Since the early 2000s, remittances have increased more than fourfold; ODA and FDI have more than doubled (Table 1.2). On average, the landlocked countries receive the highest share (13.3% of their GDP) mainly due to the contribution of ODA, remittances and FDI. Non-resource-rich countries depend more on inflows (totalling 10.7% of their GDP) than resource-rich countries (6.9% of GDP).

Remittances, ODA and FDI inflows impact African economies differently:

- Until now, remittance inflows have mostly served domestic consumption. Remittances have supported household consumption rather than private investment, partly due to underdeveloped savings mechanisms for remittance recipients. Remittance flows can increase social inequalities in countries where immigrants belong to higher income households (Anyanwu, 2011; Adams, Cuecuecha and Page, 2008). Policies to attract remittances to certain sectors, such as diaspora bonds to catalyse investment into public infrastructure projects, have met mitigated success.

- Although ODA has helped reduce poverty in many heavily indebted countries, more can be done to encourage investment in Africa's productive assets. Since 2000, the international community has focused mostly on social sectors as a mean to fight poverty. ODA may have suffered from a lack of co-ordination among donor countries. For example, analysing the data for the period 2006-11, an OECD report identified six least developed countries in Africa as potentially under-aided (OECD, 2013b). Such asymmetry in aid allocations led to the adoption of the Accra Agenda for Action in 2008. This has increased attention to countries most in need, including the African countries.
- FDI in Africa accounted for 2.5% of GDP between 2009 and 2016, but the biggest share was concentrated in the extractive sector. That share (36% of total FDI between 2003 and 2014) had limited spill-overs into the local economy. Since the extractive sector often has few linkages with the local economy, FDI has not spurred further private investment nor created a sufficient number of jobs. Moreover, FDI may lead to higher income inequality as the high skill requirements of the FDI sector may exacerbate poor returns to education (Bogliaccini and Egan, 2017).

Figure 1.24. **Total financial inflows as a percentage of GDP in Africa, Asia and LAC, 2009-16**

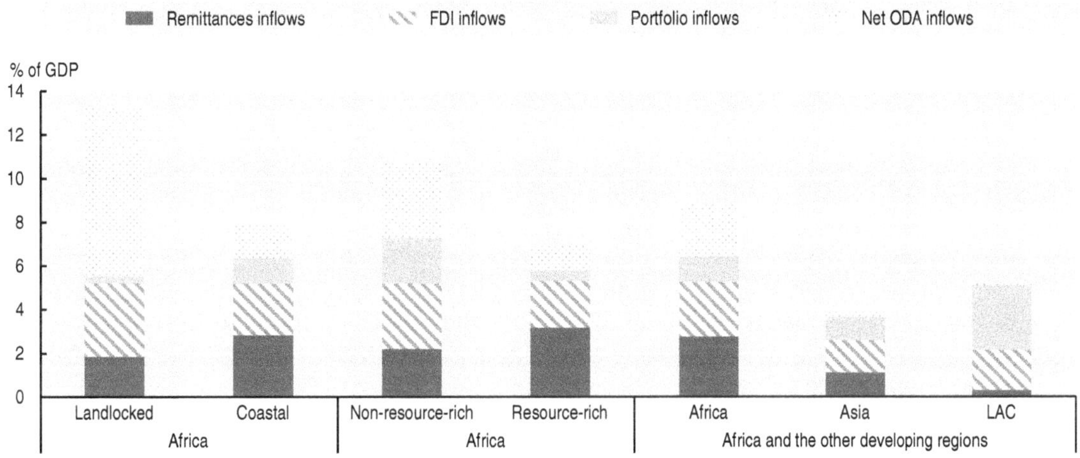

Sources: Authors' calculations based on IMF (2018), *World Economic Outlook* (database), OECD-DAC (2017), *International Development Statistics* (database), and World Bank (2017a), *World Development Indicators* (database).
StatLink http://dx.doi.org/10.1787/888933782848

Going forward, African countries can better channel these financial inflows into activities strongly linked with the local economy. Domestic savings and remittances can provide incentives to invest in activities with strong multiplier effects to generate high social returns. Leveraging on those financial resources can help reduce the cost of small capital investments. The widespread use of mobile payments and banking systems (e.g. M Pesa) creates new services to millions of customers. Such systems can increase the availability of financing and payment services for micro-enterprises and SMEs at reduced costs and risks. Improving the ability for SMEs and young companies to be listed on secondary exchanges can also help. Chapter 8 will look at policies to tap this potential.

Strategies to promote FDI should ensure that the domestic suppliers can align with lead FDI firms' needs in terms of quality and product specifications. Setting-up a national strategy for quality labelling can facilitate the interaction among different actors within the value chains. FDI can help transfer technology and knowledge, in the form of production techniques, management or marketing practices. FDI in Africa has become increasingly diversified and now targets industries such as information and communications technology, food, and financial services. Econometric analysis shows that the most significant determinants of FDI in Africa's manufacturing sector are domestic market size and the quality of infrastructure (e.g. ports, rail and road) and transport services to access local inputs. These two factors explain 28% of variations in FDI attraction to Africa (Wall, 2016).

Such linkages often make FDI's impact on economic growth and productivity more durable (OECD, 2015; Rand, 2015). Accessing technology and knowledge through linkages with lead firms is less costly and less risky for SMEs in most developing countries than building the whole capacity in research & development of new technology (OECD/World Bank, 2015). An illustrative case is the automobile industry in Morocco, where the opening of new car factories in 2005 led the Moroccan firms supplying these factories to improve their management and other techniques (Hahn and Vidican-Auktor, 2017). Calabrese (2017) finds evidence of increased firm productivity through technology transfer, particularly in the agricultural sector. A number of companies in the agro-processing industries are already engaged in important initiatives in technology transfer, working intensively with local suppliers including small farmers. This is the case for Blue Skies in Ghana; OLAM in Nigeria; SabMiller in South Africa (AfDB/OECD/UNDP, 2014: 164-166); and Cargill, Mars, Nestlé, Olam, SIFCA, and Unilever in Côte d'Ivoire's cocoa and palm-oil industries (OECD, 2016: 55, 75).

ODA to Africa can de-risk private investment and help SMEs comply with international standards. While ODA is essential to alleviate poverty and humanitarian crises, a portion of ODA can also be leveraged as a guaranty to raise more capital funds for long-term investment. For instance, since approximately USD 35 billion per year of total ODA to Africa consists of pure grants, securitising just over USD 5 billion would enable donor countries to raise USD 100 billion upfront. This sum could finance the public portion of "blended" public-private investments in major infrastructure projects in Africa (Birdsall and Okonjo-Iweala, 2017). Such solutions can help countries obtain longer maturities for loans and lower interest rates. Development finance helped mobilise USD 81 billion of private investment between 2012 and 2015 (OECD, 2018). ODA can assist local firms in accessing quality standards and product specifications. It can serve to increase technical and management skills by helping governments improve technical, entrepreneurial and vocational training programmes. ODA can also assist in revising production processes. Finally, it can promote high quality products by supporting quality label initiatives (see OECD/WTO, 2013; OECD/WTO, 2017).

Notes

1. Three-year moving average.
2. The programme decreased recipient countries' debt services by about 1.5 percentage points of GDP between 2001 and 2015.
3. The Gini index measures the extent to which the distribution of income among individuals or households within an economy deviates from a perfectly equal distribution. The index ranges from 0 in the case of "perfect equality" (each share of the population gets the same share of income) to 100 in the case of "perfect inequality" (all income goes to the share of the population with the highest income).
4. The Commitment to Equity (CEQ) project is led by Nora Lustig since 2008 and is an initiative of the Center for Inter-American Policy and Research (CIPR) and the Department of Economics, Tulane University, the Center for Global Development and the Inter-American Dialogue. The CEQ project is housed in the Commitment to Equity Institute at Tulane. See www.commitmentoequity.org.
5. For more details, see De Vries et al. (2015) and Diao, McMillan and Rodrik (2017).
6. For example, between 1991 and 2001, Indonesian manufacturing firms saw their productivity rise by 12 percentage points following a 10-percentage-point fall in tariffs of inputs they imported (Amiti and Konings, 2007).
7. See for example Allen and Heinrigs (2016) and OECD (2016:69) on the case of Western Africa, and Tschirley et al. (2015) on Eastern and Southern Africa.

References

Adams, R. H. Jr., A. Cuecuecha and J. Page (2008), "The impact of remittances on poverty and inequality in Ghana", *Policy Research Working Paper*, No. 4732, World Bank, Washington, DC, http://hdl.handle.net/10986/6940.

AfDB/OECD/UNDP (2017), *African Economic Outlook 2017: Entrepreneurship and Industrialisation*, OECD Publishing, Paris, http://dx.doi.org/10.1787/aeo-2017-en.

AfDB/OECD/UNDP (2016), *African Economic Outlook 2016: Sustainable Cities and Structural Transformation*, OECD Publishing, Paris, http://dx.doi.org/10.1787/aeo-2016-en.

AfDB/OECD/UNDP (2014), *African Economic Outlook 2014: Global Value Chains and Africa's Industrialisation*, OECD Publishing, Paris, http://dx.doi.org/10.1787/aeo-2014-en.

AfDB/OECD/UNDP/UNECA (2012), *African Economic Outlook 2012: Promoting Youth Employment*, OECD Publishing, Paris, http://dx.doi.org/10.1787/aeo-2012-en.

Allen, T. and P. Heinrigs (2016), "Emerging opportunities in the West African food economy", *West African Papers*, No. 01, OECD Publishing, Paris, http://dx.doi.org/10.1787/5jlvfj4968jb-en.

Amiti, M. and J. Konings (2007), "Trade liberalization, intermediate inputs, and productivity: Evidence from Indonesia", *American Economic Review*, Vol. 97/5, pp. 1611-1638.

Anyanwu, J.C. (2011), "International remittances and income inequality in Africa", *Working Paper*, No. 135, African Development Bank, www.afdb.org/fileadmin/uploads/afdb/Documents/Publications/WORKING%20135%20International%20Remittances%20and%20Income%20Inequality%20in%20Africa-August2011%20.pdf.

AUC/ECA (2017), *Illicit Financial Flows*, report of the High Level Panel on Illicit Financial Flows from Africa, African Union Commission and United Nations Economic Commission for Africa, www.uneca.org/sites/default/files/PublicationFiles/iff_main_report_26feb_en.pdf.

Avom, D. and D. Mignamissi (2017), "Pourquoi le commerce intra-CEEAC est-il si faible ?", *Revue française d'économie*, Vol. 32/3, pp. 136-170.

Baloy, B. (2012), "The political economy of South Africa industrial policy", *Expert Meeting Sustaining Growth in a Context of Shifting Wealth: What Role for Industrial Policy?*, presentation at OECD Development Centre, Paris.

Berg, A., J.D. Ostry and J. Zettelmeyer (2012), "What makes growth sustained?", *IMF Working Paper*, No. 08/59, International Monetary Fund, www.imf.org/en/Publications/WP/Issues/2016/12/31/What-Makes-Growth-Sustained-21769.

Birdsall, N. and N. Okonjo-Iweala (2017), "A big bond for Africa", *Project Syndicate*, www.project-syndicate.org/commentary/africa-regional-infrastructure-investment-bond-by-nancy-birdsall-and-ngozi-okonjo-iweala-2017-04?barrier=accessreg.

Bleaney, M. and D. Greenaway (2001), "The impact of terms of trade and real exchange rate volatility on investment and growth in sub-Saharan Africa", *Journal of Development Economics*, Vol. 65/2, pp. 491-500, EconPapers.repec.org/RePEc:eee:deveco:v:65:y:2001:i:2:p:491-500.

Bloom, N., R. Sadun and J. Van Reenen (2016), "Management as a technology?", *National Bureau of Economic Research Working Paper* No. 22327, www.nber.org/papers/w22327.

Boarini, R., A. Kolev and A. McGregor (2014), "Measuring well-being and progress in countries at different stages of development: Towards a more universal conceptual framework", *OECD Development Centre Working Papers*, No. 325, OECD Publishing, Paris, http://dx.doi.org/10.1787/5jxss4hv2d8n-en.

Bogliaccini J.A. and P.J.W. Egan (2017), "Foreign direct investment and inequality in developing countries: Does sector matter?", *Economics & Politics*, Vol. 29/3, pp. 209-236, https://doi.org/10.1111/ecpo.12098.

Böhme, M. and R. Thiele (2012), "Is the informal sector constrained from the demand side? Evidence for six West African capitals", *World Development*, Vol. 40/7, pp. 1369-1381, https://doi.org/10.1016/j.worlddev.2011.12.005.

Bricas, N., C. Tchamda and M.C. Thirion (2014), "Consommation alimentaire en Afrique de l'Ouest et Centrale : les productions locales tirées par la demande urbaine, mais les villes restent dépendantes des importations de riz et de blé", in *Le Déméter, Économie et stratégies agricoles*, CIRAD-Afristat-AFD, pp. 125-142, www.clubdemeter.com/.

Byerlee, D. et al. (2013), "Growing Africa: Unlocking the potential of agribusiness", World Bank, Washington, DC, http://documents.worldbank.org/curated/en/2013/03/17427481/growing-africa-unlocking-potential-agribusiness-vol-1-2-main-report.

Calabrese, L. (2017), "Chinese investment and knowledge transfer in Africa", *Growth Research Programme*, https://dl.orangedox.com/Brief-China-Africa-investment-1.

CEQ Institute (2018), *Commitment to Equity Institute Data Center on Fiscal Redistribution*, http://commitmentoequity.org/datacenter.

Christiansen, L., M. Schindler and T. Tressel (2013), "Growth and structural reforms: A new assessment", *Journal of International Economics*, Vol. 89/2, pp. 347-356.

De Vries, G., M. Timmer and K. de Vries (2015), "Structural transformation in Africa: Static gains, dynamic losses", *The Journal of Development Studies*, Vol. 51/6, pp. 674-688, https://doi.org/10.1080/00220388.2014.997222.

De Vries, G. et al. (2015), *GGDC 10-Sector Database*, https://www.rug.nl/ggdc/productivity/10-sector/.

Diao, X, M. McMillan and D. Rodrik (2017), "The recent growth boom in developing economies, a structural-change perspective", *NBER Working Paper*, No. 23132, www.nber.org/papers/w23132.

ECA (2017), *Transforming African Economies through Smart Trade and Industrial Policy*, United Nations Economic Commission for Africa, Addis Ababa, https://www.uneca.org/sites/default/files/PublicationFiles/transforming-african-economies_smart-trade_industrial-policy_eng.pdf.

El Mokri, K. (2016), "Morocco's 2014-2020 Industrial Strategy and its potential implications for the structural transformation process", *OCP Policy Center*, No. 1628, www.ocppc.ma/publications/morocco%E2%80%99s-2014-2020-industrial-strategy-and-its-potential-implications-structural.

Enterprise Surveys (2017), *World Bank Enterprise Surveys*, www.enterprisesurveys.org (accessed in April 2017).

fDi Markets (2017), *fDi Markets* (database) www.fdimarkets.com (accessed 2 June 2017).

Gallup (2017), *Gallup World Poll*, www.gallup.com/services/170945/world-poll.aspx.

Ghosh, A. and J. Ostry (1994), "Export instability and the external balance in developing countries", *International Monetary Fund Staff Papers*, Vol. 41/2, pp. 214-235, www.jstor.org/stable/3867507?origin=pubexport.

Global Financial Integrity (2015), *Illicit Financial Flows from Developing Countries: 2004-2013*, report drafted by D. Kar and J. Spanjers at the Global Financial Integrity, Washington, DC, www.gfintegrity.org/wp-content/uploads/2015/12/IFF-Update_2015-Final-1.pdf.

Hahn, T. and G. Vidican-Auktor (2017), *The Effectiveness of Morocco's Industrial Policy in Promoting a National Automotive Industry*, Deutsches Institut fûr Entwicklungspolitik, Bonn.

Hausmann, R. and C. Hidalgo (2011), "The network structure of economic output", *Journal of Economic Growth*, Vol. 16/4, pp. 309-342.

Hausmann, R., L. Pritchett and D. Rodrik (2005), "Growth accelerations", *Journal of Economic Growth*, Vol. 10/4, pp. 303-329, https://doi.org/10.1007/s10887-005-4712-0.

ILO (2018), *World Employment and Social Outlook: Trends 2018*, International Labour Organization, Geneva, www.ilo.org/wcmsp5/groups/public/---dgreports/---dcomm/---publ/documents/publication/wcms_615594.pdf.

ILO (2017), *ILOSTAT* (database), www.ilo.org/ilostat/ (accessed 1 March 2018).

IMF (2018), *World Economic Outlook, October 2018* (database), International Monetary Fund, Washington, DC, www.imf.org/external/pubs/ft/weo/2018/01/weodata/index.aspx (accessed 20 April 2018).

IMF (2017), *Regional Economic Outlook: Sub-Saharan Africa, Fiscal Adjustment and Economic Diversification*, International Monetary Fund, Washington, DC.

IMF (2016a), *Regional Economic Outlook: Sub-Saharan Africa, Time for a Policy Reset*, International Monetary Fund, Washington, DC, https://www.imf.org/en/Publications/REO/SSA/Issues/2016/04/05/Time-for-a-Policy-Reset.

IMF (2016b), *World Economic Outlook: Subdued Demand: Symptoms and Remedies*, International Monetary Fund, Washington, DC, www.imf.org/external/pubs/ft/weo/2016/02.

Kaplinsky, R. and M. Morris (2002). *A Handbook for Value Chain Research*, Institute of Development Studies, University of Sussex, Brighton, www.ids.ac.uk/ids/global/pdfs/VchNov01.pdf.

Kingombe, C. and D.W. te Velde (2013), "Structural transformation and employment creation. The role of growth facilitation policies in sub-Saharan Africa", background paper for the *World Development Report 2013*, http://citeseerx.ist.psu.edu/viewdoc/download?doi=10.1.1.862.567&rep=rep1&type=pdf.

Klinger, B. and D. Lederman (2004), "Discovery and development: An empirical exploration of 'new' products", *World Bank Policy Research Working Paper*, No. 3450, https://openknowledge.worldbank.org/handle/10986/14187.

Kowalski, P. et al. (2015),"Participation of developing countries in global value chains: Implications for trade and trade-related policies", *OECD Trade Policy Papers*, No. 179, OECD Publishing, Paris, http://dx.doi.org/10.1787/5js33lfw0xxn-en.

Lopez Gonzalez, J. (2016), "Using foreign factors to enhance domestic export performance: A focus on Southeast Asia", *OECD Trade Policy Papers*, No. 191, OECD Publishing, Paris, http://dx.doi.org/10.1787/5jlpq82v1jxw-en.

Moller, L.C. and K. Wacker (2017), "Explaining Ethiopia's growth acceleration: The role of infrastructure and macroeconomic policy", *World Development*, Vol. 96, pp. 198-215, https://doi.org/10.1016/j.worlddev.2017.03.007.

Morris, M. and J. Barnes (2009), "Globalization, the changed global dynamics of the clothing and textile value chains and the impact on sub-Saharan Africa", *Working Paper* No. 10, UNIDO Research and Statistics Branch, UNIDO, Vienna.

Nguyen, H.T.M. and M.A. Véganzonès-Varoudakis (2017), "Investment climate, outward orientation and manufacturing firm productivity: New empirical evidence", *Études et Documents*, N°17, CERDI, http://cerdi.org/uploads/ed/2017/2017.17.pdf.

Nin-Pratt, A. (2015), "Inputs, productivity, and agricultural growth in Africa South of the Sahara", *Discussion Paper* 1432, Washington, DC, International Food Policy Research Institute, http://ebrary.ifpri.org/cdm/ref/collection/p15738coll2/id/129095.

OECD (2018), *Making Blended Finance Work for the Sustainable Development Goals*, OECD Publishing, Paris, http://dx.doi.org/10.1787/9789264288768-en.

OECD (2017a), *Examen multidimensionnel du Maroc : Volume 1. Évaluation initiale*, Les voies de developpement, OECD Publishing, Paris, http://dx.doi.org/10.1787/9789264274945-fr.

OECD (2017b), *OECD Economic Surveys: South Africa 2017*, OECD Publishing, Paris, http://dx.doi.org/10.1787/eco_surveys-zaf-2017-en.

OECD (2016), *Examen multidimensionnel de la Côte d'Ivoire : Volume 2. Analyse approfondie et recommandations*, Les voies de développement, OECD Publishing, Paris, http://dx.doi.org/10.1787/9789264251670-fr.

OECD (2015), *Policy Framework for Investment, 2015 Edition*, OECD Publishing, Paris, http://dx.doi.org/10.1787/9789264208667-en.

OECD (2013a), *Interconnected Economies: Benefiting from Global Value Chains*, OECD Publishing, Paris, dx.doi.org/10.1787/9789264189560-en.

OECD (2013b), *Identification and Monitoring of Potentially Under-aided Countries*, OECD, Paris, www.oecd.org/dac/aid-architecture/Identification%20and%20Monitoring%20of%20Potentially%20Under-Aided%20Countries.pdf.

OECD/AfDB/ECA/UNDP (2011), *African Economic Outlook 2011: Africa and its Emerging Partners*, OECD Publishing, Paris, http://dx.doi.org/10.1787/aeo-2011-en.

OECD-DAC (2017), *International Development Statistics* (database), OECD Development Assistance Committee, www.oecd.org/dac/stats/idsonline.htm.

OECD/World Bank (2015), "Inclusive global value chains: Policy options in trade and complementary areas for GVC Integration by small and medium enterprises and low-income developing countries", report prepared for submission to G20 Trade Ministers Meeting, Istanbul, 6 October 2015, www.oecd.org/trade/OECD-WBG-g20-gvc-report-2015.pdf.

OECD/WTO (2017), *Aid for Trade at a Glance 2017: Promoting Trade, Inclusiveness and Connectivity for Sustainable Development*, World Trade Organisation, Geneva, and OECD Publishing, Paris, http://dx.doi.org/10.1787/aid_glance-2017-en.

OECD/WTO (2013), *Aid for Trade at a Glance 2013: Connecting to Value Chains*, World Trade Organisation, Geneva, and OECD Publishing, Paris, http://dx.doi.org/10.1787/aid_glance-2013-en.

Pierola, M.D., A.M. Fernandes and T. Farole (2017), "The role of imports for exporter performance in Peru", *The World Economy, Vol. 41/2, pp. 550-572,* doi.org/10.1111/twec.12524.

Porter, M. (1990), "The competitive advantage of nations", *Harvard Business Review,* https://hbr.org/1990/03/the-competitive-advantage-of-nations.

Rand, J. (2015), *Understanding FDI Spillover Mechanisms*, www.brookings.edu/wp-content/uploads/2015/11/L2CBrief1_FDI-linkages_FINAL.pdf.

Reardon, T. et al. (2018), "Rapid transformation of food systems in developing regions: Highlighting the role of agricultural research and innovations", *Agricultural Systems,* https://doi.org/10.1016/j.agsy.2018.01.022.

Reuter, P. (2017), "Illicit financial flows and governance: The importance of disaggregation", background paper for the *World Development Report 2017,* World Bank Group, Washington, DC, http://documents.worldbank.org/curated/en/538841487847427218/World-development-report-2017-Illicit-financial-flows-and-governance-the-importance-of-disaggregation.

Rieländer, J. and B. Traoré (2016), "Explaining diversification in exports across higher manufacturing content: What is the role of commodities?", *Journal of International Commerce, Economics and Policy,* Vol. 7/02, www.worldscientific.com/doi/abs/10.1142/S1793993316500071.

Rodrik, D. (2017), "An African growth miracle?", *Journal of African Economies*, Vol. 27/1, pp. 10-27, https://doi.org/10.1093/jae/ejw027.

Siba, E. (2015), "Returns to physical capital in Ethiopia: Comparative analysis of formal and informal firms", *World Development*, Vol. 68, pp. 215-229.

The Conference Board (2017), *Total Economy Database*, www.conference-board.org/data/economydatabase/index.cfm?id=27762 (accessed 1 February 2018).

Thorbecke, E. and Y. Ouyang (2017), "Is the structure of growth different in sub-Saharan Africa?", *Journal of African Economies*, Vol. 27/1, pp. 66-91, https://doi.org/10.1093/jae/ejw032.

UN Statistics Division (2017), *UN COMTRADE* (database), http://wits.worldbank.org/wits/ (accessed 1 February 2018).

UNDESA (2017), *World Population Prospects: The 2017 Revision (database)*, https://esa.un.org/unpd/wpp/ *(accessed 1 February 2018)*.

UNDP (2017), *Income Inequality Trends in Sub-Saharan Africa: Divergence, Determinants, and Consequences*, United Nations Development Programme, New York, www.africa.undp.org/content/rba/en/home/library/reports/income-inequality-trends-in-sub-saharan-africa--divergence--dete.html.

UNDP (2016), *Africa Human Development Report 2016: Accelerating Gender Equality and Women's Empowerment in Africa*, United Nations Development Programme, New York, www.undp.org/content/undp/en/home/librarypage/hdr/2016-africa-human-development-report.html.

Wall, R. (2016), "State of foreign direct investment to African cities", *OECD Development Centre Background Papers for the African Economic Outlook 2016*.

World Bank (2017a), *World Development Indicators* (database), http://wdi.worldbank.org (accessed 15 February 2018).

World Bank (2017b), *PovcalNet* (database), http://iresearch.worldbank.org/PovcalNet/povOnDemand.aspx (accessed 20 April 2018).

Zalk, N. (2012), "South African post-apartheid policies towards industrialization: Tentative implications for other African countries", in *Good Growth and Governance in Africa: Rethinking Development Strategies*, pp. 345, Oxford University Press, http://dx.doi.org/10.1093/acprof:oso/9780199698561.003.0012.

Chapter 2

Megatrends affecting Africa's integration into the global economy

This chapter presents five megatrends that will shape Africa's development dynamics in the coming decade. The first megatrend corresponds to the stronger role of emerging countries in the global economy (also referred to as "shifting wealth"). The second is the new production revolution brought about by technological change and digitalisation. The third megatrend relates to the continent's demographic growth, which could bring "demographic dividends" if countries implement the right policies. The fourth megatrend is rapid urbanisation, which impacts the economic structure of many countries, living conditions and multi-level governance. The fifth megatrend is climate change, which calls for innovative and sustainable "green growth" strategies. For each of these megatrends, the chapter assesses the main risks, opportunities and policy implications for African countries.

IN BRIEF

Five main megatrends pose challenges and bring new opportunities for Africa's development dynamics. How policy makers respond will significantly impact growth, job creation and inequalities.

The increasingly important role of emerging economies – known as **"shifting wealth"** – is bringing opportunities to diversify the continent's investment and trade flows. It may also affect Africa's value chain upgrading through greater international competition.

A **new industrial revolution**, brought about by technological change and digitalisation, may reshape countries' comparative advantages and industrialisation potential. African entrepreneurs can now access new modes of production and global markets. However, automation could hinder job creation in manufacturing. Investing in technological infrastructure, supporting innovation systems, and enhancing workers' skills can help countries harness this potential.

Africa's rapid demographic growth could bring **"demographic dividends"** if countries implement the right policies. Demographic growth has many implications, including migration within and outside Africa. Reaping the demographic dividends depends on creating more and better jobs, investing in human and physical capital, and increasing savings in the formal financial sector.

Africa's rapid **urban transition** brings many opportunities for industrialisation, increased productivity and well-being – through innovation, bigger regional markets, and more demand for higher value-added goods. Benefitting both rural and urban economies will require, among many policies, improving urban infrastructure and public goods provision, land management, and multi-level governance.

Although the continent contributes less than 4% to global greenhouse gas emissions, **climate change** is a big risk which African policies must address. Many African countries are now transitioning into the middle-income stage demanding more energy, often generated through fossil fuels. Policies accelerating the transition to "green growth" will make growth more sustainable and create more jobs.

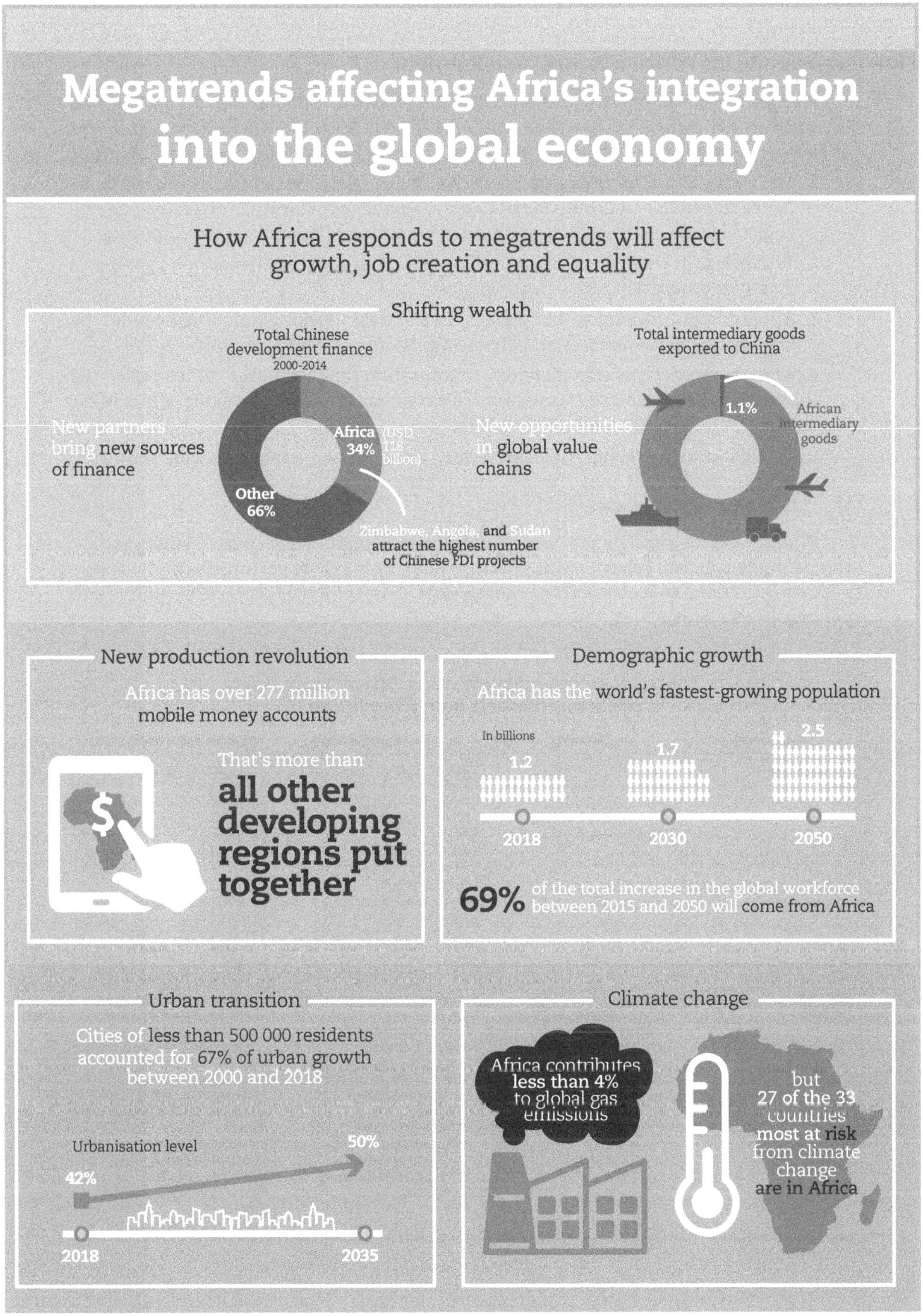
Megatrends affecting Africa's integration into the global economy
How Africa responds to megatrends will affect growth, job creation and equality
Shifting wealth
New partners bring new sources of finance
Total Chinese development finance 2000-2014
Africa 34% (USD 118 billion)
Other 66%
Zimbabwe, Angola, and Sudan attract the highest number of Chinese FDI projects
New opportunities in global value chains
Total intermediary goods exported to China
1.1%
African intermediary goods
New production revolution
Africa has over 277 million mobile money accounts
That's more than
all other developing regions put together
Demographic growth
Africa has the world's fastest-growing population
In billions
1.2
1.7
2.5
2018
2030
2050
69% of the total increase in the global workforce between 2015 and 2050 will come from Africa
Urban transition
Cities of less than 500 000 residents accounted for 67% of urban growth between 2000 and 2018
Urbanisation level
42%
50%
2018
2035
Climate change
Africa contributes less than 4% to global gas emissions
but 27 of the 33 countries most at risk from climate change are in Africa

Five megatrends for Africa's future development

At least five megatrends will shape the future of Africa's integration into the global economy in the coming decade. The way Africa deals with them will have significant impacts on growth, job creation and equality. These megatrends include the following:

1. The rising share of emerging countries in the global economy – referred to as "shifting wealth" – will offer African countries the opportunity to diversify, upgrade in global value chains (GVCs) and find new sources of finance for development.
2. Technological change and digitalisation will bring about challenges and prospects for a new production revolution in Africa.
3. Africa's rapid demographic growth can create "demographic dividends" by expanding the labour force and increasing savings and investments.
4. Africa's rapid transition towards urbanisation will continue to increase the domestic market and the necessary scale economies to provide public goods, boost competitiveness and meet SDG targets.
5. Though climate change presents many risks for vulnerable African countries, in responding to it they can become greener by capitalising on the continent's immense natural assets.

While these megatrends promise new opportunities, they also pose challenges that should guide policies. Table 2.1 summarises the main risks, opportunities and possible policy implications to harness these megatrends. Chapter 8 will propose ten important policy areas for action.

Table 2.1. **Megatrends affecting Africa: Main risks, opportunities and policy implications**

Megatrend	Main risks	Main opportunities	Possible policy implications
Shifting wealth	• Competition from other emerging markets • Creating one-dollar jobs • New "scramble for Africa" • Environmental degradation	• New markets for Africa's export products • Reallocate low-skill manufacturing from Asia to Africa • Africa's increased attractiveness for foreign direct investment (FDI) • Improved access to development finance • Access to new technologies • Transfer of skills	• Strategically engage with Africa's partners • Harmonise standards for labour rights and environment preservation • Promote FDI linkages to the local economy and knowledge transfer • Target export diversification and GVC upgrading • Help entrepreneurs upgrade their products to meet new demand
New production revolution	• Automation • Re-shoring manufacturing to advanced economies • Vulnerable technological infrastructure • Cybersecurity • Environmental degradation • Illicit financial flows	• Increase small firms' access to GVCs • Simplify economies of scale • Reduce trade costs • Create new niches and markets • Offer new off-shoring activities to "African clusters of excellence" • Use new technologies to improve access to public services, make policies more efficient and improve transparency	• Deliver quality skills for science, technology, engineering and mathematics and for technical, entrepreneurial and vocational education and training • Support new technology-based small and medium-sized enterprises (SMEs) through financing • Encourage investment in research and development, technology, and data • Promote technology-oriented clusters • Adapt fiscal policies

Table 2.1. **Megatrends affecting Africa: Main risks, opportunities and policy implications** *(cont.)*

Megatrend	Main risks	Main opportunities	Possible policy implications
Demographic dividends	• High youth unemployment and higher informal sector employment • More pressure on environmental resources • Increased demand for services and social protection, potentially lowering the quality of public services • Increased income inequality • Migration and "brain drain" • Increased social tensions and political demands	• Increase Africa's workforce • Allow the working-age population to surpass that of the dependency-age population • Increasing domestic savings, consumption and gross domestic product (GDP) growth due to higher labour supply and wealth creation • Rising middle class • Collect more fiscal revenues • Encourage the diaspora "brain gain", and remittances for private investment	• Improve the quality of education and skills to match labour market demands • Deepen the domestic financial sector by creating incentives for long-term domestic savings • Lower birth rates by improving healthcare and family planning • Promote high-potential entrepreneurship
Urban transition	• Slum urbanisation • Higher urban poverty and inequality • Inequality between rural and urban areas • Urban sprawl • Urban congestion • More air pollution and inefficient use of water and other natural resources	• Generate economies of scale and social innovation • Increase demand for high value-added goods, food and urban infrastructure • Match and share resources and knowledge among firms and citizens • Increase productivity through business clusters • Rising urban middle class	• Clarify land rights • Strengthen rural-urban linkages and develop intermediary cities • Provide public goods to business clusters • Develop mass transportation systems • Upgrade informal settlements • Apply multi-level governance reforms (capacity building, empowerment, transparency and accountability of various government levels) • Ensure citizens' participation in spatial planning
Climate change and transition to a green economy	• Increased natural disasters and droughts • Endangered ecosystems and species • Erosion of coastal zones and infrastructure damage • Loss of livelihoods and economic activities • Health hazards caused by environmental risks • Climate-induced displacement and migration	• Enjoy GDP growth due to investments in renewable energy • Gain in welfare by cutting fossil fuel (oil and coal) subsidies • Expand green sectors • Create more jobs in green sectors • Use natural resources more sustainably by efficiently sharing infrastructure in high density areas	• Invest in resilient infrastructure, including early warning systems • Develop mass transportation and reduce its costs • Implement national adaptation programmes of action and environmental regulations • Develop climate-related insurance mechanisms

Megatrend 1: Shifting wealth

The shifting wealth process – the gradual re-balancing of global wealth from OECD to non-OECD countries – entered its third phase in 2009. In 2008, the weight of emerging countries in the global economy surpassed the 50% mark (OECD, 2010). The 2008-09 global financial crisis and China's rebalancing led to a slump in oil and metals prices, burdening commodity exporters while stimulating growth in commodity-importing countries. This has created waves of changes in the global development landscape. India is forecasted to continue growing fast and contribute almost 10% to global growth. This country could become a second driver of the shifting wealth process in the coming years (see OECD, forthcoming). Other emerging economies, like the Gulf States and Turkey, may continue to grow while increasing their relations with Africa.

During its two first phases (1990-2000 and 2001-08) the shifting wealth process increased output linkages between emerging economies and developing countries. This affected the relative prices for goods, services and wages. It also changed the terms of trade and brought new sources of development finance. This process accelerated Africa's integration into the global economy, notably by diversifying its global partnerships.

Looking forward, shifting wealth offers several new opportunities to Africa. First, Africa can use its emerging partners to diversify its export basket. Several African countries can export higher value-added goods and services, such as agricultural products and tourism, to new markets as the middle class emerges.

Second, shifting wealth can allow Africa to upgrade in GVCs following China's rebalancing. China's real manufacturing wages increased about 14-fold from 1980 to 2015 (Wei and Zhang, 2017). Eastern Africa has in part benefited from this change by growing at 3.5% per year in real GDP per capita between 2013-16. With the right policies, African countries can attract labour-intensive manufacturing firms to create more jobs for the continent's upcoming youth bulge.

Third, shifting wealth brings new development finance and innovation to Africa. For example, China committed USD 118 billion, or 34% of its total development finance, to Africa during the 2000-14 period (Dreher et al., 2017). Zimbabwe, Angola, Sudan, Tanzania, Ghana, Kenya and Ethiopia (in that order) are the African countries attracting the highest number of Chinese FDI projects. Different emerging countries offer novel expertise to finance development. These include Brazil in agriculture and agro-processing, China in infrastructure, and India in affordable generics, as well as in skills and services in information communications and technology (ITC) and agriculture. Many emerging countries, especially in the Gulf States, have become attractive for African skilled workforce, which could lead to an increase in South-South knowledge transfer.

At the same time, shifting wealth brings new challenges to Africa's policy makers. African economies must boost their productivity to compete with other emerging actors. For example, countries from the Association of Southeast Asian Nations enjoy several advantages over Africa in attracting Chinese FDI. These include established global production networks, physical and cultural proximity to China, and better competitiveness especially in infrastructure and human capital. High labour costs and low productivity prevent many African countries from attracting low-skill industries (Gelb et al., 2017). At similar competitiveness ratings, countries such as the Democratic Republic of the Congo and Ethiopia have a labour cost per manufacturing worker that is comparable to that of Bangladesh (Figure 2.1). Reducing bottlenecks to private sector growth is imperative (see Chapter 8).

Figure 2.1. **Median predicted labour cost per worker in selected African countries and Bangladesh**

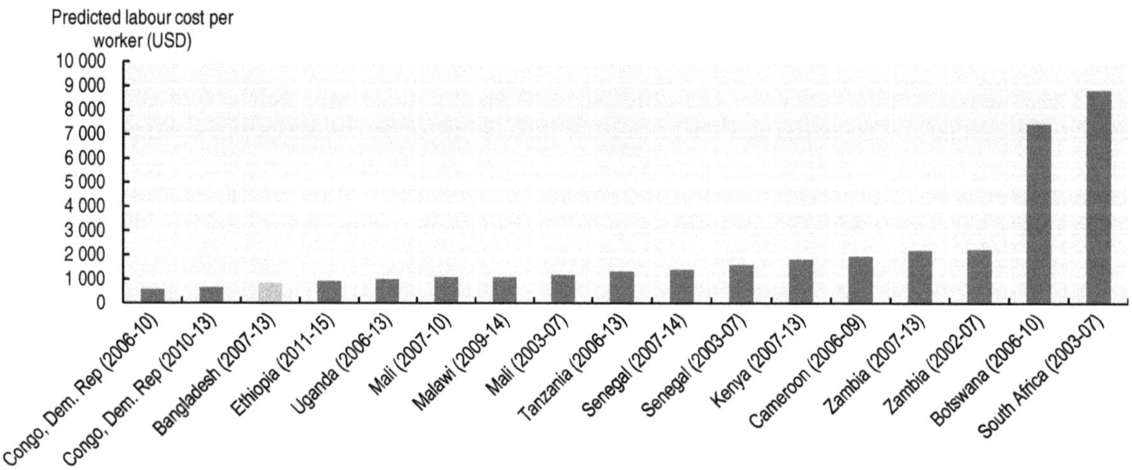

Note: Labour cost per worker is estimated after controlling for a number of firms' characteristics (including capital cost per worker, ownership, human capital and size) and the country's GDP per capita to ensure comparability.
Source: Gelb et al. (2017), "Can Africa be a manufacturing destination? Labor costs in comparative perspective".
StatLink http://dx.doi.org/10.1787/888933782867

African countries have much room to improve their levels of integration into GVCs with other emerging economies. Overall, African intermediary goods represent 1.1% of total intermediary goods exported to China. This level is significantly lower than most of China's other GVC partners. The majority of Africa's exports to Asia consist in commodities (Figure 2.2).

Figure 2.2. **Africa's exports by commodities and level of technology (shares for regional destinations), 2014**

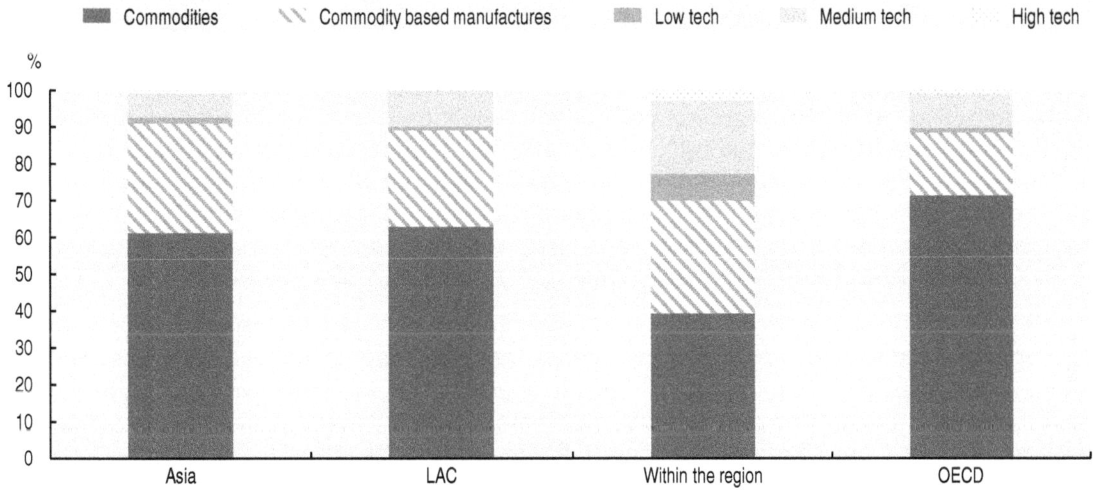

Source: Author's calculations based on UN Statistics Division (2017), *UN COMTRADE* (database).
StatLink http://dx.doi.org/10.1787/888933782886

Several policy objectives could help African governments better tap shifting wealth:

- Enhanced co-ordination can give African governments stronger bargaining power in the new global economic order, especially in trade discussions that face mounting protectionist sentiments. Pan-African organisations can play this co-ordinating role. They are already strengthening co-operation programmes with emerging partners, such as student exchanges to promote skill transfers in technical disciplines.
- By co-ordinating and harmonising regulations, African governments can avoid a "race to the bottom" in undercutting fiscal, labour and environmental regulations when attracting FDI. For instance, joining international efforts to prevent base erosion and profit shifting could make tax systems more transparent and effective.
- African countries will need to deploy strategies to diversify their export products to emerging partners. To upgrade their inputs in GVCs requires boosting competitiveness, encouraging foreign firms to create linkages with local economies and to transfer knowledge, and supporting the development of producer services such as design, marketing and branding.

Megatrend 2: The new production revolution

Over the next 15 years, the ongoing production revolution is likely to impact African economies through the following:

- New technologies (the Internet of Things, big-data analytics, cloud computing and 3D printing)
- New materials (nano- and bio-based technologies)
- New processes (artificial intelligence and data-driven production).

Digitalisation and new manufacturing technologies may reshape countries' comparative advantage in global production networks. At least 40 technologies will be key for the decades to come (OECD, 2016: 79). Taken collectively, these technological innovations can revolutionise global production networks. In this new production revolution – sometimes called "Industry 4.0" – international trade will be largely in services and data, such as bundled services and information flows through digital means.

This production revolution presents opportunities for African countries to find new development paths. First, African entrepreneurs and SMEs can enjoy better access to new modes of production and to global networks, which they could not access before. Investments in activities using digital technologies can generate economies of scale at unprecedented levels compared to traditional manufacturing. With lower equipment costs, digitalisation promises greater control and flexibility in production while reducing operational costs. Paperless trading, on-line collection of information, e-certification and on-line payment of customs duties can reduce trade costs and speed up border clearances. New technologies can enable firms to complete transactions, deliver services, and make payments faster, more efficient and more affordable. Digital communication can facilitate cross-border e-commerce and smaller firms' participation in global markets.

Second, trade in services and new technologies can largely remove logistical bottlenecks and customs barriers. Physical constraints like inadequate road networks may play a less significant role for applying these new production methods. African countries have demonstrated an impressive ability to adapt to ICT technologies. For instance, Africa uses more mobile banking than all other developing regions put together (Figure 2.3). Africa's trade in services expanded from about USD 138 billion in 2005 to almost USD 260 billion in 2015.

Figure 2.3. **Registered mobile money accounts in world regions, 2013-16**

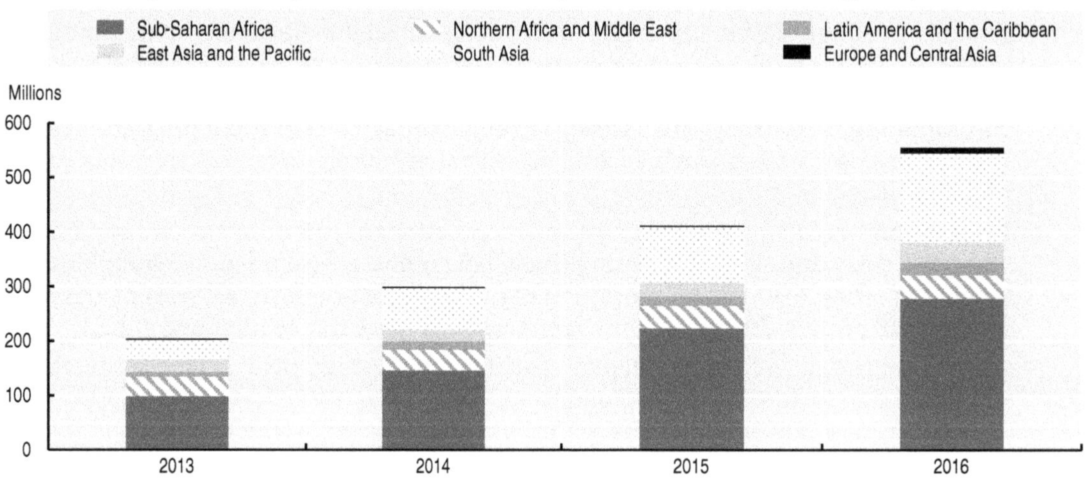

Source: GSMA (2017), *2017 State of the Industry Report on Mobile Money*.
StatLink http://dx.doi.org/10.1787/888933782905

Third, the new production revolution may bring about new niche markets, which African business clusters could tap. New technologies can boost firms' abilities to access new markets and find niches in GVCs. Within GVCs, mass production is likely to shift to mass customisation, or "manufacturing on-demand" (De Backer and Flaig, 2017). African firms could integrate into new markets with higher value added, for example hand-made products, ethical value chains or design services. Cape Town, Lagos, Nairobi, Sfax and Tangiers are emerging hubs for start-ups selling services on global markets, especially in financial technology, ICT, movies, logistics and renewable energies.

The new production revolution entails several risks for African development:

- Many low-skilled jobs in manufacturing could be automated, reducing Africa's attractiveness as a destination for manufacturing investment. Sixty-six percent of all jobs in developing countries are potentially at risk (Frey, Osborne and Holmes, 2016: 19). The risk is even higher in Ethiopia, where 85% of current jobs are in sectors susceptible to automation. In countries such as Angola, Mauritius, Nigeria, Seychelles and South Africa, more than half of current jobs are also at high risk of computerisation. In a recent survey of Chinese manufacturing firms, most said they would respond to labour shortages by investing more in capital equipment rather than by moving production out of China (Standard Chartered Research, 2017: 17).
- The less advanced African countries may not be able to provide the necessary levels of infrastructure, capital, skills and human capital to benefit from the new production revolution. In this scenario, African firms risk lagging further behind the global productivity level.
- New innovations can give rise to winner-takes-all markets that exacerbate income inequality. Rents from digital innovation are often shared among shareholders of the most successful firms, top executives and a few key employees (Guellec and Paunov, 2017).
- The increasing importance of ICT brings new risks to security (cybersecurity), data ownership and privacy, which many African countries are not prepared to face. Many countries do not yet have the legal infrastructure to protect consumer and business rights.
- New environmental risks are also appearing. For example, dumping heavy metals from electronic waste has posed an environmental threat in Ghana and Nigeria (Nnorom and Osibanjo, 2008).

The gains from the new production revolution are not automatic but call for specific policy objectives. The first is to ensure quality skills for the labour force to meet the market needs of a digital economy. Education policies should prioritise quality education with a focus on science, technology, engineering and mathematics. Technical, entrepreneurial and vocational education and training (TEVET) can be included in school curricula. Governments should encourage TEVET institutions to deliver targeted quality training with private sector engagement (e.g. through on-the-job training, apprenticeships and internships that provide certified skills).

Secondly, policies should make business clusters attractive for foreign companies and African start-ups investing in new production schemes. Providing public goods to business clusters can ensure that African firms benefit from conditions that help them grow. Business associations in clusters can facilitate knowledge transfer. Fostering linkages between industrial parks or special economic zones and the rest of the economy (through sub-contracting) is also key to facilitate productivity growth beyond clusters and reduce spatial inequalities.

Thirdly, policies should encourage knowledge transfer to African private and public companies. Agencies promoting FDI can entice foreign investors to transfer knowledge to local companies by employing the local labour force, conducting training courses and subcontracting local companies. Research and development can be scaled up in sectors where the countries have both comparative advantages and the potential to apply new technologies.

Fourthly, policies should give broader access to financing to SMEs that have growth potential. Regulatory frameworks should enable lending institutions to lower the costs and risks associated with financing SME projects while protecting macroeconomic stability.

Instruments such as credit guarantee schemes can diffuse the risks of financing SMEs by associating third party institutions. Dedicated SME authorities and business associations can facilitate connections between SMEs and credit providers. Leasing and factoring can also be used to manage risks (OECD, 2017a; AfDB/OECD/UNDP, 2017).

Finally, governments should invest in substantially upgrading backhaul infrastructure, the fixed lines that connect mobile towers to core networks for data transmission. Africa has made remarkable progress in providing mobile connectivity, but the 2G connectivity for traditional voice and text messages limits access to data services. Mobile broadband (3G, 4G and 5G) requires significant upgrading of fixed infrastructure, including power and access to high-speed broadband fibre, for transmitting data. A 2017 survey suggested that more than two-thirds of Africa's mobile connections are 2G, while 4G connections represent only 2% of the market (Connecting Africa, 2017). The choice between different business and regulatory models, the scope of public funding, the requirements for open access and wholesale service provision have significant implications for investors and the effective deployment of faster telecommunication networks (OECD, 2014). African authorities should assess those implications and design regulatory frameworks that incorporate good practices and are appropriate to their local contexts.

Megatrend 3: Demographic dividends

Africa has the world's fastest-growing population. From 2000 to 2015, Africa's population increased from 814 million to almost 1.2 billion. According to United Nations projections (medium scenario), the population will reach 1.7 billion in 2030 and 2.5 billion in 2050. Africa's share of the world population is predicted to increase from currently around 16% to almost 20% in 2030 and above 25% in 2050 (AfDB/OECD/UNDP, 2016).

Due to rapid population growth, Africa has the second largest workforce in the world after Asia, and its workforce will continue to grow. Between 2015 and 2050, Africa's working age population (defined as 15-64 year olds) will increase by 902 million people, about 69% of the total increase across the world (Figure 2.4). This growth exceeds that of India (263 million). In Europe, the figure should drop by 85 million and in China by 200 million. By 2075, Africa's population between 15 and 24 years old will reach 586 million people, exceeding that of Asia at 584 million.

Figure 2.4. **Projected workforce growth in sub-Saharan Africa, Northern Africa, China, India, Europe and the United States, 2015-50**

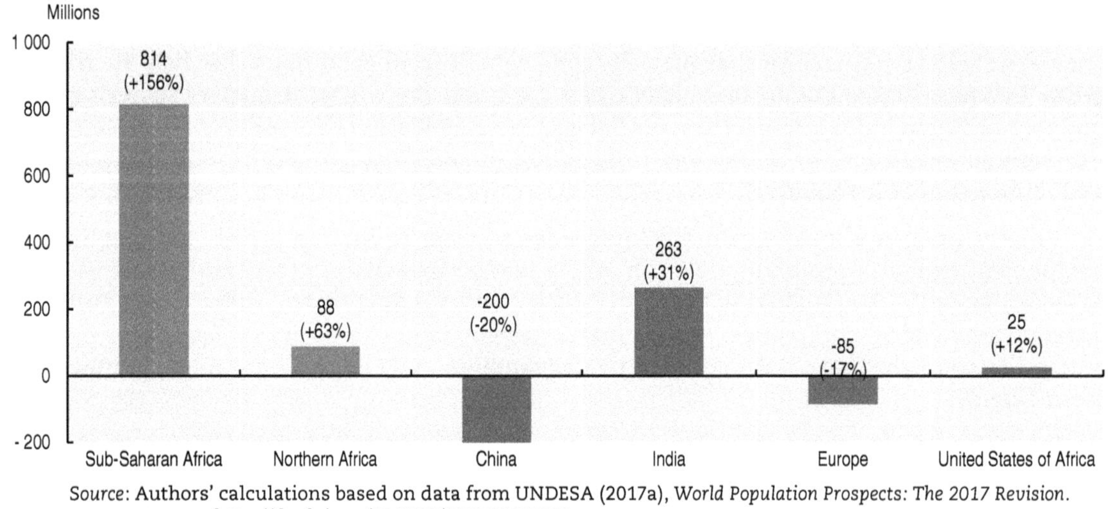

Source: Authors' calculations based on data from UNDESA (2017a), *World Population Prospects: The 2017 Revision*.
StatLink http://dx.doi.org/10.1787/888933782924

The rise in the working-age population can boost growth by increasing the effective labour supply. Activity ratios reveal that Africa has a larger working-age population than dependency-age population (defined as the population younger than 15 and older than 65) (Figure 2.5). In the 1990s, one person was economically-active for each economically-inactive person. Thanks to declining birth rates, the average activity ratio will steadily rise and continue well beyond 2050. By that time, it should reach 1.6 active people per inactive person in sub-Saharan Africa. By 2030, the increase in labour supply could create a first "demographic dividend" and boost Africa's annual growth of GDP per capita by up to half a percentage point, assuming constant output per worker (AfDB/OECD/UNDP, 2016). This demographic dividend could contribute 10-15% of Africa's gross GDP volume growth by 2030 (Ahmed et al., 2014).

Figure 2.5. **Activity ratios in sub-Saharan Africa, Northern Africa, China and India, 1950-2100**

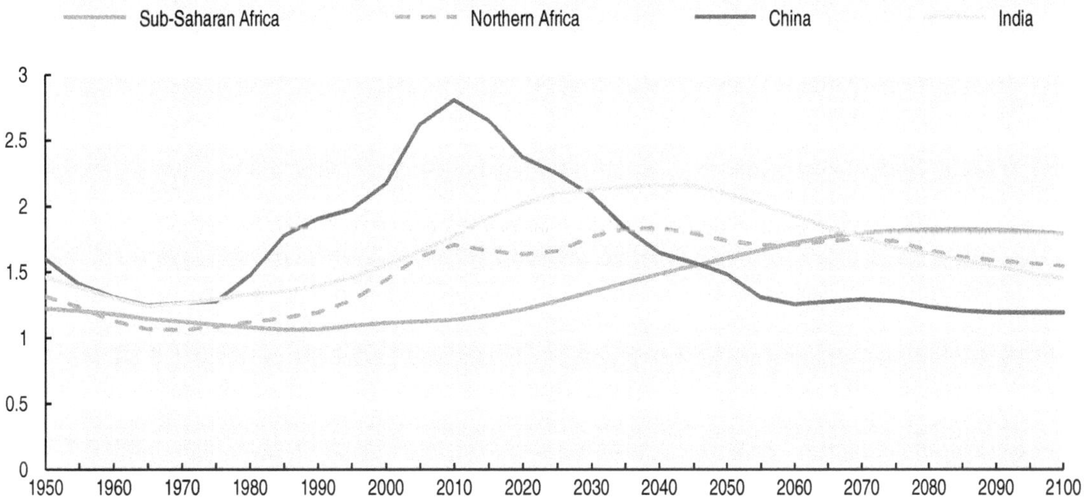

Note: Aggregate ratios are population weighted. The activity ratio is the ratio between the working-age population (ages 15-64) and the dependent-age population (under 15 and over 65). Projections are modelled using the medium fertility variant.

Source: Authors' calculations based on data from UNDESA (2017a), *World Population Prospects: The 2017 Revision.*

StatLink http://dx.doi.org/10.1787/888933782943

Africa may enjoy a second demographic dividend by accumulating savings and investing more in physical and human capital, particularly children's health and education. As activity ratios increase, families and governments have more resources available per child to provide better education and healthcare, which may strengthen productivity over time. With relatively more people of working age, the savings rate could increase and raise productivity through more investment. When the financial system works efficiently, these savings can accumulate and create a "savings glut" for re-investment into the economy.

However, these two demographic dividends depend on jobs and investment. The positive effect of labour supply on growth will only materialise if enough jobs are created. On average between today and 2030, 29 million additional young people turn 16 years old every year. This number of working-age youth is unprecedented. If not enough jobs are created, the youth may be either discouraged from actively looking for a job, causing the labour market participation rate to fall, or unable to find a job, causing unemployment and informality to rise. Rapid population growth could create high pressure on local environmental resources if resource consumption per capita grows as rapidly as in the more advanced economies (AfDB/OECD/UNDP, 2016: 41).

Even though Africa has made great strides in increasing education levels, skills mismatch remains an important challenge. The quality of education systems in Africa still requires improvements. Many African youth lack the technical and managerial skills to succeed in the labour market. Only 10.5% of secondary students are enrolled in vocational programmes, and these are often underfunded.

Reaping these demographic dividends requires fundamental policy changes. In the past, Africa has failed to create enough good jobs despite high economic growth. Policies need to achieve several objectives:

- reduce bottlenecks that still constrain demand for labour, for instance by promoting private-sector activity, including high-potential entrepreneurship, and by helping young people to obtain the skills needed to obtain decent jobs
- speed up the demographic transition towards lower birth rates by improving healthcare, universal education, family planning and women's empowerment
- deepen the domestic financial sector to facilitate savings, improve financial intermediation and attract more investment into the national economies
- create incentives for workers to save their income early on in anticipation of aging (AfDB/OECD/UNDP, 2016: 41).

Box 2.1. **Policies can help maximise migration's contribution to African development**

Emigration from Africa is at an all-time high: 36.3 million individuals born in Africa were not living in their country of birth in 2017. This is a sharp rise from the 20.3 million in 1990. However, emigration as a percentage of the total population fell from 3.2% in 1990 to 2.9% in 2017, because Africa's population is growing faster than its emigration. The causes of this absolute increase in emigration range from internal strife to a rise in income which makes migration more affordable, especially among a handful of populous countries such as the Democratic Republic of the Congo, Egypt, Morocco, Somalia and Sudan (UNDESA, 2017b). Similarly, refugee flows from Africa are highly concentrated in a small number of countries. South Sudan and Somalia alone accounted for 40% of refugees from Africa in 2016.

In terms of immigration, African migration also remains largely intra-regional. In 2017, 79% of the 24.7 million immigrants living on the continent were born in another African country. In absolute terms, South Africa hosts the most immigrants, with more than 4 million. But several other countries boast more than 1 million immigrants, including Côte d'Ivoire (2.2 million), Uganda (1.7 million), Nigeria (1.2 million), Ethiopia (1.2 million) and Kenya (1.1 million).

Migration from Africa is expected to increase due to the demands for better job prospects and living standards. Between 2015 and 2050, 69% of the increase in the global workforce will come from Africa (seeFigure 2.4). A lack of good jobs and basic infrastructure locally causes increasing numbers of young men and women to migrate to find better jobs and an urban lifestyle. The divergence in economic growth across African countries also mean that growth poles, such as Morocco, South Africa and the entire Gulf of Guinea seaboard, are attracting more African job seekers. While most emigrants from Africa continue to reside on the continent, the share has actually fallen, from 66% in 1990 to 53% in 2017.

Africa increasingly sees migration in positive terms. Migrants often send home money, for instance. Remittances were estimated at 2.8% of GDP on average between 2009 and 2016 (see Chapter 1). Remittances can help reduce poverty, and they tend to increase during economic downturns.

Box 2.1. **Policies can help maximise migration's contribution to African development** *(cont.)*

Several African countries, such as Burkina Faso, Morocco and Zimbabwe, have instituted policies or strategies to link emigration to development objectives. To increase the impact of emigration on development, policies can i) provide support to families who stay behind, ii) lower remittance costs and channel them towards productive investment, iii) encourage and integrate return migrants, and iv) bring diasporas into development initiatives. Beyond migration and development policy initiatives, more generalised public policies, such as those for labour, education, agriculture and social protection, can also help gain more from migration for better development outcomes (OECD, 2017b).

African countries can maximise the positive impact of immigration by adopting coherent policies to better manage and integrate immigrants. Among ten countries in a recent OECD-ILO report,[1] the estimated contribution of immigrants to GDP averages 7%, ranging from about 1% in Ghana to 19% in Côte d'Ivoire (OECD/ILO, 2018). Integrating immigrants into developing countries comes with different sets of challenges than those in developed countries, particularly in the context of high informality, porous borders and limited budgets (Gagnon and Khoudour-Castéras, 2012). Policy options include providing better access to basic services, ensuring the rights of immigrant workers and integrating them into the labour market so that they can invest in and contribute to the economy where they work and live.

Enhanced co-operation between origin and destination countries would lead to better managed and mutually beneficial migration. The 2030 Agenda for Sustainable Development included migration as a means for development for the first time on an international policy agenda: four Sustainable Development Goals explicitly mention migration or remittances. The current efforts towards a Global Compact for Safe, Orderly and Regular Migration can also help strengthen the global governance of international migration, which is currently limited.

Megatrend 4: The urban transition

Africa is the second fastest urbanising region after Asia. The rate of urbanisation increased from 14% in 1950 to 42% at present; by 2035, 50% of Africans are expected to reside in urban areas (Figure 2.6). The speed of this process is unmatched. Africa's urbanisation is mainly taking place in intermediate cities and towns. Cities and towns with less than 500 000 residents accounted for 67% of urban growth between between 2000 and 2018.

Figure 2.6. **Growth trends in Africa's urban, rural and total populations, 1950-2050**

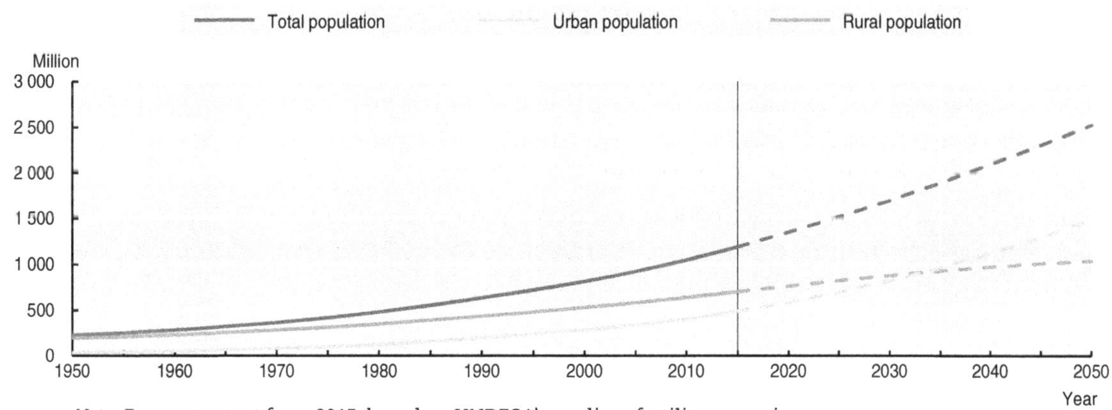

Note: Forecasts start from 2015, based on UNDESA's medium fertility scenario.

Source: UNDESA (2018), *World Urbanization Prospects: The 2018 Revision.*

StatLink http://dx.doi.org/10.1787/888933782962

Africa's urbanisation is expanding domestic markets in rural and urban areas. It is increasing demand for higher value-added goods and changing diets. The middle class, defined as those spending USD 5-20 a day, increased from 108 million people in 1990 to 247 million in 2013. The urban sector accounts for 40% of the total population but 50% of total food consumption and 60% of the food market (Reardon et al., 2013). West Africa's food economy is estimated at USD 178 billion for 2010 – 36% of the regional GDP–, over two-thirds of which were traded in markets (Allen and Heinrigs, 2016). In that region, the average distance between cities dropped from 111 kilometres to 28 between 1950 and 2010 (Moriconi-Ebrard, Harre and Heinrigs, 2016). Similarly, urban demand for goods and services in construction and supporting industries is rising.

FDI to tap African urban markets has been rising. According to Wall (2016), "Relative to GDP, sub-Saharan African cities featured in the top 10% attractors of greenfield FDI between 2002 and 2012, as often as cities in the East Asia and Pacific region. [...] Among all the jobs directly created by FDI in Africa between 2003 and 2014, 83% were located in cities".

When the enabling conditions are present, economic agglomerations and urban firm clusters across African countries can increase productivity gains. Three positive effects characterise agglomeration economies: matched inputs, shared resources and innovation through learning. For example, the entry of each new firm in an Ethiopian cluster increases their competitors' productivity by 0.91% (Siba et al, 2012). In Arusha, Dar es Salaam and Mbeya (Tanzania) and Kampala (Uganda), a 10% increase of firms in the same industry and area reduces their costs by an average of 0.3-0.4% (Iimi, Humphrey and Melibaeva, 2015).

However, many binding constraints are hindering the potential of Africa's rapid urbanisation. The high rate of urbanisation so far has not created employment outside the informal sectors or low value-added services. The informal economy accounts for 61% of urban employment and is the source of 93% of newly created jobs (Kessides, 2005). Due to gender-based discrimination and lack of opportunities, female workers are disproportionately over-represented in informal sectors, especially services.

African urbanisation takes place mostly through spatial urban expansion, without generating the benefits of densely populated areas. Between 2000 and 2010, the populations of 12 African cities rapidly expanded but into adjacent rural areas: Their density remained low at 81 inhabitants/km^2. Kampala's urban expansion at 10.6% per year was faster than its population growth at 4.6% per year, reducing its density level. Low density largely impedes cities' productivity. For instance, some estimate that a viable public transport system requires at least 15 000 inhabitants per km^2.

Africa has higher rates of urban poverty than any other region, and about 62% of urban residents live in informal settlements. Due to rapid urban population growth, many African cities face the challenge of tripling their slum populations by 2050 (UN-Habitat, 2008). People living in informal settlements often have low mobility rates, as high transportation costs can account for at least 20% of low-income households' disposable incomes.

African urban areas are exposed to high environmental risks. Mortality from air pollution costs Africa an estimated USD 447 billion in 2013, a third of its GDP. Climate change presents high risks of flooding in low coastal cities, heat extremes and changing rain patterns, threatening the livelihoods of many Africans (Roy, 2016).

Africa's intermediary cities are not yet equipped to face the rapidly-growing population (Minsat, forthcoming). Over 1 081 million Africans, 81% of the continent's population, live in a rural-urban interface defined by a continuum of rural areas, villages, towns and cities of fewer than 500 000 inhabitants. Intermediary cities would increase wealth in rural areas and strengthen rural-urban linkages: intermediary cities can create a demand pool for rural economic activities and provide services and goods in their catchment areas. However, the demand for basic services outstrips the supply. In nine African countries, the governments of intermediary cities spend on average less than USD 1 per capita per year in total (AfDB/OECD/UNDP, 2016).

Tackling these challenges and reaping the opportunities created by rapid urbanisation call for holistic development strategies and targeted policy action. While each country is unique, many countries should give priority to the following objectives for policy action:

- Continuing to upgrade urban infrastructure remains a key priority for all countries. Two-thirds of urban investments are scheduled between now and 2050. Investing in urban infrastructure adapted to the most pessimistic climate change scenarios (called the "no regrets" approach) and planning urban development would bring many benefits.
- Ensuring land rights and clarifying land ownership, including for people living in informal settlements, are essential to provide a stable environment for investment and business.
- Strengthening rural-urban linkages and linkages within the urban network can facilitate a smoother transition from a rural to an urban economy. Several countries, such as Ethiopia and Rwanda, aim to strengthen the pivotal function of intermediary cities between rural areas and primary cities.
- Governments can deliver public goods to existing business clusters in African cities more effectively. Many local companies have gathered in urban areas, forming clusters. But public goods such as a reliable electricity supply often lack in those clusters, hindering productivity growth.
- Developing mass transportation systems can help reduce pollution while positively contributing to the economy. For example, the Lagos Bus Rapid Transit system has provided 2 000 direct and 500 000 indirect jobs and has reduced the cost of public transportation by 30%.
- Multi-level governance reforms can help implement policies and better adapt them to local territories. The new rural-urban dynamics require governance structures that go beyond cities' administrative boundaries and take into account the economic functions of human settlements. Clarifying the responsibilities of different government levels and establishing co-ordinating structures are key. Multi-level governance reforms require accountability, transparency and capacity building, particularly at subnational levels.

Megatrend 5: Climate change and the transition to a green economy

Climate change represents a significant challenge for Africa's development. Increased greenhouse gas levels in the atmosphere, rising sea levels, hotter temperatures and other changing weather patterns bring concrete risks for Africa's economies and societies. Africa is more vulnerable to climate change than other world regions, although is less responsible for creating this global challenge. The continent contributes less than 4% to global greenhouse gas emissions, but 27 of the 33 countries most at risk from climate change are in Africa (FAO, 2008; Maplecroft, 2016).

Many African countries are now transitioning into the middle-income stage demanding more energy. The shift to modern energy often means a rapid reliance on electricity generated from fossil fuels, resulting in higher CO_2 emissions and other types of harmful air pollutants. As Africa's population will increase to 25.8% of the world's population in 2050 and approximately 40% in 2100, without an environmental transition towards greener growth its ecological footprint will also drastically increase.

Patterns of energy use vary among African countries. Countries such as the Democratic Republic of the Congo with low levels of energy consumption should aim for continuing on a path of sustainable energy use as their income grows (see Figure 2.7). Countries like South Africa with higher energy consumption may have to consider greener models.

Figure 2.7. **GDP and energy use per capita for selected African countries and China, 1990-2012**

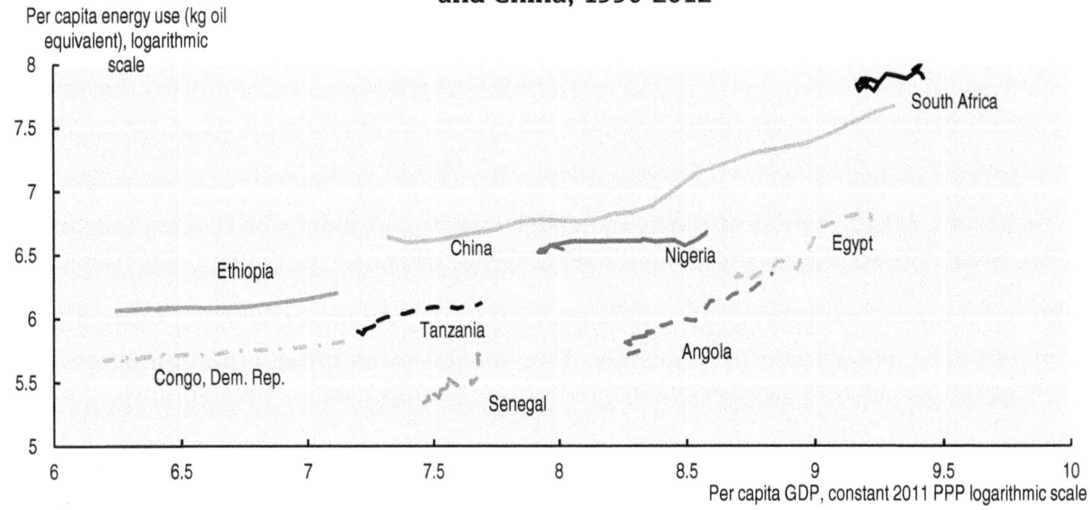

Source: Brambhatt, Haddaoui and Page (2017), "Green industrialisation and entrepreneurship in Africa".
StatLink http://dx.doi.org/10.1787/888933782981

Floods from rising sea levels can be costly. Half of African settlements with 1-5 million inhabitants lie in low elevation coastal zones and are vulnerable to flooding (Kamal-Chaoui and Robert, 2009). Egypt's coastal zone contains 40% of the country's total population; in addition to human displacement and other adverse consequences, every metre of sea level rise would decrease GDP by 6.4%. For Nigeria, estimates lay at a 0.3% GDP loss and for Senegal at 12-17% (Brown, Kebede and Nicholls, 2011).

A lack of rain, desertification and hotter temperatures seriously affect Africa. Recent droughts have had negative impacts on the agricultural sector in Eastern and Southern Africa. Global warming beyond 2°C could lead to a 40% decrease in precipitation in Southern Africa (Granoff et al., 2015). Desertification already affects two-thirds of Africa's land and 65% of its population. It contributes to rural-urban migration since African agriculture depends heavily on rainfall. A 1% decrease in precipitation could increase sub-Saharan Africa's urbanisation rate by 0.45%. Rising temperatures are already increasing the incidences of malaria in Eastern Africa's highlands (Endo, Yamana and Eltahir, 2017).

Africa faces significant costs to avoid the consequences of climate change. Present interventions to adapt to climate change will cost USD 7-15 billion a year by 2020 (Schaeffer et al., 2013). In a "below 2°C scenario", adaptation costs could reach USD 35 billion by 2050 and USD 200 billion by 2070 (Granoff et al., 2015). Adapting infrastructure projects to climate change would raise investment costs by about 15% (ICA, 2016). Retrofitting environment-unfriendly infrastructure exceeds the cost of initially investing in environment-friendly infrastructure.

African countries can mitigate the effects of climate change by targeting specific policy objectives:

- Policies should accelerate the energy transition. Africa has enormous potential for renewable energy which can help address its energy shortage (AfDB, 2017). Half of sub-Saharan Africa's growth in electricity generation will likely come from renewable energy by 2040 (OECD/IEA, 2014). The costs of renewable energy are decreasing rapidly. That of solar energy declined by 80% between 2008 and 2015. For sub-Saharan Africa in particular, "decentralised systems, led by solar photovoltaic in off-grid systems and mini-grids, are the least-cost solution for three-quarters of the additional connections needed" (OECD/IEA, 2017).

- Policies should develop green sectors. African countries can capitalise on their rich biodiversity by becoming eco-tourism destinations. Tourism already accounted for 30% of Africa's services exports in 2016 (ITC, 2016). Improving recycling and waste collection can create many jobs for low-skilled workers (AfDB/OECD/UNDP, 2016).
- Finally, policies should reduce the costs resulting from air pollution. Phasing out coal and oil subsidies would reduce deaths from air pollution by at least 50% (Coady et al., 2015: 25). Eliminating energy subsidies across six countries in East and Southern Africa would generate savings ranging from an estimated 1.5% of GDP in Uganda to 8.3% of GDP in Zambia (OECD, 2017c).

Note

1. These countries include Argentina, Costa Rica, Côte d'Ivoire, the Dominican Republic, Ghana, Kyrgyzstan, Nepal, Rwanda, South Africa and Thailand.

References

AfDB (2017), *Annual Report 2016*, African Development Bank, Abidjan.

AfDB/OECD/UNDP (2017), *African Economic Outlook 2017: Entrepreneurship and Industrialisation*, OECD Publishing, Paris, dx.doi.org/10.1787/aeo-2017-en.

AfDB/OECD/UNDP (2016), *African Economic Outlook 2016: Sustainable Cities and Structural Transformation*, OECD Publishing, Paris, dx.doi.org/10.1787/aeo-2016-en.

Ahmed et al. (2014), "How significant is Africa's demographic dividend for its future growth and poverty reduction?", *World Bank Policy Research Working Paper*, No. 7134, Washington, DC.

Allen, T. and P. Heinrigs (2016), "Emerging opportunities in the West African food economy", *West African Papers*, No. 1, OECD Publishing, Paris, http://dx.doi.org/10.1787/5jlvfj4968jb-en.

Brambhatt M., C. Haddaoui and J. Page (2017), "Green industrialisation and entrepreneurship in Africa", *The New Climate Economy/OECD Working Paper*, New Climate Economy, London and Washington, DC.

Brown, S., A.S. Kebede and R.J. Nicholls (2011), *Sea-Level Rise and Impacts in Africa, 2000 to 2100*, report by the School of Civil engineering and the Environment, www.unep.org/climatechange/adaptation/Portals/133/documents/AdaptCost/9%20Sea%20Level%20Rise%20Report%20Jan%202010.pdf.

Coady, D. et al. (2015), "How large are global energy subsidies?", *IMF Working Paper*, www.imf.org/external/pubs/ft/wp/2015/wp15105.pdf.

Connecting Africa (2017), "The economics of change in African infrastructure development", *Connecting Africa*, www.connectingafrica.com/document.asp?doc_id=736411.

De Backer, K. and D. Flaig (2017), "The future of global value chains: Business as usual or 'a new normal'?", *OECD Science, Technology and Industry Policy Papers*, No. 41, OECD Publishing, Paris, dx.doi.org/10.1787/d8da8760-en.

Dreher, A. et al. (2017), "Aid, China, and growth: Evidence from a new global development finance dataset", *AidData Working Paper*, No. 46, Williamsburg, Virginia.

Endo, N., T. Yamana and E.A. Eltahir (2017),"Impact of climate change on malaria in Africa: A combined modelling and observational study", *The Lancet*, No. 389, Issue S7, https://doi.org/10.1016/S0140-6736(17)31119-4.

FAO (2008), "Africa could reduce greenhouse gases", Food and Agricultural Organisation, Rome (accessed in January 2018).

Frey, C.B., M.A. Osborne and C. Holmes (2016), *Technology at Work v2.0: The Future Is Not What It Used to Be, Citi GPS: Global Perspectives and Solutions*, Citi GPS, Oxford, United Kingdom.

Gagnon, J. and D. Khoudour-Castéras (2012), "South-South migration in West Africa: Addressing the challenge of immigrant integration", *OECD Development Centre Working Papers 312*, OECD Publishing, Paris, http://www.oecd.org/dev/50251899.pdf.

Gelb, A. et al. (2017), "Can Africa be a manufacturing destination? Labor costs in comparative perspective", *CGD Working Paper* 466, Center for Global Development, Washington, DC.

Granoff, I. et al. (2015), "Zero Poverty, zero emissions: Eradicating extreme poverty in the climate crisis", *Overseas Development Institute*, London.

GSMA (2017), *2017 State of the Industry Report on Mobile Money*, GSM Association.

Guellec, D. and C. Paunov (2017), "Digital innovation and the distribution of income", *NBER Working Paper* No. 23987, The National Bureau of Economic Research, Cambridge.

ICA (2016), "Outcomes Statement 2016 ICA", 12th Annual Meeting of the Infrastructure Consortium for Africa (ICA), in Abidjan.

Iimi, A., R.M. Humphrey and S. Melibaeva (2015), "Firm productivity and infrastructure costs in East Africa", *Policy Research Working Paper*, No. 7278, World Bank, Washington, DC.

ITC (2016), *Trade Map* (database), International Trade Centre, https://www.trademap.org/.

Kamal-Chaoui, L. and A. Robert (2009), "Competitive cities and climate change", *OECD Regional Development Working Papers*, No. 2009/02, OECD Publishing, Paris, http://dx.doi.org/10.1787/218830433146.

Kessides, C. (2005), "The urban transition in sub-Saharan Africa: Implications for economic growth and poverty reduction", *Transport and Urban Development Department, Working Paper Series*, No. 97, World Bank.

Maplecroft (2016), *Climate Change Vulnerability Index 2017*, https://reliefweb.int/report/world/climate-change-vulnerability-index-2017.

Minsat, A. (forthcoming), "Small and intermediary cities will make or break the Sustainable Development Goals in Africa", *Urban Planning International*, 2018, 33.

Moriconi-Ebrard, F., D. Harre and P. Heinrigs (2016), *Urbanisation Dynamics in West Africa 1950–2010: Africapolis I, 2015 Update*, West African Studies, OECD Publishing, Paris, http://dx.doi.org/10.1787/9789264252233-en.

Nnorom, I.C. and O. Osibanjo (2008), "Overview of electronic waste (e-waste) management practices and legislations, and their poor applications in the developing countries", *Resources, Conservation and Recycling*, Vol. 52/6, pp. 843-858, https://doi.org/10.1016/j.resconrec.2008.01.004.

OECD (forthcoming), *"Perspectives on Global Development 2019: Rethinking Development Strategies"*, OECD Publishing, Paris.

OECD (2017a), *The Next Production Revolution: Implications for Governments and Business*, OECD Publishing, Paris, dx.doi.org/10.1787/9789264271036-en.

OECD (2017b), *Interrelations between Public Policies, Migration and Development*, OECD Publishing, Paris, http://dx.doi.org/10.1787/9789264265615-en.

OECD (2017c), *Social Protection in East Africa: Harnessing the Future*, OECD Publishing, Paris, http://dx.doi.org/10.1787/9789264274228-en.

OECD (2016), *OECD Science, Technology and Innovation Outlook 2016*, OECD Publishing, Paris, dx.doi.org/10.1787/sti_in_outlook-2016-en.

OECD (2014), "The development of fixed broadband networks", *OECD Digital Economy Papers*, No. 239, OECD Publishing, Paris, http://dx.doi.org/10.1787/5jz2m5mlb1q2-en.

OECD (2013), *Interconnected Economies: Benefiting from Global Value Chains*, OECD Publishing, Paris, dx.doi.org/10.1787/9789264189560-en.

OECD (2010), *Perspectives on Global Development 2010: Shifting Wealth*, OECD Publishing, Paris, http://dx.doi.org/10.1787/9789264084728-en.

OECD/IEA (2017), *Energy Access Outlook 2017: From Poverty to Prosperity*, OECD, International Energy Agency, Paris, www.iea.org/publications/freepublications/publication/WEO2017SpecialReport_EnergyAccessOutlook.pdf.

OECD/IEA (2014), *Africa Energy Outlook*, OECD, International Energy Agency, Paris, www.iea.org/publications/freepublications/publication/AEO_ES_English.pdf.

OECD/ILO (2018), *How Immigrants Contribute to Developing Countries' Economies*, International Labour Organization, Geneva/OECD Publishing, Paris, http://dx.doi.org/10.1787/9789264288737-en.

Reardon, T. et al. (2013), "The emerging 'Quiet Revolution' in African agrifood systems", brief for a high-level meeting on Harnessing Innovation for African Agriculture and Food Systems: Meeting Challenges and Designing for the 21st Century, African Union Conference Center, Addis Ababa.

Roy, R. (2016), "The cost of air pollution in Africa", *OECD Development Centre Working Papers*, No. 333, OECD Publishing, Paris, http://dx.doi.org/10.1787/5jlqzq77x6f8-en.

Schaeffer, M. et al. (2013), "Mid- and long-term climate projections for fragmented and delayed-action scenarios", *Technological Forecasting & Social Change*, Vol. 90, Part A, pp. 257-268, https://doi.org/10.1016/j.techfore.2013.09.013.

Siba, E. et al. (2012), "Enterprise agglomeration, output prices, and physical productivity: Firm-level evidence from Ethiopia", *Working Paper*, No. 2012/85, Africa Growth Initiative at Brookings, African Development Bank and UNU-WIDER.

Standard Charted Research (2017), "Special report: Shop talk – China, ASEAN and the future", *Standard Chartered Bank*, https://av.sc.com/corp-en/content/docs/2017-Reinventing-through-rebotics.pdf.

UN Statistics Division (2017), *UN COMTRADE* (database), accessed via http://wits.worldbank.org/wits/ (accessed 1 February 2018).

UNDESA (2018), *World Urbanization Prospects: The 2018 Revision (database)*, https://esa.un.org/unpd/wup/ (accessed 22 May 2018).

UNDESA (2017a), *World Population Prospects: The 2017 Revision (database)*, https://esa.un.org/unpd/wpp/ (accessed 1 February 2018).

UNDESA (2017b), *International Migrant Stock: The 2017 Revision (database)*, www.un.org/en/development/desa/population/migration/data/estimates2/estimates17.shtml (accessed 1 May 2018).

UNDESA (2014), *World Urbanization Prospects* (database), https://esa.un.org/unpd/wup/ (accessed 1 February 2018).

UN-Habitat (2008), *State of the World's Cities 2008/2009, Harmonious Cities.*

Wall, R. (2016), "State of foreign direct investment to African cities", *OECD Development Centre Background Papers for the African Economic Outlook 2016.*

Wei, S.-J., Z. Xie and X. Zhang (2017), "From 'made in China' to 'innovated in China': Necessity, prospect, and challenges", *Journal of Economic Perspectives*, Vol. 31/1, pp. 49-70, https://pubs.aeaweb.org/doi/pdfplus/10.1257/jep.31.1.49.

Chapter 3

Dynamics of growth, jobs and inequalities in Southern Africa

This chapter addresses the links between growth, employment and inequality in the Southern Africa region (Angola, Botswana, Lesotho, Malawi, Mozambique, Namibia, South Africa, Swaziland, Zambia and Zimbabwe). It examines the drivers of growth and the need to diversify the economy. The chapter also shows the challenges interlinking the lack of quality jobs and the inequality in Southern Africa. It highlights the heterogeneity across countries and the common problems they face.

The chapter begins with the region's economic profile. The subsequent three sections present the evolution of growth, jobs, and poverty and income inequality in the region. A discussion of the relationships between inequality, employment and economic growth follows, and the final section presents policy recommendations.

IN BRIEF

Southern Africa has registered steady **economic growth** since 2000, but sustaining it remains a challenge. Annual real gross domestic product (GDP) grew at 5.2% between 2000 and 2008 before slowing down to 2.6% between 2009 and 2016. Volatility in commodity prices and investment in the extractive sector has strongly affected this performance.

Manufacturing value added in the region dropped to 12.6% of GDP in 2015, from 18.2% of GDP in 2000. A number of countries depend heavily on the mining sector, which is volatile and creates few jobs. In other countries, subsistence agriculture still dominates. FDI in the region is increasingly moving into manufacturing and services to take advantage of growing domestic markets. The challenge remains to facilitate strong linkages and knowledge transfer between investors, lead firms and local suppliers to upgrade their capabilities and create local jobs.

Employment remains a major challenge in Southern Africa: every year between 2015 and 2030, 1.1 million people are estimated to join the labour force. Limited job creation, a skills mismatch and barriers to start and grow new businesses have contributed to unemployment rates of 15-35% in SACU member countries. Elsewhere, the majority of workers are underemployed and working in poverty, mainly in agriculture and low value-added services.

Southern Africa is characterised by high levels of income **inequality**, with the region being home to six of the world's top ten unequal countries. While Southern Africa performs relatively better than other African regions, gender inequality remains a significant hurdle. Unemployment rates for female workers are generally higher than for male workers, even among the youth, and the gap between male and female labour force participation remains wide. Social spending and decent growth have helped reduce extreme poverty, but the extreme poverty headcount in the region remains at 35.6%. The majority of the rural population still lacks access to basic services such as electricity, water and sanitation, creating a large opportunity gap with the urban population.

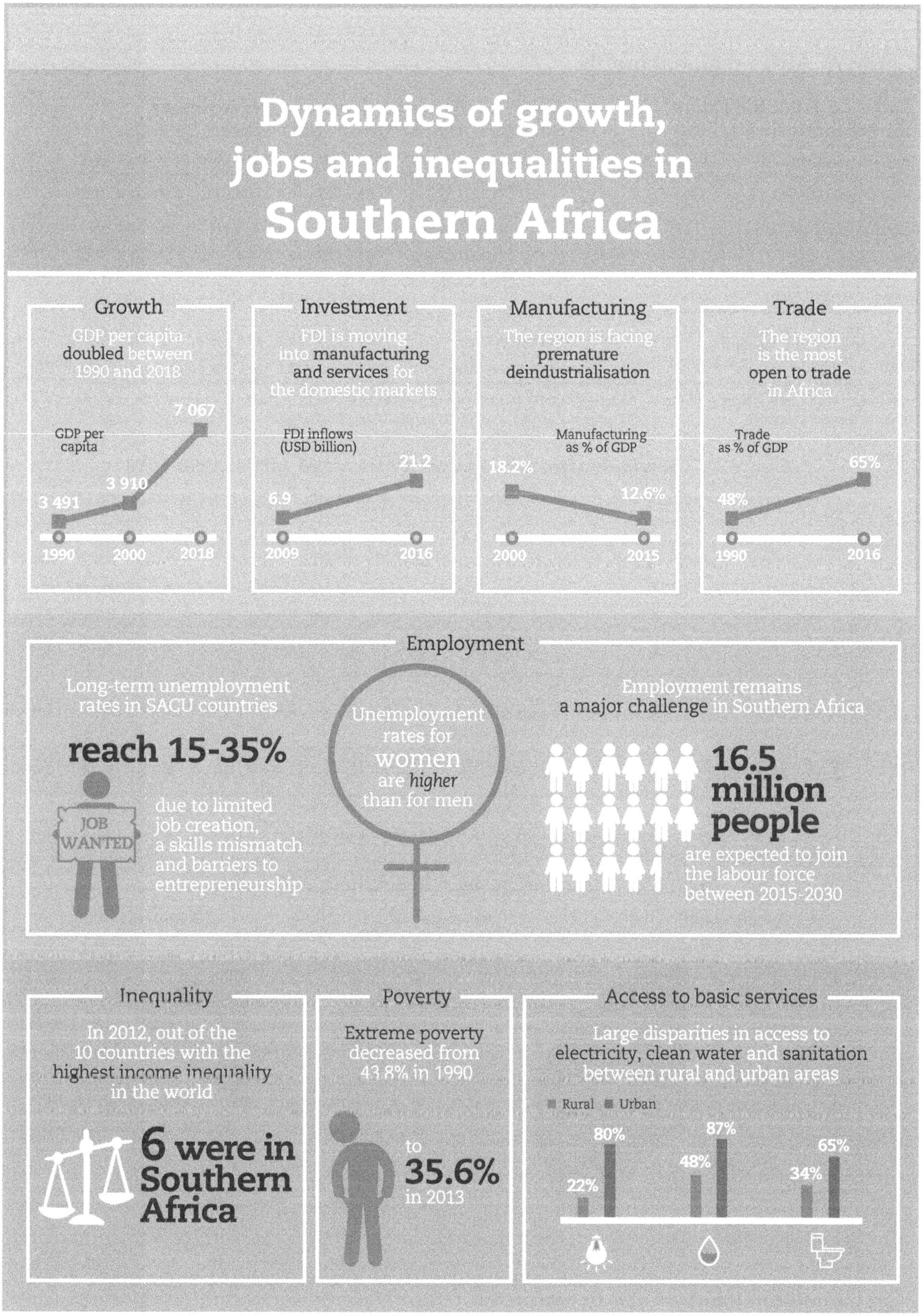
Dynamics of growth, jobs and inequalities in Southern Africa
Growth
GDP per capita doubled between 1990 and 2018
GDP per capita
3 491
3 910
7 067
1990
2000
2018
Investment
FDI is moving into manufacturing and services for the domestic markets
FDI inflows (USD billion)
6.9
21.2
2009
2016
Manufacturing
The region is facing premature deindustrialisation
Manufacturing as % of GDP
18.2%
12.6%
2000
2015
Trade
The region is the most open to trade in Africa
Trade as % of GDP
48%
65%
1990
2016
Employment
Long-term unemployment rates in SACU countries
reach 15-35%
JOB WANTED
due to limited job creation, a skills mismatch and barriers to entrepreneurship
Unemployment rates for women are higher than for men
Employment remains a major challenge in Southern Africa
16.5 million people
are expected to join the labour force between 2015-2030
Inequality
In 2012, out of the 10 countries with the highest income inequality in the world
6 were in Southern Africa
Poverty
Extreme poverty decreased from 43.8% in 1990
to 35.6% in 2013
Access to basic services
Large disparities in access to electricity, clean water and sanitation between rural and urban areas
Rural
Urban
22%
80%
48%
87%
34%
65%

Southern Africa regional profile

Table 3.1. **Basic indicators for Southern Africa, 2017**

Population (thousands)	176 842
Land area (thousands of km²)	5 908
Population density (people/km²)	30
GDP, PPP (USD billion)	1 201
GDP per capita, PPP (USD)	6 939

Source: Authors' calculations based on UNDESA (2017), *World Population Prospects* (database); World Bank (2017a), *World Development Indicators* (database) and IMF (2018), *World Economic Outlook Database*.

Table 3.2. **Financial flows and tax revenues to Southern Africa (current USD billion), 2009-16**

			2009	2010	2011	2012	2013	2014	2015	2016
Foreign	Private	Inward foreign direct investment	6.9	4.8	5.3	7.2	20.7	23.7	14.0	21.2
		Portfolio investments	12.7	14.8	16.3	23.1	14.4	15.0	13.0	10.1
		Remittances	1.7	2.0	2.1	2.0	1.8	1.7	1.5	1.3
	Public	Official development assistance (net total, all donors)	6.9	6.6	7.0	7.2	7.8	6.6	6.6	6.3
Total foreign flows			**28.2**	**28.3**	**30.7**	**39.4**	**44.7**	**47.0**	**35.1**	**38.9**
Domestic tax revenues			**106.2**	**135.5**	**164.1**	**164.1**	**156.2**	**149.0**	**123.2**	**107.1**

Source: IMF (2018), *World Economic Outlook Database*, OECD (2018a), *International Development Statistics* (database), and World Bank (2017a), *World Development Indicators* (database).

Figure 3.1. **Growth dynamics in Southern Africa and Africa, 1990-2018**

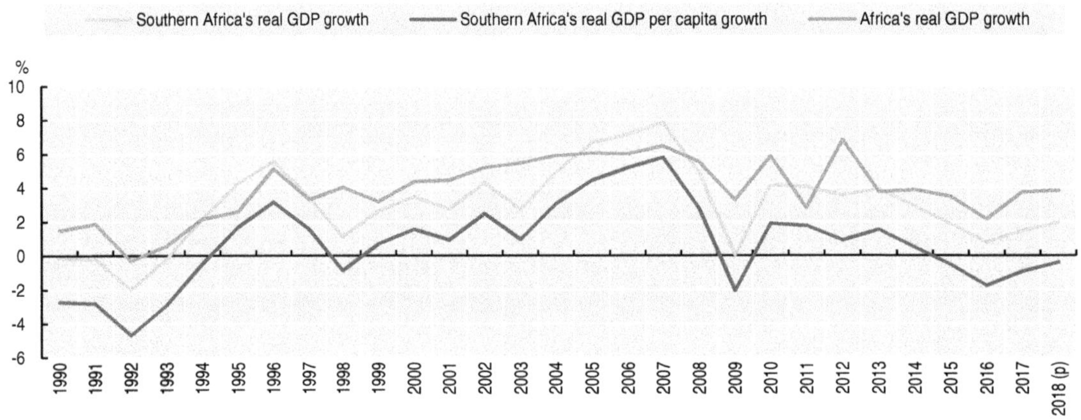

Note: (p) = projections.
Source: Authors' calculations based on IMF (2018), *World Economic Outlook Database*.
StatLink http://dx.doi.org/10.1787/888933783000

Figure 3.2. **Trade composition in Southern Africa, 2016**

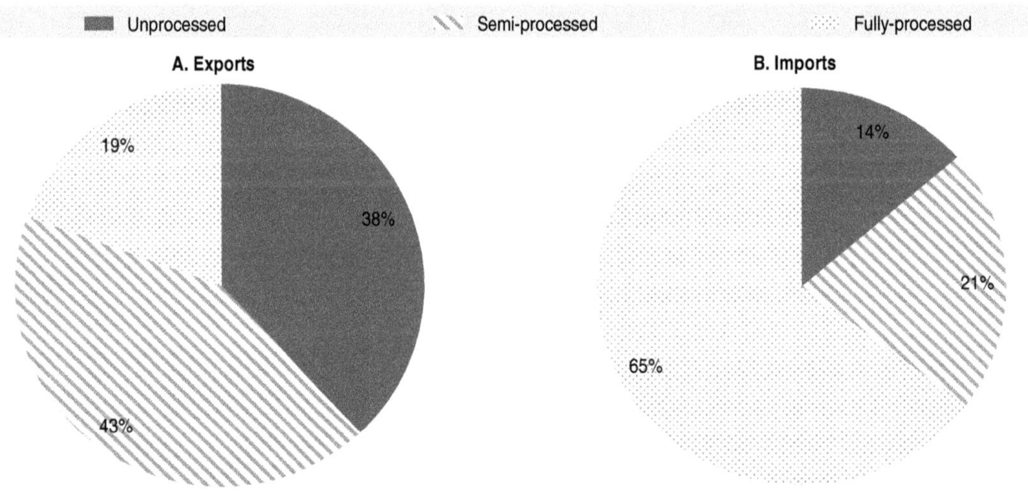

Source: Authors' calculations based on United Nations Statistics Division (2017), *UNCOMTRADE* (database).
StatLink http://dx.doi.org/10.1787/888933783019

According to the African Union's Abuja Treaty of 1991, Southern Africa comprises ten countries: Angola, Botswana, Lesotho, Malawi, Mozambique, Namibia, South Africa, Swaziland, Zambia and Zimbabwe. In 2017, the region was estimated to have a population of 177 million, representing about 14% of the African total. With a land mass of over 5.9 million km^2, Southern Africa has a population density of 30 inhabitants per square kilometre, which is lower than Africa's average of 43.

The total regional GDP at purchasing power parity (PPP) stood at USD 1 201 billion in 2017, with a per capita GDP of USD 6 939. South Africa, which makes up 64% of the regional GDP, plays a crucial role not only as a source of investment for Southern Africa but also as a market for other countries in the region, especially Southern Africa Customs Union (SACU) members. Its economic performance has profound effects on the entire region. Over the period 1990 to 2017, regional real GDP growth averaged 3.0% per annum, compared to 4.2% for Africa. During the same period, Southern Africa's annual population growth averaged 2.2%. The region's per capita GDP thus grew on average by 0.7% per annum over that period.

Over the past two decades, Southern Africa has shown decent growth rates; however, the region remains one of the most unequal in the world. In 2016, six of the ten countries with highest income inequality in the world belonged to Southern Africa (UNECA, 2017). Although some countries in the region have recorded declining inequality since 1990, it remains extremely high for the majority.

The other major problem in the region is high unemployment. It is increasing in half of the countries.

Regional Economic Communities have been critical in fostering co-operation among member countries in recent times. All ten countries in Southern Africa are members of the SADC. Botswana, Lesotho, Namibia, South Africa and Swaziland form the SACU. Malawi, Swaziland, Zambia and Zimbabwe are also members of the Common Market for Eastern and Southern Africa (COMESA). Similarly, Angola maintains dual membership in the SADC and the Economic Community of Central Africa. Intra-SADC trade lags behind intra-regional trade in other parts of the world. Increasing regional integration could help Southern Africa continue its efforts to industrialise, as laid out in the SADC Industrialization Strategy and Roadmap 2015-2063.

Most countries in Southern Africa were actively engaged in the negotiations for the Continental Free Trade Area (CFTA). Once fully operational, this CFTA trade area will facilitate increased trade among the signatory countries.

Diversifying Southern Africa's economies and links with global markets is key to sustaining long-term growth

Southern Africa has posted decent but insufficient growth and faces important constraints

Southern Africa's economies have rebounded from the economic slump at the beginning of 1990s. Growth in Southern Africa during the period 1990 to 1994 declined by -0.1% per year as a consequence of adverse weather conditions and Angola's civil war. These conditions affected non-oil production negatively, while oil production continued to register growth as it was in off-shore areas not affected by the war. Since the mid-1990s, Southern Africa has registered steady economic growth. Between 2000 and 2008, the region recorded strong growth at 5.2% annually – peaking at 7.8% in 2007. During this period, high commodity prices boosted growth in the natural resource-rich countries such as Angola, Botswana, South Africa and Zambia. Good macroeconomic management and increased investment also increased growth.

However, growth has slowed down in recent years. Between 2009 and 2016, Southern Africa's economic performance decelerated to 3.6% per annum on average. Among the African regions, the global economic recession affected Southern Africa the most. The slowdown is also a result of an electricity deficit and of reduced agricultural production due to drought. Growth is expected to have decelerated further to 1.6% per year in 2017 and 2018 due to political uncertainty and low business confidence. Beyond 2018, growth in the region should strengthen as demand for commodities is projected to increase, electricity supply is improving in most countries and investor confidence is improving.

On the supply side, capital expansion has been the main driver of growth. Figure 3.3 shows the decomposition of economic growth into the main factors of production – capital, labour and total factor productivity – from 2009 to 2015. Capital contribution to growth was steady and averaged 2 percentage points per year over the period. Labour's contribution was lower, averaging 1.2 percentage points per year. For most of the years, total factor productivity was negative and averaged -0.16 percentage points. Between 2011 and 2015, the contribution of total factor productivity was fairly low.

Figure 3.3. **Contribution to GDP growth by factors of production in Southern Africa, 2009-15**

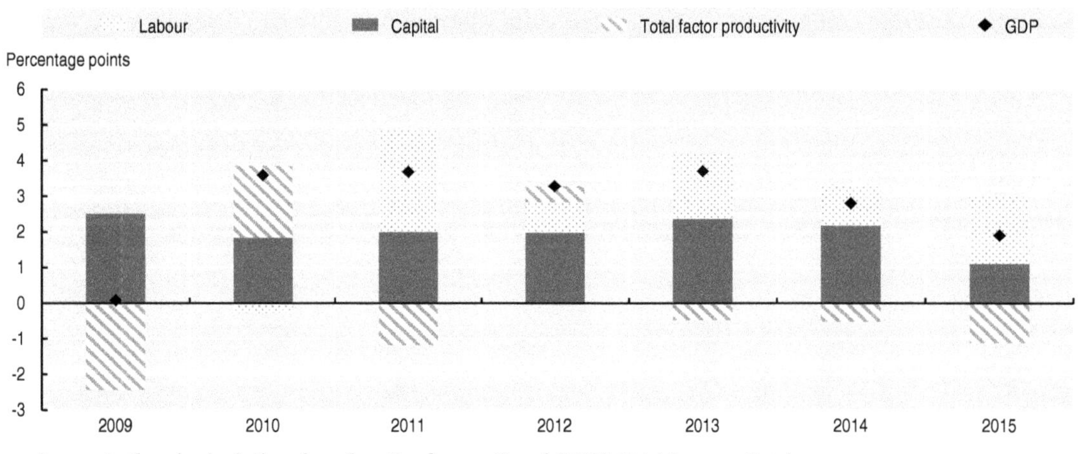

Source: Authors' calculations based on Conference Board (2017), *Total Economy Database*.
StatLink http://dx.doi.org/10.1787/888933783038

On the demand side, private and government consumption have largely supported Southern Africa's positive economic growth performance. Decomposition of economic growth by expenditure reveals that private consumption increased by 2.3% of GDP per year between 2009 and 2016 (Figure 3.4). In terms of share in GDP growth, private consumption accounted for 87.9% over this period.

The second important source of growth on the demand side is public consumption. It grew by 0.8% of GDP per year and accounted for 30% of GDP growth. In contrast, net exports were negative and external balance contributed -0.5 percentage points to GDP growth annually.

Figure 3.4. **Growth decomposition by expenditure in Southern Africa, 2009-16**

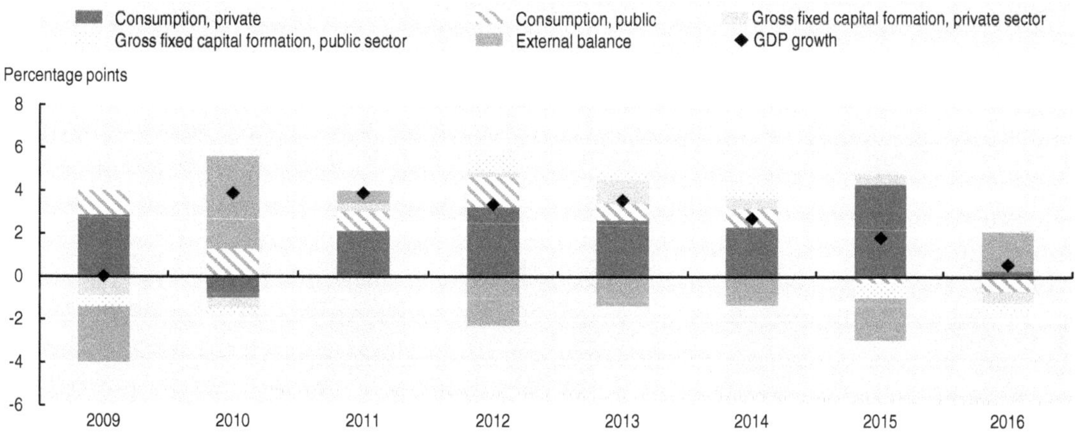

Note: Due to availability, data include Angola, Lesotho, Malawi, Namibia, Swaziland, South Africa, Zambia and Zimbabwe.
Source: Authors' calculations based on World Bank (2017a), *World Development Indicators* (database) and IMF (2018), *World Economic Outlook Database.*
StatLink http://dx.doi.org/10.1787/888933783057

The weak investment level is a cause of concern for long-term growth as accumulating capital spurs economic growth (Solow, 1956; Romer, 1986; Levine and Renelt, 1992). Investment increased marginally between 1990 and 2016. The total investment level rose from an average of 21.5% of GDP per year during the period 1990-95 to 23.3% of GDP during the period 2010-16. By 2010-16, the total investment level was higher than that for Western Africa yet lagged significantly behind Central, East and North Africa. Among Southern African countries, those with higher growth also saw high levels of investment over the 1990-2016 period (Figure 3.5).

Figure 3.5. **Annual economic growth and investment in Southern African countries, 1990-2016**

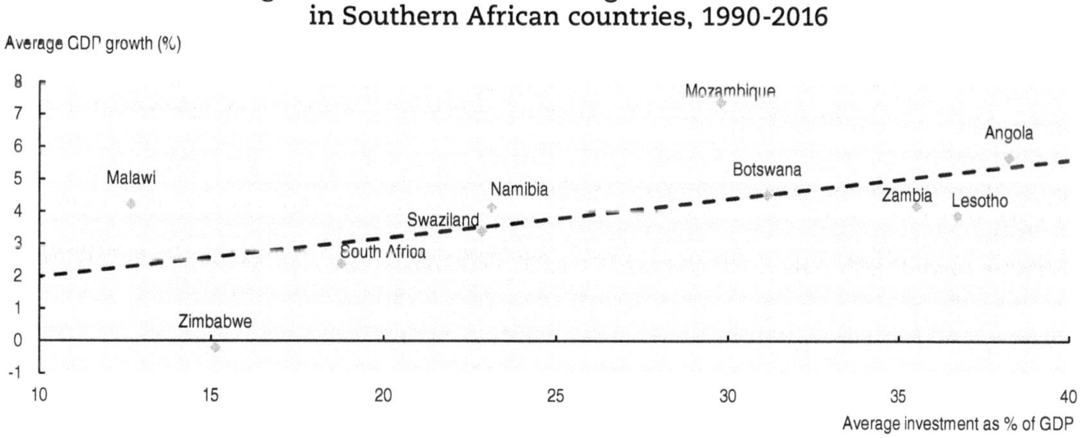

Source: Authors' calculations based on World Bank (2017a), *World Development Indicators* (database) and IMF (2018), *World Economic Outlook* Database.
StatLink http://dx.doi.org/10.1787/888933783076

Southern Africa is experiencing premature de-industrialisation

Over time, Southern Africa's share of services in GDP has increased while its industry's share has declined (Figure 3.6). The services' share of GDP increased from 59% during the first half of the 1990s to 68% during the 2010 to 2016 period. In contrast, industry's share shrunk from 38% to 29% of GDP. The share of agriculture has remained relatively low at around 5%. There is significant heterogeneity across countries, however. For example, agriculture accounts for more than a quarter of GDP in Malawi and Mozambique while the services sector accounts for more than 60% in the SACU countries. In Angola and Zambia, natural resource rents accounted for over 10% of GDP between 2005 and 2015.

Figure 3.6. **Average sector value added as a percentage of GDP in Southern Africa**

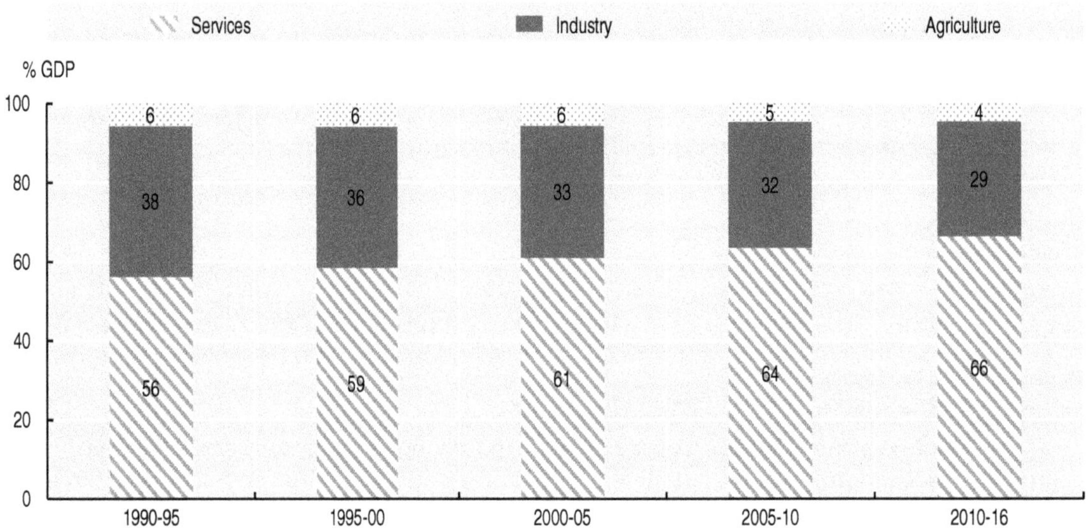

Note: This uses unweighted average to derive the regional figures. As a result, the components may not add up to 100%

Source: Authors' calculations based on World Bank (2017a), *World Development Indicators* (database).
StatLink http://dx.doi.org/10.1787/888933783095

The region shows a trend toward "premature de-industrialisation", whereby countries start de-industrialising at a lower income level than in the past (Rodrik, 2016). Even in South Africa, which has the most advanced industrial sector in the region, manufacturing value added has decreased to 13% of its GDP. Manufacturing can be crucial in providing productive jobs for relatively unskilled workers. It also allows for rapid productivity improvement to catch up with global competitors. The rising of the middle class in the region, which increases the number of urban consumers, also offers new opportunities for local producers to tap into domestic markets.

However, challenges to industrialisation remain. These include a lack of appropriate skills, a power deficit, a lack of finance, weak co-ordination and implementation of regional industrial policies, and poor infrastructure (UNECA, 2015). Southern Africa needs to tackle these constraints to ensure that its industrial sector grows.

The reduction in the share of manufacturing prompted the SADC Industrialisation Plan and Roadmap 2015-2063. Adopted in 2015, it sets out clear and ambitious targets to transition from the commodity-dependent growth path to value-adding, knowledge-intensive and industrialised economies. It aims to do so through targeted and selected industrial policies which facilitate investment in strategic economic sectors.

Southern Africa needs to expand trade and investment linkages with the rest of the world

In Africa, Southern African countries are among the most open to the global economy. With the implementation of structural adjustment programmes by most governments and the efforts towards regional economic integration, trade openness has increased significantly since 1990. Total trade increased from 48% of GDP in 1990 to 66.6% in 2009-16, the second highest in Africa behind Central Africa. In term of financial flows, the region has attracted high levels of Foreign Direct Investment (FDI) and portfolio inflows thanks to relatively stable macroeconomic conditions and developed financial markets (see Table 3.2).

Diversifying its export basket is a priority for the region. The good news is that unprocessed goods accounted for only 38% of Southern Africa's exports in 2016 (Figure 3.2, Panel A). This share is much lower than the shares for other African regions (ranging from 46% to 84% of exports). South Africa exports most of the more sophisticated products. The country accounts for 71% of the region's exports of semi-processed goods, mostly manufacture of basic metals, such as gold and platinum, and unset diamonds. It also accounts for 90% of exports of fully-processed goods, such as automobiles, machinery equipment and wine. Another example is Lesotho, which has taken advantage of the African Growth and Opportunity Act's preferential trade terms to develop a textile sector for export to the United States' market.

However, several Southern African countries depend mainly on exports of a single commodity. For example, in 2014, oil accounted for 96% of Angola's exports, copper accounted for 60% of Zambia's exports and unprocessed diamonds accounted for 73% of Botswana's exports.

So far, FDI in the region has been mostly concentrated in resource-rich economies, where it has declined due partly to the fall in global commodity prices. The majority of FDI went to Angola, Mozambique and Zambia and supported the mining and extraction sector. Angola accounted for two-thirds of FDI in Southern Africa in 2016. The country remains one the largest FDI hosts among the least developed countries.

The decline in global commodity prices in recent years and uncertainties over mineral tax policy in some countries have led to a reduction in FDI in the region. FDI flows to Botswana fell to USD 10 million in 2016, by far the lowest recorded since 2012; this is related to the fall in global diamond prices. Similarly, Zambia recorded less than half a billion US dollars in FDI inflows for the first time since 2011.

Johannesburg has emerged as the most strategically placed city for greenfield FDI (or new FDI) in Africa (AfDB/OECD/UNDP, 2016). Network analysis shows that Johannesburg has become the primary broker of greenfield FDI flows into Africa. In fact, FDI is increasingly concentrated along a development corridor linking Gauteng and Maputo which includes cities like Johannesburg, Pretoria and Maputo. This area benefits from a dense cluster of cities of various sizes. The strong development of road, rail and port infrastructure binds cities together into cohesive economic regions. Membership in the SADC plays an important role, as it offers access to markets. Further increasing regional integration could help Southern Africa attract more and more diversified FDI and support domestic firms to expand their market access.

Creating quality jobs is a major problem in Southern Africa, especially for the youth and females

Though highly diverse, the employment structures in Southern African countries can be categorised into two broad groups. In the SACU countries (Botswana, Lesotho, Namibia, South Africa and Swaziland), structural unemployment has persisted due to labour market distortions and a skills mismatch. In non-SACU countries (Angola, Malawi, Mozambique, Zambia and Zimbabwe), the unemployment rate is lower yet underemployment is a severe concern.

The following section will discuss the diverging stories of these two groups. Despite the differences in the challenges they face, all countries in the region struggle to create quality employment especially for young people and women.

Structural unemployment in the SACU countries is high due to a skills mismatch and a low rate of entrepreneurship

SACU countries are characterised by a higher level of job quality but also higher structural unemployment. In these countries, the services sector accounts for the largest share of employment, ranging from 46% in Lesotho to 71% in South Africa. Most of those employed are waged employees in the formal sector. However, the unemployment rate has remained at over 15% since the 1990s (Figure 3.7). Botswana, Lesotho, Namibia, South Africa and Swaziland even had an increase in unemployment rates between 1991 and 2016. Across all periods, unemployment is higher among females.

Figure 3.7. **Unemployment trends in Southern African Customs Union countries, 1991-2016**

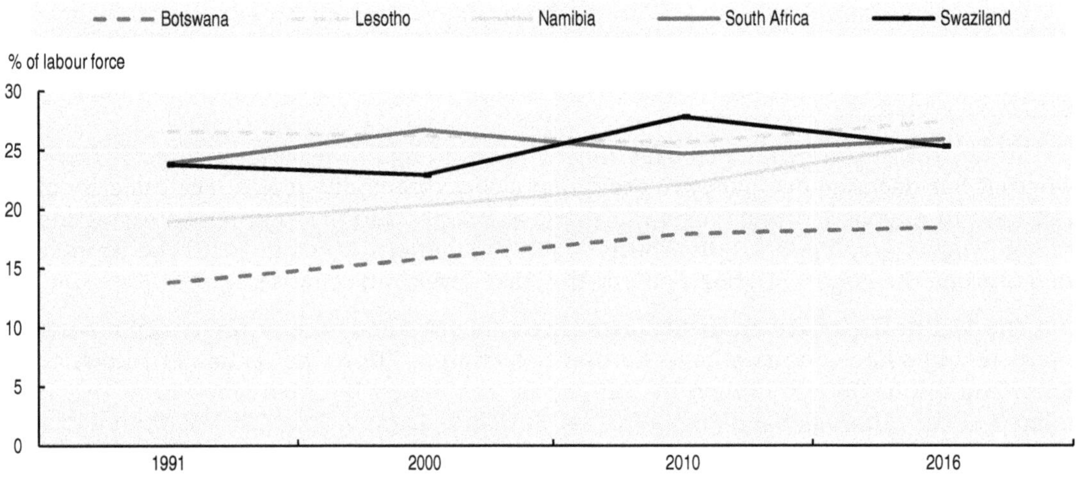

Source: Authors' calculations based on World Bank (2017a), *World Development Indicators* (database).

StatLink http://dx.doi.org/10.1787/888933783114

These countries have small informal sectors despite high unemployment rates. Lesotho had an informal sector which accounted for 9% of total employment in 2008 (Bureau of Statistics, 2008). South Africa stands out as a country with a low informal sector employment rate but with high unemployment rate. Informal sector employment in South Africa accounted for 9.8% of the labour force in 1997, and this increased to 13.1% in 2006 (Maree, 2007; Brynard, 2011).

A skills mismatch has also contributed to structural unemployment. Growth has been associated with tertiary sectors and sophisticated manufacturing which demands highly skilled labour. However, semi-skilled and unskilled labour is in oversupply. For example, in South Africa, the unemployment rate has increased despite positive economic growth during the post-apartheid period due to skill-biased technological change (Levinsohn, 2007; AfDB et al., 2012). Similarly, growth in Botswana has been accompanied by rising unemployment rates. The mining sector accounts for 35-50% of GDP in Botswana, yet it only employs 4% of the total formal labour force due to its capital-intensive nature.

A more dynamic business environment with higher rates of entrepreneurship and growth among small businesses could help create the much-needed jobs. The share of the labour force working as employers or own-account workers is significantly lower in the SACU countries than in the rest of the region (Figure 3.8). In South Africa, high barriers to entrepreneurship and labour market segmentation have prevented a large share of the unemployed population to transition to self-employment when they wanted to (Kerr, 2018; OECD, 2017a). In South Africa, labour rigidities through centralised bargaining are estimated to decrease employment in an industry by 8-13% with losses concentrated among smaller firms. Entrepreneurial skills may be also inadequate in the population, as informal employment was suppressed under apartheid (Kingdon and Knight, 2004).

Figure 3.8. **Unemployment rate and status of employment for Southern African countries**

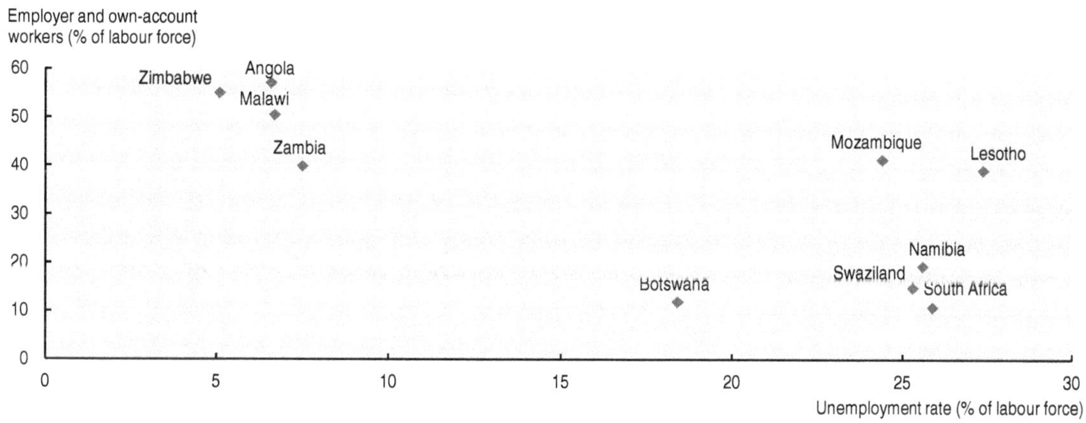

Source: Authors' calculations based on ILO (2017), *ILO Stat* (database).
StatLink http://dx.doi.org/10.1787/888933783133

In the non-SACU countries, underemployment is linked with working poverty

Unemployment rates are lower in the non-SACU than the SACU countries, but underemployment remains pervasive. This problem resembles that of many other sub-Saharan African countries. The magnitude of unemployment is masked by underemployment or disguised unemployment as people take on unsuitable jobs or work less hours. For example, 8.3% of the employed in Zambia in 2014 were underemployed. The instance of working poverty is therefore much higher in these countries (Figure 3.9).

Figure 3.9. **Sectoral employment and working poverty rate in Southern African countries**

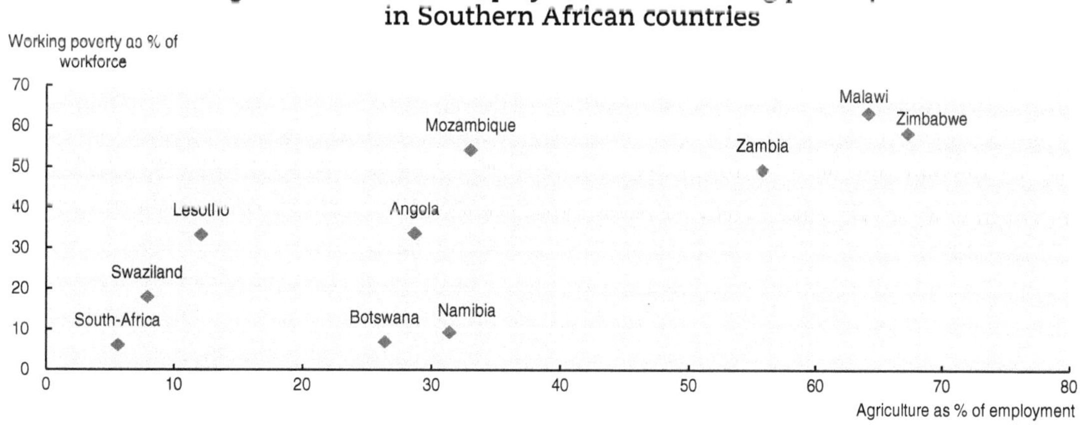

Source: Authors' calculations based on ILO (2017), *ILO Stat* (database).
StatLink http://dx.doi.org/10.1787/888933783152

In the non-SACU countries of the region, the informal sector has absorbed workers who cannot find employment in the formal sector. In Zambia, where unemployment fell from 18.9% in 1991 to 7.5% in 2016, the share of informal employment increased from 74% to 83.9% (CSO, 2015). The informal sector covered 95% of the labour force in Mozambique in 2014 and 94% in Zimbabwe the same year (Danish Trade Union Council, 2014; Zimstat, 2014).

Structural transformation is therefore an important driver for creating more and better jobs. In Malawi, Zambia and Zimbabwe, the majority of the population is still working in subsistence agriculture. In resource-dependent countries such as Angola and Zambia, the mining sector has contributed the most to growth yet little to employment. Mining accounts for only 3.5% of employment despite contributing 14% to GDP. In Angola, resource rent has attracted agricultural labour to urban services (see Chapter 1). Supporting labour-intensive activities that require relatively lower skills, such as agro-processing and light manufacturing, can create waged jobs for local labour.

Better employable skills can improve labour market outcomes for the youth in Southern Africa

The youth suffer particularly from the employment problem (Figure 3.10). Youth unemployment, especially among females, has increased over time for the majority of countries in the region. Botswana, Namibia and Swaziland had the largest increases in youth unemployment rates, each in excess of 7%, between 1991 and 2015. Apart from Zambia that recorded a large decline of 17.6% over the period, the other countries recorded small reductions.

Figure 3.10. **Youth unemployment rates in Southern Africa, 1990-2016**

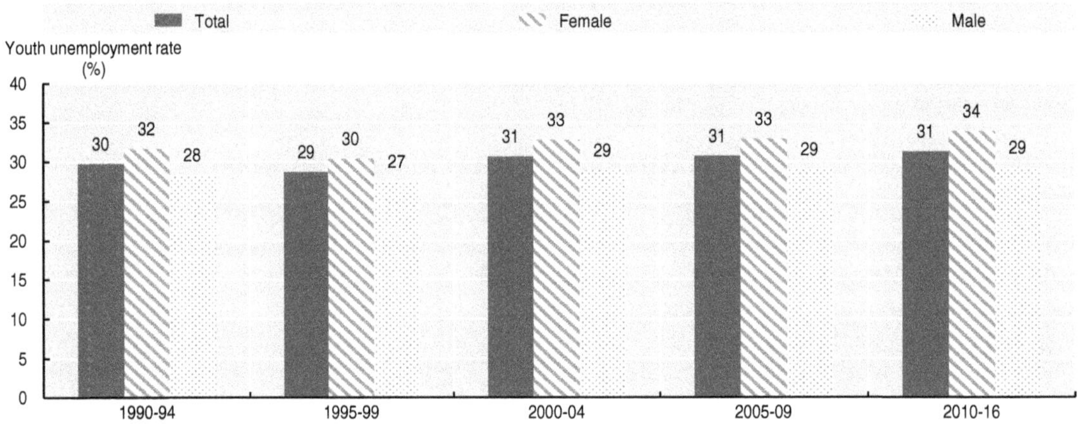

Source: Authors' calculations based on World Bank (2017a), *World Development Indicators* (database).
StatLink http://dx.doi.org/10.1787/888933783171

Youth unemployment in some countries is extremely high and has increased over time. In South Africa and Swaziland, over half of the youth aged between 15 and 24 were estimated to be unemployed in 2016. A similar pattern exists in all the region's other countries except Malawi, Zambia and Zimbabwe. Urgent measures are needed to address this growing problem, especially in light of the 1.1 million new entrants to the labour market per year between 2015 and 2030.

Women also face more challenges than men in Southern Africa's labour market. First, they are less likely to participate in the labour force. The total labour force participation rate is only 61% for women, compared to 71% for men. This gap varies across countries but is more severe in Botswana, Lesotho, South Africa and Zimbabwe. Even when women do participate in the labour force, they are more likely to be unemployed. This pattern holds also among youth (Figure 3.10).

Many youth are self-employed workers, yet they lack the necessary skills to succeed. These general trends are observed in several countries in Africa and other developing regions (OECD, 2017b). In Malawi, rural youth entrepreneurs have low education levels and 80% acquire business skills informally, either through self-teaching (44%) or by learning from family members (36%) (OECD, 2018b). In South Africa, just less than half of early-stage entrepreneurs had at least a secondary qualification in 2016, while a quarter had some secondary education (GEM, 2017).

The shortage of entrepreneurial skills lowers both the likelihood of young entrepreneurs to set up their own businesses successfully and the survival rate of youth start-ups. Indeed, the 2013 United Nations survey of 640 small and medium-sized enterprises (SMEs) in six Swaziland cities reveals a large experience and skill gap between young entrepreneurs (ages 15-35) and adult entrepreneurs (ages 36+) (Brixiová, Ncube and Bicaba, 2015). Only 40.1% of young entrepreneurs had prior work experience, relative to 60.6% of adults. Similarly, less than one out of five young entrepreneurs received business training, while a quarter of adult entrepreneurs were trained. This points to the need to better design and target entrepreneurship programmes as well education and training to better align youth aspirations with labour market realities and facilitate school-to-work transitions (OECD, 2017c).

Southern Africa has made uneven progress in reducing inequality

Income inequality remains high in Southern Africa despite a marginal reduction

Southern Africa is one of the most unequal regions in the world. Of the ten countries with the highest income inequality, six are found in Southern Africa (UNECA, 2017). South Africa had the world's highest Gini coefficient (63), followed by Namibia (61), Botswana (61), Zambia (57), Lesotho (54) and Swaziland (52) (Figure 3.11).[1] The inter-decile ratios show a similar structure (Figure 3.11). South Africa, Botswana and Lesotho, in that order, have the highest gaps between the top and bottom income deciles, implying that these countries have the greatest inequality in the region. Angola and Mozambique have the lowest gaps, as well as the lowest Gini coefficients, hence the lowest inequality in the region.

Figure 3.11. **Gini coefficients and difference in income share in Southern African countries**

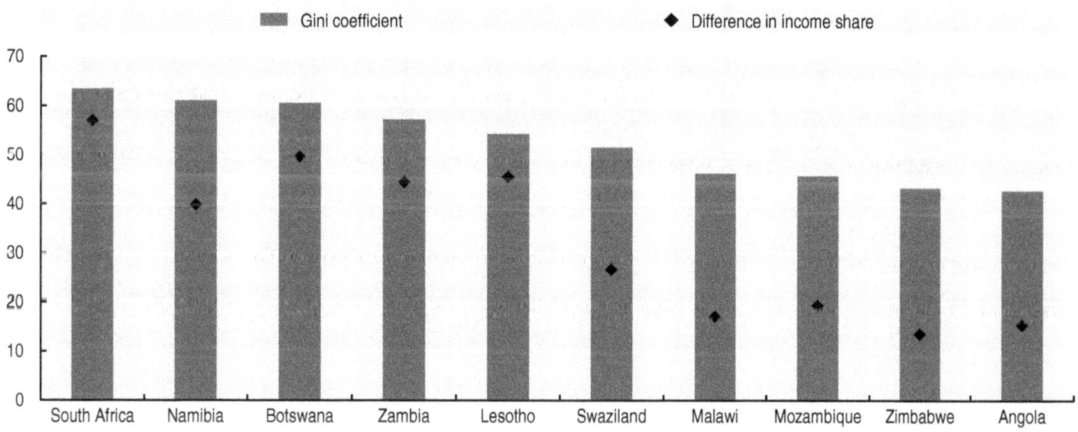

Note: The difference between the top and bottom group refers to the ratio between the income shares held by the richest 10% to the income held by the poorest 10% in the national income distribution. The latest available data is shown for each country.

Source: Authors' calculations based on World Bank (2017b), *PovcalNet* (database).

StatLink http://dx.doi.org/10.1787/888933783190

In some countries, the fiscal system has been able to reduce inequality. In particular South Africa's taxes and social spending system have achieved the largest reductions in income inequality among a sample of 29 developing countries in the Commitment to Equity database.[2] The combination of slightly progressive taxes (personal income taxes, value-added taxes, excise taxes and the fuel levy) and highly progressive spending (cash transfers, free basic services, and spending on health and education) reduced the country's Gini coefficient from 77.1 to 59.6. Similarly, fiscal policy in Zambia reduced the Gini coefficient from 59 to 48 after accounting for redistribution and tax burdens, especially through public expenditures on education (De la Fuenta, Rosales and Jellema, 2017).[3]

However, not all countries have been equally successful. In many cases, in-kind subsidies benefit the rich more than the poor due to different access and consumption patterns. In Angola, fuel subsidies cover almost 7.5% of household expenditure for the richest 20% of households, twice as much as that for the bottom 20% (World Bank, 2016). Similarly, in Zambia, benefits of tertiary education serve mostly the richest segment of society, and health spending excludes the poor without access (Cuesta, Kabaso and Suarez-Becerra, 2012).

Non-inclusive growth and high initial inequality have also led to pervasive inequality in the region. As mentioned earlier in this chapter, growth has been limited to capital intensive sectors such as mining and high-tech manufacturing, which tend to hinder sharing the fruits of growth. In South Africa, the concentration of capital and land among the wealthier groups and cultural and historical factors exacerbate the dualistic employment market. This leads to highly segmented employment outcomes among different groups in society. It creates high wage inequalities within each sector as well as a wide gap between those who are employed and those who are not (Keeton, 2014). Consequently, inequality in South Africa remains among the highest in the world despite a highly redistributive fiscal system (Inchauste et al., 2015).

Most Southern African countries have made good progress in reducing poverty

Poverty levels in the region are high. The extreme poverty headcount stands at 35.6% mostly due to very high rates in Lesotho, Malawi, Mozambique and Zambia (i.e. below USD 1.90 per day, Table 3.3). In these countries, reliance on subsistence agriculture by the large majority of the workforce and limited access to education and health services further contribute to high poverty and inequality levels (Mussa, 2015). In contrast, a number of middle-income countries in the region, such as Botswana, Namibia and South Africa, have attained lower levels of poverty. In these three countries, almost a quarter of the population lives on USD 1.90-3.20 a day (2011 PPP), but this income group is vulnerable to falling back into extreme poverty.

Table 3.3. **Poverty rates in Southern African countries**

Country	Headcount poverty, USD 1.90/day			Poverty gap, USD 1.90/day		
	Earliest year	Latest year	% change	Earliest year	Latest year	% change
Angola (first: -; last: 2008)	-	30.1	-	-	9.6	-
Botswana (first: 1993; last: 2009)	34.8	18.2	-16.6	13.5	5.8	-7.7
Lesotho (first: 1994; last: 2010)	69.6	59.7	-9.9	44.8	31.8	-13.0
Malawi (first: 1997; last: 2010)	63.6	70.9	7.3	24.9	33.3	8.4
Mozambique (first: 1996; last: 2008)	85.4	68.7	-16.6	47.3	31.4	-15.9
Namibia (first: 2003; last: 2009)	31.5	22.6	-8.9	10.2	6.7	-3.6
South Africa (first: 1993; last: 2011)	29.3	16.6	-12.7	9.5	4.9	-4.6
Swaziland (first: 1994; last: 2009)	81.7	42.0	-39.6	51.0	16.6	-34.4
Zambia (first: 2000; last: 2015)	54.1	64.4	10.4	34.7	29.5	-5.2
Zimbabwe (first: -; last: 2011)	-	21.4	-	-	5.2	-
Southern Africa (first: 1990; last: 2013)	43.8	35.6	-8.2	20.8	14.2	-6.6

Note: Regional average for Southern Africa is generated by estimations from World Bank (2017b), *PovCal Net*.
Source: World Bank (2017b), *PovCal Net* (database).

Poverty rates and severity have decreased for most countries, with Botswana, Mozambique, South Africa and Swaziland having reduced them the most. In Botswana, for example, increasing agricultural incomes and demographic changes have reduced extreme poverty by 11.6 percentage points, from 29.8% in 2002/03 to 18.2% in 2009/10. Increases in agricultural incomes, including agricultural subsidies, accounted for 47.8% of poverty reduction over this period (World Bank, 2015a). Decreased demographic ratios accounted for 24.3% of the poverty reduction. Other factors, such as increased wages in non-agricultural sectors and improved households' access to finance, also helped alleviate poverty.

Looking forward, broad-based employment growth will be necessary to strengthen the income of the poor and move them firmly into the middle class. The rising middle class will be important to create a skilled and educated workforce and provide the consumption base for local entrepreneurs to tap into (see Chapter 2, Megatrend 4).

Malawi and Zambia saw their poverty rates increase between 1996 and 2016. In Zambia, the poverty rate peaked at about 73% in 1998 and only started declining thereafter. The increase in poverty was driven by economic decline and the closure of state-owned enterprises that had become uncompetitive as the country liberalised its economy. A review of Zambia's 2015 fiscal policy shows that fiscal policy has been able to reduce inequality, but it has also contributed to increasing the poverty headcount (De la Fuente, Rosales and Jellema, 2017). Indeed, the poor receive only a small portion of in-kind benefits such as fuel, electricity, education and health subsidies, and the various direct cash transfers programmes are too small to reduce poverty. Furthermore, the poor pay more into the fiscal system than they receive from it, in the form of higher prices due to value-added taxes and alcohol and tobacco excises.

While income-based poverty has been reduced significantly in Southern Africa, a large share of the rural population still do not have access to basic services such as water, sanitation and electricity. During the period 2010-16, on average the proportion of the population with access to electricity was 46% (Figure 3.12). Slightly over three-quarters (78%) of the population in urban areas had electricity, while rural access on average stood at 20%. Similarly, only 59% of the rural population had access to an improved water source compared to 92% in urban areas. And only 33% of the rural population had access to improved sanitation facilities, compared to 65% of the urban population.

Figure 3.12. **Access to basic services in Southern Africa, 2010-16**

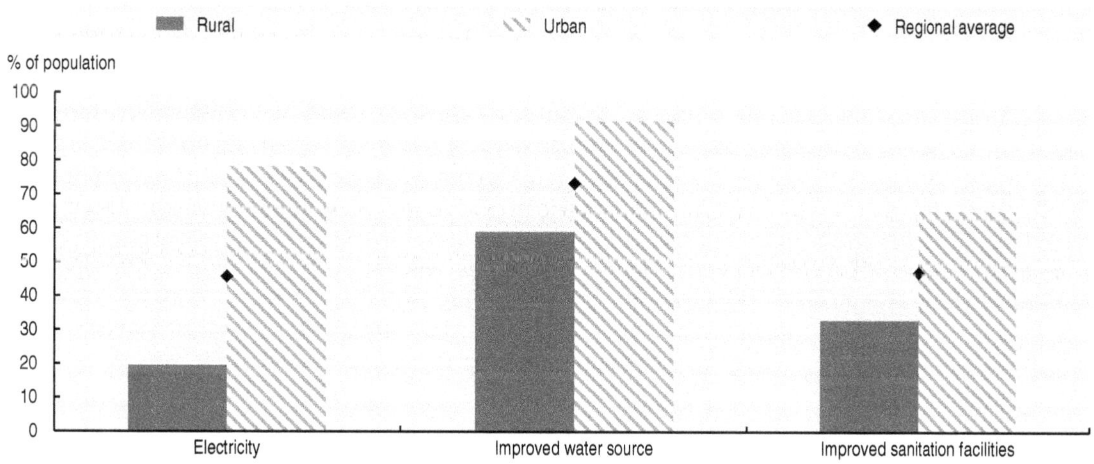

Source: Authors' calculations based on World Bank (2017a), *World Development Indicators* (database).
StatLink http://dx.doi.org/10.1787/888933783209

Tackling the inequality and employment challenges is the key to unlock long-term development in Southern Africa

Reducing high inequality and unemployment will facilitate long-term growth in Southern Africa

Addressing inequality can boost long-term growth through several channels. First, it enables the poor to accumulate productive assets and invest in human capital. Second, it increases their purchasing power and thus changes the structure of domestic demand for higher-quality goods and services. Third, it helps ensure social cohesion and political stability. The analysis presented in Figure 3.13 shows a negative association between long-term economic growth and income inequality. While this association does not imply causality, it does show the link between the two variables in the region.

Figure 3.13. **GDP per capita growth versus Gini coefficient in Southern African countries, 1990-2016**

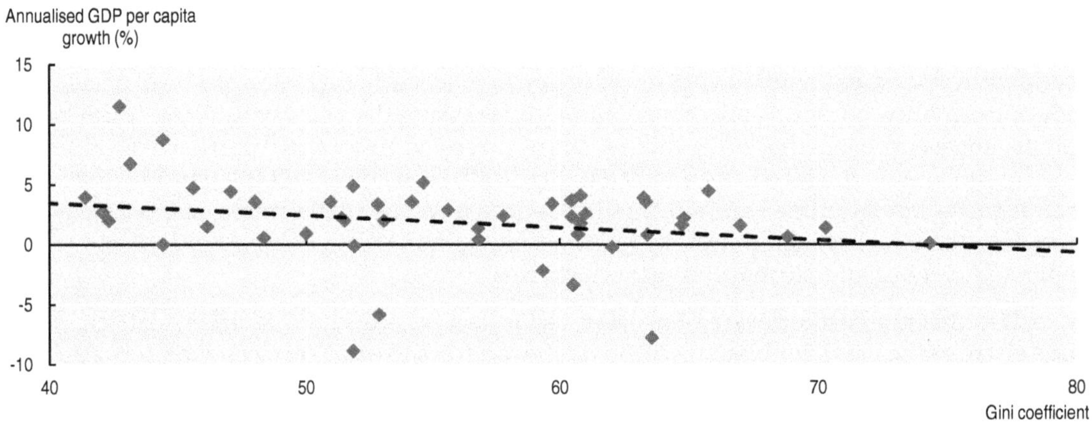

Note: Each scatter point represents a five-year average of growth and Gini coefficients for each country in Southern Africa.

Source: Authors' calculations based on World Bank (2017a), *World Development Indicators* (database).

StatLink http://dx.doi.org/10.1787/888933783228

Reducing income inequalities can have a positive impact on the duration of growth (IMF, 2012). SACU countries could almost double the duration of growth periods if they had the same level of inequality as other countries with the same level of GDP per capita.[4] For most growth spells, the average duration could have been increased from about 5-8 years (e.g. Namibia) to 15 years and more (e.g. Botswana).

According to this analysis, income inequality appears to play a statistically more significant role in explaining the length of growth spells than other factors, such as investment, infrastructure, external shocks (e.g. terms of trade), the quality of public institutions and the financial sector. This result is important because of the nature of growth in the region. Since most countries depend on primary agricultural and/or mineral exports, they have experienced growth spells that are driven by external shocks and, therefore, that may not last long. However, targeting inequality will help to lengthen those growth spells.

Addressing inequality and unemployment in Southern Africa requires an integrated approach

In Southern Africa, unemployment and inequality are interlinked. Unemployment is higher among the bottom 40% of the income distribution compared to the top 10%. Inequality and unemployment also reinforce each other. The five-year averages of Gini coefficients positively correlate with the unemployment rates for each Southern African country. In South Africa, a 10 percentage point reduction in unemployment would lower the Gini coefficient by 3%; but to achieve the same Gini results solely through government transfers would require increasing them by 40% (Anand, Kothari and Kumar, 2016).

High inequality can lead to unemployment in several ways. High inequality leads to liquidity constraints that prevent the poor from investing in health, education and skills. This underinvestment creates a large pool of low-skilled workers that the economy cannot absorb, driving up structural unemployment. Furthermore, labour force participation rates are highest among top income deciles, those that also have access to better opportunities (Leibbrandt and Levinsohn, 2011). In South Africa, for example, most new entrants in the labour market do not have the necessary skills to find a job or, if employed, to earn decent wages. This has led to a situation where 3 million youth are not in employment, education or training and 600 000 university graduates are unemployed. At the same time, the private sector cannot fill the existing 800 000 job vacancies (The Economist, 2012).

Boosting employment opportunities will have to stay at the forefront of addressing inequality and unemployment. Namibia provides a case in point. Although its Gini coefficient dropped from around 63 in 2003 to 61 in 2009, partly owing to generous social safety nets, the country's level of income inequality remains high. Income inequality in Namibia is linked to high unemployment due to inadequate skills and a skills mismatch. The national development agenda thus needs to further encourage the creation of low-skill jobs on a large scale, namely through industrialisation. Unlocking the barriers to entrepreneurship can also allow motivated entrepreneurs to create jobs. Better education and training, especially for the youth, will be critical to address the skills mismatch and the unemployment trap.

At the same time, the entrenched nature of inequality and unemployment calls for combining labour market policies and social assistance programmes. Well-targeted direct redistribution policies can effectively reduce inequalities as seen in the case of South Africa. Countries in the region have increasingly used cash and in-kind transfers (Garcia and Moore, 2012). However, creating broad-based employment growth through structural transformation will be necessary to tackle income inequality at the source. The decomposition of income shows that employment income is the most important source of income inequality. Relying on social assistance alone may not be enough to eliminate the root cause of inequality (Leibbrandt, Finn and Woolard, 2015; Leite, McKinley and Osorio, 2006).

Policy recommendations

Pushing Southern Africa's industrialisation agenda remains key

The SADC Industrialization Strategy and Roadmap 2015-2063 has set out a clear and ambitious plan to transition from a commodity-based to a technology-based industrial sector. In following up, SADC has adopted further regional strategies and protocols including the SADC Finance and Investment Protocol (FIP) Revised Annex 1 on Investment and the SADC Protocol on Trade.

Despite some early encouraging signs, implementation remains challenging. Recent benchmarking of the SADC FIP shows that regional integration strategies have helped firms in many countries join the regional and global value chains and attract more and better-quality FDI (SADC/OECD, 2017). For example, general retailers such as Shoprite or Pick and Pay as well as more specialised retailers such as Ellerines (furniture) or Mr. Price and Foschini (clothing) have been able to expand into the SACU market (World Bank, 2015b). Other retailers from outside of South Africa such as Choppies (Botswana) have also established 28 supermarkets in South Africa and 13 in Zimbabwe. However, not all countries have reaped the benefits, partly due to the lack of implementing and of monitoring such strategies. At the same time, the lack of a harmonised dispute settlement and of an arbitration mechanism may deter further increases in FDI (Chidede, 2017).

Two major priority areas for reforms stand out. One is to create opportunities for learning from FDI. This could be achieved by increasing co-ordination between national and regional actions especially through linking FDI to the local economy. A review of good practices in effectively using local content and local value-added provisions could help identify practices to implement at the regional level. Global experience shows that these policies need to be complemented with supply-side support for local firms to upgrade and meet the standards and requirements of lead firms. Monitoring effectiveness is also essential to avoid unconditional support of uncompetitive local firms.

The opportunities and challenges are sector specific, so policies must be targeted to each sector. Table 3.4 presents a recent review of the challenges and opportunities for each key cluster identified by the SADC Industrial Strategy. For example, the automotive sector is largely constrained by its small market size while the textiles and garments sectors lack the skilled labour and capacity to manage the supply chain. As a consequence, policies to facilitate local value chain development will be effective only when they are industry and country specific (AfDB/OECD/UNDP, 2014).

Table 3.4. **Challenges and opportunities for several key clusters identified by the SADC Industrial Strategy**

Value chain	Challenges	Opportunities
Automotive	• Production is limited to South Africa • Local capacity is constrained by small market size	• Vehicles tailored to African needs (durable, affordable) can jump-start production
Textiles and garments	• Lack of skills and co-ordination capabilities • Local content requirements place undue burden on manufacturers	• Industry may shift from Asia to the African continent, as production costs rise in Asia
Medical devices	• Lack of adequate regulatory and accreditation framework undermine efforts of local manufacturers	• Need to focus on research and development, education and vocational training to capitalise on value added through human capital
Pharmaceuticals	• Long registration time for drug licensing • Regionally fragmented regulations • Over-reliance on foreign drugs	• Regional initiatives to increase capacity for local generic drug development and production
Agro-processing	• Small-holder farmers impede economies of scale, mechanisation and fail to meet national and international standards	• Initiatives to support small-holder farmer • Investment in climate smart agriculture

Source: SADC/OECD (2017), *FDI-SME Linkages in Regional and Global Value Chains and the Development Dimension in SADC.*

The other priority area for reform is to advance intra-SADC integration and increase intra-African trade. Better implementation of existing SADC protocols and agreements would advance integration and create jobs. At the continental level, the Southern African countries need to fast-track the process to adopt and implement the CFTA. Reducing non-tariff barriers by improving customs procedures and simplifying rules of origin would lower trade costs in the region. These trade agreements should also expand to services, which have been growing significantly in Southern Africa.

Building key infrastructure, supporting the development of support services and reducing non-tariff barriers are essential to facilitate trade. SADC can follow the lead of the EAC and COMESA by adopting a simplified trade regime with instruments tailored to the needs and requirements of small-scale traders (Fundira, 2018). Such measures would help create jobs and boost income for informal cross-border traders.

Education and training programmes can increase the employability of Southern Africa's youth population

Governments should ensure that sufficient resources are devoted to building human capital through education. Education must be transformed to not only increase enrolment but also improve quality so that the imparted skills match those demanded by industry. The region should make efforts to close its skills gap, for instance by establishing centres of excellence to generate important technical skills that Africa is currently importing.

Developing an effective vocational system will help address skills shortages and redirect the youth back into training. Only 12% of South African students in upper secondary education were enrolled in vocational programmes in 2013. The technical and vocational education and training (TVET) sector can be further strengthened in terms of qualifications and training of staff, resources and curriculum content to make it more viable and attractive to students and businesses (Field, Musset and Alvarez-Galvan, 2014). Generalising apprenticeships and internships as part of the education curriculum in TVET colleges and universities may favour youth entry into the labour market.

Governments can also support local entrepreneurs to start new businesses. Reforms to ease the cost of doing business, lift competition barriers in many sectors and facilitate the expansion of firms in the region would boost productivity and help create jobs. Integrating SMEs into local value chains can expand the demand and learning opportunities for entrepreneurs to develop their businesses. Supply-side policy can also increase the capabilities of domestic entrepreneurs through improving management skills, access to finance/start-up capital and the business environment.

Concentrating the limited resources available on a narrow range of cases maximises the chances of having a real impact. In Angola, Botswana, South Africa and Zambia, the majority of entrepreneurs are motivated by new business opportunities. Identifying those entrepreneurs and providing them with targeted support proves more effective than indiscriminate measures. By contrast, in Malawi and Namibia, the lack of formal employment opportunities pushed the majority of job seekers into self-employment. To help such entrepreneurs transition back to labour markets, entrepreneurship policies will need to co-ordinate with social protection and training.

Southern African governments need to gradually invest in integrated social protection systems and mobilise domestic finance

The current social protection systems are highly uneven across Southern Africa, reflecting countries' unique economic structures and challenges. In particular, South Africa has developed a relatively comprehensive system with social grants for vulnerable groups, unemployment insurance, public works programmes and other progressive social policies. This is in response to the consequences of former apartheid regimes. Other SACU countries have successfully implemented universal non-contributory pension schemes. In contrast, the non-SACU Southern African countries have much smaller social protection systems due to weaker institutional and fiscal capacities and to the prevalence of informal and agricultural workers. In recent years, these countries have succeeded in reducing poverty using cash transfer programmes, yet the overall systems remain fragmented and under-articulated.

In all cases, developing an integrated social protection system can help ensure a basic level of coverage for all. Expanding coverage remains a challenge, even in countries with more advanced systems. In Botswana, the social protection system comprises more than 29 programmes by 10 government agencies; many overlap each other. Despite the complex and fairly comprehensive system, 80% of children who are deprived in any one dimension of poverty live in households that do not benefit from either state pensions or governmental assistance (Social Policy Research Institute, 2017).

Countries in Southern Africa also can increase operational efficiencies by avoiding duplication and by capitalising on synergies between programmes. In the near future, governments in the region may not have the fiscal space to expand social spending further because commodity prices are unlikely to return to the high levels of the mid-2000s and low growth is likely to persist. Improving the effectiveness of social spending is thus especially important. Zambia, for example, has done so by introducing the National Social Protection Policy in 2014 which includes both social assistance and social insurance. In the long run, governments will need to gradually develop social assistance, social insurance and labour market policies in an integrated system.

Domestic fiscal mobilisation will be crucial to boost social protection spending. Figure 3.14 shows spending on social assistance programmes across Southern African countries, excluding expenditure on social insurance and labour market programmes. Lesotho, Namibia and South Africa have fared much better than the average for developing countries. On the contrary, Zambia and Zimbabwe spend less than 0.5% of GDP on social assistance.

The African Union's Agenda 2063 targets increasing public spending on social protection to 5%. Governments will need to diversify financing schemes in order to boost their budgets for social protection. Malawi and Zambia largely rely on donor funding for social protection. In resource-dependent countries such as Angola and Botswana, resource rents account for 50-80% of government revenues (Ulriksen, 2013). While resource rents can provide an immediate boost and incite new entrants to participate in voluntary schemes, funding social protection systems cannot rely solely on resource revenue due to its volatility. Increasing direct taxation is the most important tool in the long term, yet it requires sustained investment in administrative and institutional capabilities (OECD, 2017d).

Figure 3.14. **Public spending on social safety net programmes in Southern African countries**

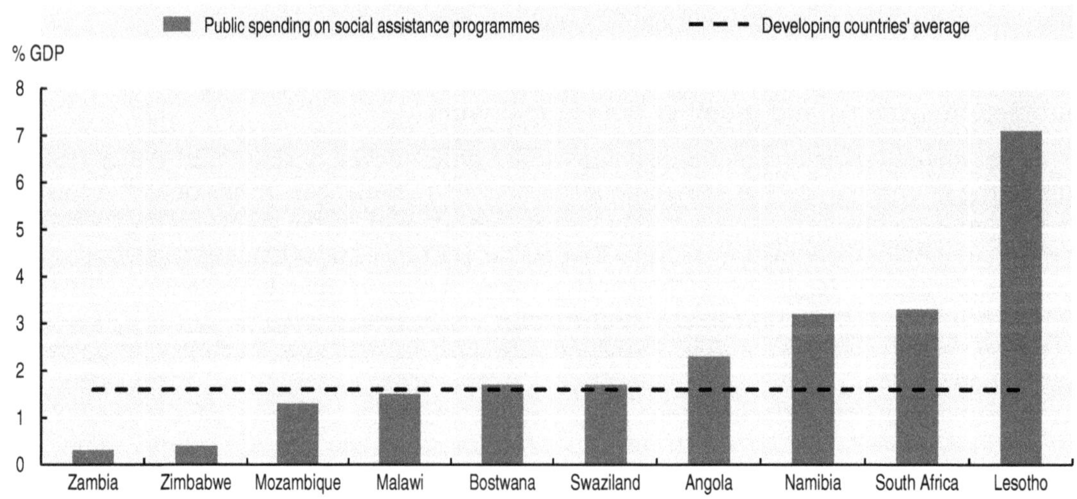

Note: The figure shows data for the latest available year.
Source: World Bank (2018), *ASPIRE* (database).
StatLink http://dx.doi.org/10.1787/888933783247

Annex 3.A1. Additional statistical tables and figures on Southern Africa

Table 3.A1.1. Sector distribution of employment in Southern African countries

	Agriculture	Industry	Services
Angola (2017)	28.7	21.5	49.7
Botswana (2010)	26.4	17.5	56
Lesotho (2008)	12.1	41.7	45.5
Malawi (2011)*	64.1	4.4	31.5
Mozambique (2012)*	33	14.4	52.6
Namibia (2013)	31.4	14.4	54.2
South Africa (2015)	5.6	23.9	70.5
Swaziland (2011)*	7.9	43.5	48.6
Zambia (2012)	55.8	10.1	33.7
Zimbabwe (2014)	67.2	7.3	25.4

Source: World Bank (2017a), *World Development Indicators* (database) and * National Labour Force Surveys.

Table 3.A1.2. National unemployment rates in Southern African countries, 1991-2016

	National unemployment rates*				Change 1991-2016
	1991	2000	2010	2016	
Angola	6.7	6.8	6.8	6.6	-0.2
Botswana	13.8	15.8	17.9	18.4	4.6
Lesotho	26.6	26.2	25.6	27.4	0.9
Malawi	6.9	7.4	6.5	6.7	-0.2
Mozambique	24.7	23.2	23.5	24.4	-0.3
Namibia	19.0	20.3	22.1	25.6	6.6
South Africa	23.9	26.7	24.7	25.9	2.0
Swaziland	23.8	22.9	27.8	25.3	1.5
Zambia	18.9	12.9	10.8	7.5	-11.4
Zimbabwe	5.8	4.8	6.3	5.1	-0.7

Note: * World Bank estimate using the International Labour Organization (ILO) method.
Source: World Bank (2017a), *World Development Indicators* (database).

Notes

1. The Gini index measures the extent to which the distribution of income among individuals or households within an economy deviates from a perfectly equal distribution. The index ranges from 0 in the case of "perfect equality" (each share of the population gets the same share of income) to 100 in the case of "perfect inequality" (all income goes to the share of the population with the highest income).
2. The Commitment to Equity (CEQ) project has been led by Nora Lustig since 2008. It is an initiative of the Center for Inter-American Policy and Research and the Department of Economics, Tulane University, the Center for Global Development and the Inter-American Dialogue. The CEQ project is housed in the Commitment to Equity Institute at Tulane. See www.commitmentoequity.org.
3. The Gini coefficients for South Africa and Zambia are based on data on revenue or consumption and years that differ from those shown in previous sections (calculated based on *PovCal* data).
4. Each SACU country is compared to the countries having the next three higher levels of income per capita (in constant USD, averaged over the period 2008-10) and the next three lower levels of income per capita.

References

AfDB/OECD/UNDP (2016), *African Economic Outlook 2016: Sustainable Cities and Structural Transformation*, OECD Publishing, Paris, http://dx.doi.org/10.1787/aeo-2016-en.

AfDB/OECD/UNDP (2014), *African Economic Outlook 2014: Global Value Chains and Africa's Industrialisation*, OECD Publishing, Paris, http://dx.doi.org/10.1787/aeo-2014-en.

AfDB et al. (2012), *African Economic Outlook 2012: Promoting Youth Employment*, OECD Publishing, Paris, http://dx.doi.org/10.1787/aeo-2012-en.

Altman, M. (2004), "The state of employment", in J. Daniel, R. Southall and J. Lutchman (eds.), *State of the Nation 2004-2005*, HSRC Press, Cape Town, pp. 423-454.

Anand, R., S. Kothari and N. Kumar (2016), *South Africa Labour Market Dynamics and Inequality*, International Monetary Fund.

Brixiová, Z., M. Ncube and Z. Bicaba (2015), "Skills and youth entrepreneurship in Africa: Analysis with evidence from Swaziland", *World Development*, Vol. 67, pp. 11-26.

Brynard, A. P. (2011), "The implementation of unemployment policies in South Africa", *Journal of African Public Affairs*, Vol. 4(2).

Bureau of Statistics (2008), *Lesotho Integrated Labour Force Survey Report for 2008*, Maseru, http://catalog.ihsn.org/index.php/catalog/4531/download/57895.

Chidede, T. (2017), "Intellectual property governance in Africa", *Tralac trade brief* No. S17TB14/2017, July 2017.

Conference Board (2017), *Total Economy Database*, https://www.conference-board.org/data/economydatabase/index.cfm?id=27762 (accessed 31 January 2018).

CSO (2015), *Labour Force Survey Report 2014*, Central Statistical Office, Government of the Republic of Zambia, Lusaka.

Cuesta, J., P. Kabaso and P. Suarez-Becerra (2012), "How pro-poor and progressive is social spending in Zambia?", *Policy Research Working Paper* 6052, April 2012, World Bank, Washington, DC, https://openknowledge.worldbank.org/bitstream/handle/10986/6054/WPS6052.pdf?sequence=1&isAllowed=y.

Danish Trade Union Council (2014), *Mozambique Market Profile*, Copenhagen.

De La Fuente, A., M. Rosales and J. Jellema (2017), "The impact of fiscal policy on inequality and poverty in Zambia", *Policy Research Working Paper*, No. 8246, World Bank, Washington, DC, https://openknowledge.worldbank.org/handle/10986/28907.

Department of Finance (1996), *Growth Employment and Redistribution: A Macroeconomic Strategy*, Department of Finance, Pretoria.

Field, S., P. Musset and J. L. Alvarez-Galvan (2014), *A Skills Beyond School Review of South Africa*, OECD Reviews of Vocational Education and Training, OECD Publishing, http://dx.doi.org/10.1787/9789264223776-en.

Fundira, T. (2018), "Informal cross-border trading – review of the simplified trade regimes in east and southern Africa", *TRALAC Trade Brief* No. S18TB5/2018.

Garcia, M. and C.Moore (2012), *The Cash Dividend : The Rise of Cash Transfer Programs in Sub-Saharan Africa*, Directions in Development, World Bank, https://openknowledge.worldbank.org/handle/10986/2246.

GEM (2017), *South Africa 2016-2017 Report*, Global Entrepreneurship Monitor, http://gemconsortium.org/report/49833.

ILO (2017), *ILO Stat* (database), www.ilo.org/ilostat.

IMF (2018), *World Economic Outlook Database*, International Monetary Fund, http://www.imf.org/external/pubs/ft/weo/2018/01/weodata/index.aspx.

IMF (2012), *Botswana Country Report*, International Monetary Fund, Washington, DC.

Inchauste, G. et al. (2015), *The Distributional Impact of Fiscal Policy in South Africa*, World Bank, Washington, DC.

Keeton, G. (2014), "Inequality in South Africa", *Journal of Helen Suzman Foundation*, Vol. 74.

Kerr, A. (2018), "Job flows, worker flows and churning in South Africa", *South African Journal of Economics*, Vol. 86(S1), pp. 141-166.

Kingdon, G. and J. Knight (2004), "Unemployment in South Africa: The nature of the beast", *World Development*, Vol. 32(3), pp. 391-408.

Leibbrandt, M., A. Finn and I. Woolard (2012), "Describing and decomposing post-apartheid income inequality in South Africa", *Development Southern Africa*, Vol. 29(1), pp. 19-34.

Leibbrandt, M. and J. Levinsohn (2011), "Fifteen years on: Household incomes in South Africa", in *National Bureau of Economic Research Working Paper No. 16661*, National Bureau of Economic Research, Cambridge.

Leite, P.G., T. McKinley and R.G. Osorio (2006), *The Post-Apartheid Evolution of Earnings Inequality in South Africa, 1995-2004*, International Poverty Centre.

Levine, R. and D. Renelt (1992), "A sensitivity analysis of cross-country growth regressions", *American Economic Review*, Vol. 82(4), pp. 942-963.

Levinsohn, J. (2007), *Two Policies to Alleviate Unemployment in South Africa*, National Bureau of Economic Research, Cambridge.

Maree, J. (2007), "Strategies for reducing unemployment in South Africa and the role of organized labour", paper presented at the Labour and the Challenges of Development Conference, Johannesburg, 1-3 April 2007.

Mussa, R. (2015), *A Dangerous Divide: The State of Inequality in Malawi*, Oxfam, Lilongwe.

Nattrass, N. (2001), "High productivity now: A critique of South Africa's growth strategy", *Transformation*, Vol. 45, pp. 1-24.

OECD (2018a), *International Development Statistics* (database), www.oecd.org/dac/stats/idsonline.htm.

OECD (2018b), "Youth Well-being Policy Review of Malawi", EU-OECD Youth Inclusion Project, Paris, https://www.oecd.org/countries/malawi/Youth-well-being-policy-review-Malawi.pdf.

OECD (2017a), *OECD Economic Surveys: South Africa 2017*, OECD Publishing, Paris, http://dx.doi.org/10.1787/eco_surveys-zaf-2017-en.

OECD (2017b), *Unlocking the Potential of Youth Entrepreneurship in Developing Countries: From Subsistence to Performance*, OECD Publishing, Paris, http://dx.doi.org/10.1787/9789264277830-en.

OECD (2017c), *Youth Aspirations and the Reality of Jobs in Developing Countries: Mind the Gap*, OECD Publishing, Paris, http://dx.doi.org/10.1787/9789264285668-en.

OECD (2017d), *Social Protection in East Africa: Harnessing the Future*, OECD Publishing, Paris http://dx.doi.org/10.1787/9789264274228-en.

Rodrik, D. (2016), "Premature deindustrialization", *Journal of Economic Growth*, Vol. 21(1), pp. 1-33.

Romer, P.M. (1986), "Increasing returns and long-run growth", *Journal of Political Economy*, Vol. 94(5), pp. 1002-1037.

SADC/OECD (2017), *FDI-SME Linkages in Regional and Global Value Chains and the Development Dimension in SADC*, Southern African Development Community, December 2017.

Social Policy Research Institute (2017), *Profiling of Social Protection Beneficiaries in Botswana*, July 2017.

Solow, R.M. (1956), "A contribution to the theory of economic growth", *Quarterly Journal of Economics*, Vol. 70(1), pp. 65-94.

Streak, J. (2004), "The GEAR legacy: Did GEAR fail or move South Africa forward", *Development Southern Africa*, Vol. 21(2), pp. 271-288.

The Economist (2012a), "Education in South Africa still dysfunctional: Standards still leave a lot to be desired", 21 January 2012.

Ulriksen, M. (2013), "The Politics of Social Protection Expenditure and Financing in Southern Africa, *Development Southern Africa*, Vol. 30(1), pp. 39-53, DOI: 10.1080/0376835X.2013.756097.

UNDESA (2017), *World Population Prospects* (database), https://esa.un.org/unpd/wpp/ (accessed 1 March 2018).

UNECA (2017), *Economic Report on Africa 2017,* United Nations Economic Commission for Africa, Addis Ababa.

UNECA (2015), *Accelerating Industrialization in Southern Africa through Beneficiation and Value Addition*, United Nations Economic Commission for Africa, Addis Ababa.

United Nations Statistics Division (2017), *UNCOMTRADE* (database), https://wits.worldbank.org/ (accessed 1 February 2018).

World Bank (2018), *ASPIRE* (database), http://datatopics.worldbank.org/aspire/indicator/social-expenditure (accessed 13 March 2018).

World Bank (2017a), *World Development Indicators* (database), World Bank Group, Washington, DC, https://data.worldbank.org/products/wdi (accessed 1 March 2018).

World Bank (2017b), *PovcalNet* (database), World Bank Group, Washington, DC, http://iresearch.worldbank.org/PovcalNet (accessed 1 March 2018).

World Bank (2016), *Republic of Angola Poverty and Social Impact Analysis*, Report No. ACS19693, 22 June 2016, World Bank, Washington, DC, https://openknowledge.worldbank.org/bitstream/handle/10986/25105/ACS19693.pdf?sequence=4&isAllowed=y.

World Bank (2015a), *Botswana Poverty Assessment*, Report No. 88473-BW, World Bank, Washington, DC, http://documents.worldbank.org/curated/en/351721468184754228/pdf/88473-REVISED-WP-P154659-PUBLIC-Box394819B.pdf.

World Bank (2015b), *Factory Southern Africa? SACU in Global Value Chains: Summary Report*, November 2015, World Bank, Washington, DC, https://www.saiia.org.za/non-saiia-publications/969-2016-01-21-saiia-world-bank-factory-southern-africa-full-report/file.

Zimstat (2014), *Zimbabwe Labour Force Survey,* Zimstat, Harare.

Chapter 4

Dynamics of growth, jobs and inequalities in Central Africa

This chapter presents trends and determinants of growth, employment and inequalities in Central Africa (Burundi, Cameroon, the Central African Republic, Chad, Congo, the Democratic Republic of Congo, Equatorial Guinea, Gabon, Sao Tome and Principe). It looks at the sectoral composition of the economies in the region as well as the dynamics of productivity, of job creation and of inequality of opportunity and income. It also analyses the role of structural transformation in reducing the region's vulnerability to international commodity price fluctuations.

The chapter addresses four topics: growth dynamics, employment dynamics, dynamics of inequalities, and concludes with recommendations that take into account national specificities.

IN BRIEF

Between 2000 and 2016, Central Africa had a strong **growth** dynamic – at 5.6% on average – but with a volatility almost twice as high as the rest of Africa, due to its vulnerability on global commodity prices. Without any structural transformation, the prospects of sustainable growth reducing poverty and inequalities remain weak.

Despite their heterogeneity, all countries in the region share a dependence on oil and minerals. Since the start of the 1990s, the services sector has contributed around 40% of GDP. The agricultural sector's contribution fell from 21% of GDP in 1990 to 11% in 2015 in favour of the industrial sector's expansion, with a rising contribution to GDP from 34% to 49%. This improvement is based on extractive activities and does not signal a deep structural change.

While the unemployment rate is stable at 7% since 2000, the informal economy dominates the labour market. Based on a production profile dominated by minerals, growth is more capital intensive than labour intensive. Only the services sector has managed to create jobs, without being able to offset **employment** losses in other sectors.

Pro-poor policies have led to a reduction in poverty and **inequality** of opportunity in most countries in the region, without eradicating them entirely. However, income inequality has not fallen. The Gini coefficient has remained constant at 42 since 2000, the highest level on the continent. Yet, Central Africa diverges from the rest of the continent in terms of its positive results in combatting gender inequality even though this remains high. Countries must persevere in their efforts to ensure that gender inequality does not start to rise again.

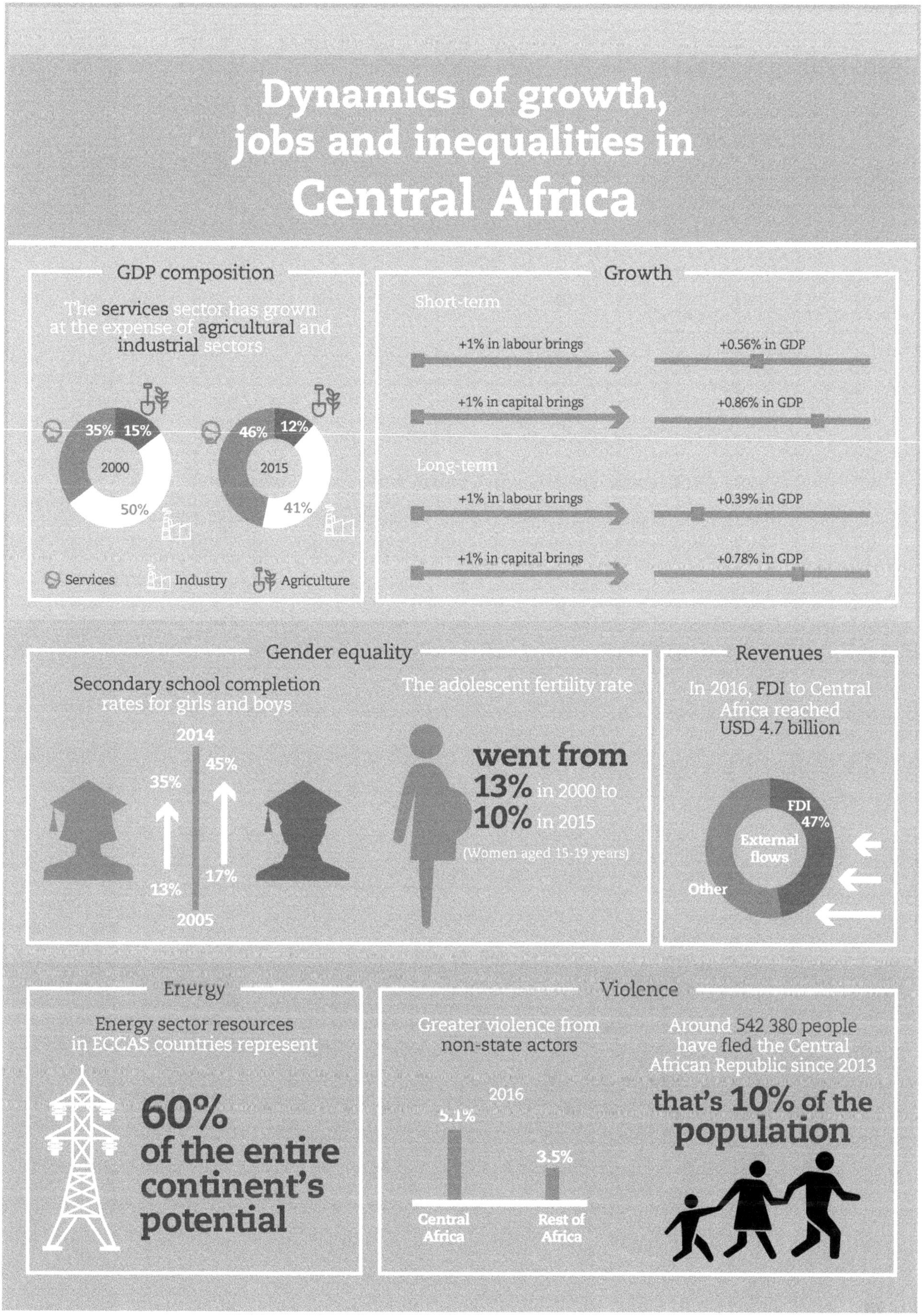
Dynamics of growth, jobs and inequalities in Central Africa
GDP composition
The services sector has grown at the expense of agricultural and industrial sectors
35%
15%
2000
50%
46%
12%
2015
41%
Services
Industry
Agriculture
Growth
Short-term
+1% in labour brings
+0.56% in GDP
+1% in capital brings
+0.86% in GDP
Long-term
+1% in labour brings
+0.39% in GDP
+1% in capital brings
+0.78% in GDP
Gender equality
Secondary school completion rates for girls and boys
2014
35%
45%
13%
17%
2005
The adolescent fertility rate
went from 13% in 2000 to 10% in 2015
(Women aged 15-19 years)
Revenues
In 2016, FDI to Central Africa reached USD 4.7 billion
FDI
47%
External flows
Other
Energy
Energy sector resources in ECCAS countries represent
60% of the entire continent's potential
Violence
Greater violence from non-state actors
2016
5.1%
3.5%
Central Africa
Rest of Africa
Around 542 380 people have fled the Central African Republic since 2013
that's 10% of the population

Central Africa regional profile

Table 4.1. Basic indicators for Central Africa, 2017

Population (thousands)	144 575
Land area (thousands of km²)	5 276
Population density (pop./km²)	27
GDP, PPP (USD billion)	294
GDP per capita, PPP (USD)	2 009

Source: Authors' calculations based on UNDESA (2017) database, World Bank (2017a), *World Development Indicators*, IMF (2017a), *World Economic Outlook* (database of October 2017).

Table 4.2. Financial flows and tax revenues to Central Africa, 2009-16 (current USD billions)

			2009	2010	2011	2012	2013	2014	2015	2016
Foreign	Private	Inward foreign direct investment	5.2	7.5	7.2	8.7	7.5	8.7	5.6	4.7
		Portfolio investments	0.3	0.3	-2.2	-3.5	1.3	0	0	0
		Remittances	0.2	0.2	0.4	0.3	0.3	0.4	0.3	0.3
	Public	Official development assistance (net total, all donors)	4.8	7.0	7.9	4.9	4.9	5.0	5.0	4.9
Total foreign flows			**10.6**	**14.9**	**13.3**	**10.4**	**14.0**	**14.1**	**10.9**	**10.0**
Domestic tax revenues			**10.8**	**10.8**	**13.4**	**14.6**	**15.8**	**17.2**	**14.2**	**11.5**

Source: Authors' calculations based on World Bank (2017a), *World Development Indicators* database, IMF (2018), *World Economic Outlook* database (October 2017), and OECD/DAC (2017), *Online Statistics on International Development* database.

Figure 4.1. Growth dynamics in Central Africa and Africa, 1990-2018

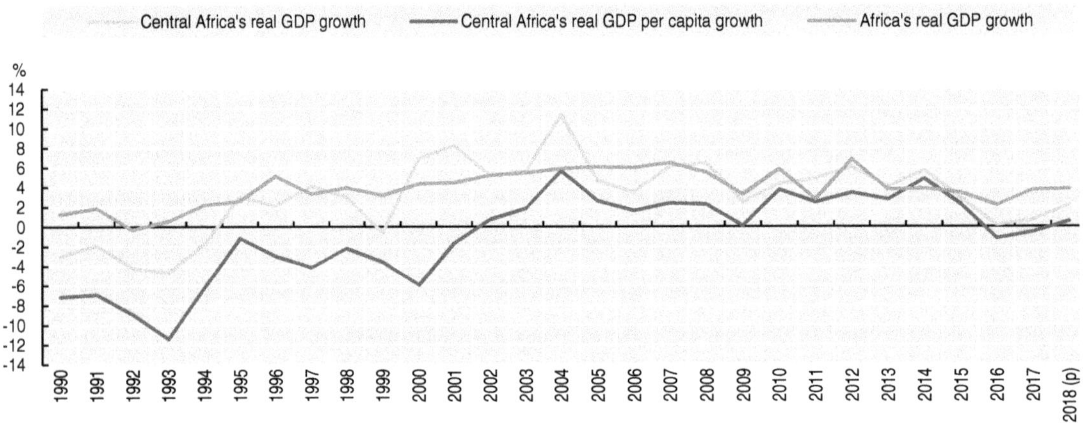

Source: Authors' calculations based on IMF (2017a) World Economic Outlook database (April 2018).

StatLink http://dx.doi.org/10.1787/888933783247

Figure 4.2. Trade composition in Central Africa, 2016

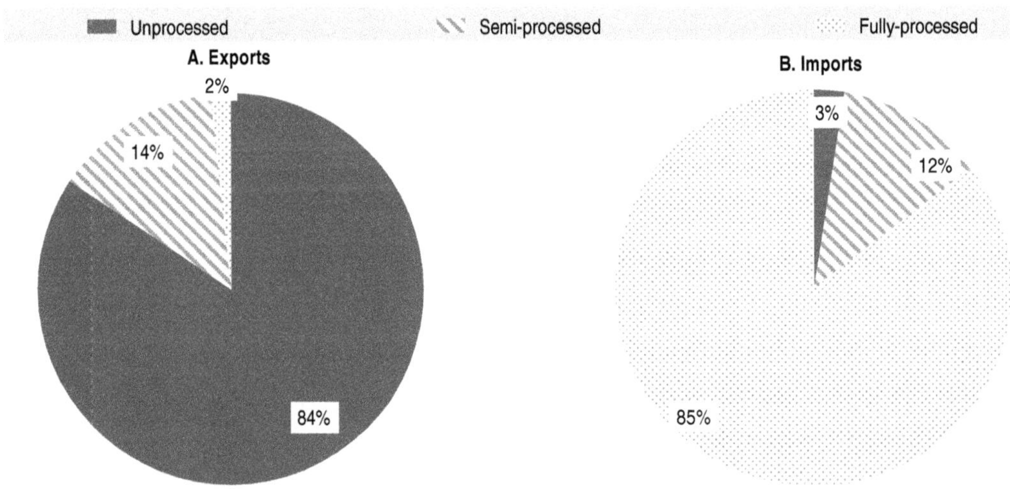

Source: Authors' calculations based on UNCOMTRADE database (2017).

StatLink http://dx.doi.org/10.1787/888933783285

Central Africa is made up of nine countries that differ greatly in terms of size, population and geography. The region includes landlocked countries such as Burundi and Chad as well as smaller insular states such as Equatorial Guinea and Sao Tome and Principe. Cameroon, the Central African Republic, Congo, the vast Democratic Republic of Congo (DRC) and Gabon are also part of the region.

With 144.6 million people in 2017, 53% of which were aged between 15 and 64 years, Central Africa represents 11.5% of the continent's population. Central Africa's land covers 5.3 millions of square meters (km^2) and has the lowest population density with 27 inhabitants/km^2. It is lower than Africa's 39 inhabitants/km^2. Varying from country to country, the rural population went from representing 73% to 55% of the total between 1980 and 2016.

Central Africa's GDP is the smallest one of the continent, at USD 294 billions at purchasing parity power (PPP). The sub region's contribution to Africa's GDP fluctuates from 4% to 11%, depending on the global economy and international prices for oil products. These latter represent more than 80% of the region's total exports.

All the region's countries are members of the Economic Community of Central African States (ECCAS), a free trade area created in 1983. Six of the nine countries are additionally members of an economic and monetary area created in 1994, the Economic and Monetary Community of Central Africa (CEMAC).

Unstable and fragile growth

More volatile growth compared to the continent

Growth in Central Africa generally shadows that of the continent, both in periods of growth and recession, although it is more erratic. From 1989 to 1993, the region experienced a harsh economic crisis caused by the 1986 petrol crisis, the depletion of oil deposits (particularly for Cameroon) and the collapse in prices of raw materials. After the devaluation of the CFA franc (XAF) in 1994, growth followed a broadly positive trajectory, at times above that of Africa. Since 2015, economic activity, unsettled by the fall in prices of primary materials, has been lower.

The instability of this growth appears more pronounced than elsewhere, with volatility almost twice as high as in the rest of Africa. Volatility is here measured via a standard deviation of the rate of economic growth. This was 4.11 and 2.6 for Central Africa over the 1971-2016 and 2000-16 periods, versus 1.84 and 1.63 for Africa over the same periods.

Since 1994, the extractive sector has driven growth

The sectoral contribution to growth highlights the dominance of the extraction of primary products, despite deindustrialisation in the 1990s and 2000s.

- The agricultural sector contributed less to regional production, its share having collapsed since the start of the 2000s to stabilise around 10% of GDP at the end of the decade.
- The services sector appeared to drive growth up until 1993, before stabilising at 40% of GDP.
- Since 1994, industry has propelled growth, associated with the extraction of primary products rather than the real creation of value added. In fact, the share of manufacturing production included in the industrial sector is low and stable, around 10% of GDP over the 1970-2015 period (Figure 4.3).

Figure 4.3. **Sectoral contribution to GDP in Central Africa (percentage)**

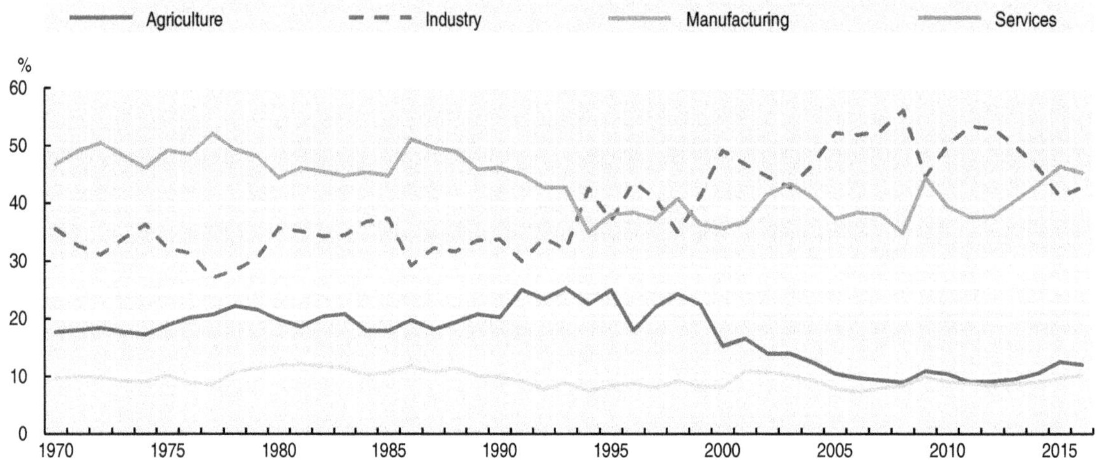

Source: Authors' calculations based on UNCTAD (2017), *UNCTADStat* database.
StatLink http://dx.doi.org/10.1787/888933783304

Since 1999, the rise in the price of raw materials (Figure 4.4) has encouraged the exploitation of natural resources, particularly oil. It also led countries to turn away from other sectors such as agriculture, a dynamic that impedes development of other branches of the economy that could create real value added, such as manufacturing.

Figure 4.4. **Evolution of prices of main primary products**

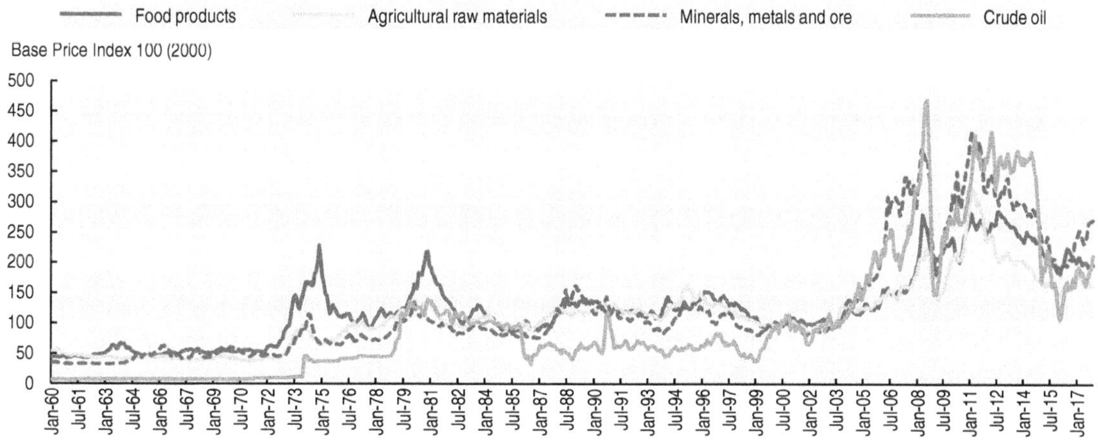

Source: Authors' calculations based on UNCTAD (2017), *UNCTADStat* database.
StatLink http://dx.doi.org/10.1787/888933783323

Given the weight of raw materials in the national economies, two types of structural transformation are common favouring either the industrial sector or services. In Congo, Equatorial Guinea and Chad, mining production underpins growth in the industrial sector. In contrast, Burundi and Sao Tome and Principe experienced an expansion of services to the detriment of agriculture. In all the countries of Central Africa apart from Burundi, the primary sector contributes less to growth than the secondary and service sectors.

Since 2000, the economic performance of the region has been dependent on the evolution of prices for raw materials, the collapse of which in 2014-15 resulted in a recession. The lack of diversification in the economies weakens growth.

Capital: The engine of economic growth

An analysis of factors of production shows that capital contributed more to economic growth than labour and total factor productivity (TFP), both in the short and long term (Table 4.3).

Table 4.3. **Factoral contribution to growth**

VARIABLES	Production	Variation in production
	Long term	Short term
Labour	0.385*** (0.0167)	
Capital	0.784*** (0.0217)	
Variable Labour		0.564** (0.234)
Variable Capital		0.864*** (0.202)
TFP	0.987*** (0.211)	-0.00951 (0.0110)
Observations	315	306
Square root	0.926	0.163

Notes: The symbols ***, **, and * refer to statistical significance of 1%, 5% and 10%, respectively. The standard deviations are found in parentheses. The model used for estimates considered problems of autocorrelation and heteroscedasticity. Annex 4.A1 describes the steps taken to break production down into labour, capital and total factor productivity (TFP).
Source: Authors' calculations based on GGDC/UC Davis 2017, *Penn World Table* 9.0 database.

- Over the short term, variations in growth are driven by labour and capital. A 1% rise in the employment growth rate is associated with a 0.56% rise in the overall growth rate. The impact of capital is larger: a 1% rise in capital growth brings with it an improvement of growth of 0.86%. There is no significant effect of productivity on growth.
- Over the long term, capital has a more important role in production than labour. A 1% rise in the labour factor causes a 0.39% rise in production while a 1% rise in capital brings about an increase in production of 0.78%.

Economic drivers unconducive to sustainable growth

Since 2009, growth has been driven by private consumption and private investment. Private consumption has been the most stable determinant of growth since 2003 (Figure 4.5). Investment also has a positive effect on growth in Central Africa, similar to the dynamics for all of Africa (Figure 4.6).

However, the low level of public investment in infrastructure undermines long-term growth. Variations in oil prices render public finances unstable and the countries have experienced difficulties in committing to long-term public investment, notably in infrastructure. Access to electricity in Central Africa is close to that of the continent, at 30%, despite large regional differences. Burundi, Gabon, Equatorial Guinea and Sao Tome and Principe have good levels of electrification (between 50% and 70%, compared with less than 10% in the Central African Republic, DRC or Chad).

Figure 4.5. **Components of growth in Central Africa**

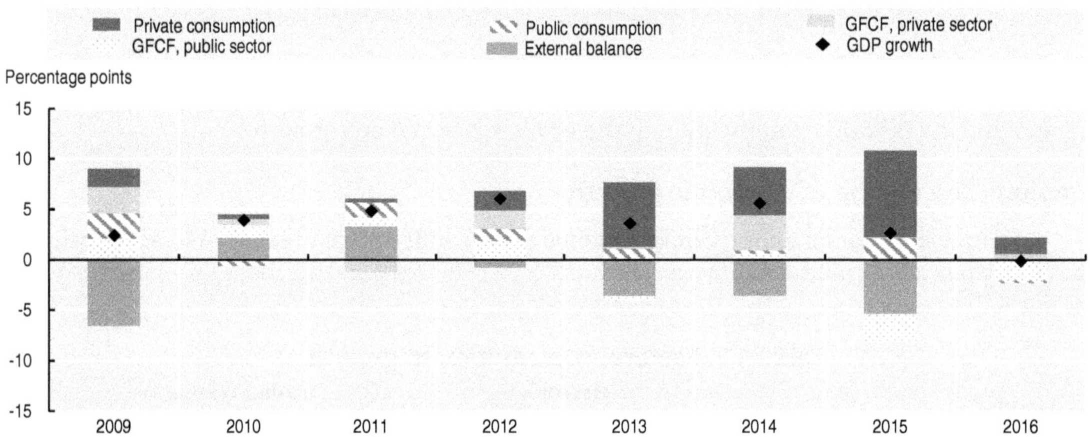

Source: Authors' calculations based on World Bank (2017a), *World Development Indicators* database and IMF (2018), *World Economic Outlook* database (October 2017).
StatLink http://dx.doi.org/10.1787/888933783342

Since 2015, an improvement in the business environment has encouraged the growth of private investment. The reforms of the Ohada Treaty and Uniform Acts and national legislation brought new protection for minority investors and promoted the acquisition of loans (World Bank, 2017b). However, the countries of the region have consistently lower performances internationally in the World Bank's *Doing Business* index, which each year evaluates the business environment around the world. Cameroon, the region's leading country, is thus in 163rd place in 2018 out of a list of 190 countries (World Bank, 2018). The adoption of new legislation should thus go hand in hand with the effective implementation of reforms.

The countries with the highest levels of growth also have the highest levels of openness to trade and financial flows (Figure 4.6). This relationship, often highlighted in the literature (Barro, 1991; Barrow, 2000), depends on the structure of national economies although the correlation does not strictly imply a cause and effect link.

Mining and oil countries benefiting from relative institutional stability attract more FDI (Figure 4.6). Congo, Equatorial Guinea and Sao Tome and Principe receive on average more FDI thanks to the extractive sector, while FDI remains very low in other countries of the region.

Figure 4.6. **The principal determinants of growth in Central Africa (averages from 1980 to 2014)**

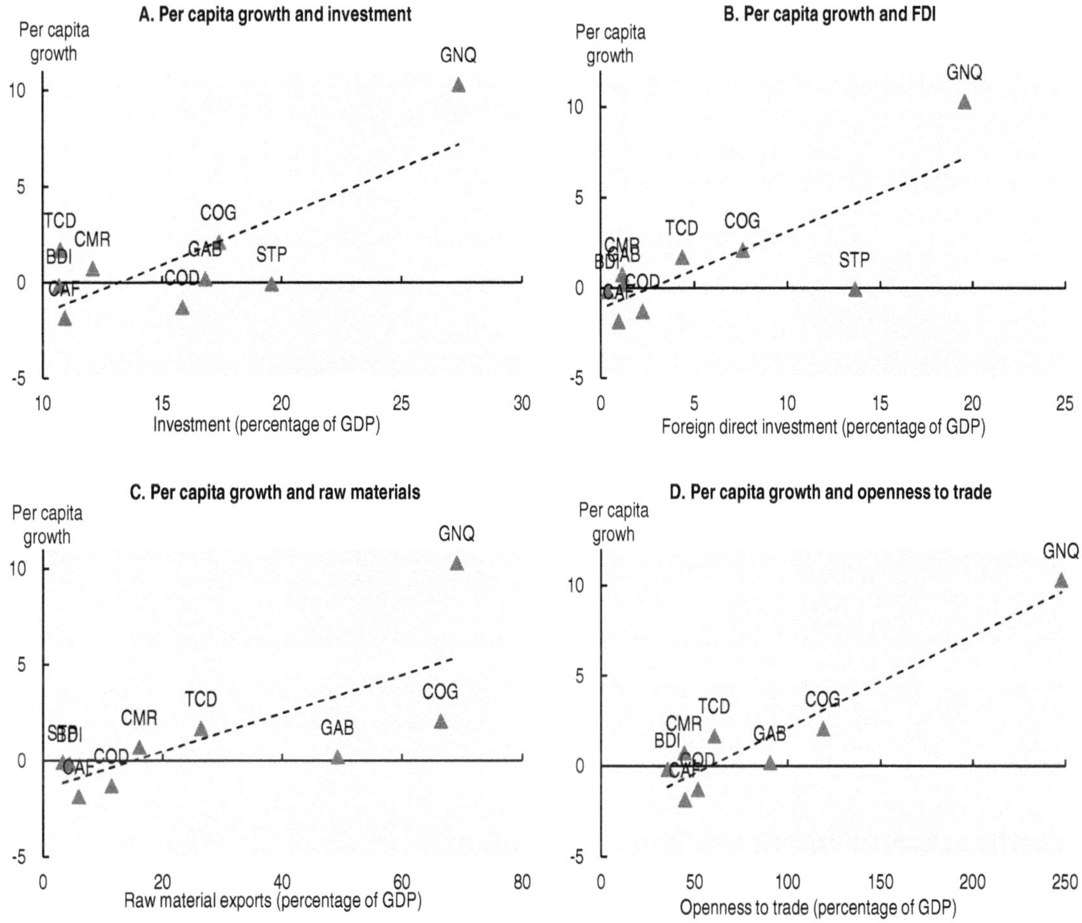

Source: Authors' calculations based on World Bank (2017a), *World Development Indicators* database; GGDC/UC Davis (2018), *Penn World Table 9.0* database; and UNCTAD (2017), *UNCTADStat* database.
StatLink http://dx.doi.org/10.1787/888933783361

Economic openness has a positive and significant effect on growth, despite strong heterogeneity between countries (Figure 4.6). Equatorial Guinea, with 10% growth, represents an exceptional case compared with the regional average, due to its very high level of investment, exports and openness to trade.

Exports of raw materials remain one of the principal sources of revenue and of foreign currency, but they hinder economic diversification. The countries that depend on the export of raw materials, such as Congo, Gabon and Equatorial Guinea, have poorly diversified economies that are more vulnerable to variations in international oil prices. Other economies are also exposed by their dependence in the sense that 75% of their exports derive from three products (Central African Republic, DRC, and Sao Tome and Principe), or even a single product (oil in Chad).

While not all the countries have experienced a period of conflict, the region has been affected by serious security risks (Figure 4.7). Since 2000, Burundi, Cameroon, the Central African Republic, DRC and Chad have either experienced or still experience conflict, whether internal or cross-border. The correlation between conflicts and economic development is not clear. A country that lives with conflict could have a good level of growth, like DRC between 2011 and 2016.

Despite this, security problems have negative repercussions on the drivers of growth. The wars in Central Africa have destroyed physical capital, reduced investment in health and the education of human capital and curbed the accumulation of social capital, notably trust-building between investors and governmental institutions (Hugon, 2006). These conflicts also lead to forced displacement of the population, which prevents all stable productive activity. As such, more than 400 000 people have fled Burundi since 2015 (UNHCR, 2017) and 542 380 the Central African Republic since 2013 (UNHCR, 2018), or around 4% and 10% of the population, respectively.

Figure 4.7. **Violence by non-state actors in Africa**

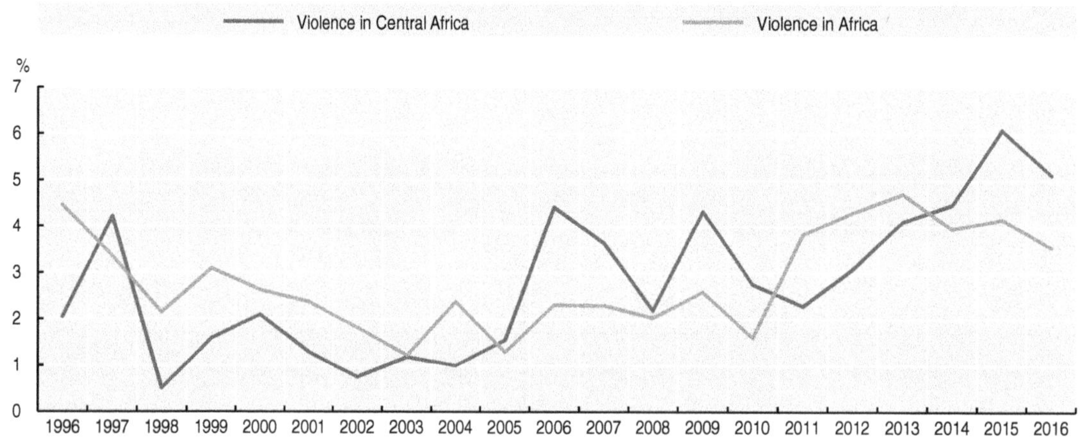

Source: OECD Development Centre indicators based on information collected by the Reuters and AFP press agencies in Africa.

StatLink http://dx.doi.org/10.1787/888933783380

Growth without employment weakens the economy

In 15 years, the labour market has remained predominantly informal

With a booming labour market, employment levels appear to be slightly higher than the African average over the 2000-15 period. By 2030, the working age population should increase by 4.3 million people a year. Today, 68% of the total population of Central Africa is economically active, compared with 61% for the entire continent. The employment rate of women in Central Africa exceeds that of the continent, although gender inequality persists (Annex 4.A2). Women have an employment rate of 64.8%, versus 71.7% for men in the region and 48.7% on average for women on the continent.

However, these statistics should be interpreted with caution, given the size of the informal sector. It is very difficult to gain an accurate overview of the labour market overlooking this sector, estimated at around 38% of GDP on average in Africa (IMF, 2017b). According to the same source, the available figures for Central Africa between 2010 and 2014 go from just under 30% for Cameroon (the lowest in the region) to almost 45% in Gabon. Jobs in the informal sector represent a reserve that makes it possible to absorb growth of the working-age population. However, insecurity linked to jobs – which includes income instability and lower salaries – are an argument for the encouragement of formal activities.

Unemployment figures do not account for underemployment, thus underestimating the extent of unemployment in the economy. However, to evaluate and improve the efficacy of public policy, complete and current databases are necessary. As such, unemployment data appear insufficient for capturing the reality of the labour market and its development over time. For example, between 2000 and 2015, average unemployment varied little in the region and on average was fairly low at 7% (Figure 4.8). Unemployment by category barely changed either, at 14.6% among youth, 9.8% for women and 7% for men.

Figure 4.8. **Average unemployment, 2000-15 (percentage)**

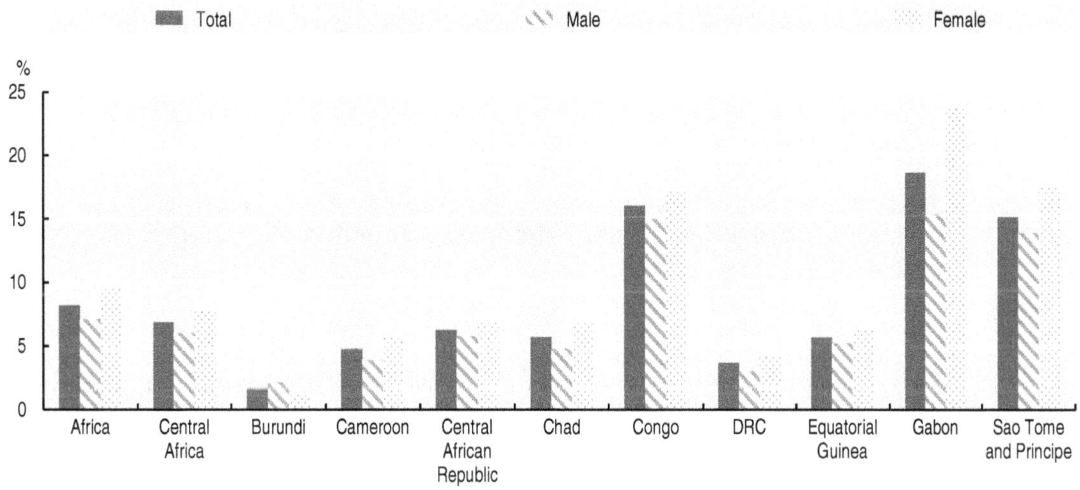

Source: Authors' calculations based on ILO (2017), *ILOStat* database.
StatLink http://dx.doi.org/10.1787/888933783399

Capital-intensive growth has not succeeded in creating employment

As in other low-income countries, jobs in Central Africa are concentrated in the agricultural sector. Almost all countries have agricultural sector employment rates well in excess of other sectors, with a regional average of 70.9%. Only Gabon (43%) and Sao Tome and Principe (26%) are exceptions to the rule (Figure 4.9).

Figure 4.9. **Employment distribution by sector 2000-15 (percentage)**

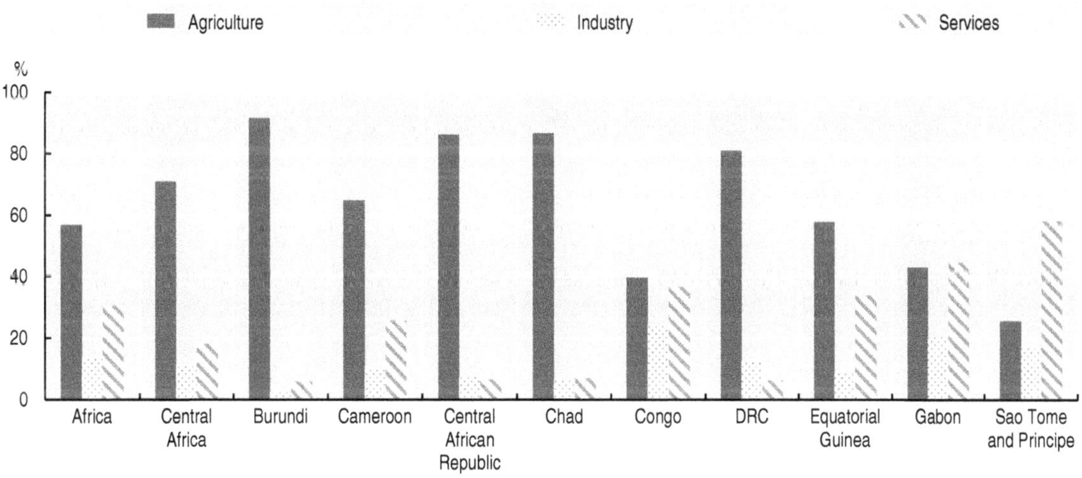

Source: Authors' calculations based on ILO (2017), *ILOStat* database.
StatLink http://dx.doi.org/10.1787/888933783418

According to the Vector Auto Regressive (VAR, Annex 4.A1) model, the relationship between the labour market and economic growth in Central Africa is certainly positive, but with very different temporal dynamics (Figure 4.10).

- Positive shocks to the economy have an immediately positive, although relatively low, impact on job creation. In fact, the magnitude of the reaction of employment (called the *impulse response*) is relatively low, according to the results in Central Africa between 2008 and 2014. For example, a 1% increase in economic activity results in a marginal rise of 0.03% in employment in the same year. The effect gradually diminishes, becoming zero after two years.
- Inversely, a positive shock to the labour market has a delayed effect – after two years – that is sustained on economic growth, until the fourth year after the shock. In this instance, a 2% rise in employment will lead to a 1% rise in economic activity during the second year and a 0.5% rise during the third year. This effect is still positive the fourth year after a shock.

Figure 4.10. **Interaction between growth and employment in Central Africa (impulse response to shocks), 1980-2014**

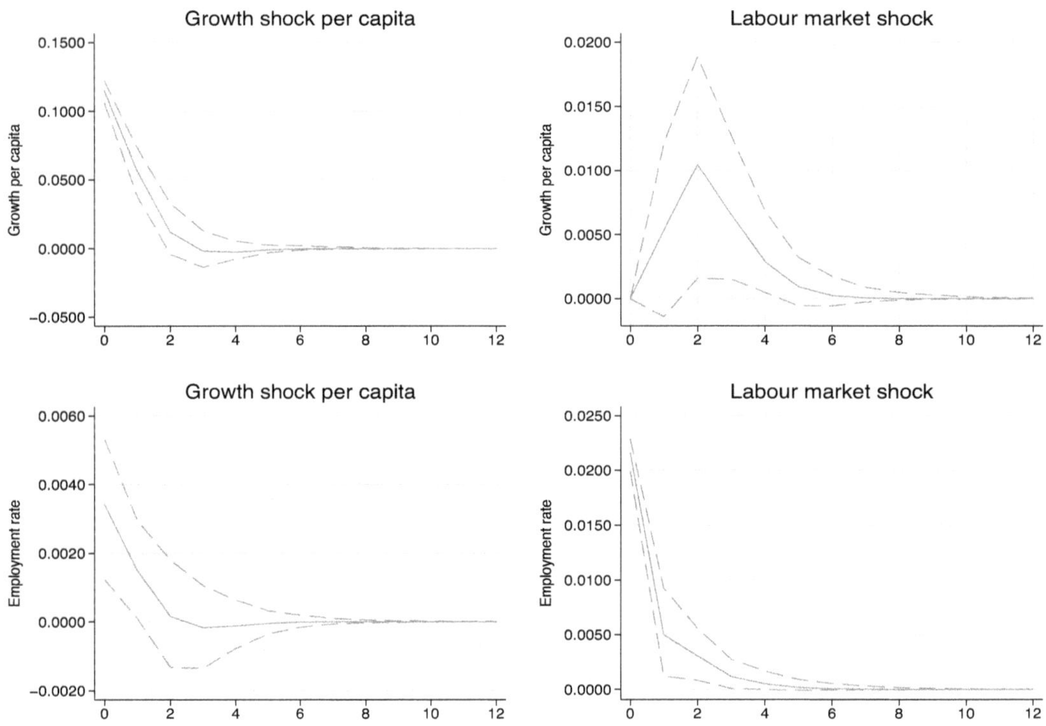

Source: Authors' calculations based on GGDC/UC Davis (2018), *Penn World Table 9.0* database.
StatLink http://dx.doi.org/10.1787/888933783437

Growth over the past seven years has also not created sufficient jobs, especially in the countries dependent on natural resources (Figure 4.11). At the start of the 2000s, structural transformation led to the creation of low-wage jobs in the extractive sector, which employs less than 1% of the active population and has not succeeded in recruiting sufficient numbers of local workers for high value added jobs (UNDP, 2017).

The various sectors are unable to create sufficient employment. Agricultural sector employment fell, particularly between 1999 and 2005. This could be an indication of structural transformation or a redistribution of the labour force. Still, this decline is not offset by a proportional number of new jobs in industry and services. The lack of opportunity remains worrying while the working age population continues to increase, at a rate of 16% between 2010 and 2015 (UNDESA, 2017).

Figure 4.11. **Annual job creation by sector, 1999-2017**

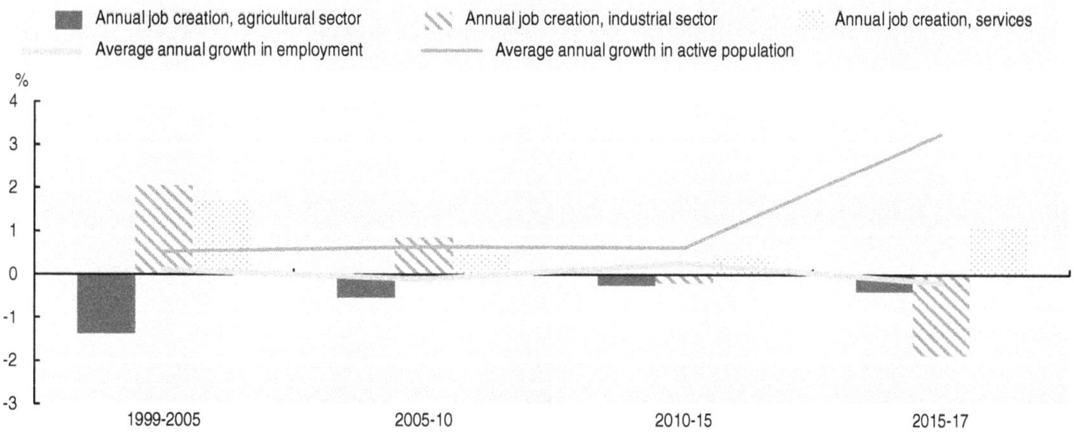

Source: Authors' calculations based on World Bank (2017a), *World Development Indicators* database.
StatLink http://dx.doi.org/10.1787/888933783456

The structures of the economies increase inequality

Inequality and poverty have stalled at alarming levels

The Gini coefficient for Central Africa has remained fixed at 42 (Table 4.4) for the past 15 years and it remains the highest of all the regions of the continent. The capacity of countries to allocate resources and redistribute income appears limited by, among other things, the low level of tax revenue: only 11% of GDP in 2016, compared with an average of 16% for all of Africa (IMF, 2018). The inconsistency of statistical measurements however does not allow for a precise and complete overview of the scale of poverty and inequality. Still, several trends emerge for the countries listed here in alphabetical order.

Table 4.4. **Income inequality in Central Africa**

Country	Year	Gini coefficient
Burundi	2006	33.4
	2013	39.2
Cameroon	2001	42.1
	2007	42.8
	2014	46.5
Central African Republic	2003	43.6
	2008	56.2
Chad	2003	39.8
	2011	43.3
DRC	2004	42.2
	2012	42.1
Congo	2005	47.3
	2011	48.9
Equatorial Guinea	-	-
Gabon	2005	42.2
Sao Tome and Principe	2000	32.1
	2010	30.8
Central Africa	**2000-08**	**42**
	2009-16	**42**

Source: Adapted by the authors from World Bank (2017a), *World Development Indicators* database.

The level of poverty remains high in Central Africa in the absence of strong systems of social security (Tables 4.5 and 4.6). The countries of the region have not managed to sustain inclusive growth, despite redistributive policies. Where these exist, it is necessary to assess the impact of social security reforms, such as in Gabon, where a human investment strategy was launched in 2014.

Table 4.5. **Poverty rates in Central Africa (threshold of USD 1.90)**

Country	Year	Rate
Burundi	2006	77.7
	2013	73.7
Cameroon	2001	23.1
	2007	29.3
	2014	24
Central African Republic	2003	64.8
	2008	66.3
Chad	2003	62.9
	2011	38.4
Congo	2005	50.2
	2011	37
DRC	2004	94
	2012	77.1
Equatorial Guinea	-	-
Gabon	2005	8
Sao Tome and Principe	2000	29.8
	2010	32.3

Source: Adapted by the authors from World Bank (2017a), *World Development Indicators* database.

Table 4.6. **Poverty rates in Central Africa (national thresholds)**

Country	Year	Rate
Burundi	2006	67.1
	2014	64.6
Cameroon	2001	40.2
	2007	39.9
	2014	37.5
Central African Republic	2008	62
Chad	2002	54.8
	2011	46.7
Congo	2004	69.3
	2011	46.5
DRC	2004	69.3
	2012	63.9
Equatorial Guinea	2006	76.8
Gabon	2005	32.7
Sao Tome and Principe	2000	68.3
	2010	66.2

Source: Adapted by the authors from World Bank (2017a), *World Development Indicators* database.

Once again, these statistics must be interpreted with caution given the inconsistency of the studies carried out. The fight against poverty and inequalities begins with a precise assessment of the situation. But little current data are available, which decreases the reliability of existing statistics. Administrative systems extending to the far reaches of each country and that enable the systematic collection of basic data on the population (for example, the birth certificate for each child) remain to be established.

Income inequality is reinforced by inequality of opportunity (Table 4.7). Despite progress achieved in terms of access to basic services, education and healthcare in all countries, and notably Gabon, the region could improve further. The rate of primary school enrolment (68%) is good, despite a low rate of secondary school enrolment (25%), and could attract further commitment. Since 1999, the infant mortality rate has been approximately halved in almost all countries, except for Chad and DRC. Rural areas remain underprivileged, as the example of Cameroon shows, where 86% of citizens have access to electricity, compared with just 22% in rural areas. In addition, access to Internet is low, 10% of the population, worse than in the rest of the continent, 24% (Annex 4.A2).

Table 4.7. **Inequalities of opportunity in the countries of Central Africa, 1999-2015**

	Burundi	Cameroon	Central African Republic	Chad	Congo	DRC	Equatorial Guinea	Gabon	Sao Tome and Principe	Central Africa
Education indicators										
Primary school enrolment rate	71.3	87.9	60.4	58.5	35.8	72.8	60.5	-	94.1	**67.1**
Secondary school enrolment rate	19.4	41.6	12.7	8.6	-	-	22.7	-	41.1	**25.3**
Girls enrolment share in primary	69.2	85.4	51.5	48.2	34.4	73.8	58.3	-	92.9	**63.5**
Girls enrolment share in secondary	18.5	38.8	9.0	4.3	-	-	15.4	-	43.4	**22.2**
Health indicators										
Infant mortality rate (‰)	70.3	76.7	103.5	88.9	90.2	53.7	85.6	45.0	39.3	**72.9**
Life expectancy at birth	53.8	53.7	46.7	49.3	54.7	57.2	55.0	61.6	65.0	**55.4**
Decent standards of living indicators (percentage of the population)										
Access to electricity	5.1	49.2	9.2	5.2	10.7	35.3	63.7	81.6	57.1	**39.0**
Access to basic services, sanitation	46.2	39.2	20.8	9.7	21.0	13.8	77.0	40.0	30.4	**31.5**
Access to basic services, water	54.2	60.4	73.4	40.7	62.1	38.1	49.1	83.7	53.2	**57.6**
Technological indicators (per 100 people)										
Access to fixed line telephone	0.3	2.0	0.1	0.2	0.0	0.4	1.6	2.1	4.1	**1.3**
Access to mobile telephone	13	32	13	17	10	53	33	85	34	**35.7**

Note: Access to technology indicators were taken as averages for the 2010-15 period, to better reflect reality. These indicators were almost 0 in the 1990s and rose rapidly in the 2000s.
Source: Adapted by the authors from World Bank (2017a), *World Development Indicators* database.

Since 2000, gender inequality has declined (Figure 4.12), particularly in the labour market, although progress remains to be made in terms of health, education, labour market participation and political representation.

Figure 4.12. **Evolution of gender inequality index in Central Africa (percentage)**

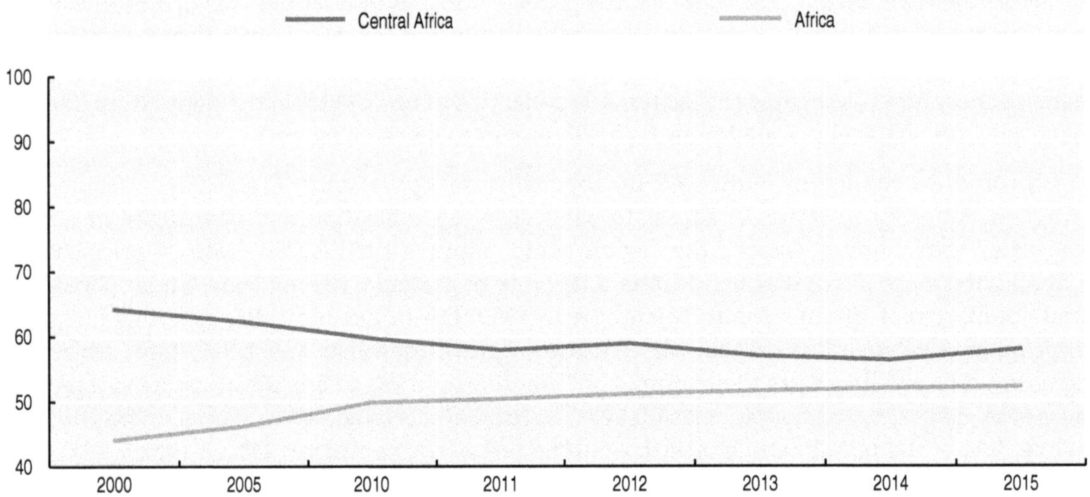

Source: Authors' calculations based on UNDP (2016), *Human Development Report* database.
StatLink http://dx.doi.org/10.1787/888933783475

The number of teenage pregnancies and the rate of maternal mortality fell throughout the region (Figure 4.13) thanks to urban migration and the higher level of education for girls (UNICEF, 2015), but they remain too high.

Figure 4.13. **Maternal mortality and teenage birth rates in Central Africa**

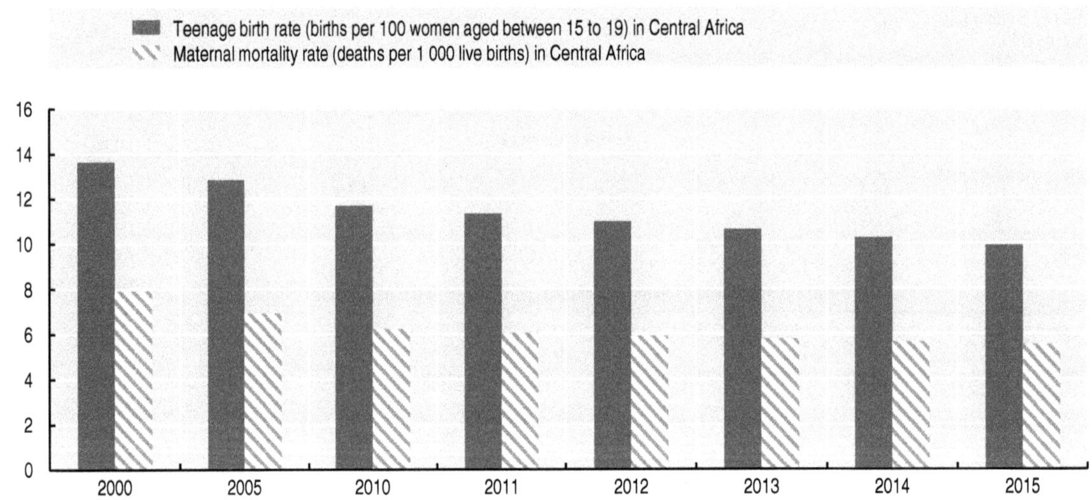

Source: Authors' calculations based on UNDP (2016), *Human Development Report* database.
StatLink http://dx.doi.org/10.1787/888933783494

In terms of education, the countries must continue their efforts to promote female access to education. Everywhere the share of men over 25 years with a minimum of secondary level education is higher than that of women, except in Gabon (Figure 4.14). In Burundi and Chad, less than 10% of men have higher level education, versus 5.6% and 1.7% of women, respectively.

Figure 4.14. **Average school enrolment rates by gender (average 2000-15)**

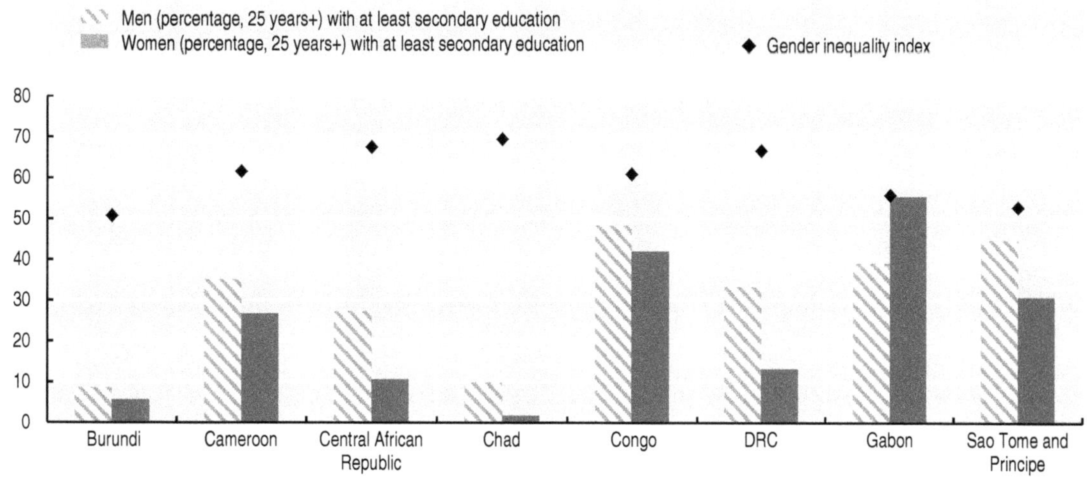

Note: Incomplete data for Equatorial Guinea.

Source: Authors' calculations based on UNDP (2016), *Human Development Report* database.

StatLink http://dx.doi.org/10.1787/888933783513

The labour market appears less unequal than in the rest of the continent (Figure 4.15). Apart from Gabon and Sao Tome and Principe, all the countries of the region have female employment rates that are above the African average. In addition, the agricultural sector employs marginally more women than men, demonstrating that women succeed in becoming engaged in food-producing economic activities. These activities provide low value-added jobs that are more flexible, which facilitates female integration into the labour force.

However, the gender pay gap has not materially diminished since 2000 (Figure 4.16). Burundi has the lowest gap, with women earning on average 84% as much as men, compared with less than 50% in Sao Tome and Principe and around 66% (two thirds) in Cameroon, the Central African Republic, Chad, Equatorial Guinea and Gabon.

Figure 4.15. **Female/male employment rates by sector (average over 2000-15 period, percentage)**

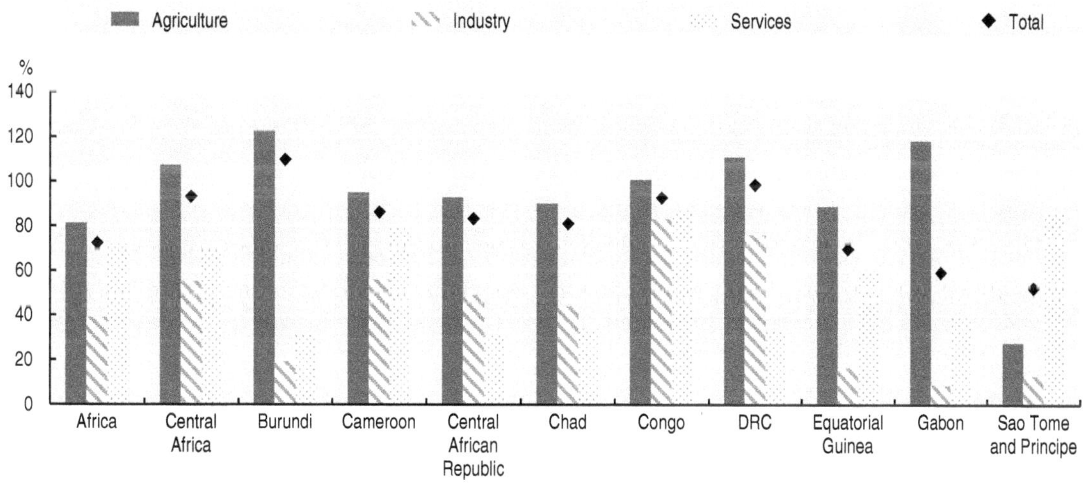

Source: Authors' calculations based on ILO (2018), *ILOStat* database.

StatLink http://dx.doi.org/10.1787/888933783532

Figure 4.16. **Male/female income inequality (average over 2000-15 period)**

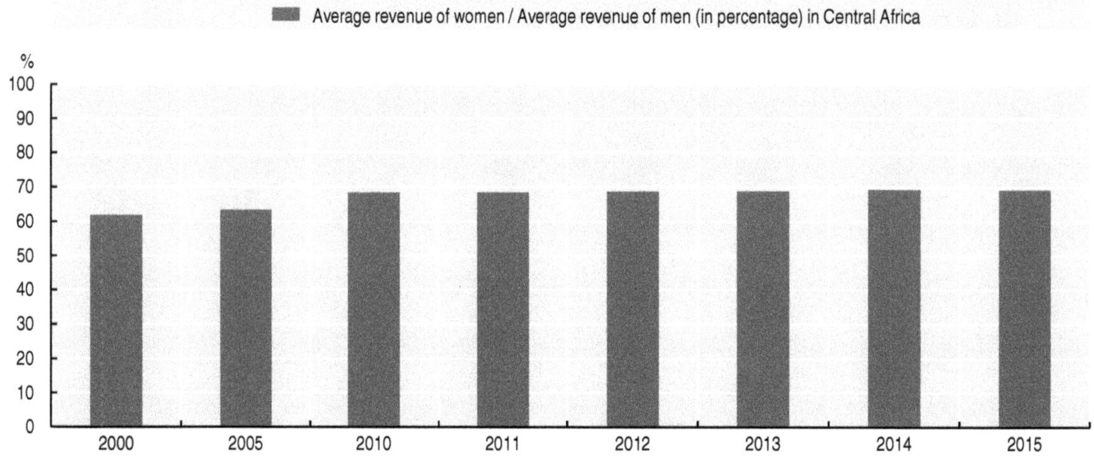

Source: Authors' calculations based on UNDP (2016), *Human Development Report* database.
StatLink http://dx.doi.org/10.1787/888933783551

Women are very poorly represented in institutions of power (Figure 4.17). The country that has made the most effort on this front remains Burundi, where almost one third of Parliamentary delegates are women, a level three times that of the Central African Republic (11%).

Figure 4.17. **Female representatives in Parliament (average 2000-15)**

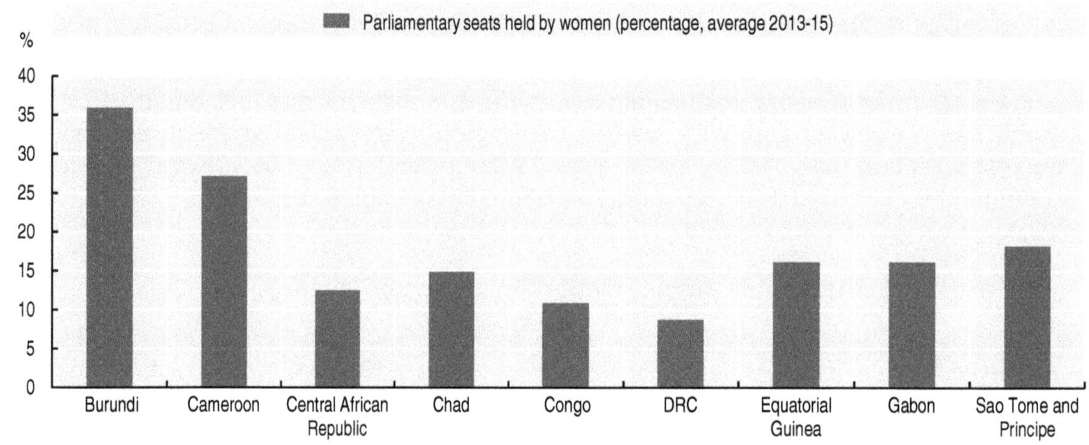

Source: Authors' calculations based on UNDP (2016), *Human Development Report* database.
StatLink http://dx.doi.org/10.1787/888933783570

Productivity gains in the extractive sector have not reduced income inequality

Central Africa has not managed to maintain inclusive and sustainable growth. Redistribution policies have not succeeded in capitalising on the growth at the start of the 2000s. Also, inequalities have stalled, or even increased in Burundi, Cameroon, the Central African Republic and Chad.

Economic growth has been driven by an industrial sector that fails to create jobs and generates inequality. In effect, inequalities fell in those African countries where growth is driven by progress in modern agriculture, the service sector or highly labour-intensive industrial production (UNDP, 2017). But, the industrial sector in Central Africa depends on mining and oil, which are both capital intensive.

In maintaining diversification efforts, Cameroon has succeeded in lowering the poverty rate. With the fall in oil prices at the start of the 1990s, Cameroon's dependence on primary products triggered an economic recession. To build the foundations of a resilient economy, the government encouraged investment in services and agriculture. Productivity gains in the agricultural sector and job creation in services caused a reduction in the poverty rate, from 29% in 2007 to 24% in 2014.

In countries dependent on natural resources, inequalities are reinforced by institutional instability. The exploitation of these resources weakens the governance of certain countries such as DRC. Conversely, weak institutions increase dependence on natural resources. Yet, the extractive sector, which is highly capital intensive, is an incentive for state monopolies or oligopolies. The small number of operators with the financial means to invest lets them benefit from rents and informal institutional protection (UNDP, 2017).

Figure 4.18. **Economic growth and income inequality (2000-15)**

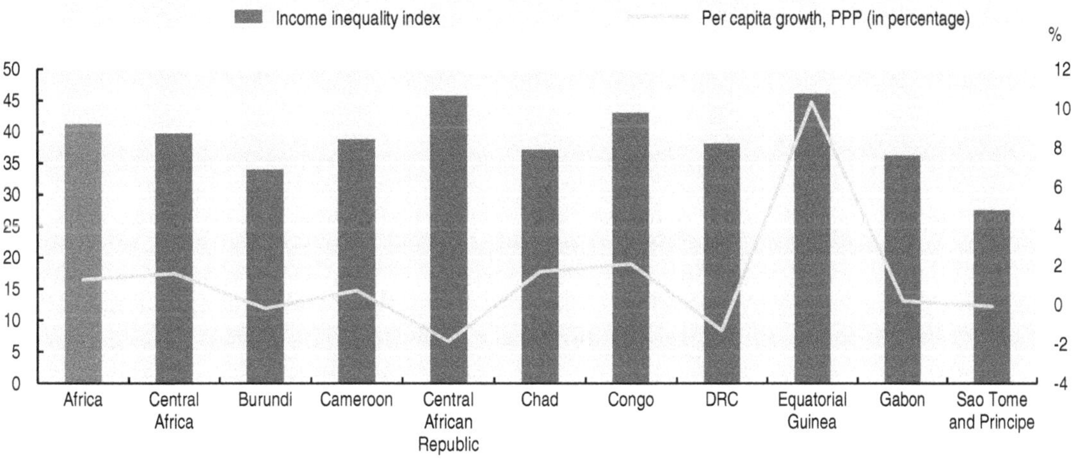

Source: Authors' calculations based on UNDP (2016), *Human Development Report* database.
StatLink http://dx.doi.org/10.1787/888933783589

Policy recommendations

Addressing the challenges of the region involves supporting structural transformation that increases economic capacity and resists the distortions associated with the domination of the extractive sector. The manufacturing, services and agricultural sectors could create jobs and make economic growth more sustainable over the long term. This section proposes measures aimed at bolstering and diversifying activity, and reducing unemployment and inequalities in the region. Specific and detailed policies should be tailored to the specific needs of each country.

Promote more diversified, productive and job-creating growth

By focusing on the management of natural resources and the business environment, a well-designed policy of raw material transformation could increase the value of exports and create jobs in industry, notably agro-food. First, trade policies could lift financial and material barriers for small and medium-size enterprises (SMEs) seeking to invest in secondary processing inputs. Secondly, policies should promote investment in electricity, transport and agro-food research infrastructure. Furthermore, the countries should invest in training labour qualified for jobs in construction and maintenance of processing machinery. The goal once again is to set up the conditions necessary for local transformation of raw materials. As such, it will be possible to avoid a situation like in

Gabon when the decision to ban exports of lumber (cut but not squared timber) resulted in high costs for companies. They had to adapt their production to transform wood, while coping with a low-skilled workforce (AfDB/OECD/UNDP/UNECA, 2013).

To be effective, these policies must incorporate the social and environmental challenges linked to the exploitation of natural resources (oil and minerals). The sector's actors, both nationally and internationally, should collectively define the conditions on which extractive activities will remain beneficial to the region's economy. To channel the negative externalities of the exploitation of raw materials, governments, companies, industries and representatives of civil society all have a role to play in the sustainable management of these resources (OECD, 2016a). With a high level of engagement of OECD members since 2010, 11 African members of the International Conference of the Great Lakes Region (ICGLR), industry, civil society, as well as UN experts on the DRC, the OECD drew up a practical guide on the due diligence of responsible supply chains in minerals from conflict or high risk zones. This guide sets out norms to be respected and evaluation tools aimed at helping extractive industry companies respect human rights (OECD, 2018). In DRC, this engagement has already resulted in a fall in conflict financing by the mining of minerals including tin, tantalum and tungsten, to name but a few (OECD, 2015).

In agriculture, policies should boost the sector's productivity, which remains low. In Cameroon and DRC, agriculture has become more productive thanks to public programmes to upgrade and develop infrastructure (AfDB/OECD/UNDP, 2017).

However, agricultural production policies should also reconcile the need to create jobs in rural areas as well as in medium-sized towns, as the agricultural sector employs more than 70% of the region's workforce. Creating non-agricultural rural employment is a priority in some countries such as Burundi where between 1989 and 2015 demographic pressure has divided by one and a half times the area of agricultural land available per inhabitant. This is thus estimated at 0.12 hectares in 2015 (World Bank data, 2017a). Developing the agro-food, logistics and distribution value chains more could create numerous jobs whilst facilitating the growth of more productive activities. DRC, for example, began to create agro-industrial parks focusing on cassava, palm oil, processed fruit and fisheries products.

Facilitating the business environment should be a priority for attracting investment and enabling the private sector to develop. Countries could improve governance and transparency, for example by reducing corruption and bureaucracy. These are measures for which Central Africa remains far behind other African regions (IIAG, 2017). To improve the quality of institutions, governments could establish agencies to promote investment by guaranteeing transparency, reducing procedures – if necessary via points of single contact – and by consulting the private sector to respond to its needs and attract investors.

Prioritise infrastructure investment

Despite its great need, the region invests the least in infrastructure per inhabitant in Africa. In 2016, just USD 6.3 billion – or 2% of regional GDP – was used to finance projects. This is two times lower than elsewhere in Africa (ICA, 2017).

Increasing electricity production remains imperative. Paradoxically, the energy sector in the region is the least developed in Africa, despite the ECCAS countries having a potential that corresponds with 60% of that of the entire continent (AfDB, 2011). The Grand Inga dam project on the Congo River in DRC will have a 40 GW capacity (AfDB/OECD/UNDP, 2016). However, the absence of co-operation between public enterprises dramatically curbs intra-African energy exchanges and affects the reliability of supply (AfDB/OECD/UNDP, 2015).

Public-private partnerships (PPP) to finance infrastructure could be broadly improved. Most projects with private participation are found outside Central Africa, due to the smaller size of these markets and a weak institutional framework. In 2016, only 6.2% of infrastructure financing for the region came from the private sector (ICA, 2017). For example, the Egis Group and the Republic of Congo invested in three airports in the country, including Maya-Maya airport in Brazzaville. However, these partnerships must guarantee transparency, in particular in the granting of contracts by public actors and in cost management by operators throughout the life of the contract. Ground rules consist of retaining as much simplicity in contracts, avoiding unconditional commitment clauses and carrying out realistic projections of revenue expected by the partnership.

At the inter-regional level, several opportunities exist in the transport sector. The region could invest in an electric cross border rail network, such as the Eastern African Railway Masterplan (EAM) which should connect Burundi, Kenya, Tanzania, Rwanda and Uganda. Since 1999, the International Commission of the Congo-Oubangui-Sangha Basin (CICOS), created by Congo and DRC, has been promoting sustainable use of water (AfDB/OECD/UNDP, 2015). Its role could include better regulation of trade via river transportation, as this method of transport is the most polluting after road transport. Monitoring the application of better regulations could protect the ecosystems of Central Africa.

Include regional integration in economic policy

The ECCAS free trade agreement should be introduced as part of a coherent regional economic policy. Without the two regional organisations of CEMAC and ECCAS, Central Africa has the lowest rate of internal trade of all regional African communities (De Melo, Nouar and Solleder, 2017). However, the states are furthering integration efforts. In October 2017, they all ratified a free movement of people agreement. Before the end of 2018, it is envisaged that the citizens of CEMAC member states will be able to travel effectively visa-free for up to three months. The liberalisation of regional trade should increase trade flows by 15% (Djemmo Fotso, 2014). Given the lack of complementarity of goods produced in the region, ECCAS countries should support trade liberalisation by co-ordinating their industrial plans. Regional integration has been boosted by the signing of the Continental Free Trade Area agreement in March 2018.

Monetary policy could help countries to better withstand the market distortions produced by the predominance of the extractive industries. Following the 2007-08 crisis, the fixity of the exchange rate and the guarantee of convertibility have reduced speculation around the XAF. The CEMAC countries have a stable inflation rate of below 3%, but it is important to maintain room for manoeuvre in case of shocks associated with prices of raw materials. The Bank of Central African States (BEAC) should be able to strengthen its balance sheet, particularly by building up foreign exchange reserves, which suffered due to the collapse in oil prices (IMF, 2016).

The countries could facilitate regional trade by harmonising both quality standards and the productive capacities of the private sector. Burundi and Equatorial Guinea could rejoin the Quality Infrastructure Programme for Central Africa (PIQAC), a shared public-private action plan to develop rules and quality-control systems to attain international standards.

Improve tax revenue mobilisation

This priority for all Africa turns out to be particularly important in Central Africa. Except for Cameroon, the countries of the region remain highly dependent on official development assistance (ODA) and revenue from natural resource extraction. In 2015, ODA represented XAF 1 200 billion while public receipts from oil production contributed XAF 78 billion (OECD/ATAF/AUC, 2017).

It is essential to redirect income from natural resources while reducing dependence on them. A redistribution of wealth could serve to finance priority investments better in the region and to reduce inequality. Sound financial management could also reduce the impact of price volatility of raw materials. A fund to accrue revenue could enable the adoption of counter-cyclical policies during periods of macroeconomic shock or simply better redistribution. Gabon and Equatorial Guinea have thus had sovereign wealth funds since 1998 and 2002, respectively.

Fiscal discipline policies, necessary as they are, should not impede the consumption potential of households. Since 2016, Chad has implemented a restrictive policy to reduce the structural public deficit, particularly by reducing public sector spending. Also, crucial fiscal stabilisation should not take place at the expense of middle class vectors. In 2018, spending reached XAF 1 343 billion while receipts reached XAF 846 billion.

Countries should continue to optimise the tax structure to increase public revenue minimising costs for the population. This entails effective tax reforms that eliminate taxes and allowances that are no longer justified. Fiscal reforms should avoid over dependence on a single type of tax, and their regressive effects could assist underprivileged parts of the population.

These measures could help countries better collect economic data. Thus, most fiscal revenues from consumption taxes have risen in Cameroon and DRC since 2000 (OECD/ATAF/AUC, 2017). The countries in the region could also follow the example of the Small and Medium Taxpayers Office (SMTO) in Rwanda, which has permitted informal businesses to register and has simplified the registration process. This reform has made it possible to increase the tax compliance rate to 97% (OECD/ATAF/AUC, 2017).

Primary and secondary schooling is vital for boosting growth

An ambitious education policy for Central Africa could entail mandatory schooling to the age of 16. In DRC for example, the 2016-25 sectoral strategy on education and training (*Stratégie sectorielle de l'éducation et de la formation*, SSEF) provides for mandatory schooling to increase to eight years. While the secondary school completion rate has improved in Central Africa, gender disparities are strong. In 2005, 13% of girls and 17% of boys finished secondary school. This increased to 35% for girls and 45% for boys in 2014.

The gender gap in education must be reduced, particularly in secondary schooling. Throughout this level of education, girls achieve parity with boys in just one country: Sao Tome and Principe. The lowest rates of secondary school enrolment are in the Central African Republic (51%), DRC (59%) and Chad (46%) (UNESCO, 2015). Policies could encourage families to educate young girls. Gender issues could also be incorporated into the training curriculum of teachers. Hiring more female teachers and evaluating student performance along gender are other potential tools.

Reduce gender inequality

Achieving the African Union (AU) Agenda 2063 goals entails the promotion of gender parity at all levels and in all domains. All the more as this agenda aspires to: "an Africa whose development is people-driven, relying on the potential of African people, especially its women and youth, and caring for children."

Women's empowerment policies remain to be implemented. Countries could adopt legislation penalising businesses for wage discrimination for equal work and discouraging income disparities between traditionally female and male occupations, encouraging individuals to work where his or her gender is a minority. Equally, governments could encourage women's access to financial services and property (OECD, 2016b).

Reducing child marriage and pregnancy requires better protection of young women. Teenage marriage remains a common problem throughout the region, with a minimum of 10% of youth married before the age of majority in Burundi and a maximum of 45% in Chad (OECD, 2014). Health policies focused on contraception and increased education could yield results (Odejimi and Bellingham-Young, 2014).

Figure 4.19. **Gender inequality in Africa**

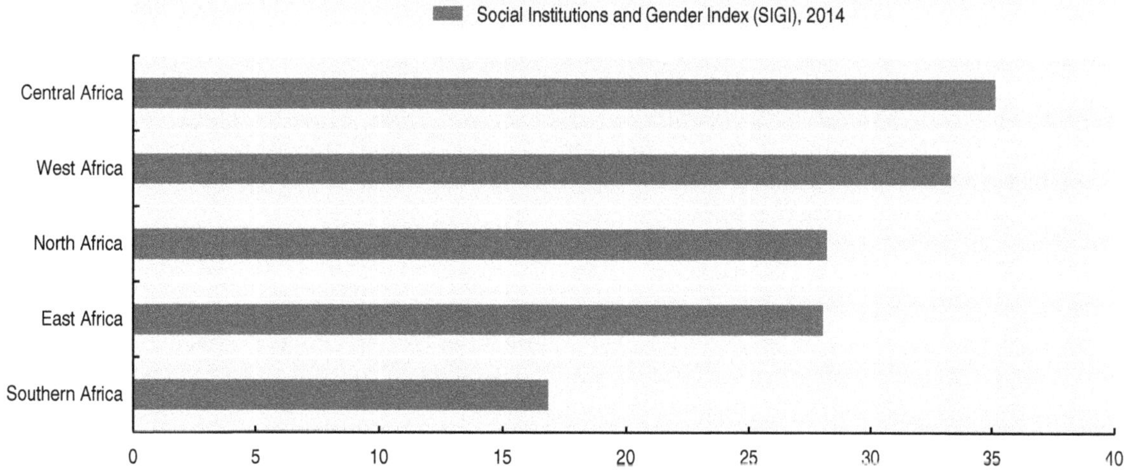

Note: The SIGI ranges from 0, for very low discrimination to 100 for very high discrimination. Higher SIGI values indicate higher inequality.

Source: OECD (2016b), Gender, Institutions and Development Database.

StatLink http://dx.doi.org/10.1787/888933783608

Introduce pro-poor growth policies

A pro-poor growth policy focused on rural areas is important. Aside from Gabon, no country in the region possesses a social safeguarding programme that targets at least some of the poorest families (World Bank, 2015). The countries could envisage:

- **Conducting surveys and censuses to update data available on the labour market as well as on inequalities of income, gender and opportunity.** These studies could be conducted through a partnership between national statistical institutions and international organisations.
- **Map out social security and poverty reduction policies in a coherent way, with the aim of implementing universal lifelong coverage.** For example, the new social security system in Gabon is comprised of four types of insurance: health, workplace accidents, family benefits and pensions.
- **Combine social security programmes,** public works to generate employment, assistance to non-active women and financial aid for childhood education.
- **Increase spending on health services and improve their quality.** Only Burundi and Sao Tome and Principe achieve spending levels on health that are above the average of Sub-Saharan Africa (7.5% and 8.4% of GDP, respectively, versus 5.5% for south of the Sahara). The Central African Republic, Equatorial Guinea, DRC and Chad have the highest rates of neonatal, infant and under-fives mortality south of the Sahara. In the Central African Republic and Chad, life expectancy is lower by 8.5 and 7.3 years than the average in Sub-Saharan Africa (59.9 years in 2015). Equally, health is one of the three major problems often cited by Cameroonians (AfDB/OECD/UNDP, 2017).
- **Devote public funding to social security programmes** to free them from dependence on international aid. Real systems of social protection also financed by domestic resources remain to be developed in the region.

Annex 4.A1. Methodological annex

Box 4.A1.1. Factoral contribution to growth: labour, capital and TFP

To examine the contribution of traditional factors of production to growth, we rely on a Cobb Douglas type function of production in which production Y is expressed as labour (L) and capital (K) as indicated in the equation below:

$$Y_{i,t}=A_{i,t}\, L^{\alpha}_{i,t}\, K^{\beta}_{i,t} \qquad (1)$$

where i (i = 1, ..., N) denotes the country, and t (t = 1, ..., T) time. $A_{i,t}$ is the total factor productivity (TFP). By linearising this function by a logarithmic transformation, we obtain the below equation which enables us to calculate the sensitivity of production to the variation of each factor of production.

$$y_{i,t}=\delta+\alpha l_{i,t}+\beta k_{i,t}+\varepsilon_{i,t} \qquad (2)$$

$Y_{i,t}=(ogap_{i,t},\ CA\_gap_{i,t},\ mis_{i,t})' y_{i,t}=ln(Y_{i,t}),\ \delta=ln(A_{i,t})$. In effect, we are making the reasonable hypothesis that total factor productivity is comparable between countries and does not vary in time as it depends on institutional and organisational factors that are comparable and relatively stable in time. α is the elasticity of the production of labour and β is the elasticity of production of capital. Here we impose no limits on these parameters; which leaves us the possibility of decreasing, constant or increasing returns to scale. Lastly, to examine the short-term effects of factors of production on economic growth, we consider equation (2) in variation, that is, in first difference as follows:

$$\Delta y_{i,t}=\delta+\alpha\Delta l_{i,t}+\beta\Delta k_{i,t}+\varepsilon_{i,t} \qquad (3)$$

Box 4.A1.2. Modelling the *Vector Auto Regressive in Panel* (PVAR) to estimate the relationship between the labour market and economic growth

Combining a traditional VAR approach (Sims, 1980) with panel data econometrics, the panel VAR model (PVAR) is particularly suited for analysing interactions between macroeconomic variables. In effect, the impulse response functions (IRF) inferred from the PVAR valuation are very useful for analysing how growth and labour interact. The reduced-form PVAR model is established as:

$$X_{i,t}=\alpha_i+\Gamma(L)\, X_{i,t}+\varepsilon_{i,t} \qquad (1)$$

where i (i = 1, ..., N) denotes the country, and t (t = 1, ..., T) time. $X_{i,t}$ is the vector of endogenous stationary variables, $\Gamma(L)$ represents the matrix polynomial in the operator of delay L, α_i denotes the vector of country fixed effects and $\varepsilon_{i,t}$ is an error vector. The vector $X_{i,t}$ is comprised here of our two macroeconomic variables – the variations (or cycles) of real GDP per inhabitant in PPA (varPIB) and the variation of labour from its long-term trend (varemploi):

$$X_{i,t}=(varPIB_{i,t},varemploi_{i,t})' \quad (2) Y_{i,t}=(ogap_{i,t},CA\_gap_{i,t},mis_{i,t})'$$

Box 4.A1.2. **Modelling the *Vector Auto Regressive in Panel* (PVAR) to estimate the relationship between the labour market and economic growth** *(cont.)*

From a methodological point of view, the application of the VAR process on panel data necessitates imposing the same underlying structure for each transversal unit (country); a constraint that could be violated in practice (see Love and Zicchino, 2006). The fixed effects by country introduced in equation (1) are a mean of overcoming the restriction on the parameters to the extent they capture individual heterogeneity. It is nevertheless well known that the use of an estimator of fixed effects in autoregressive panel data models is not appropriate, fixed effects being correlated with regressors due to deviations of the dependent variable (Nickell, 1981). To overcome this problem, we consider the generalised method of moments (GMM). More specifically, to suppress fixed effects, we use the differentiation procedure known as the Helmert procedure as in Love and Zicchino (2006) among others. This transformation preserves orthogonality between transformed variables and delayed regressors, which enables us to use delayed regressors as tools and to estimate the coefficients of the GMM procedure. Once coefficients are estimated, we calculate the IFR using the Cholesky decomposition.

The VAR approach has several advantages. It enables the analysis of the relationship between growth and labour without a priori postulating a direction to the causality. This leaves the possibility that growth could be explained by labour and conversely. In addition to the advantages of traditional VAR models, the panel VAR method makes it possible to collect a number of larger observations necessary for reliable results. This is particularly important in the context of this study given the limited time dimension of variables by country.

Annex 4.A2. Central Africa's statistical annex

Figure 4.A2.1. **Average employment by gender, 2000-15 (percentage)**

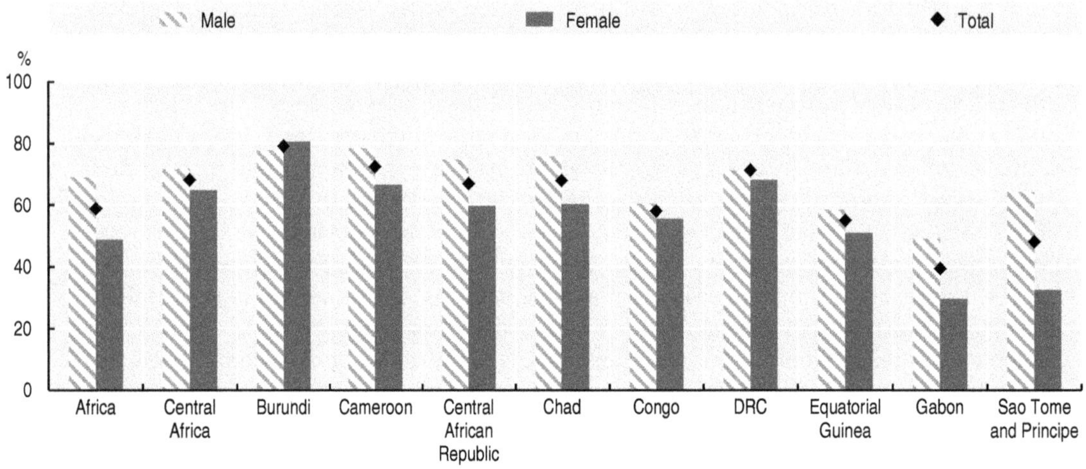

Source: Authors' calculations based on ILO (2017), *ILOStat*.
StatLink http://dx.doi.org/10.1787/888933783627

Figure 4.A2.2. **Internet penetration rates in Central Africa (percentage of the population), in 2016**

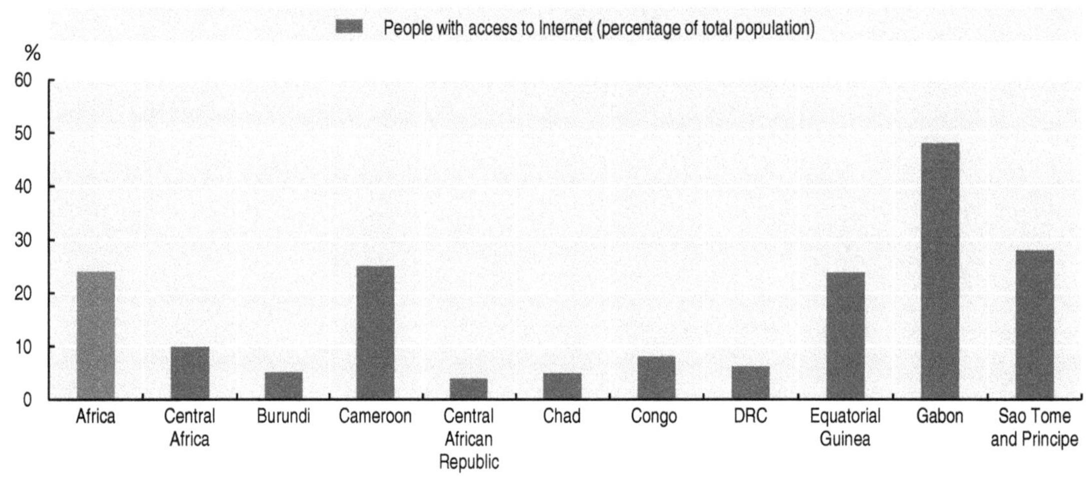

Source: Authors' calculations based on UNDESA (2017) and ITU (2016) databases.
StatLink http://dx.doi.org/10.1787/888933783646

References

AfDB (2011), "Central Africa", *Regional Integration Strategy Paper* (RISP) 2011-15, African Development Bank, Abidjan, https://www.afdb.org/fileadmin/uploads/afdb/Documents/Policy-Documents/RISP%20CENTRAL%20AFRICA-ECCAS%20English%20FINAL.pdf.

AfDB/OECD/UNDP (2017), *African Economic Outlook 2017: Entrepreneurship and* Industrialisation, OECD Publishing, Paris, http://dx.doi.org/10.1787/aeo-2017-en.

AfDB/OECD/UNDP (2016), *African Economic Outlook 2016: Sustainable Cities and Structural Transformation*, OECD Publishing, Paris, http://dx.doi.org/10.1787/aeo-2016-en.

AfDB/OECD/UNDP (2015), *African Economic Outlook 2015: Regional Development and Spatial Inclusion*, OECD Publishing, Paris, http://dx.doi.org/10.1787/aeo-2015-en.

AfDB/OECD/UNDP/UNECA (2013), *African Economic Outlook 2013: Structural Transformation and Natural Resources*, OECD Publishing, Paris, http://dx.doi.org/10.1787/aeo-2013-en.

Barro, R. (2000), "Inequality and growth in a panel of countries", *Journal of Economic Growth*, Vol. 5(1), pp. 5–32.

Barro R.J. (1991), "Economic growth in a cross-section of countries", *Quarterly Journal of Economics*, vol. 106(2), pp. 407-443.

De Melo, J., M. Nouar and J-M. Solleder (2017), "Integration along the Abuja road map", *FERDI Working Paper* n° 191, July 2017, www.ferdi.fr/fr/node/3850.

Djemmo Fotso, A. (2014), "The potential effects of the ECCAS free trade area on trade flows", *MPRA Paper*, n° 59863, https://mpra.ub.uni-muenchen.de/59863/.

GGDC/UC Davis (2017), *Penn World Table 9.0*, Groningen Growth and Development Centre, https://www.rug.nl/ggdc/productivity/pwt/ (database consulted January 2018).

Hugon, P. (2006), "Conflits armés, insécurité et trappes à pauvreté en Afrique", *Afrique contemporaine*, vol. 218(2), De Boeck Supérieur, pp. 33-47, doi:10.3917/afco.218.47.

ICA (2017), *Infrastructure Financing Trends in Africa – 2016*, Infrastructure Consortium for Africa, Abidjan.

IIAG (2017), *2017 Ibrahim Index of African Governance: Index Report*, Mo Ibrahim Foundation, London.

IMF (2018), *World Economic Outlook*, International Monetary Fund, Washington, DC, http://www.imf.org/external/pubs/ft/weo/2017/02/weodata/index.aspx, (database consulted April 2018).

IMF (2017a), *World Economic Outlook*, International Monetary Fund, Washington, DC, http://www.imf.org/external/pubs/ft/weo/2017/02/weodata/index.aspx, (database consulted January 2018).

IMF (2017b), *Regional Economic Outlook: Sub Saharan Africa – Restarting the growth engine*, International Monetary Fund, Washington, DC, http://www.imf.org/en/Publications/REO/SSA/Issues/2017/05/03/sreo0517

IMF (2016), *Central African Economic and Monetary Community (CEMAC) Common policies of member countries – Press release, staff report and statement by the executive director*, International Monetary Fund Country Report n°16/277, Washington, DC, https://www.imf.org/external/pubs/ft/scr/2016/cr16277.pdf.

ITU (2016), *Country ICT data* (database), International Telecommunication Union, https://www.itu.int/en/ITU-D/Statistics/Pages/stat/default.aspx

Odejimi, O. and D. Bellingham-Young (2014), "A policy pathway to reducing teenage pregnancy in Africa", *Journal of Human Growth and Development*, vol. 24(2), pp. 135-141, http://dx.doi.org/10.7322/jhgd.79915.

OECD (2018), *Alignment Assessment of Industry Programmes with the OECD Minerals Guidance*, OECD Publishing, Paris, http://mneguidelines.oecd.org/Alignment-assessment-of-industry-programmes-with-the-OECD-minerals-guidance.pdf

OECD (2016a), *Collaborative Strategies for In-Country Shared Value Creation: Framework for Extractive Industries*, OECD Development Policy Tools, OECD Publishing, Paris, http://dx.doi.org/10.1787/9789264257702-en

OECD (2016b), *Sub-Saharan Africa – The Social Institutions and Gender Index (SIGI) Regional Report*, OECD Publishing Paris, https://www.genderindex.org/.

OECD (2015), *Annual Report on the OECD Guidelines for Multinational Enterprises 2014: Responsible Business Conduct by Sector*, OECD Publishing, Paris, https://www.oecd-ilibrary.org/governance/annual-report-on-the-oecd-guidelines-for-multinational-enterprises_19990952.

OECD (2014), *Social Institutions and Gender*, https://data.oecd.org/inequality/social-institutions-and-gender.htm (database accessed January 2018).

OECD/ATAF/AUC (2017), *Revenue Statistics in Africa 2017*, OECD Publishing, Paris, http://dx.doi.org/10.1787/9789264280854-en-fr.

OECD/DAC (2017), *Global Aid Prospects and Projections*, http://www.oecd.org/dac/financing-sustainable-development/global-aid-prospects-and-projections.htm (database consulted January 2018).

UNCOMTRADE (2017), *United Nations Commodity Trade Statistics*, http://comtrade.un.org/db/ (database consulted January 2018).

UNCTAD (2017), *UNCTADstat*, United Nations Conference on Trade and Development, Geneva, http://unctadstat.unctad.org/wds/TableViewer/tableView.aspx?ReportId=95 (database consulted January 2018).

UNDESA (2017), *World Population Prospects: The 2017 Revision* (customised searches of the Internet site), Population Division, United Nations Department for Economic and Social Affairs, New York, NY.

UNDP (2017), *Income Inequality Trends in sub-Saharan Africa: Divergence, Determinants and Consequences*, United Nations Development Programme, Paris.

UNDP (2016), Human Development Report, http://hdr.undp.org/en/data (database consulted January 2018).

UNESCO (2015), *Education for All Global Monitoring Report 2015 - Regional Overview: Sub-Saharan Africa*, United Nations Educational, Scientific and Cultural Organisation, Paris.

UNHCR (2018), "CAR: Displacement reaches unprecedented levels in 2017", United Nations High Commission for Refugees (UNHCR), http://www.unhcr.org/uk/news/briefing/2018/1/5a6701184/car-displacement-reaches-unprecedented-levels-2017.html (consulted 28 March 2018).

UNHCR (2017), "UNHCR launches urgent appeal to help Burundian refugees", United Nations High Commission for Refugees (UNHCR), http://www.unhcr.org/fr/news/briefing/2018/1/5a672ae8a/rca-deplacements-populations-precedent-2017.html (consulted 28 March 2018).

UNICEF/ICRW (2015), *Child Marriage, Adolescent Pregnancy and Family Formation in West and Central Africa: Patterns, trends and drivers of change*, United Nations Children's Fund and International Center for Research on Women, Dakar.

World Bank (2018), *Doing Business: Reforming to Create Jobs*, World Bank, Washington, DC. http://www.doingbusiness.org/~/media/WBG/DoingBusiness/Documents/Annual-Reports/English/DB2018-Full-Report.pdf.

World Bank (2017a), *World Development Indicators* (database), https://datacatalog.worldbank.org/dataset/world-development-indicators.

World Bank (2017b), *Doing Business in OHADA 2017*, World Bank, Washington DC, http://www.doingbusiness.org/Reports/regional-reports/ohada.

World Bank (2015), *The State of Social Safety Nets 2015*, World Bank, Washington, DC. http://documents.worldbank.org/curated/en/415491467994645020/The-state-of-social-safety-nets-2015.

Chapter 5

Dynamics of growth, jobs and inequalities in East Africa

This chapter seeks to investigate the links between growth, employment and inequalities in East Africa (Comoros, Djibouti, Eritrea, Ethiopia, Kenya, Madagascar, Mauritius, Rwanda, Seychelles, Somalia, South Sudan, Sudan, Tanzania and Uganda). Specifically, the chapter analyses the evolution of economic growth, the drivers behind the growth process and the impact of growth on living standards of the people in the region. The chapter gives a comparative overview of the trends in economic growth, labour market outcomes and income inequality since the 1980s in East Africa.

The chapter is structured as follows. The first section provides key facts on East Africa. The second section gives an overview of the economic performance in the region. The third section focuses on the evolution of employment and unemployment outcomes. The fourth section analyses the main trends in poverty and income inequality. The final section provides policy recommendations.

IN BRIEF

Gross domestic product (GDP) has expanded at a fair pace in East Africa in recent years. However, economic growth is not translating into rapid structural transformation or job creation. Many East African countries have large and growing informal sectors, condemning many workers to low wages, lack of job security and limited opportunities to acquire skills. Rapid economic growth is not reducing poverty or income inequality at an equally rapid pace.

Since 1990, annual **growth** rates in the region have exceeded 4%. The services sector has grown to almost 60% of GDP, driven mostly by informal and non-tradable services, while industry has remained constant at 20% of GDP. GDP growth increasingly results from private consumption, while the role of public and private investment is diminishing. The region's trade is skewed towards primary commodity exports (52% of total exports) and imports of finished products (70% of total imports).

Despite agriculture's low productivity and declining contribution to GDP, it employs almost 60% of the labour force. The gender gap in **employment** (the ratio of male-to-female employment) has been decreasing slowly, from 1.41 in 1991 to 1.39 in 2017, with large disparities across sectors and countries. Growth has not increased the number of "good" jobs offering higher wages and better working conditions.

Income **inequality** varies across countries, but overall is on an upward trend. On average, only 37% of the population has access to electricity, 48% to drinking water and 20% to sanitation services, though large variations exist across countries and between urban and rural populations. Poverty remains high in the region at 35%, in spite of its decline since 1999. Several countries are addressing poverty by enhancing social protection programmes and by investing in education and skills development. Such investments will have to significantly increase for these programmes to deliver on their objective of supporting more inclusive development.

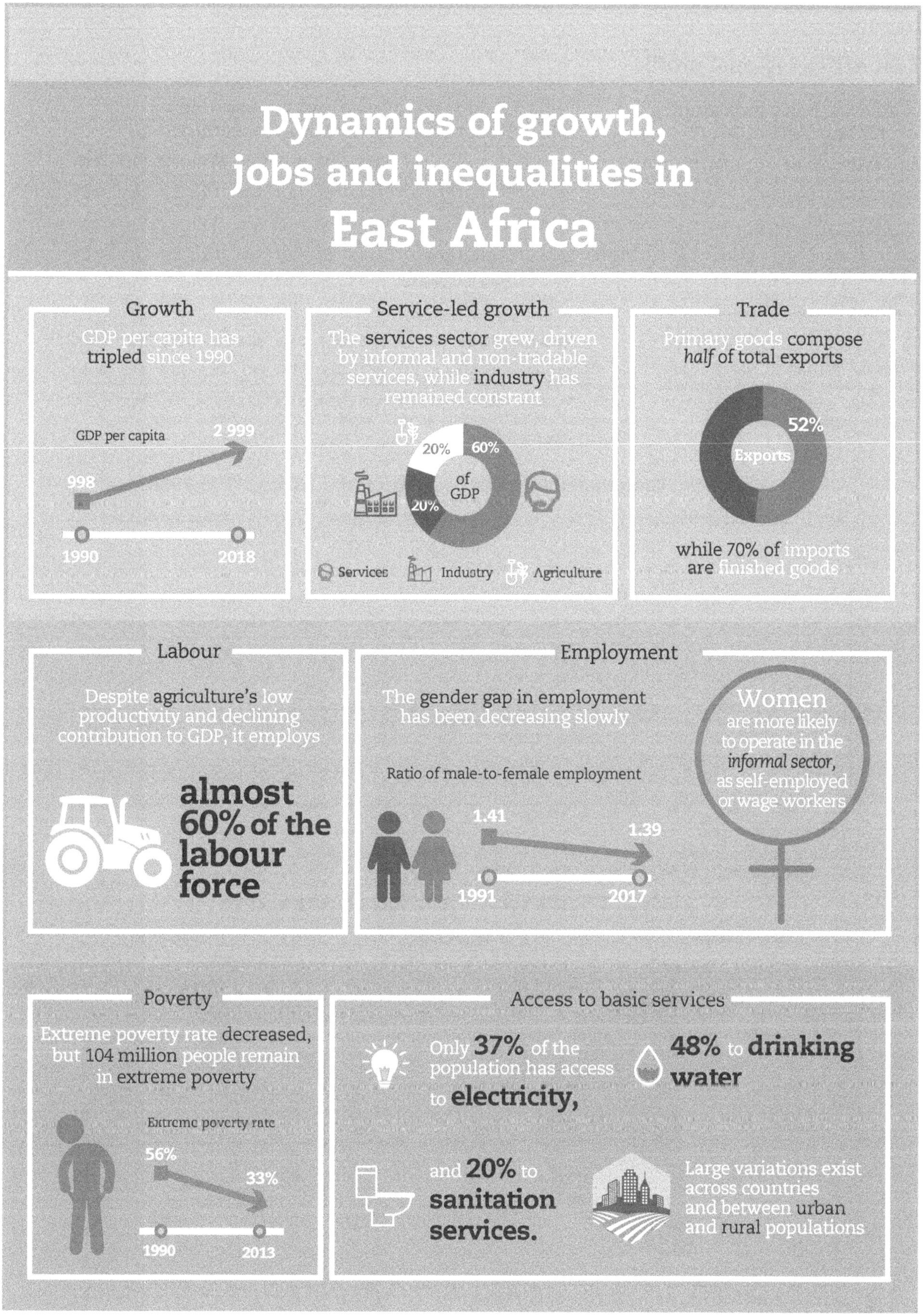
Dynamics of growth, jobs and inequalities in East Africa
Growth
GDP per capita has tripled since 1990
GDP per capita
998
2 999
1990
2018
Service-led growth
The services sector grew, driven by informal and non-tradable services, while industry has remained constant
20%
60%
of GDP
20%
Services
Industry
Agriculture
Trade
Primary goods compose half of total exports
52%
Exports
while 70% of imports are finished goods
Labour
Despite agriculture's low productivity and declining contribution to GDP, it employs
almost 60% of the labour force
Employment
The gender gap in employment has been decreasing slowly
Ratio of male-to-female employment
1.41
1.39
1991
2017
Women are more likely to operate in the informal sector, as self-employed or wage workers
Poverty
Extreme poverty rate decreased, but 104 million people remain in extreme poverty
Extreme poverty rate
56%
33%
1990
2013
Access to basic services
Only 37% of the population has access to electricity,
48% to drinking water
and 20% to sanitation services.
Large variations exist across countries and between urban and rural populations

East Africa regional profile

Table 5.1. **Basic indicators for East Africa, 2017**

Population (thousands)	368 661
Land area (thousands of km²)	6 394
Population density (people/km²)	58
GDP, current (USD billion)	947
GDP per capita, current (USD)	2 840

Source: Authors' calculations based on UNDESA (2017), *World Population Prospects* (database); World Bank (2017a), *World Development Indicators* (database) and IMF (2018), *World Economic Outlook Database*.

Table 5.2. **Financial flows and tax revenues to East Africa (current USD billion), 2009-16**

			2009	2010	2011	2012	2013	2014	2015	2016
Foreign	Private	Inward foreign direct investment	7.1	7.9	7.7	9.3	8.4	8.6	8.3	8.6
		Portfolio investments	0.0	7.6	5.7	2.5	1.1	4.7	0.0	-1.1
		Remittances	3.9	4.6	4.5	4.7	4.8	5.9	5.0	5.0
	Public	Official development assistance (net total, all donors)	15.4	14.3	15.5	15.8	18.4	16.5	15.9	16.0
Total foreign flows			**25.2**	**33.4**	**26.5**	**34.4**	**33.4**	**32.3**	**32.7**	**35.8**
Domestic tax revenues			**21.1**	**23.7**	**21.1**	**23.7**	**25.2**	**28.6**	**33.0**	**36.8**

Source: IMF (2018), *World Economic Outlook Database*, OECD (2018a), *International Development Statistics* (database), and World Bank (2017a), *World Development Indicators* (database).

Figure 5.1. **Growth dynamics in East Africa and Africa, 1990-2018**

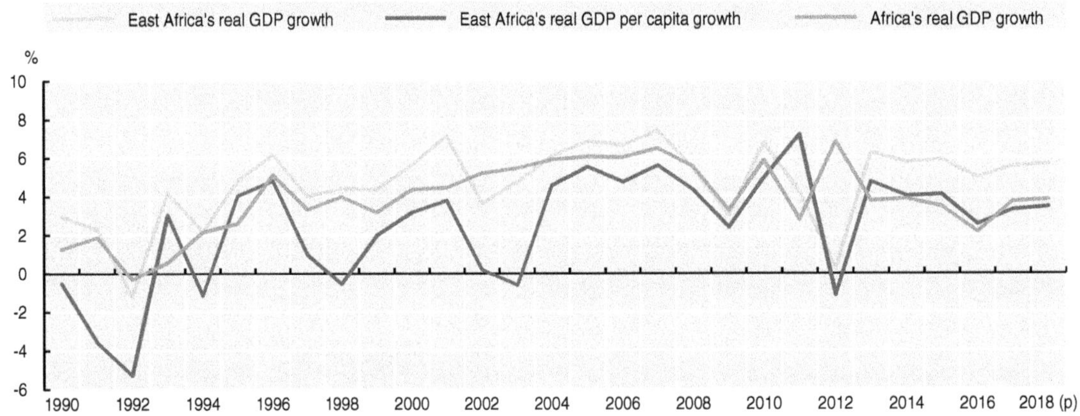

Note: (p) = projections.

Source: Authors' calculations based on IMF (2018), *World Economic Outlook Database*.

StatLink http://dx.doi.org/10.1787/888933783665

Figure 5.2. **Trade composition in East Africa, 2016**

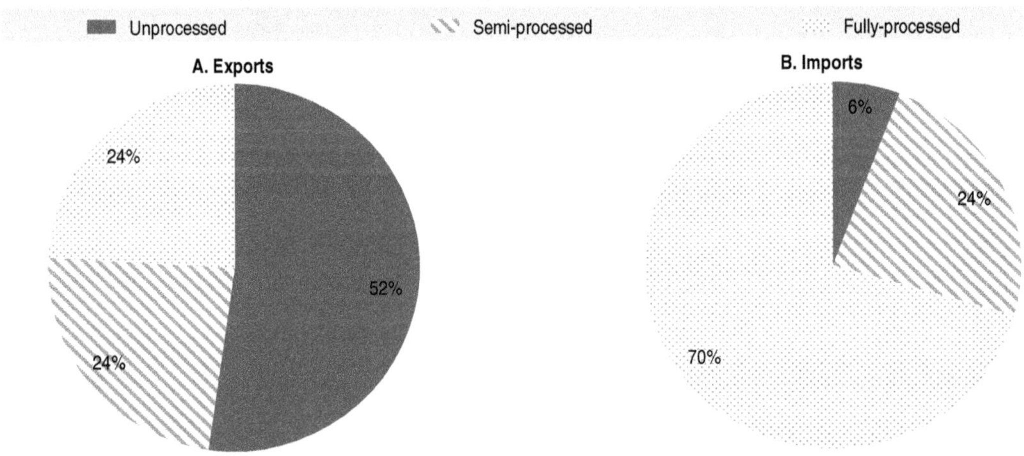

Source: Authors' calculations based on United Nations Statistics Division (2017), *UNCOMTRADE* (database).

StatLink http://dx.doi.org/10.1787/888933783684

According to the African Union grouping (under the Abuja Treaty, 1991), the East Africa region consists of 14 countries: Comoros, Djibouti, Eritrea, Ethiopia, Kenya, Madagascar, Mauritius, Rwanda, Seychelles, Somalia, South Sudan, Sudan, Tanzania and Uganda.[1]

East Africa covers a total land area of 6 394 000 km^2, which is about 22% of Africa's total land area. It has a population of 369 million people (about 29.3% of the continent's total population) and a population density of 58 people/km^2. The region's population growth has averaged 2.9% per annum since 1990. The median age for the region is 18 years old.

The region's GDP at purchasing power parity (PPP) is USD 947 billion in 2016. The GDP per capita is USD 2 840. Real GDP growth has averaged 4.8% over the years 1990-2018, compared to 3.9% for Africa.

Two decades of sustained economic growth in East Africa

Economic performance in the East Africa region during the past two decades has been strong. Since 1995, the region has enjoyed annual growth rates of over 4%, well above the continental average (Figure 5.1). The services sector makes up the largest share of GDP in all countries except Ethiopia, Tanzania and Uganda, where the size of agriculture remains substantial. Informal and non-tradable services account for most of the recent growth in services but have had a limited impact on the economy. Private consumption is increasingly driving economic expansion, while the role of investment is diminishing. The region's trade concentrates on primary commodity exports and imports of finished products, thus slowing growth. Finally, macroeconomic stability and inflationary pressures in the region depend largely on fuel and food price fluctuations, to which economies remain vulnerable.

The region's countries vary significantly in terms of growth performance and demographic dynamics. The early 1980s to the mid-1990s was a period characterised by low and volatile GDP growth. Since the mid-1990s, the region has experienced sustained growth rates and lower demographic growth, which translate into increases in per capita incomes.

Different sectors have underpinned the growth of the region's top performers. Ethiopia has contributed to regional growth mainly through increased government expenditure on infrastructure (roads and hydro-power). Since 1980, Rwanda has contributed to regional growth via agricultural production, particularly of commodities such as coffee and tea. While huge investments in the energy sector have driven Uganda's growth, investments in the services sector have raised Mauritius' growth rates. In addition to these top performers, other countries have increased the region's growth like Kenya (infrastructure investment and household consumption), Seychelles (tourism) and Tanzania (manufacturing and services).

Changing composition of East Africa economic growth

The overall sectoral composition of GDP across the region has changed little since 1980 (see Figure 5.3). Until recently, the contribution of agriculture to GDP had declined steadily, and that of the services sector had increased. On average, the contribution of agriculture to GDP is higher in the top performing countries. In the early 1980s and 1990s, agriculture was the largest contributor to growth. Since the mid-1990s, the economies of most countries have shifted to the services sector. While the contribution of the manufacturing sector has remained fairly stable, there have been slight gains in the contribution of total industry to GDP.

The increases in the shares of the services and industrial sectors to GDP appear to coincide with the macro-economic reform period for most of the countries in the region. Low productivity activities such as informal and non-tradable services largely explain this increasing role played by the services sector. Therefore, the increase in the share of this sector has not transformed the economy. Since the 2000s, several of the top performers in the region have experienced a reduction in the contribution of the industrial sector towards GDP. This coincides with the slowdown in the global economy.

The decline in the share of agriculture could translate into economy-wide gains in productivity. Agriculture tends to have lower value-added than other sectors (McMillan and Rodrik, 2011; Gollin et al., 2014). Moreover, income and consumption are lower in agriculture than in any other sector (McMillan and Verduzco, 2012; Gollin et al., 2014). Thus, as workers leave agriculture for other sectors, value-added, income and consumption should increase.

Figure 5.3. **Average sector value added as a percentage of GDP in East Africa, 1991-2016**

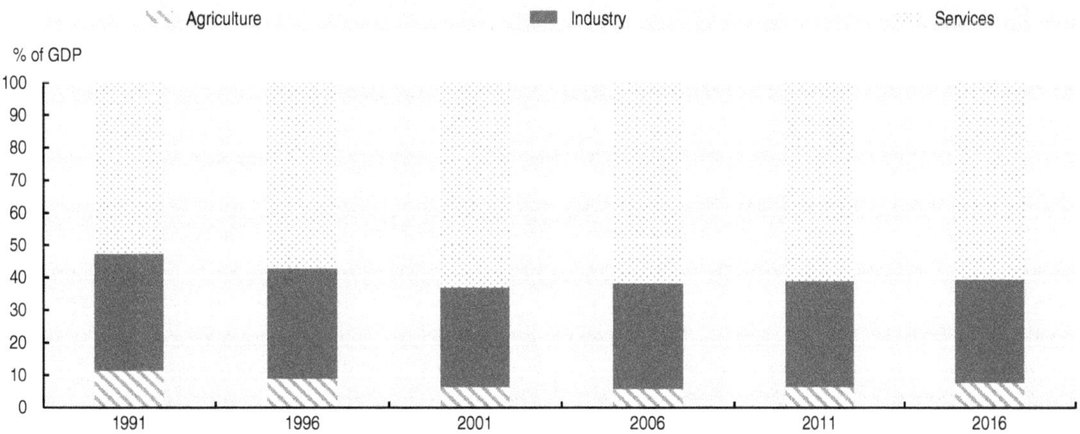

Source: Authors' calculations based on World Bank (2017a), *World Development Indicators* (database).
StatLink http://dx.doi.org/10.1787/888933783684

Services-led growth can take different forms. In Seychelles, tourism leads economic growth and the services sector, which accounts for approximately 80% of GDP. In recent years the government has encouraged foreign investment in order to upgrade hotels and other services. Djibouti, benefiting from its strategic location on the Red Sea, provides services as a transit port for the region and as an international trans-shipment and refuelling centre. Mauritius, on the other hand, has growing industrial, financial, information and communications technology (ICT) and tourist sectors. It developed from a low-income, agriculture-based economy (mainly sugarcane) to a middle-income diversified economy.

Factor contribution to growth in East Africa

Capital accumulation explains growth in the region more than gains in total factor productivity (TFP) (see Figure 5.4). In the early 1990s, decreasing TFP partly slowed East Africa's growth. In the mid-1990s, labour played a key role. However, since the late 1990s, capital has increasingly driven growth. Labour and TFP growth have posted minimal contributions to growth in GDP, with TFP growth also registering volatility over time.

Figure 5.4. **Decomposition of economic growth by factors of production in East Africa, 2009-15**

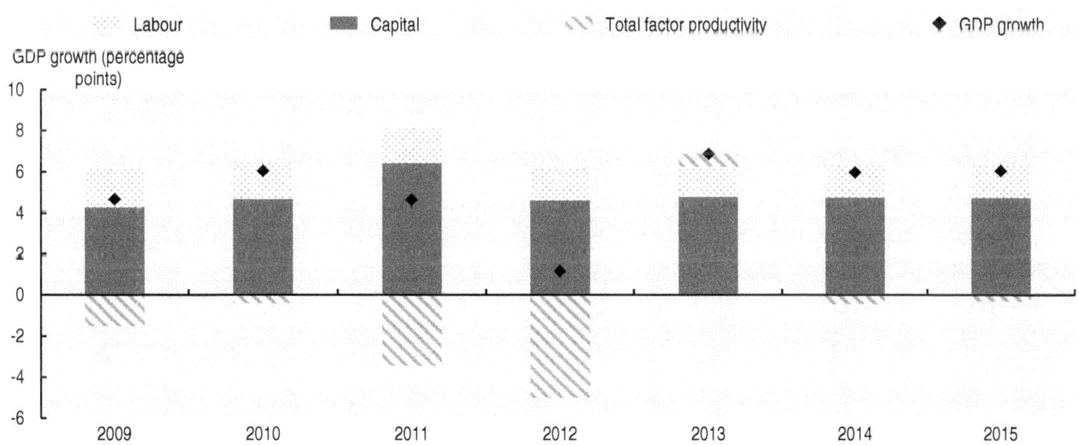

Source: Authors' calculations based on Conference Board (2017), *Total Economy Database.*
StatLink http://dx.doi.org/10.1787/888933783722

Recent drivers of East Africa economic growth

The strong economic growth performance in East Africa in the past decade was largely driven by increased investment and by private and public consumption. Exogenous drivers of growth, or those that are outside the control of individual countries, include the global price shocks and demand for commodities. Endogenous drivers include development strategies adopted by governments in the region, macroeconomic stability, investment, trade, and demographic and social factors. They will be briefly analysed below.

Investment in the region has been increasing since 2000. Investment rates in East Africa improved from 18.4% of GDP in 2000 to 25.6% in 2014. Countries that have managed to sustain increases in growth have also experienced steady increases in investment rates. Within the region, average investment is highest in Seychelles at 27.2% of GDP while it is lowest in Djibouti at 7.4%. However, East Africa's region witnessed a slight decrease in average investment rates in years 2015 and 2016 (respectively at 24.3% and 24.5% of its GDP).

Figure 5.5. **Growth decomposition by expenditure in East Africa, 2009-16**

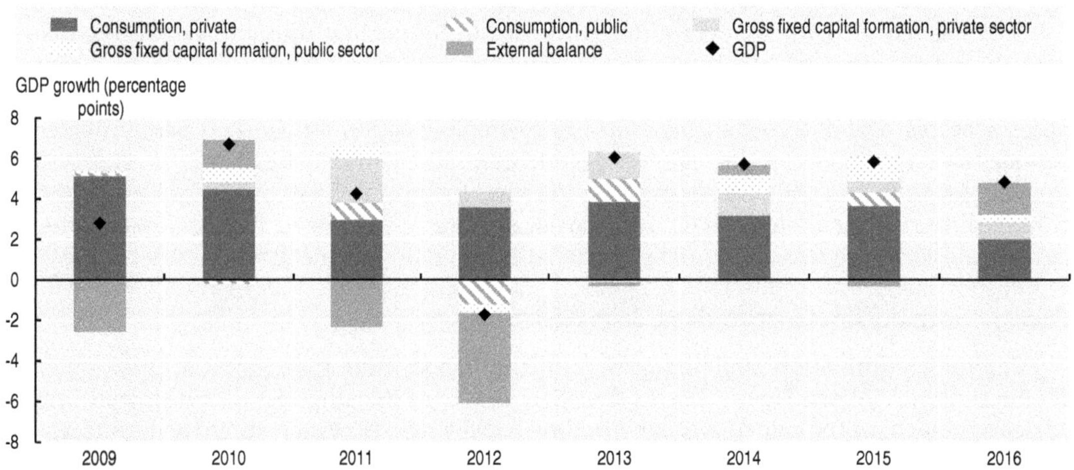

Source: Authors' calculations based on IMF (2018), *World Economic Outlook Database* and World Bank (2017a), *World Development Indicators* (database).

StatLink http://dx.doi.org/10.1787/888933783741

Consumption is the main driver of GDP growth and, despite some volatility, has rebounded since 2014. Private consumption almost consistently makes up over half of GDP growth in the region, growing on average at 4.7% between 2009 and 2016. The dip in private consumption between 2009 and 2014 can be partly attributed to the slowdown in global demand in the aftermath of the global financial crisis. East Africa is at least partially integrated into the global economy and is exposed to external economic shocks. Public consumption has been more volatile and less strong at 0.6% on average (Figure 5.5).

The contribution of the external sector (net exports) to recent GDP growth was largely negative until 2015. This negative contribution can be explained by the higher import price of energy between 2011 and 2014, and by suppressed external demand in part caused by the global financial crisis. Regional exports are still dominated by primary agricultural commodities (more than half the exports in 2016), while fully-processed goods dominate imports (at about 70% in 2016). Since 2000, exports have been progressively rising as a share of GDP and becoming more geographically diversified. This trend reflects rapid growth and a relative degree of structural transformation of regional economies, as they expand to a wide range of goods and services outside the traditional agricultural sector (see Annex 5.A1).

Dynamics of employment and unemployment in East Africa

Economic growth in East Africa is not sufficiently diversifying the economy or creating enough jobs, both of which are key to inclusiveness and sustainability. Agriculture still employs almost 60% of the labour force, despite its declining contribution to GDP. The services sector is absorbing most of the workers moving out of agriculture, leaving employment in industry almost unchanged. This hampers development and employment prospects since most jobs in services are informal and unproductive and offer low wages and poor working conditions (UNECA, 2015). Youth unemployment remains a major challenge.

Growth strategies should aim to create increasingly attractive business environments that can enhance employment. Policies should encourage the private sector to grow, invest and employ workers, including small businesses such as start-ups and entrepreneurs that can create jobs. A case in point is Rwanda which, in parallel with macroeconomic and business reforms, has embedded entrepreneurship development into its policy frameworks. These include its employment policy in 2007, small and medium-sized enterprises policy in 2010 and Private Sector Development Strategy in 2013.

Trends in employment and unemployment in East Africa

Employment rates vary significantly across countries. In three countries, less than half of the labour force is employed. Almost half of the countries have employment rates of about 80%. Unemployment in the region has remained fairly constant, falling slightly from 7.5% in 1991 to just under 7.2% in 2017 (Figure 5.6).[2,3]

Figure 5.6. **Employment and unemployment rates in East African countries**

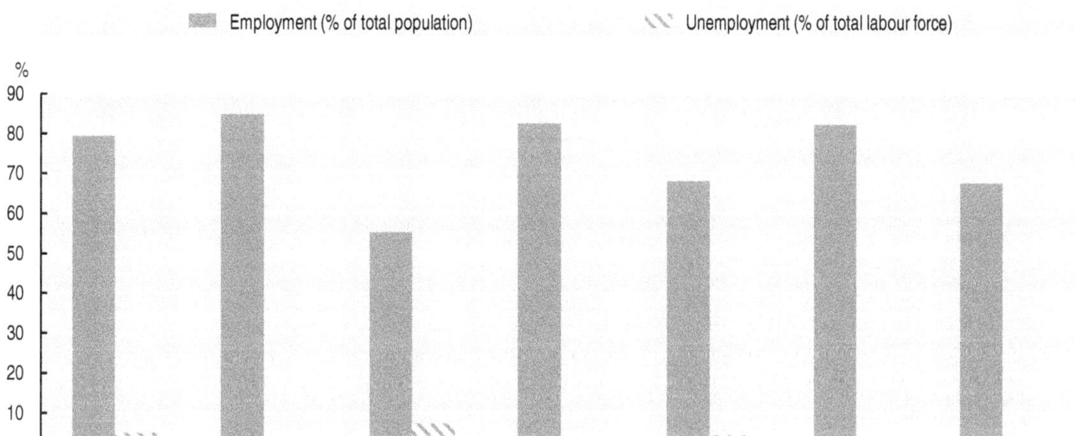

Note: Only the latest data available after 2009 for each country is shown.
Source: Authors' calculations based on World Bank (2017a), *World Development Indicators* (database).
StatLink http://dx.doi.org/10.1787/888933783760

The reallocation of labour to the services sector has not led to productivity increases. The agricultural sector still employs the largest proportion of the labour force, though its share has marginally decreased. In recent years, the services sector has absorbed most of the workers leaving agriculture and industry. Employment in services tends to be in low productivity activities such as retail trade and hospitality, limiting the gains of labour reallocation (see Chapter 1).

In recent years, women's participation in the labour force has increased in many developing countries including those in East Africa. There are at least three factors that explain this trend. With economic development and the ensuing shift of the population from rural and agricultural sectors to other sectors, more women choose to participate in the labour force. Second, with rising levels of education, women tend to work in greater numbers in order to capture returns on their investment. Third, falling household income and rising poverty in certain countries seem to have persuaded more women to join the labour force (Tandrayen-Ragoobur, Ummersingh and Bundhoo, 2011).

Inequalities in employment are decreasing, but women and youth remain at a disadvantage. Female employment is increasing while male employment is decreasing, although the gender gap is still significant. The overall gender gap (measured as the ratio of male-to-female employment) has been decreasing slowly, from 1.41 in 1991 to 1.39 in 2017, and large disparities exist across sectors and countries (see Table 5.3 for a sector breakdown). Youth remain vulnerable to unemployment in East Africa. The youth unemployment rate is higher than overall unemployment, at 13.5% in 2017.

Both women and men work mostly in agriculture. The sector employs 62% of the female labour force and 55% of the male labour force. However, female employment is shifting from agriculture and industry towards services, while male employment is moving to industry and services (see Table 5.3). This is consistent with men being more likely to undertake wage employment. In Uganda and Tanzania, for example, respectively almost 50% and over 62% of employed women work in the informal sector (ILO, 2015). The share reaches 80% in Kenya and Rwanda (UNECA, 2015). East Africa therefore follows the same trend as sub-Saharan Africa where over 75% of women are likely to engage in informal work (ILO, 2016).

Table 5.3. **Sector shares in East Africa's employment by gender, 1995-2017 (percentage)**

	Agriculture		Industry		Services	
	Female	Male	Female	Male	Female	Male
1995	63.1	55.4	10.6	11.5	26.4	33.1
2005	62.2	54.1	9.5	12.1	28.2	33.8
2017	60.1	52.8	8.7	13.7	31.2	33.5
Average (1991-2017)	62.1	54.4	9.8	12.4	28.1	33.1

Source: Authors' calculations based on World Bank (2017a), *World Development Indicators* (database).

Box 5.1. Explaining the disparity in gender employment in Mauritius

Mauritius has often been cited as an outlier in sub-Saharan Africa with stable growth and sound macroeconomic conditions. Nonetheless, female unemployment remains a major problem of the Mauritian society. In 2010,[4] 64% of the unemployed were women. The economy has become more service-oriented and knowledge-based, and many lower-skilled jobs have been lost. Those who lost their jobs were mostly women, hence increasing the gender unemployment gap. Married women in Mauritius tend to remain outside of the labour force. Additionally, many women do not enter the labour force due to inflexible working hours and inadequate childcare options (Tandrayen-Ragoobur, Ummersingh and Bundhoo, 2011).

Dynamics of inequality and poverty in East Africa

This section analyses two main factors that prevent economic well-being: inequality and poverty. Income inequality varies across East Africa but overall is on an upward trend (see Table 5.4). Most countries also lag behind in providing access to electricity, water and sanitation, with large gaps between urban and rural populations. Poverty has declined in the region but remains high.

Inequality and poverty can decrease with growth, but policies for the long term are also required, since growth alone does not systematically reduce them. To reduce vulnerability and promote greater participation in the growth process, some countries have put in place social protection programmes (e.g. Tanzania). Others are investing in education, skills and entrepreneurship development to create better jobs in the longer term (e.g. Rwanda). Mauritius offers an example of policies to reduce poverty and inequality through education – such as targeted skills training for disenfranchised groups in particular women and youth –, health services and social safety nets.

High poverty rates do not necessarily imply high inequality. For example, despite an increase in Madagascar's poverty headcount ratio between 2001 and 2010, inequality decreased, driven by a return to agriculture as the economy failed to grow.

Inequality in East Africa

Looking at inequality of income and of opportunity, some countries are performing badly in terms of one indicator but perform well in others. For instance, Comoros has the highest Gini coefficient, meaning the most wealth inequality, but a high percentage of its population has access to electricity. Ethiopia, on the other hand, has a low Gini coefficient, but few citizens have access to basic services. These incongruences can be explained by different social protection programmes (or a lack thereof) across countries (World Bank, 2015).

Table 5.4. **Inequality in East Africa as measured by the Gini index**

	1999	2005	2010	2012	2013
Comoros	-	55.9	-	-	45.0
Djibouti	39.1	41.5	44.1	45.1	44.1
Ethiopia	30.0	29.8	33.2	-	-
Kenya	46.9	48.5	-	-	-
Madagascar	38.6	39.9	42.4	42.7	-
Mauritius	37.7	35.7	35.7	35.8	-
Rwanda	48.5	52.0	51.3	49.7	50.4
Seychelles	42.8	42.8	43.4	45.7	46.8
Tanzania	37.3	40.3	36.4	37.8	-
Uganda	43.0	42.9	44.2	41.0	-

Note: - = data unavailable. The Gini index measures the extent to which the distribution of income among individuals or households within an economy deviates from a perfectly equal distribution. The index ranges from 0 in the case of "perfect equality" (each share of the population gets the same share of income) to 100 in the case of "perfect inequality" (all income goes to the share of the population with the highest income).
Source: Authors' calculations based on World Bank (2017a), *World Development Indicators* (database).

Comparing the income shares held by the highest- and lowest-earning 20% of the population shows that inequality is generally high in East Africa (Figure 5.7). Rwanda, Comoros and Kenya have the highest levels of income inequality according to this measurement (see Annex 5.A2 for more detailed data). In comparison with the other regions in Africa, East Africa's inequality level is almost equivalent to that of the Central and West Africa. North Africa has the smallest difference between the highest and lowest quintiles, while Southern Africa has the largest.

Figure 5.7. **Gini coefficients and difference in income share in East African countries**

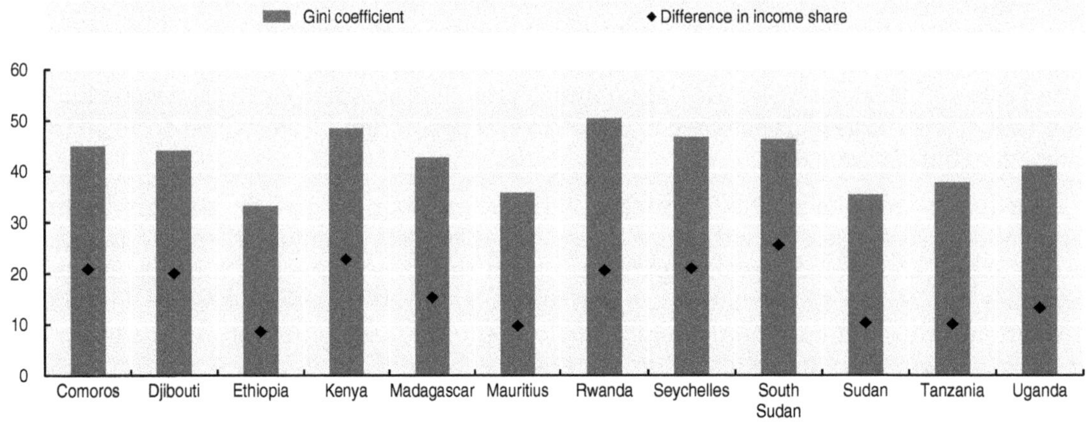

Note: The difference between the top and bottom group refers to the ratio between the income shares held by the richest 10% to the income held by the poorest 10% in the national income distribution. The latest available data is shown for each country.

Source: Authors' calculations based on World Bank (2017b), *PovcalNet* (database).

StatLink http://dx.doi.org/10.1787/888933783779

Inequality can also be analysed in terms of access to basic amenities, and, on average, countries in East Africa lag behind. In the region, 37% of the population have access to electricity, 48% to drinking water and 20% to sanitation services (see Annex 5.A2 for breakdowns by country). A number of countries exhibit large gaps in access to basic amenities between the rural and urban populations, particularly in providing electricity and sanitation. By contrast, in Mauritius and Seychelles over 90% and 85% respectively of their rural populations have access to electricity.

Poverty in East Africa

Poverty has declined in East Africa but remains high. Generally East African countries have seen reductions in extreme poverty since they started their economic reforms in the 1990s (Table 5.5).

Table 5.5. **Poverty rates in East Africa, 1999-2013**

	Poverty headcount ratio at USD 1.90/day (% of population)				
	1999	**2005**	**2010**	**2012**	**2013**
Comoros	-	13.5	-	-	17.7
Djibouti	-	20.6	-	18.3	22.5
Ethiopia	55.4	36.3	33.5	-	-
Kenya	21.5	33.6	-	-	-
Madagascar	63.9	72.0	78.5	77.8	-
Mauritius	-	0.4	-	0.5	-
Rwanda	77.0	68.0	60.3	-	60.4
Tanzania	86.0	55.1	49.1	-	-
Uganda	64.1	53.2	41.5	34.6	-
	Poverty headcount ratio at national poverty lines (% of population)				
	1999	**2005**	**2010**	**2012**	**2013**
Comoros	69.0	44.8	-	-	-
Ethiopia	44.2	38.9	29.6	-	-
Kenya	-	45.9	-	-	-
Madagascar	70.8	73.2	71.4	70.7	-
Rwanda	-	56.7	44.9	-	39.1
Seychelles	-	37.8	-	-	39.3
Uganda	33.8	31.3	24.5	19.5	-

Note: - = data unavailable.

Source: World Bank (2017b), *PovCalNet* (database).

Countries in the region have taken various approaches to tackling poverty:

- **Mauritius has a generous welfare system, a solid education system, and policies to support low-income families and the unemployed.** The country has focused its poverty reduction strategy on education (e.g. training to enhance employability) and health services, targeting the most vulnerable segments of the population – women and youth – through improved social safety nets. Mauritius' development in the early 2000s succeeded in reducing poverty through growth at roughly no cost in terms of inequality.
- **Rwanda's poverty reduction efforts are anchored in long-term and medium-term strategies.** The country put in place a monitoring mechanism for poverty through household surveying (i.e. the Integrated Household Living Condition Survey and the Demographic and Health Survey). Several factors contributed to rapidly reducing poverty: peace and political stability; high and sustained real GDP growth; sound macroeconomic management; and improved social services and social protection programmes (such as the 2020 Umurenge Programme). The Rwandan government is strengthening its efforts to create jobs through education, skills and entrepreneurship to further reduce poverty to the target of 20% of the population by 2020.
- **Tanzania has reduced poverty and inequality by increasing disposable income for the poorest households.** The government supports poor households through social safety net programmes (such as the Tanzania Social Action Fund and the Productive Social Safety Net Programme), conditional cash transfers and public works programmes.

Peace and stability are also key factors for poverty reduction. The two political crises that hit Madagascar in the 2000s cost the country dearly in terms of poverty reduction. Had Madagascar avoided the crises, almost 11% less of the country's population would have been poor in 2010 compared to 2001 (i.e. the poor population would have dropped from 70.8% in 2001 to 59.8% in 2010) (World Bank, 2014).

Policy recommendations

Most of East Africa has benefited from sustained economic growth as a result of a diversified economic profile, particularly compared to regions such as Central Africa and West Africa. Nevertheless, a large agriculture sector and an export-led growth model that focuses on a narrow set of products (e.g. coffee, tea and minerals) make the region vulnerable to commodity price fluctuations and currency depreciations. The region's growth has not created jobs nor substantially reduced poverty or inequality.

The following policy recommendations will try to direct countries towards greater economic diversification, job creation, inclusive growth and structural transformation. Governments can achieve these by enhancing the role of the growing domestic consumer base, increasing the productivity of sectors that employ large parts of the population and supporting job creation in higher productivity sectors. These recommendations address problems shared by all or most countries in the region. They aim to propose actions for a regional development agenda that is coherent with the commonalities across countries and their regional integration needs. As countries have different starting points, approaches, capacities and national priorities, they will have to prioritise and sequence policies according to their own specificities.

Countries in the region should pursue responsible fiscal and monetary policies, as these directly affect inflation rates and currency volatility. Macroeconomic stability matters for sustained economic growth, especially in the long run. Maintaining low and stable inflation rates requires *i)* controlling the supply of money, which influences price indices in the short term, and *ii)* shielding the economy from inflation spill-overs and changes in oil and food prices, which impact inflation in the longer term (Nguyen et al., 2015; Simpasa and Gurara, 2011).

As the region increasingly integrates into the global economy, shielding the economy is particularly important to reduce poverty and could also be complemented by measures to protect low-income households from price shocks. Regional Economic Communities can help. For instance, the 2015 Monetary Union Protocol of the East African Community sets out macroeconomic convergence criteria that in the long term would lead to inflation below 5%, a regional tax-to-GDP ratio of 25%, a debt-to-GDP ceiling of 50% and a minimum reserve cover of 4.5 months of imports.

Improving the policy and regulatory framework and the overall business environment is crucial to foster diversification and more sustainable growth. Policy makers can stimulate productive investment in the economy through a number of structural and institutional measures:

- **Introduce reforms to improve the business climate.** Only four countries in the region – Kenya, Mauritius, Rwanda and Seychelles – rank among the top 100 globally for ease of doing business (World Bank, 2018). Specifically, these countries have somewhat consistently reduced the number and cost of procedures to register businesses and property and to obtain permits and public goods (e.g. electricity). Additional actions could include aligning investment, infrastructure and human capital development plans; centralising regulatory information and making it easily accessible to domestic and foreign investors; and empowering regulatory authorities to avoid government influence in certain sectors (e.g. electricity price setting) (OECD, 2013; 2014).
- **Investment promotion agencies (IPAs) are needed to cater for the needs of private investors, big and small.** Effective IPAs require a clear mission with strategic objectives as well as strong leadership (Morisset and Andrews-Johnson, 2004). For instance, Rwanda has set up an investment promotion agency with the clear mandate to attract and assist investors who can create jobs and foster economic activity in the country. The agency also benefits from a seat in cabinet, to ensure direct contact with other ministries and the president.
- **Governments can streamline trade policy to facilitate importing intermediate and capital goods and exporting final products.** According to the OECD Trade Facilitation Indicators, East Africa could prioritise removing trading fees and charges as well as involving more of the trade community in the decision-making process (OECD, n.d.). Lowering tariffs on intermediate inputs and capital goods that are essential for industrialisation can enhance the competitiveness of firms in the region. For example, in the East African Community (EAC), nearly 400 tariff lines for industrial inputs are misclassified as finished goods and therefore taxed at 25% instead of 10% (Frazer, 2017). Supporting firms with an export promotion agency or other trade facilitation measures can help countries increase exports and tap into value chains (WTO, 2014).
- **To further attract investment, governments in the region can support projects and services that crowd in private capital.** Governments should provide assistance and services such as seed funding and business support services and should facilitate interactions between domestic and foreign firms. Donors and development partners can contribute by providing technical assistance and funding to specific programmes (Powers and Butterfield, 2014). Governments could promote private sector participation in sectors and activities that offer good prospects for returns on investment such as infrastructure (e.g. toll roads) and public services (e.g. transport).

Developing quality infrastructure projects will enhance sustained growth. EAC countries alone will need approximately USD 100 billion by 2021 to close their infrastructure gap, which is hindering growth and keeping business costs at uncompetitive levels.[5] Co-ordinated investment in basic infrastructure can overcome the most salient constraints in electricity and logistics. Projects such as the East African Power Pool (EAPP) will help reduce the region's infrastructure deficit and strengthen cross-border co-operation. The EAPP aims to generate surplus capacity by 2030 as well as to create an integrated electricity exchange market among the six countries in the region that are part of the project (Deloitte, 2015). Countries should also aim to improve enabling infrastructure for the services sector (e.g. ICT connectivity), which can help firms to grown. Kenya's "Silicon Savannah", for example, is attracting entrepreneurs and has now expanded beyond Nairobi, partly thanks to the fast mobile broadband available across the country.[6]

Given the importance of human capital in promoting growth, countries should improve their education systems. Between 2005 and 2014, the share of boys graduating from secondary school increased by 24 percentage points and the share of girls by 27 percentage points, almost closing the gender gap. Nevertheless, the quality and job market relevance of education need improving.

Young people require at least a lower secondary education to have foundation skills to find work that pays a decent wage (UNESCO, 2013). In Ethiopia, however, over 75% of those aged 15-19 do not have foundation skills. The same is true for around two-thirds of young Ugandans. To provide the necessary education, governments should work towards increased learning outcomes in primary and secondary school and higher enrolment rates in science, technology, engineering and mathematics. They should promote specialised education and vocational training and involve the private sector in designing curricula and engaging with students.

Increasing coverage of social protection programmes can help countries manage the possible negative effects of growth on the more vulnerable. The region's demographic growth is not slowing down enough to prevent vulnerable people from facing inequality and falling into poverty. Governments can nevertheless extend coverage of social protection programmes to benefit the most vulnerable (see Chapter 8), including women, who often constitute a disproportionate share of the poor. Programmes could be designed to promote women's access to health and education services as well as to support them when they are out of the labour force caring for dependents. While financing such programmes will pose a serious challenge, estimates for four countries in the region show that removing fuel subsidies alone could free up to 2.1% of GDP (OECD, 2017).

Countries need to boost agricultural productivity and support the growth of high-potential firms in the industrial and services sectors. Agriculture remains the largest employer in the region. Increasing its productivity and competitiveness can create jobs in the sector beyond mere subsistence. Low productivity and non-tradable services also employ a large share of the population. Allowing firms in this sector to grow and encouraging workers to move into more productive industries could help countries accelerate their economic transformation.

- Interventions in agriculture could include introducing affordable and scalable technology and improved farm inputs to increase productivity, developing financial products (i.e. credit and insurance) tailored to the sector, and creating value chains to increase value addition (which can also generate additional jobs). For instance, the cut flower industry in Ethiopia has greatly benefited from investments by small foreign companies to develop trade with Europe, transferring knowledge and generating spill-overs to the local economy. Place-based and multi-sectoral approaches can also help improve farming productivity. As part of their development strategies, Ethiopia and Rwanda are targeting the growth of secondary cities to strengthen the productivity of local food markets.

- Modern technology solutions can enable own-account workers to reduce costs and increase the productivity of their enterprises, as well as provide opportunities to diversify activities and sectors (AfDB/OECD/UNDP, 2017). Tourism is a key industry for East Africa and has the potential to create many jobs, particularly for women (UNCTAD, 2017). Promoting tourism (e.g. through private sector platforms and single tourist visas, such as in the EAC) can help establish linkages across economic sectors, reduce poverty and create more inclusive growth.

Mobilising more domestic revenue will allow countries to increase investment in key areas such as infrastructure and education. Several countries in the region have been able to increase their domestic resources mobilisation. For instance, Kenya and Rwanda have increased their tax-to-GDP ratios by 2 and 6.5 percentage points, respectively, between 2000 and 2015. In 2015, Kenya's tax-to-GDP ratio was at 18.4% and Rwanda's at 16.7%. The Rwandan government has expanded its tax base by registering informal businesses and simplifying compliance processes. It established a Small and Medium Taxpayers Office in 2006 and introduced a value-added tax in 2001 and new income tax laws and tax rates in 2005 and 2006 (OECD/ATAF/AUC, 2017).

Annex 5.A1. Trade profiles

Figure 5.A1.1. **Composition of exports and imports in East Africa**

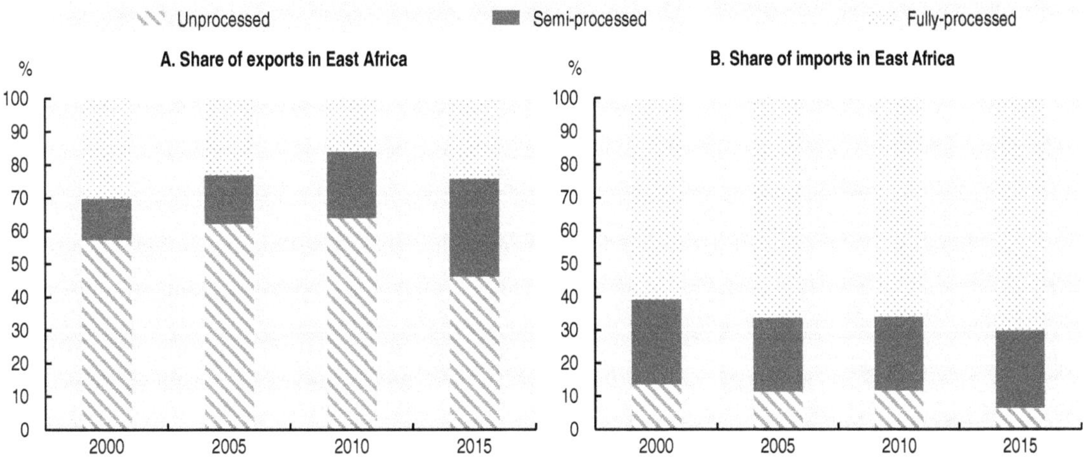

Source: Authors' calculations based on on United Nations Statistics Division (2017), *UNCOMTRADE* (database).
StatLink http://dx.doi.org/10.1787/888933783798

Although primary commodities dominate exports in the East Africa region, fully-processed commodities dominate imports (Figure 5.A1.1). The exported primary commodities include, among others, coffee, cut flowers, tea, tobacco, fish and vegetables. The imported fully-processed commodities are mainly heavy machinery, automobiles and chemicals.

Evidence shows that exports are playing an increasing role in GDP. This is consistent with the region's economies becoming more internationally integrated and thus their production processes and outputs becoming more modern (Gigineishvili, Mauro and Wang, 2014).

Annex 5.A2. Inequality profiles

Figure 5.A2.1. **Access to electricity in East African countries**

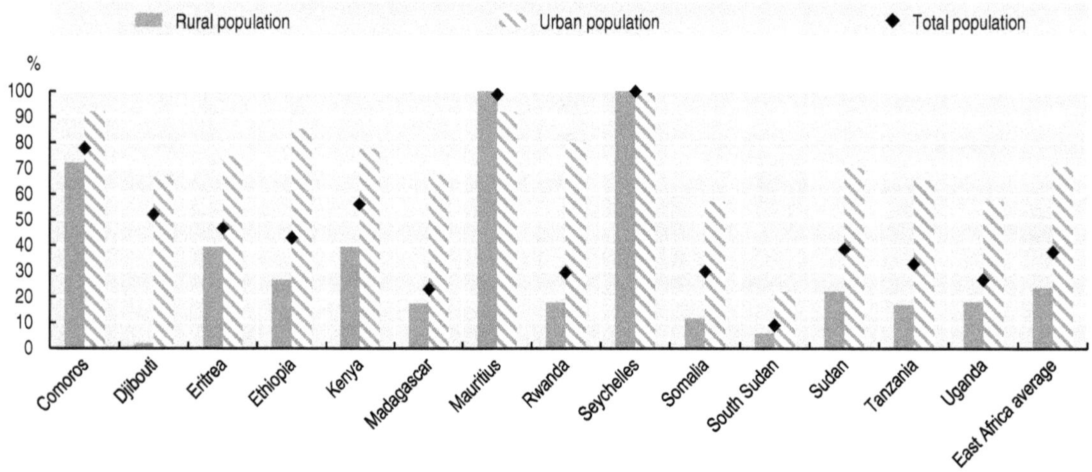

Note: Total = access to electricity (% of total population); Rural = access to electricity (% of rural population); Urban = access to electricity (% of urban population).

Source: Authors' calculations based on World Bank (2017a), *World Development Indicators* (database).

StatLink http://dx.doi.org/10.1787/888933783817

Figure 5.A2.2. **Access to basic sanitation in East African countries**

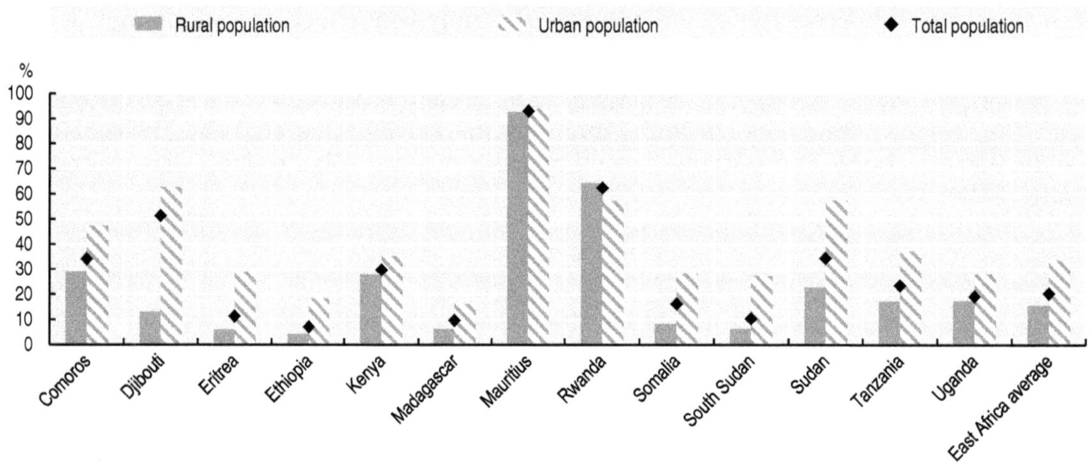

Note: Total = access to basic sanitation (% of total population); Rural = access to basic sanitation (% of rural population); Urban = access to basic sanitation (% of urban population).

Source: Authors' calculations based on World Bank (2017a), *World Development Indicators* (database).

StatLink http://dx.doi.org/10.1787/888933783836

Figure 5.A2.3. **Access to drinking water in East African countries**

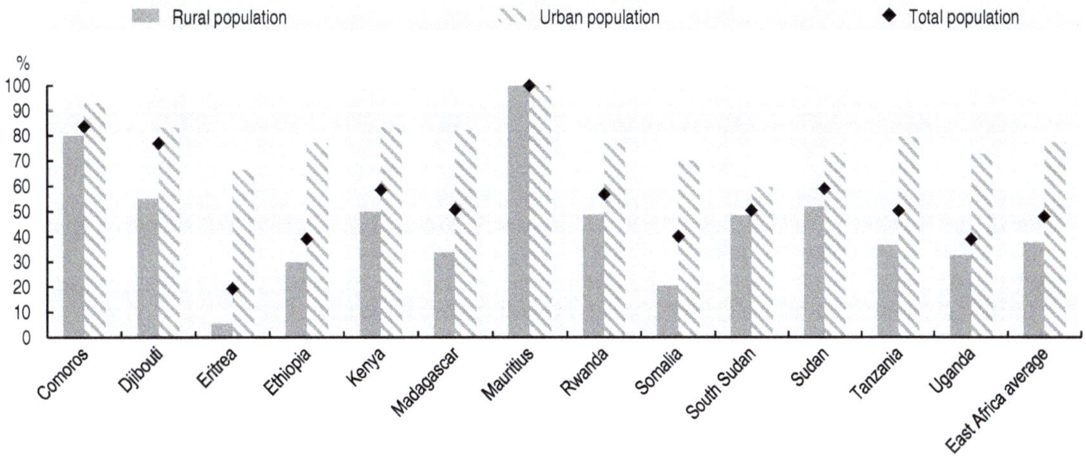

Note: Total = access to drinking water (% of total population); Rural = access to drinking water (% of rural population); Urban = access to drinking water (% of urban population).

Source: Authors' calculations based on World Bank (2017a), *World Development Indicators* (database).

StatLink http://dx.doi.org/10.1787/888933783855

Notes

1. Data availability determines the countries included in particular sections.
2. In this section, the study period has been adjusted to 1991-2017 due to data availability.
3. Unemployment rate as a percentage of the total labour force (modelled International Labour Organization estimate) (World Bank, 2017).
4. More recent data are not available.
5. www.theeastafrican.co.ke/business/EA--region-needs-100b-dollars-for-infrastructure/2560-4003018-nuwd1mz/index.html
6. https://qz.com/1059305/kenyas-newest-tech-hubs-are-sprouting-outside-its-silicon-savannah-in-nairobi/

References

AfDB/OECD/UNDP (2017), *African Economic Outlook 2017: Entrepreneurship and Industrialisation*, OECD Publishing, Paris, http://dx.doi.org/10.1787/aeo-2017-en.

Conference Board (2017), *Total Economy Database*, https://www.conference-board.org/data/economydatabase/index.cfm?id=27762 (accessed 31 January 2018).

Deloitte (2015), "The roadmap to a fully integrated and operational East African Power Pool", 2015 Edition, Deloitte & Touche.

Frazer, G. (2017), "Examining the impact of the common external tariff of the East African Community in Uganda", *IGC Policy Paper.*

Gigineishvili, N, P. Mauro and K. Wang (2014), "How solid is economic growth in the East African Community?", *IMF Working Paper*, WP/14/150, International Monetary Fund.

Gollin, D., D. Lagakos, and M. E. Waugh (2014), "The agricultural productivity gap in poor countries", *Quarterly Journal of Economics*, 129(2), pp. 939–993.

ILO (2016), *Women at Work: Trends 2016*, International Labour Organization, www.ilo.org/wcmsp5/groups/public/---dgreports/---dcomm/---publ/documents/publication/wcms_457317.pdf.

ILO (2015), "Engaging informal women entrepreneurs in East Africa: Approaches to greater formality", *Issue Brief*, International Labour Organization, www.ilo.org/global/docs/WCMS_430945/lang--en/index.htm.

IMF (2018), *World Economic Outlook Database*, International Monetary Fund, http://www.imf.org/external/pubs/ft/weo/2018/01/weodata/index.aspx.

McMillan, M. S. and I. Verduzco (2012), "Measuring the Impact of Structural Change on Labor's Share of Income", Background Paper for the World Development Report 2013, World Bank.

McMillan, M. and D. Rodrik (2011), "Globalization, structural change and productivity growth", in M. Bacchetta and M. Jansen (eds.), *Making Globalization Socially Sustainable*, International Labour Organization and World Trade Organization, Geneva.

Morisset, J. and K. Andrews-Johnson (2004), "The effectiveness of promotion agencies at attracting foreign direct investment", *FIAS Occasional Paper 16*, World Bank.

Nguyen, A.D.M. et al. (2015), "On the drivers of inflation in sub-Saharan Africa", *IMF Working Paper*, WP/15/189, International Monetary Fund.

OECD (n.d.), *OECD Trade Facilitation Indicators: Sub-Saharan Africa*, Paris, www.oecd.org/tad/facilitation/Sub-Saharan-Africa_OECD-Trade-Facilitation-Indicators.pdf.

OECD (2017), *Social Protection in East Africa: Harnessing the Future*, OECD Publishing, Paris, http://dx.doi.org/10.1787/9789264274228-en.

OECD (2014), "Executive summary", in *OECD Investment Policy Reviews: Mauritius 2014*, OECD Publishing, Paris, http://dx.doi.org/10.1787/9789264212619-5-en.

OECD (2013), "Executive summary", in *OECD Investment Policy Reviews: Tanzania 2013*, OECD Publishing, Paris, http://dx.doi.org/10.1787/9789264204348-5-en.

OECD/ATAF/AUC (2017), *Revenue Statistics in Africa 2017*, OECD Publishing, Paris, p. 34, http://dx.doi.org/10.1787/9789264280854-en-fr.

Powers, C. and W.M. Butterfield (2014), "Crowding in private investment", *Frontiers in Development*, USAID.

Simpasa, A. and D. Gurara, (2011), *Inflation Dynamics in Selected East African Countries: Ethiopia, Kenya, Tanzania and Uganda*, African Development Bank.

Tandrayen-Ragoobur, V., S. Ummersingh and Y. Bundhoo (2011), "The power to choose: Women and labour market decisions in Mauritius", *Journal of Emerging Trends in Economics and Management Sciences*, Vol. 2(3), Scholarlink Research Institute Journals, pp. 193-205.

UNCTAD (2017), *Economic Development in Africa Report 2017: Tourism for Transformative and Inclusive Growth*, UNCTAD/ALDC/AFRICA/2017, United Nations Conference on Trade and Development, United Nations Publication.

UNDESA (2017), *World Population Prospects* (database), https://esa.un.org/unpd/wpp/ (accessed 1 March 2018).

UNECA (2017), *Economic Report on Africa 2017: Urbanization and Industrialization for Africa's Transformation*, United Nations Economic Commission for Africa, https://www.uneca.org/publications/economic-report-africa-2017.

UNECA (2015), *Economic Report on Africa 2015: Industrializing through Trade*, United Nations Economic Commission for Africa, https://www.uneca.org/sites/default/files/PublicationFiles/era2015_eng_fin.pdf.

UNESCO (2013), "Regional fact sheet: Education in Eastern Africa", in *Education for All Global Monitoring Report*, United Nations Educational, Scientific and Cultural Organisation, http://unesdoc.unesco.org/images/0021/002193/219351e.pdf.

United Nations Statistics Division (2017), *UNCOMTRADE* (database), https://comtrade.un.org/ (accessed 1 February 2018).

World Bank (2018), *Doing Business 2018: Reforming to Create Jobs*, World Bank Group, Washington, DC.

World Bank (2017a), *World Development Indicators* (database), World Bank Group, Washington, DC, https://data.worldbank.org/products/wdi (accessed 1 March 2018).

World Bank (2017b), *PovcalNet* (database), World Bank Group, Washington, DC, http://iresearch.worldbank.org/PovcalNet (accessed 1 March 2018).

World Bank (2015), *State of Social Safety Nets 2015*, World Bank Group, Washington, DC, http://documents.worldbank.org/curated/en/415491467994645020/pdf/97882-PUB-REVISED-Box393232B-PUBLIC-DOCDATE-6-29-2015-DOI-10-1596978-1-4648-0543-1-EPI-1464805431.pdf.

World Bank (2014), "Face of poverty in Madagascar: Poverty, gender and inequality assessment", *World Bank Report*, No. 78131-MG, March 2014, World Bank Group, Washington, DC.

WTO (2014), *World Trade Report 2014 – Trade and Development: Recent Trends and the Role of the WTO*, World Trade Organization, Geneva.

Chapter 6

Dynamics of growth, jobs and inequalities in North Africa

Growth has proved to be broadly unstable in North Africa with volatile domestic investment and inadequate productivity gains. Jobs and inequality remain major challenges, despite the vitality of labour markets in some countries and falling inequality. This chapter reconsiders the dynamic and determinants of these aggregates in the countries for which data are available. It then suggests ways of invigorating economic activity while reducing unemployment and inequality. The primary solutions suggested by this chapter include: promoting political stability, accelerating the structural transformation of the economy, and introducing new policy levers targeting youth and female employment.

IN BRIEF

In North Africa growth has brought about a decline in both poverty and **inequality**, enabling the emergence of a middle class in the region. Over the period extending from 1990 to 2015, the Gini index fell by seven points from 40.3 to 33.0. Inequality of opportunity (access to health, education, electricity and sanitation) has diminished significantly in most countries. Income inequality however persists, as the richest 20% earn 7.5 times more than the poorest 20%.

According to the available data, since 2010 North Africa has been broadly characterised by unstable economic performance. **Growth**, which averaged 2.6% between 2010 and 2015 (compared with 4% between 1995 and 2009), has not been sufficient to deal with unemployment or significantly reduce inequality. Productivity gains contributed just 17.6% to growth, versus 42.6% for capital and 39.8% for labour. These figures suggest poor innovation capacity.

Structural transformation in the region remains fairly slow, with services dominating (47.4% of GDP), the industrial sector rising slightly (35.9%) and the agricultural sector contracting (16.7%). Growth remains dependent on external factors such as developments in European demand and international oil prices, as well as domestic factors linked to institutional stability.

In terms of **employment**, official unemployment is moderate at about 13%, while the average level of employment is a low 40.9%, suggesting a strong potential of underutilised labour. Labour markets offer few prospects for high-skilled jobs that would be capable of injecting new dynamism into the economy. Youth unemployment (age 15-24) is 28.8%, which is double the world average. Only 16.6% of young women are employed or seeking employment, compared with 46.8% of young men. Around one-quarter of these young workers live in poverty.

To overcome these challenges, policies will need to improve and strengthen political stability and institutional accountability, accelerate the structural transformation of economies, and target job creation for women and youth via structural policy levers.

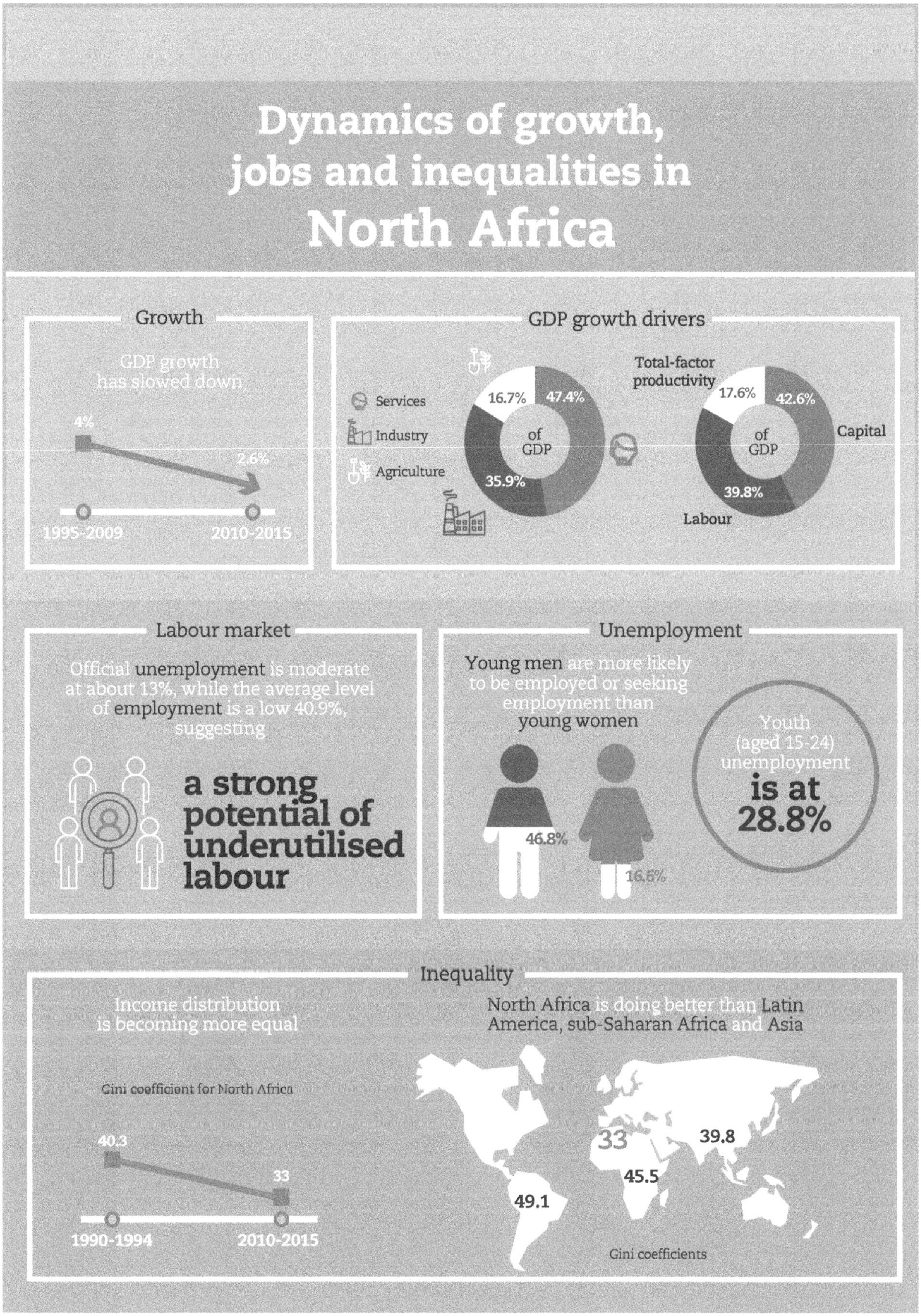
Dynamics of growth, jobs and inequalities in North Africa
Growth
GDP growth has slowed down
4%
2.6%
1995-2009
2010-2015
GDP growth drivers
Services
Industry
Agriculture
16.7%
47.4%
35.9%
of GDP
Total-factor productivity
17.6%
42.6%
39.8%
of GDP
Capital
Labour
Labour market
Official unemployment is moderate at about 13%, while the average level of employment is a low 40.9%, suggesting
a strong potential of underutilised labour
Unemployment
Young men are more likely to be employed or seeking employment than young women
46.8%
16.6%
Youth (aged 15-24) unemployment is at 28.8%
Inequality
Income distribution is becoming more equal
Gini coefficient for North Africa
40.3
33
1990-1994
2010-2015
North Africa is doing better than Latin America, sub-Saharan Africa and Asia
33
39.8
45.5
49.1
Gini coefficients

North Africa regional profile

Table 6.1. Basic indicators for North Africa, 2017

Population (thousands)	197 490
Land area (thousands of km²)	6 769
Population density (people/km²)	29
GDP, PPP (USD billion)	2 350
GDP per capita, PPP (USD)	12 172

Source: Authors' calculations based on UNDESA (2017), *World Population Prospects* (database); World Bank (2017a), *World Development Indicators* (database) and IMF (2018), *World Economic Outlook Database.*

Table 6.2. Financial flows and tax revenues to North Africa (current USD billion), 2009-16

			2009	2010	2011	2012	2013	2014	2015	2016
Foreign	Private	Inward foreign direct investment	16.4	13.8	6.4	14.7	12.2	11.3	11.8	13.7
		Portfolio investments	-0.7	0.7	-0.7	1.5	1.2	3.1	1.3	-0.2
		Remittances	17.4	23.0	25.5	30.0	29.0	31.7	29.2	27.6
	Public	Official development assistance (net total, all donors)	3.2	2.7	4.0	5.0	8.9	7.3	5.0	5.4
Total foreign flows			**36.4**	**40.2**	**35.3**	**51.0**	**51.2**	**53.4**	**47.4**	**46.5**
Domestic tax revenues			**107.9**	**117.9**	**140.9**	**145.3**	**145.6**	**141.5**	**119.2**	**111.8**

Source: IMF (2018), *World Economic Outlook Database*, OECD (2018a), *International Development Statistics* (database), and World Bank (2017a), *World Development Indicators* (database).

Figure 6.1. Growth dynamics in North Africa and Africa, 1990-2018

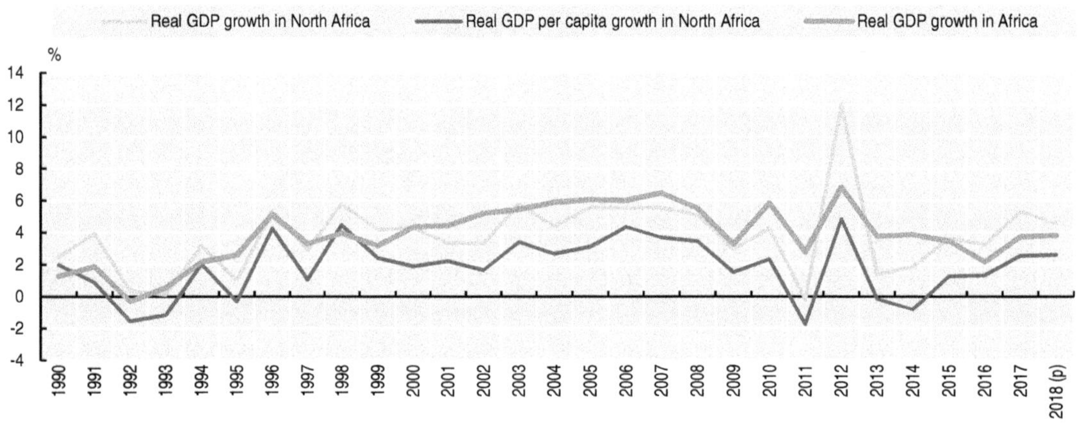

Note: (p) = projections.
Source: Authors' calculations based on IMF (2018), *World Economic Outlook Database.*
StatLink http://dx.doi.org/10.1787/888933783874

Figure 6.2. Trade composition in North Africa, 2016

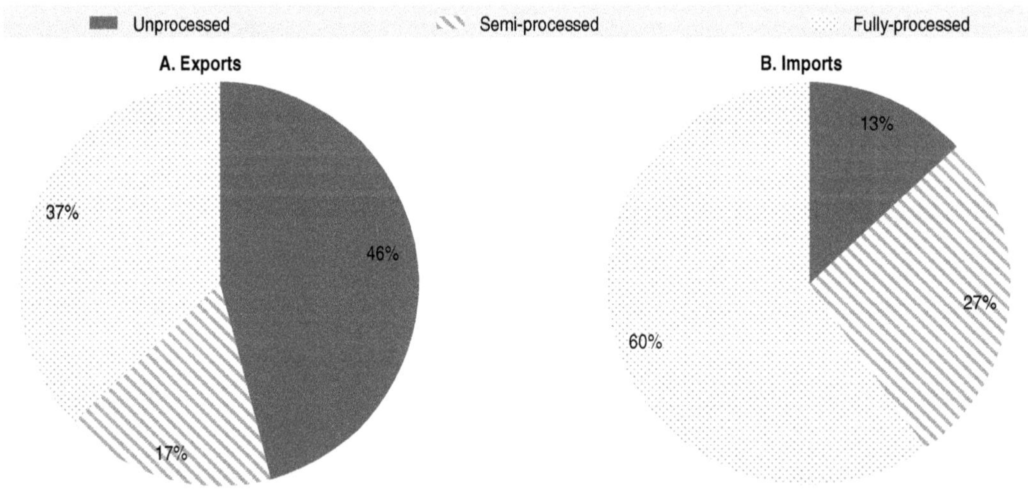

Source: Authors' calculations based on United Nations Statistics Division (2017), *UNCOMTRADE* (database).
StatLink http://dx.doi.org/10.1787/888933783893

North Africa occupies a strategic position in the southern Mediterranean, just a few hours from Europe. The population of the region is 197.5 million (15.7% of the population of Africa) spread over 6 769 000 km^2 (23% of the total African continent), giving a population density of 29 inhabitants per km^2. It is the richest region in Africa, with GDP of USD 2.35 trillion, or more than one third (36.8%) of that of the continent. GDP per capita was USD 12 172 in 2017, more than double the African average. The countries of North Africa share several common features: religion, language, culture and source of law. However, a number of differences exist in terms of population trends and economic and social trajectories.

Dynamics and determinants of growth in North Africa

Broadly unstable growth

Growth remains inadequate and volatile. Over the study period, in those countries for which data were available, economic growth was between 2.6% and 5% (Table 6.3), significantly below the double-digit growth of emerging economies. The highest growth was achieved between 2005 and 2009, and the lowest between 2010 and 2015.

After noteworthy progress in the 2000s, growth of GDP per capita weakened over the past five years, given the deterioration of the economic and institutional environment. The region's members were confronted variously with volatility in oil prices, sluggish European demand after the 2008 crash, as well as repercussions of the Arab Spring, the conflict in Libya and waves of terrorist attacks. In addition, average growth was higher in oil importing countries (4%), than in exporters (2.5%), which were left exposed to volatility in oil prices. Growth was most lacklustre in 2011, with the political turmoil of the Arab Spring. This year also marked the start of the fall in GDP per capita.

Table 6.3. **Average GDP growth in North African countries, 1990-2015**

	1990-2015	1990-94	1995-99	2000-04	2005-09	2010-15
Algeria	2.9	-0.3	3.5	4.8	3.0	3.4
Egypt	4.2	3.6	5.1	3.7	6.1	3.1
Libya	2.1	-	-	3.7	5.3	-1.9
Mauritania	3.9	0.9	4.4	2.8	6.1	4.7
Morocco	4.0	3.7	2.8	4.6	4.9	3.9
Tunisia	4.1	5.0	5.2	4.2	4.5	2.1
Mean	**3.6**	**2.6**	**4.2**	**4.0**	**5.0**	**2.6**

Source: Authors' calculations based on World Bank (2017), *World Development Indicators* (database).

This general trend in growth conceals several differences, linked to the trajectories of each country.

- Between 1990 and 1994, **Algeria** recorded negative average growth (-0.3%), due to high political instability and the civil war. The election of President Abdelaziz Bouteflika and the introduction of the Civil Concord contributed to an improvement in the economic situation. Oil price instability however contributed to rendering growth volatile.
- Led by tourism, growth in **Egypt** was the highest during the period, at over 3.5% between 1990 and 2009. This sector remains one of the country's growth motors (11% of GDP in 2017, according to the World Travel and Tourism Council, WTTC, 2018), a provider of employment (2.5 million direct and indirect jobs, or approximately 1 in 10) as well as of foreign exchange earnings. Despite government efforts to strengthen economic and employment dynamics, growth has been hampered in recent years by the unfavourable exchange rate, low foreign exchange reserves, a vulnerable banking system and sluggish growth in Europe (the country's principal trade partner).
- In **Libya**, growth has fluctuated strongly as a function of oil production. Oil extraction and refinement are the primary source of income, which depend on the security conditions in the country.
- Growth was stable in **Morocco** and almost always above average for the region, save between 1995 and 1999. It was driven by exports of phosphates and fruit and vegetables to Europe, the boom in competitive services, as well as a rapidly transforming industrial sector. The relatively stable growth contributed to halving the poverty rate in seven years (from 8.9% in 2007 to 4.2% in 2014). The reinstatement of Morocco

into the African Union and its application to join the Economic Community of West African States (ECOWAS) in 2017 are testament to the country's wish to open up to the continent and to further economic integration in West Africa.

- After an extended sluggish period, growth in **Mauritania** has recovered, exceeding 5% between 2003 and 2015, thanks to historic high international prices of raw materials. Revenue from iron ore exports boomed, going from USD 318 million to USD 2.7 billion between 2003 and 2013, without any increase in export volumes. However, the country has difficulty taking full advantage of its natural resources, particularly fishing and livestock, which restricts the prospect of diversification, sustainable growth and job creation.
- In **Tunisia**, a period of exceptional growth (over 5%) between 1990 and 2010 made it one of the best performing countries of Africa. However, over the 2010-15 period its growth was the weakest in the region (2.1%). Political instability and terrorist attacks undermined the productive sectors, particularly tourism.

Over the past 25 years, apart from Mauritania, the dynamics of North African economies reveal notable progress in terms of GDP per capita. In Tunisia, Algeria and Morocco, per capita income grew by more than 50% between 1990 and 2015 (Table 6.4). In Egypt however, growth has been slower due to tremendous population pressure. Income levels there increased by around USD 1 100 on average between 1990 and 2015, compared with USD 1 200 in Algeria, USD 1 500 in Morocco and USD 1 900 in Tunisia. Mauritania in contrast remains on the margins as GDP per capita did not effectively increase between 1990 and 2004, due to demographic growth (at 2.9%) exceeding production growth (2.7%). As it became an oil producing nation, the country experienced a slight uplift (up USD 318 between 2004 and 2014), although this far from compensates for the accumulated arrears.

Table 6.4. **GDP per capita in North Africa (USD at constant prices)**

	1990-94	1995-99	2000-04	2005-09	2010-15	1990-2015
Algeria	3 360.3	3 331.4	3 792.3	4 338.3	4 594.1	3 910.6
Egypt	1 576.4	1 768.9	1 999.8	2 328.9	2 609.0	2 077.7
Libya	-	8 782.8	9 033.2	11 404.9	8 349.6	9 821.0
Mauritania	1 006.6	1 023.9	994.2	1 199.6	1 268.2	1 105.0
Morocco	1 764.5	1 880.8	2 147.1	2 576.9	3 026.0	2 307.8
Tunisia	2 337.3	2 665.6	3 166.9	3 798.8	4 168.2	3 263.5
Mean	**2 009.0**	**2 389.7**	**3 522.2**	**4 274.6**	**3 459.1**	**3 195.5**

Source: Authors' calculations based on World Bank (2017), *World Development Indicators* (database).

Despite sustained internal demand, inward investment remains volatile

Overall, growth remained buoyed by public and private spending from 2009 to 2016 (Figure 6.3). The contribution of investment (public and private) was often negative, given the various internal and external shocks. The negative contribution of investment in 2009 is due to the international financial crisis which impacted on FDI flows, while those of 2011 and 2014 were linked to the uncertainty following the Arab Spring. This volatile contribution of investment underscores the limited effectiveness of certain large public investment projects as well as a low level of transversal coherence in sectoral policies (OECD, 2017a).

Similarly, the trade balance remained negative over this period, apart from 2013 and 2015. Despite an increase in international trade, imports often were higher than exports, indicating a structural imbalance in growth. Reliant on external factors (such as European demand and international oil prices), economic activity remained characterised by poor domestic investment.

Figure 6.3. **Growth decomposition by expenditure in North Africa, 2009-16**

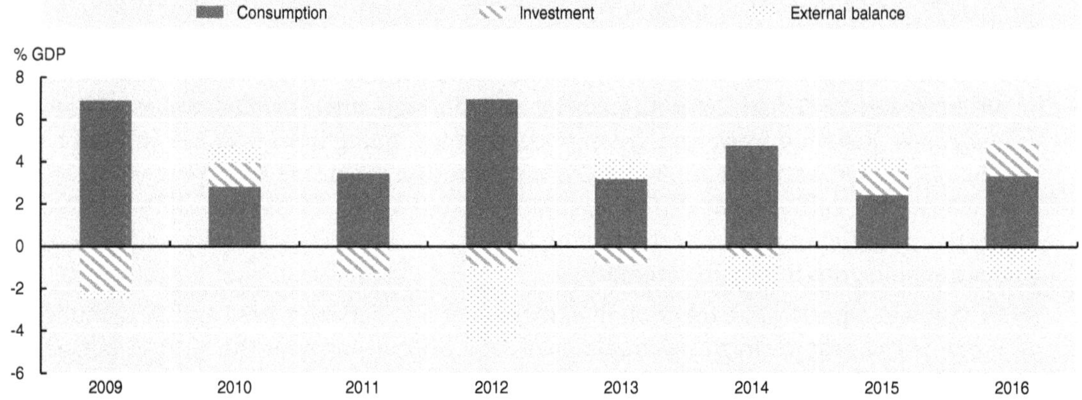

Source: Authors' calculations based on World Bank (2017), *World Development Indicators* (database) and IMF (2018), *World Economic Outlook Database*.

StatLink http://dx.doi.org/10.1787/888933783912

Productivity gains too low to support sustainable development

Labour and capital are not the sole determinants of growth. A third factor, technical progress or total factor productivity (TFP), also contributes. The growth of TFP, identified by a multi-factor approach, represents the share of GDP growth not explained by labour and capital growth.

Productivity gains have not accelerated strongly (Figure 6.4). Countries with good growth prospects post productivity gains between 1 and 1.5% per annum. This broadly poor dynamic is attributable to socioeconomic and political pressures (poor participation of women in the workforce, political instability and dependence on international prices of raw materials).

Figure 6.4. **Total factor productivity by country, 1990-2015**

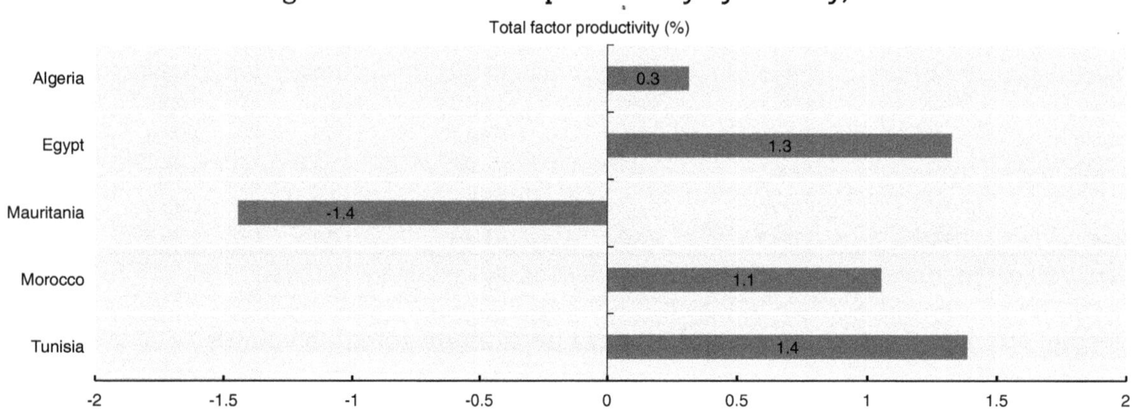

Source: Authors' calculations based on World Bank (2017), *World Development Indicators* (database).

StatLink http://dx.doi.org/10.1787/888933783931

Low levels of productivity and its volatility contribute to the poor macroeconomic performance of several North African countries (Table 6.5). Between 1990 and 2015, capital was the leading contributor to growth (42.6%), followed by labour (39.8%) and finally TFP (17.6%), which contributes almost half of growth in developed countries.

- The strong contribution of capital could be attributed to massive public investment as well as by FDI. The lower contribution of labour is due to the predominance of unskilled labour.
- The negative contribution of TFP to growth in recent years is due to the repercussions of the 2008 international financial crisis, but also to the Arab Spring, social protests

and waves of terrorist attacks. It is also testimony to the poor capacity for innovation and research and development (R&D) in companies.

- These results attest that these countries must not rely solely on the strong accumulation of capital based on large public infrastructure projects to lift growth and employment.

Table 6.5. **Sources of economic growth in North African countries, 1990-2015**

		Sources of GDP growth		
Period	GDP growth rate	Capital	Labour	Total factor productivity
1990-94	2.6	0.9 [34.9]	1.4 [54.1]	0.3 [11.0]
1995-99	4.2	1.2 [29.2]	1.8 [43.7]	1.1 [27.1]
2000-04	4.0	1.6 [39.0]	1.5 [38.3]	0.9 [22.8]
2005-09	4.9	2.3 [46.1]	1.5 [29.4]	1.2 [24.5]
2010-15	3.4	2.2 [63.7]	1.4 [40.8]	-0.2 [-4.5]
1990-2015	3.6	1.6 [42.6]	1.5 [39.8]	0.7 [17.6]

Note: Bracketed figures present the percentage contribution of each factor.
Source: Authors' calculations based on World Bank (2017), *World Development Indicators* (database).

Box 6.1. **Sectoral analysis of growth**

Services contributed most strongly to growth, as far as 47.4%, followed by industry and manufacturing (35.9%) then agriculture (16.7%, Figure 6.5).

Mauritania is the only country in which each of these three sectors made an almost identical contribution to growth, whilst services dominated in Tunisia (57.3%) and Morocco (55.4%), and industry and manufacturing in Algeria. Industry and manufacturing increased throughout the period in the region, except in Morocco where only the services sector increased, with the other sectors remaining stable.

Figure 6.5. **Sectoral contribution to GDP in North African countries, 1990-2015**

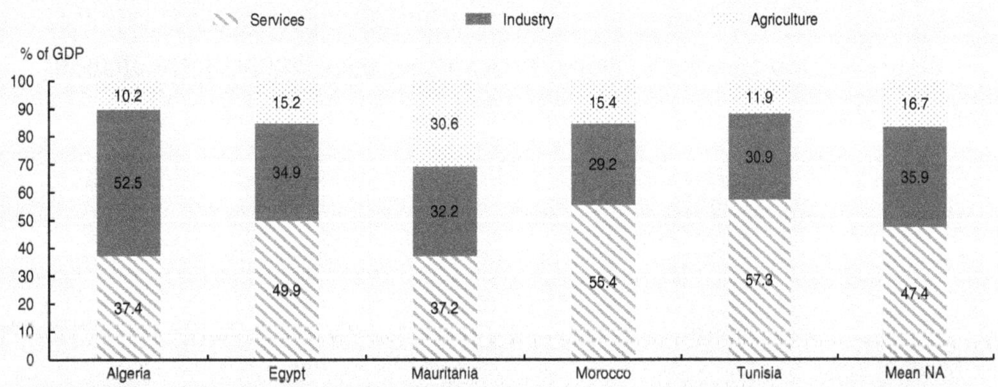

Source: Authors' calculations based on World Bank (2017), *World Development Indicators* (database).
StatLink http://dx.doi.org/10.1787/888933783950

Specialised clusters emerge as a function of each country's resources: phosphates in Morocco, oil in Libya and Algeria, fishing in Mauritania, and agriculture and transportation via the Suez Canal in Egypt. Countries with oil resources posted a strong contribution of the industrial sector, while an agricultural specialisation coupled with the development of services characterised Egypt and Morocco. Stimulated primarily by services, North African economic growth is taking an unconventional path. The boom in the tertiary sector (commerce, hotels, tourism, ICT, services to individuals, etc.) is attributable to the fact that these require neither significant investment nor skilled labour, in contrast to the industrial sector. The geographical proximity of the region to Western Europe was also an asset for the development of services. However, these countries are aware that they cannot truly develop without industry. Hence the notable efforts made by Morocco to establish primary and secondary processing industries.

Jobs and inequalities: Major challenges

This section first sets out the dynamic of employment and unemployment, followed by developments in inequalities.

A reorientation towards job-creating sectors for youth

The informal sector dominates the labour market exacerbating the vulnerability of those on the margins of society, specifically women and the poorest. The employment rate – the proportion of the active population in work – was relatively low (40.9%) from 1990 to 2015. In 2014, 52% of those of working age were reliant on the informal economy (ILO, 2014). As such, in Morocco 60% of all employment was informal and the informal sector accounted for between 11% and 33% of GDP (High Commission for Planning, HCP, 2011; General Confederation of Enterprises, CGEM, 2014). For workers, informal jobs create insecurity in terms of income and social security. In North Africa, these jobs exist primarily in the construction, transport, service to individuals and commerce sectors. Women and the poorest are overrepresented in these industries (World Bank, 2011). For states, informal activities represent a loss of potential tax revenue, the negative externalities of which impact on the country's growth, as well as that of GDP per capita, public investment and wealth redistribution.

A large portion of the population are excluded from the labour market, in particular youth. Between 2009 and 2016, the proportion of young people not in employment, education or training was 26.5% in Algeria, versus 29.5% in Egypt (ILO, 2017). Gender disparities are also significant: 36.1% of women are not in the labour market in Algeria, and this rises to 42.3% in Egypt. That said, education levels are rapidly rising. The region's economies must create skilled jobs to absorb new entrants into the labour market. The active population of North Africa will effectively expand by 10 million people between 2010 and 2020 according to the ILO, a slightly lower level of growth than that of the 2000-10 period (11 million people).

Figure 6.6. **Job creation in North African countries, 2000-15 (thousands)**

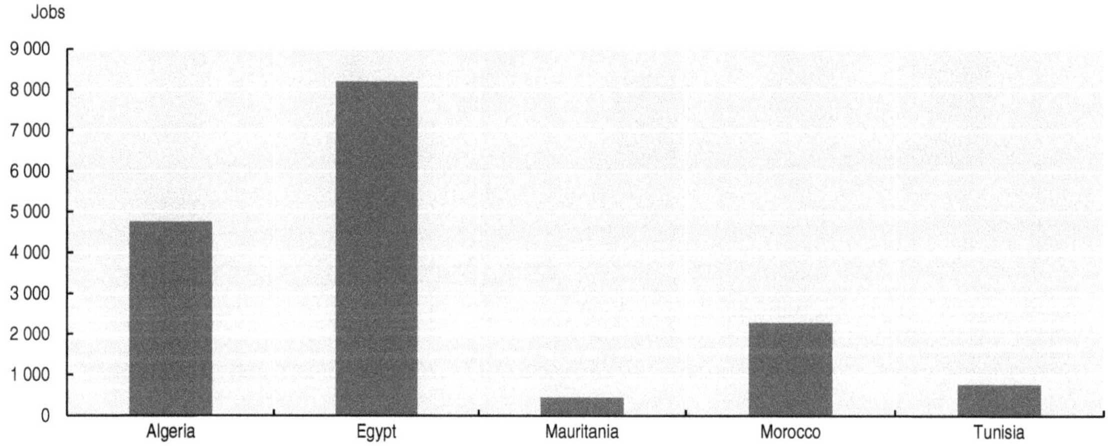

Source: Authors' calculations based on World Bank (2017), *World Development Indicators* (database) and ILO (2017).
StatLink http://dx.doi.org/10.1787/888933783969

Growth remains insufficient to converge towards full employment. Despite the job creation of the previous years (Figure 6.6), the situation remains difficult for every country in the region (Figure 6.7, and Box 6.2). On average, between 1990-2015 the unemployment rate was 12.8%, while the employment rate[1] remained relatively low (40.9%). This result highlights the high rate of latent labour. By comparison, in OECD countries in 2016 the employment rate was 67.2%, versus 66.9% in European Union (EU) countries. Only two-fifths of the labour force is employed in North Africa, while the remaining three-fifths are unemployed. This situation is even more troubling given that the countries of North Africa (apart from Egypt and Mauritania) have started the demographic transition and have increasingly lower dependency ratios (number of dependents for each active member of the workforce). These were 64% on average in 1990 and 52.4% in 2015 (UN DESA, 2017).

Figure 6.7. **Employment and unemployment rates in North African countries, 1991-2015**

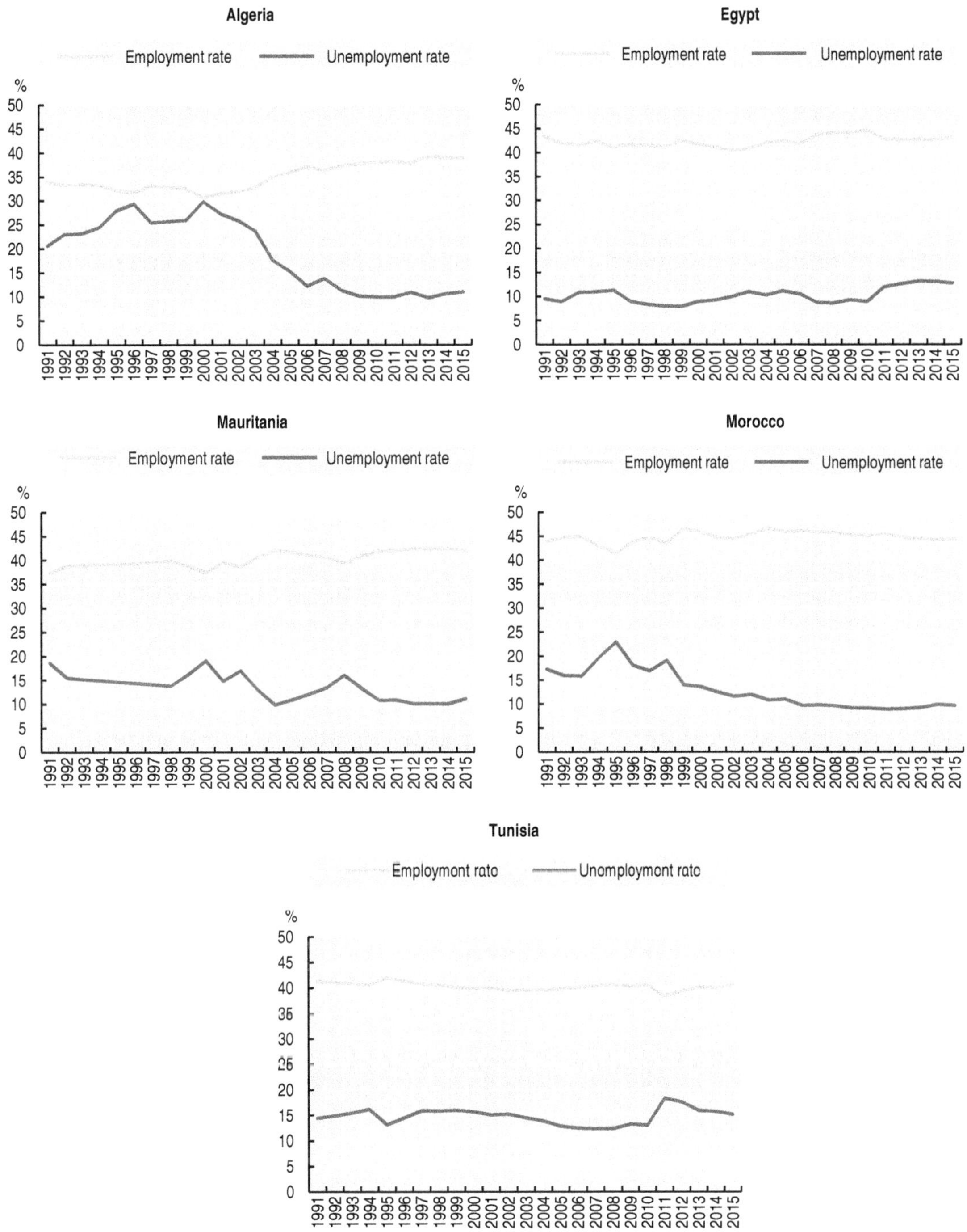

Source: Authors' calculations based on World Bank (2017), *World Development Indicators* (database) and ILO (2017).

StatLink http://dx.doi.org/10.1787/888933783988

Box 6.2. Mixed labour market development by country

In **Algeria**, the return of political stability injected some dynamism into the job market throughout the 2000s (Figure 6.7). Although official policies to boost entrepreneurship have not achieved all their objectives, they have resulted in an increase of self-employment over the last 15 years that has had a positive impact on the unemployment rate (AfDB/OECD/UNDP, 2017). The number of employers and freelancers grew by 235 000 between 2013 and 2015, or by 8.2%, compared with a more modest rise in the number of permanent waged jobs (+203 000 between 2013-15) and temporary jobs (+166 000). Two out of three workers are salaried (69% of the total, of which 35.9% are in permanent positions).

The job situation in **Egypt**, in contrast, remains poor. Despite a relatively high employment rate (42.6%) and an average unemployment rate of 10.7%, strong demographic growth has prevented any improvement of the overall situation. As such, the 8.2 million jobs created between 2000 and 2015 were unable to absorb the active population, which grew by 10.6 million. The unemployment and employment rates have not moved much over the past 20 years (Figure 6.7). This stagnation is also evident in workforce participation by gender; between 2000 and 2015, 80% of jobs were held by men.

Disparities also exist as a function of education: in 2015, 45.2% of jobs were carried out by people with a low level of education, compared with 37.6% of jobs requiring an intermediate level and 17.2% requiring an advanced level of education. Growth in waged employment has also been rapid, accounting for around 60% of all jobs (up from 10.9 million in 2000 to 16.5 million in 2015), while self-employment rose from 5.2 million to 6.6 million between 2000 and 2015. As such, the labour market is dominated by low-skilled jobs and waged employment, rather than self-employment.

In **Morocco**, both the active population and jobs increased proportionally between 2000 and 2015, at 2.3 million. This dynamic is reflected by an average employment rate of 45.3% over the period, the highest in North Africa, and by falling unemployment at 10.3%, which is the lowest in the region (Figure 6.7). However, the unemployment rate remains very high among urban youth (38.8%). Dominated by waged positions (45.2% of the total) followed by self-employed workers (30%), family workers (22%) and employers (2.8%), the labour market is characterised by a low level of education. Around 75% of workers have at most a basic education, 18% an intermediate level and only 7% higher education. Men occupy 77.8% of jobs, giving a female employment rate of 26.2% in 2015 (versus 22.2% in 2000), concentrated largely in low-skilled jobs. Most active women lack even basic education, 55% versus 24% of men. Only 23% of active women have basic education (compared with 49% for men).

In 2016, the participation rate fell from 47.4% to 46.4% in one year, declining by 1 point while the employment rate dropped by 0.8 points, from 42.8% to 42%. In this respect, the national economy lost 37 000 net jobs (with 26 000 created in urban areas and 63 000 lost in rural ones), compared with an annual average creation of 27 000 jobs in 2015 and 95 000 during the 2008-13 period. Lastly, it should be highlighted that Morocco has made itself more attractive to business and is now ranked as the most attractive in Africa according to the Ernst & Young 2017 barometer, ahead of Kenya and South Africa, which share second place. None of the other North African countries appear in the list of the top ten African countries in which to invest.

Although job creation almost equalled growth in the active population between 2000 and 2015 in **Mauritania** (444 000 jobs compared with 467 498 additional active people), the employment rate has gradually risen, while the unemployment rate has fallen (Figure 6.7). As in most of the other countries in the region, labour market participation remains

Box 6.2. **Mixed labour market development by country** *(cont.)*

imbalanced for women: of 1 024 000 total jobs in 2015, 715 000 (69.8%) were occupied by men, compared with 309 000 (30.2%) by women. This poor female participation is an illustration of the relatively low employment rate in Mauritania (40.9%). According to a study by the National Office of Statistics (ONS) of Mauritania, just over 45.5% of the employed population possessed a general, vocational or technical education. While half of active workers attained at least secondary level and only 12.2% higher level. More than half of active men (52.9%) went beyond primary level, compared with 57.1% for women. Jobs are primarily created in the private sector (86%) versus 14% in the public sector. Private employment drives the job market in Mauritania, with self-employment (42.8%) predominating.

In contrast to the dynamic Moroccan and Algerian labour markets, the **Tunisian** market has remained stable. The employment rate has stagnated while the unemployment rate has gradually risen to more than 15%, compared with around 10% in Algeria and Morocco (Figure 6.7). Between 2000 and 2015, Tunisia only created 756 000 jobs, while the active population rose by 877 470 people. This imbalance hit young graduates hardest, for whom unemployment persists at worrying levels (31.2% in 2015). Of the 70 000 jobs created each year between 2005 and 2010, only 30 000 went to graduates of tertiary education, despite an average of 65 000 graduates being produced each year.

This situation is tied to the fact that the secondary and tertiary sectors rely primarily on unskilled labour. In 2010, the five leading sectors of the economy outside of government (banking and insurance, telecommunications, oil, production and distribution of electricity, and real estate) had very few university graduates among their workforce (6.7% of total employees). Construction represented 14.8% of all jobs, followed by textiles (11.7%) and hotels and restaurants (4.1%). Waged employment dominates, rising from 65.2% in 2000 to 72.1% in 2015, while self-employed numbers plummeted from 25.1% to 17.3% between 2000 and 2015. Female participation in the labour force remains relatively low (25.5% of jobs in 2015, versus 22.7% in 2000).

In all, the current structure of employment offers few opportunities for highly skilled jobs. The large majority of jobs are created in agriculture and services. These sectors together concentrate more than 72% of all jobs, versus 28% on average for the industrial sector (Figure 6.8).

Figure 6.8. **Employment structure in North African countries, 2000-15**

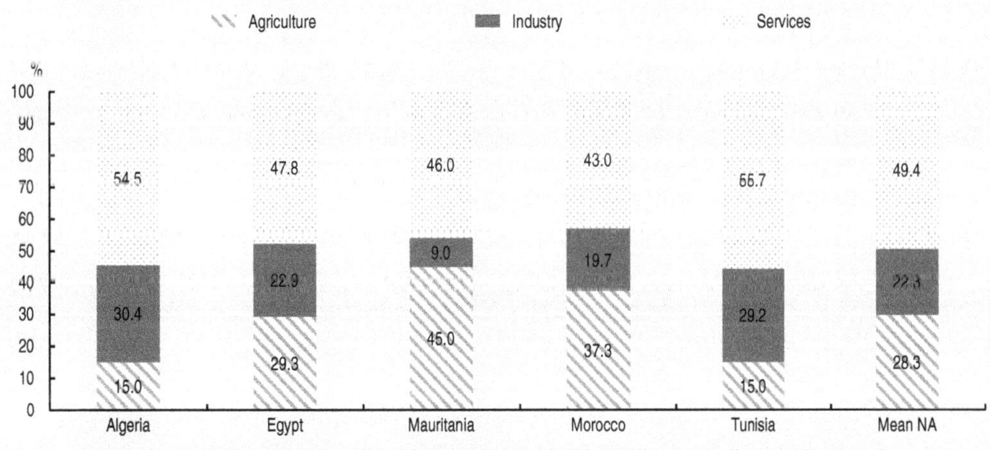

Source: Authors' calculations based on World Bank (2017), *World Development Indicators* (database).
StatLink http://dx.doi.org/10.1787/888933784007

The challenge of youth employment could be overcome. Demographic growth has in fact slowed in all North African countries. Algeria, Morocco and Tunisia have achieved demographic transition. As noted earlier, the rise in the active population is gradually slowing although pressure on job markets remains intense as young people are increasingly educated. According to ILO forecasts, by 2025, 65% of Moroccans and 73% of Egyptians aged 20-24 years will have attended secondary school (compared with 44% and 65%, respectively today). This trend could create unique opportunities for economic and social development, provided that these reserves of human capital are effectively used.

The creation of added value through innovative industries remains a key challenge. In addition, entrepreneurship should be encouraged among youth and women, as the rate at which companies are created is lower than in other regions internationally. To this end, the countries of the region should incentivise companies to innovate more, and should lift barriers to both the creation of companies and the growth of small businesses. Also, given the existing FDI-friendly investment codes, the countries of the region could move towards sectors in need of qualified labour and join global value chains.

- For example, the logistics and automobile clusters of Tangier in Morocco attracted large investors. These include a 20 000 m^2 logistics platform for Decathlon Group, aimed at supplying 11 stores in Morocco and at exporting to 10 countries from Tangier-Med (including Côte d'Ivoire, Senegal, Tunisia, Turkey, South America and Russia).
- An automobile logistics platform was established in Malloussa, around 20 km from Tangier, to supply spare parts to Ford, PSA Peugeot-Citroën (PSA Group) and Renault. Renault has been present in Tangier since 2007 producing entry-level cars there that are sold in 70 countries. In 2016, automobile production on the two Renault sites in Morocco (Tangier and Casablanca) was estimated at 348 000 vehicles, up from 288 053 vehicles in 2015. In 2016, 118 000 people were employed by the automobile sector in Morocco with 165 000 projected by 2020. Renault's expansion in Morocco drew the attention of PSA Group, and it is now planning on opening a factory in Morocco at the start of 2019 to produce around 200 000 vehicles and engines by 2024.
- Algeria has also had a Renault factory since 2014, capable of producing 25 000 vehicles a year at start up, and this should eventually reach 75 000 units. Already in 2017, the factory produced its 100 000th car. In addition, the German manufacturer Volkswagen opened an assembly plant in Algeria in July 2017.

Developing marks of quality could boost niche markets or new prospects for local businesses and absorb unemployed young graduates in North Africa. Numerous examples exist in the sub-region of small businesses (often with government support) having developed local resources using quality or ethical certifications, or developing their products by targeting specialised markets like that of the North African diaspora. In Algeria, examples include dried figs of Beni Maouche, Ighil Ali pepper and in Morocco, ecotourism, and in Tunisia, Beni Khedache weaving (Giordano et al., 2015).

The level of income inequality remains low

Changes in inequality must be linked to the labour market and economic development over the last 20 years. Since the 1990s, there are both greater numbers of young people arriving on the labour market and, equally, they are better educated. However, there is a lack of skilled jobs to absorb these numbers. With a growing population, difficulties related to employment and wealth creation translate into growing inequality.

The level of income inequality is moderate in North Africa. The average level of the Gini index went from 40.3 between 1990-94 to 33.0 between 2010-15 (Table 6.6), a level closer to that of Western Europe (30.7) or Eastern Europe (33.9) than Latin America (49.1), Sub-Saharan Africa (45.5) or Asia (39.8).

Table 6.6. **Dynamics of inequality in North Africa (percentage, Gini index)**

	1990-94	1995-99	2000-04	2005-09	2010-15	1990-2015
Algeria	40.2	35.3	31.1*	27.3*	24.1*	31.6
Egypt	32.0	30.1	32.5	31.5	31.3*	31.5
Mauritania	50.1	37.8	39.6	35.7	32.4	39.1
Morocco	39.2	39.5	40.6	40.7	41.2*	40.3
Tunisia	40.2	41.7	40.8	37.7	35.8	39.3
Mean	**40.3**	**36.9**	**36.9**	**34.6**	**33.0**	**36.3**

Note: The data required for calculating the Gini index are microeconomic and are collected from household surveys, which are infrequent in North African countries. The values marked with * indicate authors' estimates based on the average growth rate of the Gini index over the preceding periods.
Source: Authors' calculations based on World Bank (2017), *World Development Indicators* (database).

Despite this overall trend, disparities exist: inequalities remained almost stable in Egypt and Morocco over the 1990-2015 period, while in Tunisia they fell slightly (-12.4%) and fell more significantly in Mauritania (-35.2%). It must be noted that two of the three countries in which inequalities fell only slightly between 1990 and 2015 – Egypt and Tunisia – were affected by popular risings at the start of the 2010s. Additionally, the Gini index is an imprecise tool as it can produce the same result from situations with wildly different income distributions. Hence the necessity of supplementing the Gini index analyses with studies of income distribution by decile (Figure 6.9).

Figure 6.9. **Income distribution by quintile in North Africa**

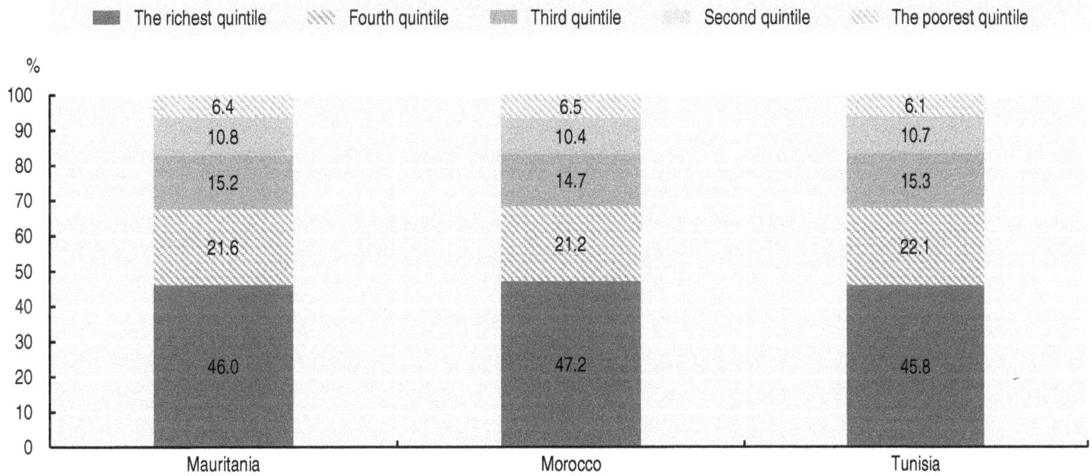

Source: Authors' calculations based on World Bank (2017), World Development Indicators (database).
StatLink http://dx.doi.org/10.1787/888933784026

One feature stands out in the three North African countries for which data is available: the emergence of a middle class. Wealth distribution by decile of the population is almost identical from one country to the next (Figure 6.9). The other remarkable fact is the constancy of statistical data over time. In fact, in most countries over the study period these proportions varied hardly at all. This suggests that the reduction of inequalities noted earlier has not resulted in a reduction in the revenue share of the richest, nor a growth in the revenue share of the poorest, but rather the constitution of a middle class under the combined effect of improved education and booming services.

The constitution of a middle class explains the falling Gini index, while gaps between the richest and poorest remain large. A certain number of people still live on less than USD 1.90 and USD 3.10 a day (Table 6.7), which points to complex social dynamics. While economic growth and job creation are important, it is also necessary to direct growth to benefit the poorest and to ensure that jobs are aimed at the most vulnerable. Indeed, although it might appear that rising inequality is difficult to avoid during a period of transition, such disparities must be contained to avoid living standards falling.

Table 6.7. **Dynamics of poverty in North African countries**

	Number of people with income below USD 1.90/day (2011 PPP, millions)				
	1990-94	1995-99	2000-04	2005-09	2010-15
Mauritania	0.9	0.5	0.5	0.4	0.2
Morocco	0.7	2.1	1.8	1.0	-
Tunisia	0.8	1.0	0.5	0.3	0.2
	Number of people with income below USD 3.10/day (2011 PPP, millions)				
	1990-94	1995-99	2000-04	2005-09	2010-15
Mauritania	1.5	1.1	1.2	1.1	0.9
Morocco	4.5	7.5	7.5	4.8	-
Tunisia	2.2	2.6	1.9	1.3	0.9

Source: Authors' calculations based on World Bank (2017), *World Development Indicators* (database).

In spite of decreasing inequality, part of the population remains vulnerable to poverty.

- Algeria had almost completely eradicated extreme poverty through welfare programmes and the gradual improvement in the security situation, but the collapse in international oil prices after 2015 has undermined the State's ability to engage in social redistribution. According to the World Bank, 4 million people – or 10% of the population – face insecurity and risk falling below the national poverty line.
- In Libya, an increasingly large part of the population lives in poverty, with more than 435 000 people displaced and 1.3 million living in food insecurity at the end of 2016.
- In Morocco, around 19% of the rural population is at risk of, or lives in, poverty.
- In Tunisia, extreme poverty remained constant at 1.9% over the period 2013-16 and moderate poverty fell from 8.3% in 2013 to 7.9% in 2015. Regional disparities in terms of standards of living and employment remain significant.

Inequality of opportunity disappears with targeted public policy

Beyond persistent income inequality, inequalities of opportunity can exist within countries and between them. These are primarily linked to disparities in accessing social goods (education, health, decent living conditions and technology). Inequalities of opportunity are perforce correlated to income inequalities, as only the most affluent households can secure social goods. However, public programmes in social sectors (education, health, sanitation) can reduce inequalities of opportunity and mitigate adverse effects despite the persistence of income inequality.

Improved access to social services underlies the net fall in poverty and extreme poverty (Table 6.8).

The results show a convergence not just in the level of human capital, but also a reduction in inequalities around access to education. Apart from Mauritania, the primary and secondary schooling rates were relatively high in all North African countries. These rates improved remarkably over the past two decades. Furthermore, disparities between male and female access to education remains marginal, as on average 46% of students were girls between 1990 and 2015, largely due to a variety of programmes promoting female schooling. In contrast, there are important differences in gender participation rates in economic life. While the region possesses a growing talent pool of educated women who want to work, their employment rate remains one of the lowest in the world (OECD, 2017b).

Table 6.8. **Inequalities of opportunity in North African countries, 1990-2015**

	Algeria	Egypt	Mauritania	Morocco	Tunisia	Mean North Africa
			Education index			
Primary school enrolment rates	93.8	93.3	69.0	88.0	97.7	88.4
Secondary school enrolment rates	70.6	77.1	19.8	46.0	73.7	57.4
Girls' primary school enrolment rates	46.7	46.6	48.0	44.7	47.4	46.7
Girls' secondary school enrolment rates	49.7	46.9	41.5	43.9	49.7	46.3
			Health indicators			
Infant mortality rates (‰)	30.9	36.5	66.3	40.1	25.0	39.8
Life expectancy at birth	71.4	68.6	60.6	70.2	73.2	68.8
			Decent living conditions indicators (percentage of population)			
Access to electricity	97.1	97.6	20.0	70.3	95.3	76.1
Access to sanitation	84.2	86.3	27.0	66.1	83.3	69.4
Access to drinking water	88.4	96.5	44.9	79.5	91.1	80.1
			Technology indicators (per 100 people)			
Fixed line telephone access	8.1	9.5	1.6	9.3	10.0	7.7
Mobile phone access	99.3	110.4	93.1	120.4	118.6	108.4

Note: Technology indicators were taken using averages over the 2010-15 period as pre-1990s these were almost zero, before rising rapidly after 2000.
Source: Authors' calculations based on World Bank (2017), *World Development Indicators* (database).

The performance of North African countries in terms of health and living standards indicators is also remarkable. The average rate of infant mortality (39.8 per thousand), life expectancy at birth (68.8 years), as well as access to electricity (76.1%), sanitation (69.4%) and clean water (80.1%) surpass the standards of developing countries. These average levels however mask both the under-performance of Mauritania in terms of decent living conditions and health, and better progress elsewhere. For example, since 2013 in Algeria, Egypt and Tunisia, electricity coverage is 99%, more than 90% of the population has access to water and sanitation in Egypt and Tunisia, and life expectancy is over 75 years in Egypt, Morocco and Tunisia.

Access to technology represents a shared opportunity in North Africa. The average rate of access to a mobile telephone is 108.4%, while access to fixed line telephony has declined over the past 15 years. Equal access to mobile telephony has thus facilitated access to information and training, as well as to mobile banking and financial services (money transfers and microcredit).

For some opportunities such as rural access to electricity or transportation, inequality reduction could be co-ordinated with large public investments. For example, the average GDP/public investment ratio between 2010 and 2015 was over 20% in Algeria and Morocco, compared with just 9.3% in Mauritania.

Employment and inequalities can influence economic growth

Depending on levels of unemployment, analysing the links between growth, unemployment and inequality can yield two types of correlation:

- For low levels of unemployment, economic growth is accompanied by an increase in income inequality, which in turn feeds economic growth. This situation corresponds with a transition phase, marked by the accumulation of capital and investment to support stronger economic growth.
- In contrast, when the unemployment rate is higher than 15%, higher growth reduces inequality and social programmes to reduce inequality have a positive

effect on growth. This situation particularly corresponds to periods of crisis or crisis recovery, characterised by socioeconomic deterioration, when measures aimed at supporting a reduction in poverty and inequality are necessary to relaunch economic growth.

As such, in North African countries, a growth promotion strategy could generate or eradicate income inequality depending on the employment situation.

Policy recommendations

Improve and reinforce political stability and institutional accountability

Over the past few years, the countries of North Africa have been characterised by a relatively high level of political instability as well as a growing demand for governmental transparency and civic engagement in democratic processes. Broadly, measures of both governmental stability and political risk have deteriorated, particularly in Tunisia, suggesting an increase in political risk (PRS, 2018). Furthermore, the periods of sluggish growth have been characterised by episodes of political instability, which discourages investors.

Recent studies corroborate the negative impact of political instability on growth. This loss of growth could reach 2% according to Aisen and Veiga (2013), by impacting human and physical capital, TFP and FDI. It is thus necessary to guarantee a climate of political stability and a transparent regulatory framework to encourage strong, durable and more inclusive growth to reduce inequality. Greater political stability can be achieved via a firm commitment to combat extremist groups implicated in attacks and kidnappings. In addition, the fight against corruption and the improvement of democratic processes (freedom of expression, transparent electoral processes, strong checks and balances and institutions) are also elements that could improve social tensions and encourage political stability.

Although more progress could still be made, Morocco succeeded in rising to certain political expectations by adopting a new constitution in 2011 that gave new authority to the head of government and embraced a policy of "advanced" regionalisation. Tunisia managed to improve its stability through a national dialogue that gave civil society an important role in resolving social conflict. Four civil society organisations[2] were thus awarded with a Nobel peace prize in 2015 for their "decisive contribution to the construction of multi-party democracy in Tunisia" (Norwegian Nobel Committee, 2015).

Accelerate the structural transformation of economies

The countries of North Africa have already reached an important milestone by achieving demographic transition and by urbanising (AfDB/OECD/UNDP, 2016). However, the real challenge is to shift their economies towards sectors that create added value and offer employment to young and qualified workers. Consolidating the development of the manufacturing sector and expanding the exportable offer to emerging countries, particularly in Africa could help achieve this goal. This route could not only open new growth opportunities for medium-sized organisations, but also reduce dependence on international prices of primary materials and tourism, whilst compensating for sluggish demand from traditional partners.

The case of the automotive sector with the car assembly platforms in Morocco and Algeria provide an example other sectors could follow, including domestic appliances, electronics, textiles and others. The medium-term objective is to establish a real industrial sector, unachievable without foreign investment. Of course, the legal regime is already favourable to FDI and state contributions played a determining role in the automobile sector. This dynamism and political determination should promote the development of public private partnership (PPP) agreements to facilitate the creation of new industries or the offshoring of foreign industries.

In Morocco, the Industrial Acceleration Plan 2014-20 (*Plan d'accélération industrielle*, PAI) aims to increase industry's contribution to GDP to 23% before 2020, as well as to create 500 000 jobs. With a fund of USD 2.2 billion, the PAI aims for massive infrastructure construction, the creation of industrial clusters and targeted support for Moroccan companies to attract FDI in the manufacturing sector.

Local government participation in national agencies enables the promotion of local SMEs to investors, as for example, in the automobile cluster in Tangier. However, the capacity of local businesses to subcontract tasks and meet quality standards of international investors still needs to be improved. Closer co-operation with the private sector and the development of targeted training in a number of sectors could be useful.

Similarly, industrial clusters could facilitate the emergence of productive zones, but these must create links with the surrounding areas to limit geographic disparities which remain high in the region, particularly between the richer coastal regions and the hinterland. In Tunisia, while the Sfax cluster brings together 60 000 companies from relatively productive sectors, these have few links with local companies in other sectors and regions of the country.

To address these shortcomings, governments could work on the functional zones of regions rather than administrative districts. Thus in 2015, under regionalisation reforms, Morocco created the region of Casablanca-Settat which enabled neighbouring towns to benefit from infrastructure and services in proximity to Casablanca, a city with more than 10 million inhabitants. Lastly, the adoption of sectoral strategies adapted to the conditions of each region could create more skilled jobs linked to the needs of the local and national markets.

Target jobs for women and youth via structural catalysts

Female employment rates are still very low in all North African countries, representing a loss of potential productivity. Although these countries have made progress in terms of female education, women's access to the job market is still limited to unskilled or part-time positions. Furthermore, the proportion of women entrepreneurs remains low in Algeria (15%), Egypt (25%) and Morocco (11%).

Bold politics that promote flexibility in the workplace are important for female participation. For example, families must be helped access low-cost childcare by supporting public nurseries thus enabling women to envisage full-time work as a profitable activity (OECD, 2018b). Similarly, longer maternity leaves also have beneficial effects. Currently, in most North African countries maternity leave is 90 days. As demographic transition has been achieved, maternity leave could be extended to six months if desired, accompanied by a 20-30% reduction in salary for the last three months. More generous parental leave is currently offered in North America and Scandinavian countries, with very encouraging results for female employment.

Encouraging female entrepreneurship is also a way of embedding employment policies and reducing gender disparities in the labour market. Despite relative emancipation, the gender gap in entrepreneurship remains higher in Tunisia (10%), Libya (8%) and Egypt (7%) than in other African countries where the gap is on average 3% (AfDB/OECD/UNDP, 2017). To reduce this gap, female-led projects should be supported by banking and decentralised financial institutions (EU/ETF/OECD, 2014). This will improve female employment rates as female entrepreneurs hire more women than men.

Youth employment should also be a defining element of employment policy via three key themes aimed at harmonising education with market needs:

- **The development of skilled vocational training programmes in line with labour market needs.** Skills required to service the primary sector and industrial processing should be encouraged, via among other things supporting industrial and technological research, which is still nascent in these countries. These programmes could aim to support structural transformation via provision of technically qualified labour to work in secondary industries.
- **The introduction of business incubators for young graduates between 20 and 30 years of age.** In effect, young people graduating from vocational training that wish to start a company in their area of training should benefit from support. This support should extend from setting up the project to the first three years of its execution, emphasising a search for matched funding. It is essential to monitor and evaluate the projects to guarantee the success of these programmes and to ensure that entrepreneurs make good use of the funds and create jobs.
- **Professional retraining for long-term unemployed youth.** Additional training could make people competitive in the labour market once more. This assumes that technical and vocational training courses will first be developed.

Notes

1. The employment rate is not directly correlated to the unemployment rate, as unemployment counts labour that is not in work but is available and actively seeking employment. It excludes those who have ceased looking for work or are in education.
2. The Tunisian General Union of Work (*Union générale tunisienne du travail*, UGTT), Tunisia Union of Industry, Commerce and Craft (*Union tunisienne de l'industrie, du commerce et de l'artisanat*, UTICA), the Tunisian human rights league (*Ligue tunisienne des droits de l'homme*, LTDH) and the National Order of Lawyers (*Ordre National des Avocats de Tunisie*).

References

Aisen, A. and F.J. Veiga (2013), "How does political instability affect economic growth?", *European Journal of Political Economy*, Vol. 29/C, Elsevier, Amsterdam, pp. 151-167, https://econpapers.repec.org/article/eeepoleco/v_3a29_3ay_3a2013_3ai_3ac_3ap_3a151-167.htm.

AfDB/OECD/UNDP (2017), *African Economic Outlook 2017: Entrepreneurship and Industrialisation*, OECD Publishing, Paris, http://dx.doi.org/10.1787/aeo-2017-en.

AfDB/OECD/UNDP (2016), *African Economic Outlook 2016: Sustainable Cities and Structural Transformation*, OECD Publishing, Paris, http://dx.doi.org/10.1787/aeo-2016-en.

CGEM (2014), Étude sur les leviers de la compétitivité des entreprises marocaines, Commission investissement, compétitivité et émergence industrielle, Confédération générale des entreprises du Maroc, Casablanca, www.cgem.ma/upload/392118863.pdf.

De Long, B. and H.L. Summers (1992), "Equipment investment and economic growth: How strong is the nexus ?", *Brookings Papers on Economic Activity (BPEA)*, N° 2, Brookings Institution, Washington D.C., pp. 157-211, https://www.brookings.edu/bpea-articles/equipment-investment-and-economic-growth-how-strong-is-the-nexus/.

Devarajan, S., V. Swaroop and H.F. Zou (1996), "The composition of public expenditure and economic growth", *Journal of Monetary Economics*, N° 37, World Bank, Washington D.C., pp. 313- 344, http://www1.worldbank.org/publicsector/pe/pfma07/ShantaVinayHengfu.pdf.

Edwards, S. (1998), "Openness, productivity and growth: What do we really know?", *The Economic Journal*, Vol. 108/447, Royal Economic Society, London, pp. 383-398.

Engelbrecht, H-J. (1997), "International R&D spillovers, human capital and productivity in OECD economies: An empirical investigation", *European Economic Review*, Vol. 41/8 (August 1997), pp. 1479-1488, Elsevier, Amsterdam.

Giordano, T., B. Losch, A. Minsat and H. B. Solignac Lecomte (2015), "Unlocking the potential of African regions", in *Recent Trends in Banking in Sub-Saharan Africa: From Financing to Investment*, Stijns Jean-Philippe and Revoltella Debora (eds.), European Bank of Investment (EIB), Luxembourg, pp. 87-106, http://dx.doi.org/10.2867/361551.

HCP (2011), *Enquête nationale démographique à passages répétés 2009-10 : principaux résultats*, Haut-commissariat au plan, Rabat, www.hcp.ma/Etude-Nationale-Demographique-a-Passages-Repetes-2009-2010_a749.html.

ILO (2017), *ILO Stat* (database), www.ilo.org/ilostat.

IMF (2018), *World Economic Outlook Database*, International Monetary Fund, http://www.imf.org/external/pubs/ft/weo/2018/01/weodata/index.aspx.

IMF (2016a), "Financial development in Sub-Saharan Africa: Promoting inclusive and sustainable growth", *Departmental Papers*, N°16/11, African Department, International Monetary Fund, Washington D.C., http://www.imf.org/en/Publications/Departmental-Papers-Policy-Papers/Issues/2016/12/31/Financial-Development-in-Sub-Saharan-Africa-Promoting-Inclusive-and-Sustainable-Growth-44220.

IMF (2016b), *World Economic Outlook*, International Monetary Fund, Washington D.C., https://www.imf.org/external/pubs/ft/weo/2016/02/weodata/index.aspx.

Jorgenson, D. and E. Yip (1999), "Whatever happened to productivity investment and growth in the G-7?", *Institute for Monetary and Economic Studies (IMES) Discussion Paper* N°99-E-11, Bank of Japan, Tokyo, http://www.imes.boj.or.jp/edps99/99-E-11.pdf.

Kato, H. (2016), "Population, economic growth, and TFP in developed countries", in *An Empirical Analysis of Population and Technological Progress*, Population Studies of Japan, Tokyo.

Mankiw, N.G., D. Romer and D. Weil (1992), "A contribution to the empirics of economic growth", *Quarterly Journal of Economics*, Vol. 107/2, Harvard University Department of Economics, Harvard, pp. 407-437 https://doi.org/10.2307/2118477.

Mohapatra, S. and D. Ratha (2011), *Remittance Markets in Africa*, International Bank for Reconstruction and Development, World Bank, Washington D.C.

Norwegian Nobel Committee (2015), "The Nobel Peace Prize for 2015", *Press release*, https://www.nobelprize.org/nobel_prizes/peace/laureates/2015/press.html.

OECD (2018a), *International Development Statistics* (online database), Development Assistance Committee (DAC), www.oecd.org/dac/stats/idsonline.htm.

OECD (2018b), *OECD Economic Surveys: Tunisia 2018*, OECD Publishing, Paris, http://dx.doi.org/10.1787/eco_surveys-tun-2018-en.

OECD (2017a), *Examen multidimensionnel du Maroc: Volume 1. Évaluation initiale*, Les voies de développement, OECD Publishing, Paris, http://dx.doi.org/10.1787/9789264274945-fr.

OECD (2017b), *Women's Economic Empowerment in Selected MENA Areas: The Impact of Legal Frameworks in Algeria, Egypt, Jordan, Libya, Morocco and Tunisia*, Competitiveness and Private Sector Development, OECD Publishing, Paris, http://dx.doi.org/10.1787/9789264279322-en.

OECD (2001), *Measuring Productivity: Measurement of Aggregate and Industry-level Productivity Growth*, OECD Publishing, Paris, http://www.oecd.org/sdd/productivity-stats/2352458.pdf.

OECD/European Commission/ETF (2014), *SME Policy Index: The Mediterranean Middle East and North Africa. Implementation of the Small Business Act for Europe*, OECD Publishing, Paris, http://dx.doi.org/10.1787/9789264218413-en.

The Political Risk Services (PRS, 2018), *Database on political instability*, PRS Group, East Syracuse, N.Y., https://www.prsgroup.com/explore-our-products/international-country-risk-guide/

Toussaint, E., D. Munevar, P. Gottiniaux and A. Sanabria, (2015), *Les inégalités dans le monde. Dans les chiffres de la dette 2015*, Comité pour l'abolition des dettes illégitimes (CADTM), Liège, Belgique, http://www.cadtm.org/Les-chiffres-de-la-dette-2015, p. 271.

UNDESA (2017), *World Population Prospects* (database), https://esa.un.org/unpd/wpp/ (accessed 1 March 2018).

United Nations Statistics Division (2017), *UNCOMTRADE* (database), https://comtrade.un.org/ (accessed 1 February 2018).

World Bank (2017), *World Development Indicators*, World Bank Group, http://databank.worldbank.org/data/reports.aspx?source=world-development-indicators.

World Travel and Tourism Council (WTTC) (2018), *Travel & Tourism Economic Impact 2018 Egypt*, World Travel and Tourism Council (WTTC), March 2018 https://www.wttc.org/-/media/files/reports/economic-impact-research/countries-2018/egypt2018.pdf.

Chapter 7

Dynamics of growth, jobs and inequalities in West Africa

This chapter examines the economic dynamics of 15 West African countries (Benin, Burkina Faso, Cabo Verde, Côte d'Ivoire, Gambia, Ghana, Guinea, Guinea-Bissau, Liberia, Mali, Niger, Nigeria, Senegal, Sierra Leone and Togo) from 1990 to 2015. Strong regional growth could be undermined by youth unemployment, while inclusive and endogenous growth relies on strengthening regional integration. Growth of the population, of regional demand and of an emerging middle class offer important opportunities for West Africa's development. Harnessing these calls for implementing efficient policies and generating more jobs in the formal economy.

IN BRIEF

Growth in West Africa reached over 5% on average between 2000 and 2014, but it remains to be consolidated. Led by demand fuelled by population increases and the rise of the middle class, economic growth depends on raw materials and agriculture, and remains driven by the large economies of the region (e.g. Nigeria, Côte d'Ivoire, Ghana).

In ten countries for which data was available, informal activities accounted for between 68% and 90% of **jobs**. The lack of formal employment, poor education levels and the gap between skills and jobs contribute to unemployment, particularly among youth, for whom periods of unemployment are often long. By 2035, the population aged between 15 and 24 years will increase by 73% to reach 117 million. Improving private sector capacity is thus crucial for supporting growth and jobs.

The **poverty** rate declined from 55.4% in 1990 to 43.8% in 2013. Access to basic services has improved: 79% of the population thus had access to clean water in 2017 (according to available data). However, with demographic growth, the number of people living in poverty has increased to 144.4 million of a total population of 367.6 million. **Inequalities** also remain high, with a Gini coefficient of 0.39 in 2014, and this is higher in several countries. The human development index (HDI) is the lowest of the continent, at 0.47. Social security remains insufficient and half of West African countries display strong gender inequality.

Inclusive growth will require **development strategies** along three principal areas. First, rural-urban links must be developed through intermediate cities, cross-border corridors, agro-food chains, fair access to land and redistribution policies. Secondly, local products could be upgraded by encouraging companies to come together, as well as via education and training in skills required by the labour market, and investment in the private sector. Lastly, inclusive growth necessitates improvements in institutional capacity, the business regulatory framework and taxation.

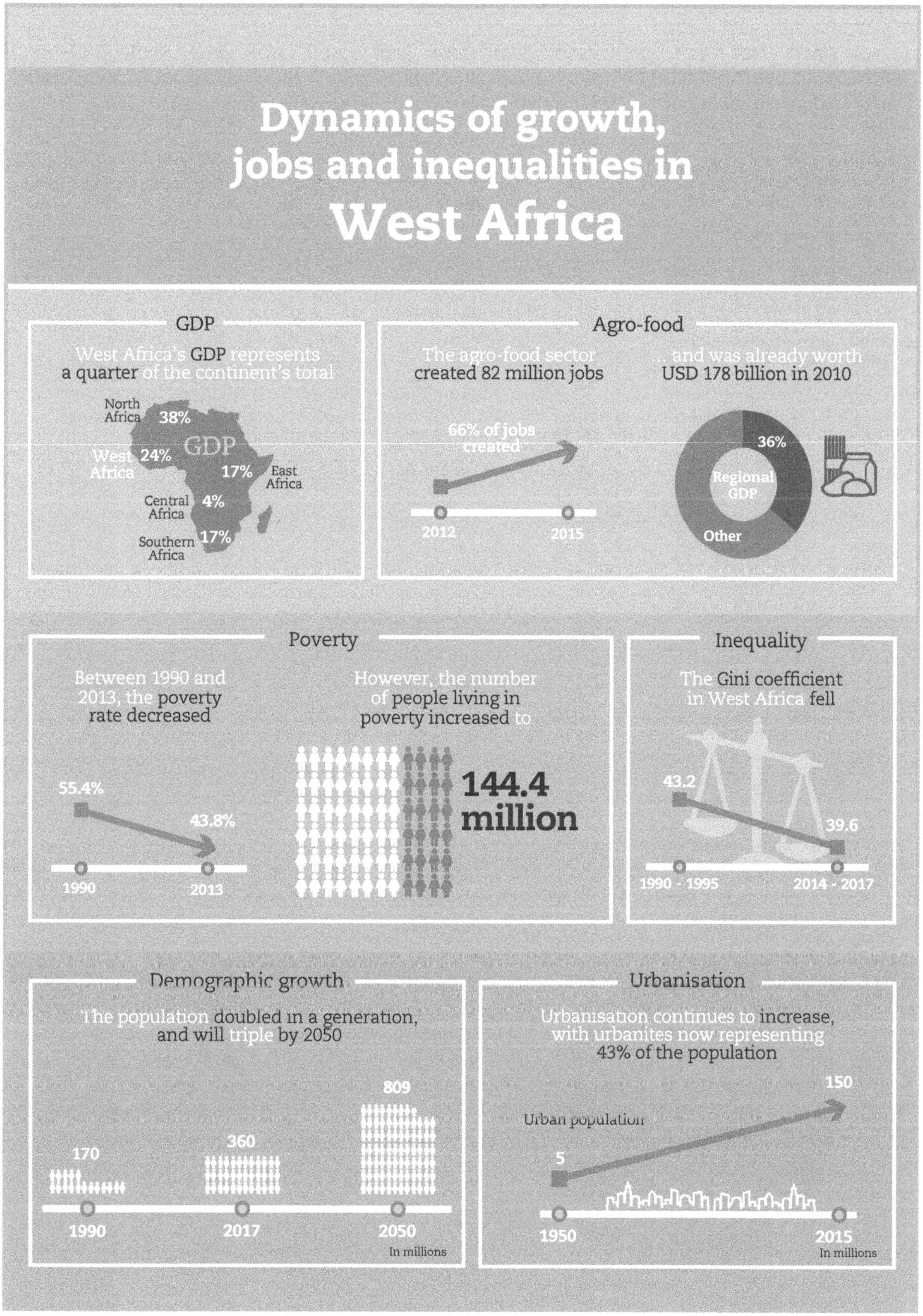
Dynamics of growth, jobs and inequalities in West Africa
GDP
West Africa's GDP represents a quarter of the continent's total
North Africa 38%
GDP
West Africa 24%
17% East Africa
Central Africa 4%
Southern Africa 17%
Agro-food
The agro-food sector created 82 million jobs
66% of jobs created
2012
2015
... and was already worth USD 178 billion in 2010
36%
Regional GDP
Other
Poverty
Between 1990 and 2013, the poverty rate decreased
55.4%
43.8%
1990
2013
However, the number of people living in poverty increased to
144.4 million
Inequality
The Gini coefficient in West Africa fell
43.2
39.6
1990 - 1995
2014 - 2017
Demographic growth
The population doubled in a generation, and will triple by 2050
170
360
809
1990
2017
2050
In millions
Urbanisation
Urbanisation continues to increase, with urbanites now representing 43% of the population
Urban population
5
150
1950
2015
In millions

West Africa regional profile

Table 7.1. **Basic indicators for West Africa, 2017**

Population (thousands)	367 566
Land area (thousands of km2)	5 033
Population density (people/km2)	73
GDP, PPP (USD billion)	1 584
GDP per capita, PPP (USD)	4 370

Source: Authors' calculations based on UNDESA (2017), *World Population Prospects* (database); World Bank (2017), *World Development Indicators* (database) and IMF (2018), *World Economic Outlook Database.*

Table 7.2. **Financial flows and tax revenues to West Africa (current USD billion), 2009-16**

			2009	2010	2011	2012	2013	2014	2015	2016
Foreign	Private	Inward foreign direct investment	14.8	11.9	18.3	15.4	13.4	11.7	9.7	11.2
		Portfolio investments	0.8	5.0	6.6	18.8	14.4	8.1	5.5	4.7
		Remittances	21.6	23.3	27.2	27.4	27.6	28.5	28.7	27.8
	Public	Official development assistance (net total, all donors)	12.0	12.2	12.1	13.6	12.2	12.4	12.4	11.5
Total foreign flows			**49.2**	**52.5**	**64.2**	**75.3**	**67.6**	**60.7**	**56.3**	**55.2**
Domestic tax revenues			**35.3**	**43.9**	**63.3**	**68.9**	**67.3**	**67.7**	**47.8**	**39.7**

Sources: Authors' calculations based on IMF (2018), *World Economic Outlook* (database), OECD-DAC (2017), International Development Statistics (database), and World Bank (2017), *World Development Indicators* (database).

Figure 7.1. **Growth dynamics in West Africa and Africa, 1990-2018**

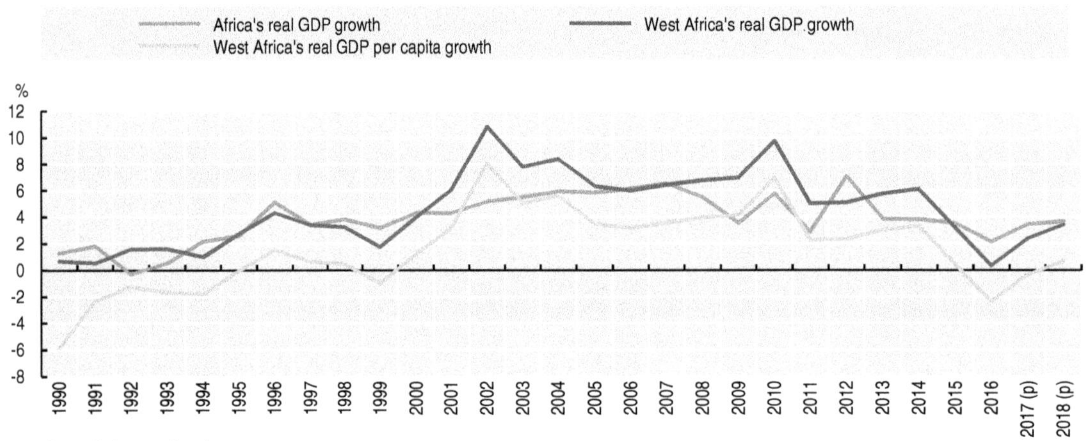

Note: (p) = projections.

Source: Authors' calculations based on IMF (2018) *World Economic Outlook* database.

StatLink http://dx.doi.org/10.1787/888933784045

Figure 7.2. **Trade composition in West Africa, 2016**

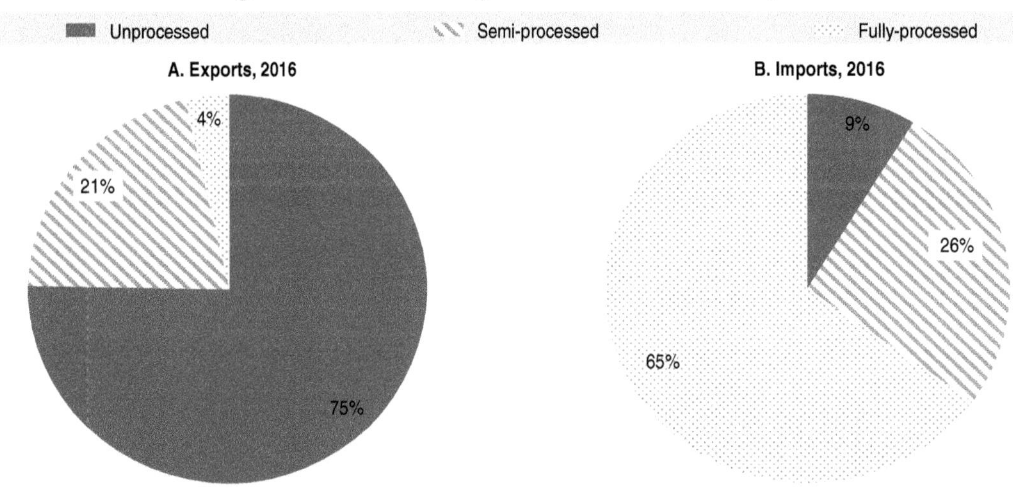

Source: Authors' calcuations based on *UNCOMTRADE* (2017) data.

StatLink http://dx.doi.org/10.1787/888933784064

The 15 countries of West Africa are diverse culturally, linquistically and ecologically, with a marked difference between the Sahelien North and the Southern coast along the Gulf of Guinea. Politically, almost all of the countries have experienced democratic changes of government, although stability remains a challenge. There are also sizeable economic differences: the region includes both countries held up as examples of development, such as Ghana (ranked 120th by the World Bank's *Doing Business* 2018) and Côte d'Ivoire (139th), as well as countries that rank among the poorest in terms of GDP per inhabitant, such as Liberia, Niger, Mali, Togo, Guinea, Guinea-Bissau and Burkina Faso.

The population doubled in the space of one generation, rising from 170 to almost 360 million inhabitants between 1990 and 2017 (30% and 5% of the African and world populations, respectively). According to UN projections, the population of the region will reach 809 million by 2050, representing 31.7% of the African population and 8.2% of the world population (UNDESA, 2018). The population is concentrated along the Atlantic coastline, leaving vast empty and almost-desert spaces. More than four in ten people (44%) are under the age of 15, a higher proportion than average for the continent (41%).

In terms of regional integration, progress has been made both in harmonising economic policy and in free circulation of goods and people. The Economic Community of Western African States (ECOWAS), founded in 1975, is comprised of two regional economic organisations (Box 7.A1.1). It also plays a political role with achievements in terms of peace and security. However, the terrorist threat persists in Mali, Burkina Faso, Côte d'Ivoire, Niger and Nigeria.

As the second largest regional economy in Africa, West Africa accounts for 24% of total GDP of the continent, behind North Africa (38%) and ahead of Southern Africa (17%), East Africa (17%) and Central Africa (4%) (IMF, 2017a). In 2016, growth plumeted to 0.4%, having been over 5% between 2000 and 2014, but it subsequently recovered to 3.4% in 2018. The region remains exposed to climate events that affect agricultural production, as well as to fluctuations in international prices for raw materials. Activity is focused around the largest economy in the region (Annex 7.A1), Nigeria (77% of total GDP and 52% of the West African population). Activity has also proven sustained in countries such as Côte d'Ivoire and Senegal, but remains very weak, or even negative elsewhere.

Economic structural transformation and intra-community trade remain necessary in order to contain inequalities between and within countries, while also addressing the shortage of decent jobs.

Dynamics and determinants of growth

A favourable momentum to be consolidated

Over the 2000-14 period, West Africa experienced stronger growth than the rest of the continent, although this was relatively unstable. For example, growth collapsed to 0.4% in 2016 (Figure 7.1). It then recovered in 2017 and should reach around 3.4% in 2018. These strong variations are due in part to external factors, such as the economic situation in main trade partners and fluctuations in prices of raw materials. ECOWAS countries export products in high global demand, but in 2016 up to 75.3% of them remained unprocessed (Figure 7.2). Thus, oil and bitumen represent 81% of Nigeria's exports, cocoa 48% of Ivoirian exports while Ghana's external trade is comprised mainly of oil (32.5%), cocoa and gold (20%, respectively) (OECD, 2016). Internal shocks also play a role, as with the Ebola virus in 2014-15 (World Bank, 2014) or in the wake of political or security crises.

However, growth dynamics vary between WAEMU and non-WAEMU countries. After the international financial crisis of 2008 and 2009, activity within WAEMU increased in a more or less sustained manner between 2010 and 2015 compared with non-WAEMU countries. Nigeria in particular fell into recession (Figure 7.3). The control of inflation, based on a maximum threshold of 3% in the WAEMU zone results in growth that is not as strong – half that of non-WAEMU countries between 1995 and 2004 – but more stable. In contrast, Ghana, Nigeria and Sierra Leone suffered inflation rates higher than 10% in 2016 (ECOWAS, 2016).

Figure 7.3. **Comparative real growth in ECOWAS economic areas**

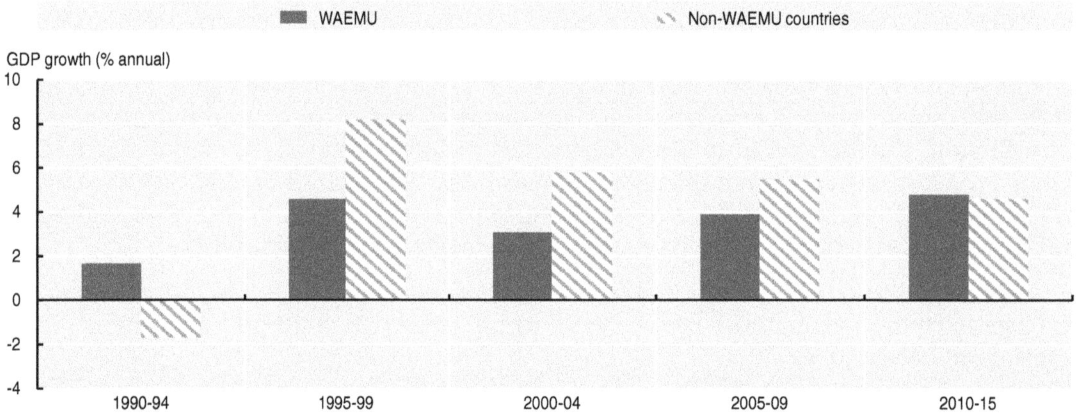

Note: The seven non-WAEMU countries are Cabo Verde, Gambia, Ghana, Guinea, Liberia, Nigeria and Sierra Leone
Source: Authors' calculations based on World Bank (2017), *World Development Indicators*.
StatLink http://dx.doi.org/10.1787/888933784083

Private consumption and public investment support growth

Regional demand, underpinned by demographics and the growth of a middle class, increasingly drives growth. Since 2000, private consumption has been the principal contributor to growth (Figure 7.4). It should continue both to broaden with demographic growth and deepen with the growth of a relatively well-off middle class. Here, the middle class is defined as households spending between USD 5 and USD 20 per person per day at purchasing power parity. According to the PovCal database, in West Africa the middle class counted 44.6 million people in 2013 concentrated in a number of countries, including 18.6 million Nigerians and a total of 17.2 million Ghanians, Ivoirians and Senegalese together. However, 53% of the intermediate class – defined here as spending between USD 2 and USD 10 per person per day (AfDB, 2011) – remains vulnerable to falling back into poverty (Staatz and Hollinger, 2016).

Under certain conditions, local production could benefit from demographics and the middle class expansion. Increasingly, middle class demand calls on local producers for high value-added goods and services that are progressively being integrated into consumption (processed goods and meat in particular). On average, expenditure on food represents 39% of revenue in Côte d'Ivoire and 65% in Nigeria (Staatz and Hollinger, 2016: 8).

Figure 7.4. **Growth composition in West Africa, 2009-16**

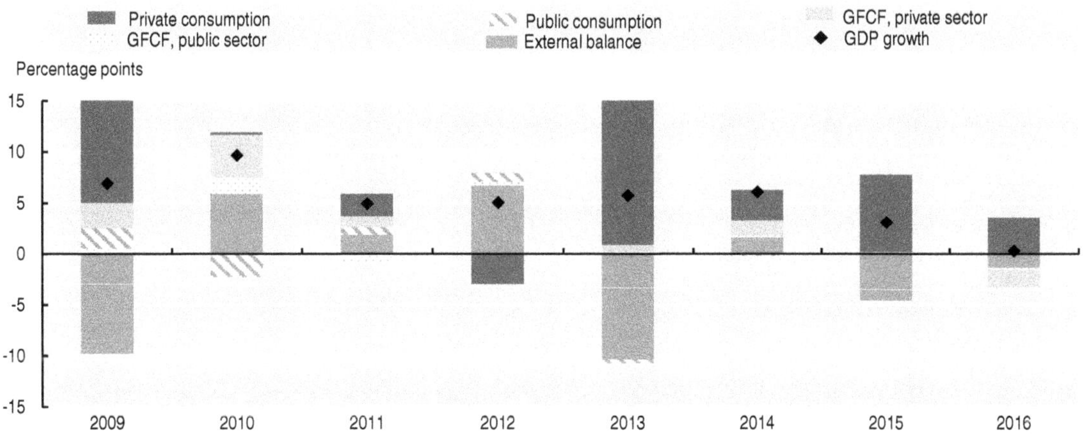

Source: Authors' calculations based on IMF (2018), *World Economic Outlook* database.

StatLink http://dx.doi.org/10.1787/888933784102

The countries of the region would benefit from stabilising their public accounts in order to release resources for public investment. In the decade starting from 2000, better macroeconomic stability policies, debt cancellation and improved fiscal policy helped governments to gain a margin that enabled them to launch public investment programmes. The debt-to-GDP ratio of the zone, estimated at 41.7% in 2016, remains below the threshold of 70% fixed by the convergence criteria. Several States in ECOWAS have also demonstrated a better capacity to access international debt markets. Côte d'Ivoire, Nigeria and Senegal's issuing of Eurobonds provide a case in point. However, the pace of debt accumulation has proven fairly high for certain countries (IMF, 2017b). According to the IMF (2017c), four countries have resumed levels of debts significantly higher than the convergence criteria: Cabo Verde (129% of GDP in 2016), Gambia (120%), Ghana (73%) and Togo (80%). These levels of public indebtedness call into question the medium-term sustainability of public investment.

Local provision of consumer goods and services remains limited

Rapid urbanisation helps economic structural transformation but often via the informal sector. Between 1950 and 2015, the number of urban areas with more than 10 000 inhabitants increased from 152 to 1 800. The urban population also increased 30 fold, from 5 to 150 million (Staatz and Hollinger, 2016). Urbanites now represent 43% of the population (Allen and Heinrigs, 2016). As a result, demand for processed agro-food products has proven more dynamic in West Africa than the global average (OECD, 2016). However, if the offer of goods and services does not improve via a dual process of industrialisation and local transformation of raw materials, an important driver of growth could be lost. Without local supply, demographic growth may result in increased imports of food stuffs and other consumer goods, to the detriment of the trade balance.

Since 2000, labour and capital accumulation have contributed positively to growth, while global productivity has often proven negative. Over the 2000-15 period, labour contributed more to growth than capital, explained by strong demographic growth and the weight of agricultural activity (Figure 7.5).

Figure 7.5. **Factoral contribution to growth, 1990-2015**

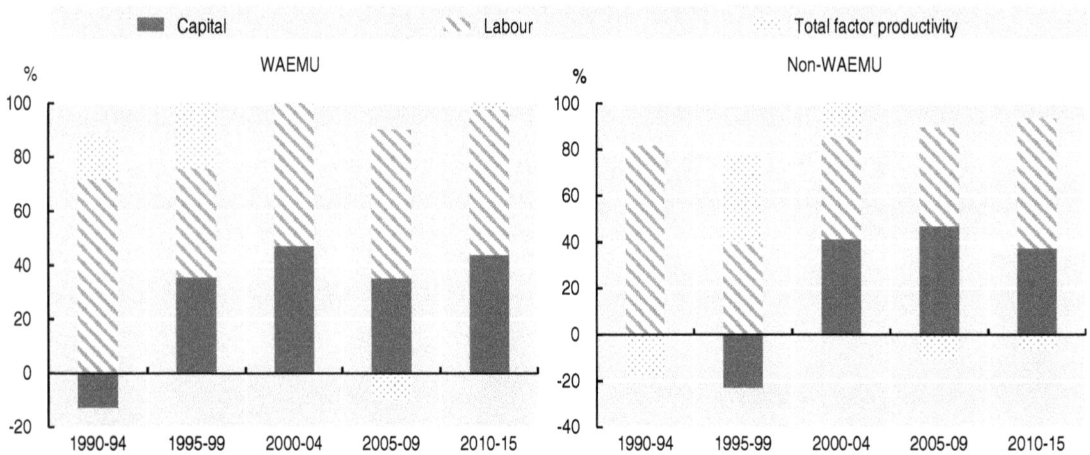

Source: Authors' calculations based on World Bank (2017), *World Development Indicators* database.
StatLink http://dx.doi.org/10.1787/888933784121

Dynamics and determinants of employment and unemployment in West Africa

Employment, buoyed by the agro-food sector, is dominated by the primary and services sectors

The agricultural sector is the leading source of employment in ECOWAS, followed by services and industry. In 2000, it represented between 33% (Gambia) and 77% of jobs (Niger). While agriculture's share has either stagnated or declined in all countries, it still accounts for almost 51% of jobs (simple average, Figure 7.6). In contrast, jobs in the services sector have increased in nearly all countries with the exception of Mali and Senegal. The tertiary sector represents more than 40% of jobs in Gambia, thanks to hotels and restaurants, as well as in Ghana due to tourism (UNCTAD, 2015). In Burkina Faso, the agricultural sector contracted to the benefit of services, particularly the manufacturing sector which accounted for 32% of jobs in 2017 versus 4% in 2000. This surge in the industrial sector is linked to the expansion of informal mining activity, primarily of small-scale gold panning.

Figure 7.6. **Employment structure in ECOWAS (percentage of total, 2017)**

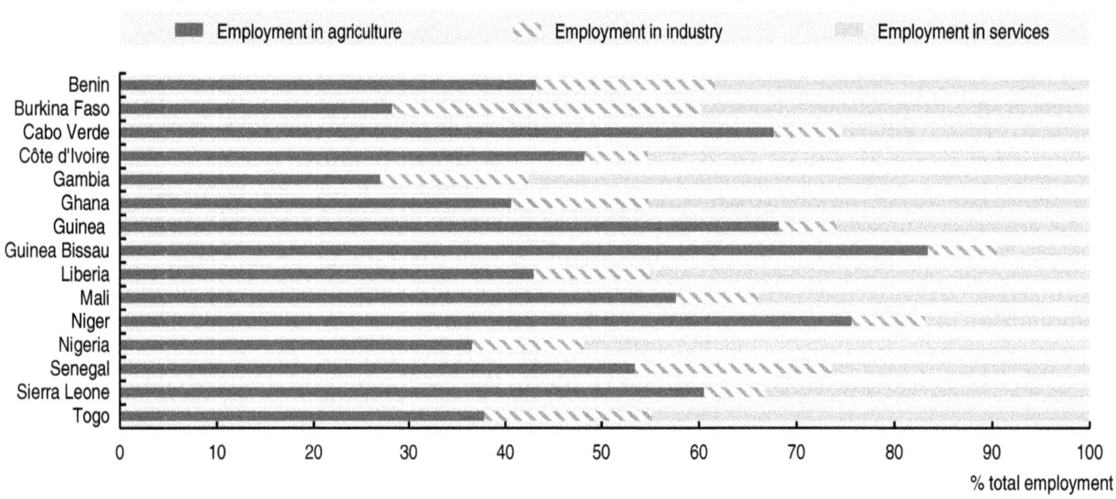

Source: Authors' calculations based on ILO (2017) ILOStat database.
StatLink http://dx.doi.org/10.1787/888933784140

The agro-food sector offers good employment perspectives, with more than 66% of jobs created between 2012 and 2015 – or 82 million positions (Allen et al., 2018: 8). It is the largest sector, with production representing USD 178 billion in 2010, or 36% of regional gross domestic product (GDP). One quarter of the rural population in West Africa is involved in non-agricultural activities (OECD, 2013). The activities of transformation, logistics and retail generate employment in transportation, packaging and distribution to urban areas. These activities are rapidly expanding and are generally more productive than agricultural activities. According to Sahel Club and ECOWAS estimates, they represent 40% of the sector's value added, and will continue to expand as the region urbanises (Allen and Heinrigs, 2016).

The jobs market remains primarily informal

On the whole, a large part of the population is employed, either formally or informally. The employment rate varies from 80% in Burkina Faso to 51% in Senegal (Figure 7.7).

Figure 7.7. **ECOWAS labour market participation, percentage of active population (2015-17)**

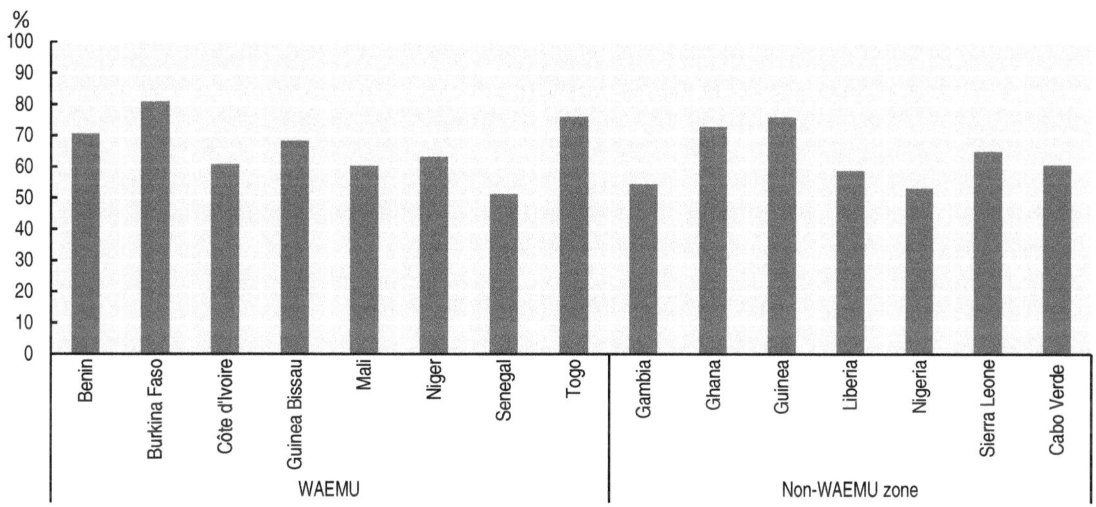

Source: Authors' calculations based on ILO (2017), ILOStat database.
StatLink http://dx.doi.org/10.1787/888933784159

The jobs market, however, remains dominated by a dynamic informal sector. Throughout the sub-region, the informal sector represents between 30% (Togo) and 50% (Benin) of the national economy (IMF, 2017b). In Senegal, the informal economy has created between 80% and 97% of jobs over the past 20 years (Minister of the Economy and Finances of Senegal, 2011). Of the 407 000 companies surveyed in Senegal, 97% formed part of the informal sector (ANSD, 2015). In Côte d'Ivoire, more than 80% of the labour force is in the informal sector, while this exceeds 90% in Mali and Burkina Faso. In Ouagadougou (Burkina Faso), almost 45% of unemployed people are unaware of the public employment agency (*Bureau public pour l'emploi*) (DIAL, 2007, cited in Nordman and Pasquier Doumer, 2015). The most vulnerable groups work in the informal sector, namely, the poorest, young people (AfDB/OECD/UNDP, 2012) and women. Table 7.3 shows the share of informal sector in non-agricultural employment.

Table 7.3. **Informal sector share of non-agricultural employment by gender**

Country	Year	Informal sector share (%)	Gender share (%)	
			Women	Men
Benin	2011	94.5	97.7	90.2
Côte d'Ivoire	2016	87.7	93.8	82.4
Gambia	2012	68.2	77.6	62
Ghana	2015	83.2	88.3	75.9
Liberia	2010	77.6	86.3	68.8
Mali	2015	92.1	96.9	87.9
Niger	2011	86.4	95.2	76.4
Senegal	2015	90.4	93.5	88.2

Source: Authors' calculations based on ILO (2017), *ILOStat* database.

Although they drive economic activity, informal activities do not perforce provide decent jobs. They do allow for a degree of flexibility however, which could facilitate participation in economic life (AfDB/OECD/UNDP, 2012). The informal sector has thus furthered female and youth integration into the labour market. In Nigeria, 40% of women were self-employed in 2013 (AfDB/OECD/UNDP, 2017: 185). Often, small companies benefit from a highly structured social network, which enables them to withstand economic shocks. However, the informal sector also acts as a poverty trap by relegating workers, particularly women and youth, into time-consuming and poorly productive activities, whilst depriving them of social protection. In Côte d'Ivoire, 86% of young entrepreneurs between the ages of 15 and 29 years earn less on average than young salaried workers, while 43.9% of young people also create their own businesses (OECD, 2017a). These informal companies in the services and trade sectors are often exposed to variations in the prices of raw materials, primarily oil and agricultural inputs. They provide unstable incomes that represent a loss of tax revenue for the State.

Unemployment and job insecurity primarily affect youth

At first glance, the unemployment rate appears to have stagnated at a low level in all ECOWAS countries, although much of the population is excluded from unemployment statistics, given most work in the informal sector. Countries such as Benin, Burkina Faso and Sierra Leone have unemployment rates fluctuating between 1% and 5% (World Bank, 2017). Only Cabo Verde, Gambia, Ghana and Mali present rates higher than 10%.

Faced with bottlenecks in the formal employment market, young people instead resort to the informal sector. This employs 94% of workers in Mali and 93% in Benin, with the remainder divided between the public and private sectors (ILO, 2012). The public sector is the largest provider of formal employment in Mali (4% of all jobs, versus 2% for the private sector). These posts are concentrated in urban centres particularly in Bamako, the capital, where they account for around one quarter of all employment (ILO, 2012). In Côte d'Ivoire, entrepreneurs represent 43.9% of youth employment outside of agriculture (OECD, 2017b). Unable to find better salaried work, young people prefer self-employment in the informal sector, where they combine several insecure jobs.

Those aged 15-25 are most affected by job insecurity. Unemployment among youth reached 12% in 2017 and has stagnated for 25 years, and this does not account for young people in the informal sector who are often less educated. The employment rate for youth reached 41% in 2017, having declined from 47% in 2000. Several structural factors explain youth unemployment: low levels of education and training and the mismatch between skills and labour market needs (UNECA, 2015). Other factors could exacerbate the situation, be they social (cronyism), political (nepotism), ethnic and religious (preferences) or specific networks of solidarity.

The uneducated represent the largest category of young unemployed, but young graduates are also liable to be unemployed (AfDB/OECD/UNDP, 2012). Between 2010 and 2015, the unemployment rate of those with basic education in all the countries was under 8%, except for Gambia (16%). In contrast, over the same period, unemployment among those with higher education was higher than 9% in all the countries, except Ghana, Liberia and Nigeria. The lack of employment prospects in the public and private sectors encourages young graduates to emigrate. This brain drain in the region will constrain public sectors such as healthcare, which is indispensable for human development (IMF, 2016).

Young graduates are victims of the mismatch between training and jobs. The average duration of unemployment among first-time job seekers is 4.4 years (Kouakou and Koba, 2015). Aligning training with employability of candidates constitutes a major challenge. The low level of qualifications, the education system's focus on supply rather than demand, and basic training that is considered overly theoretical limit the employability of young people. A survey of 27 multinationals in Côte d'Ivoire carried out by the ILO (11 companies of which were in the agro-food industry, 8 in the banking sector, 4 in mining and 4 in telecommunications) indicated a mismatch between youth skills and the labour market (UNDP, 2013). In order to develop competences, the quality of training must be improved, if the gap between the needs of the productive system and the products of the education system is to be closed.

With rural exodus underway, urban areas are increasingly affected by youth unemployment. As rural youth seek professional and financial opportunities, they migrate towards urban areas raising the number of young urban dwellers. In Mali, 19% of the urban population is young compared to 13% in rural areas (AfDB/OECD/UNDP, 2012: 128). But, the education level of young rural residents is lower than that of urban youth, which hinders their integration into the labour market.

Demographic growth poses an unprecedented challenge

Faced with demographic pressure, it will be difficult for the West African labour market to absorb new entrants. Despite sustained growth, the average levels of employment and unemployment in Africa have varied little since the 1990s. Between 1990 and 2017, the average employment rate in the region went from 58% to 62%. By 2035, young people aged 15 to 25 will represent 20% of the West African population, versus 15% globally (UNDESA, 2018) – a pressure that fuels intra-African and international migratory flows.

Inequality dynamics in West Africa

Access to basic social services has greatly improved

Overall, standard of living indicators have improved in the region, despite demographic growth of 3.5% per annum. Although the Human Development Index (HDI) is the lowest in Africa (along with East Africa), it is rising and in 2017 was 0.47 for the entire region, compared with 0.33 in 1990. Within the region, HDI ranges from 0.35 in Niger to 0.65 in Cabo Verde. Life expectancy at birth was 60 (for both men and women) on average over the 1990-95 period, compared with 51 at the start of the 1990s (UNDP, 2017a).

Access to basic services has also improved, although progress remains to be made. Access to drinking water (Figure 7.8), sanitation, electricity and mobile telephones is rising (Annex 7.A3). Thus, in Liberia after a long civil war, between 2000-07 only 0.4% of the population had access to electricity, rising to 8.4% between 2008-17.

Figure 7.8. **Access to drinking water in West Africa, 1990-2015 (% of the population)**

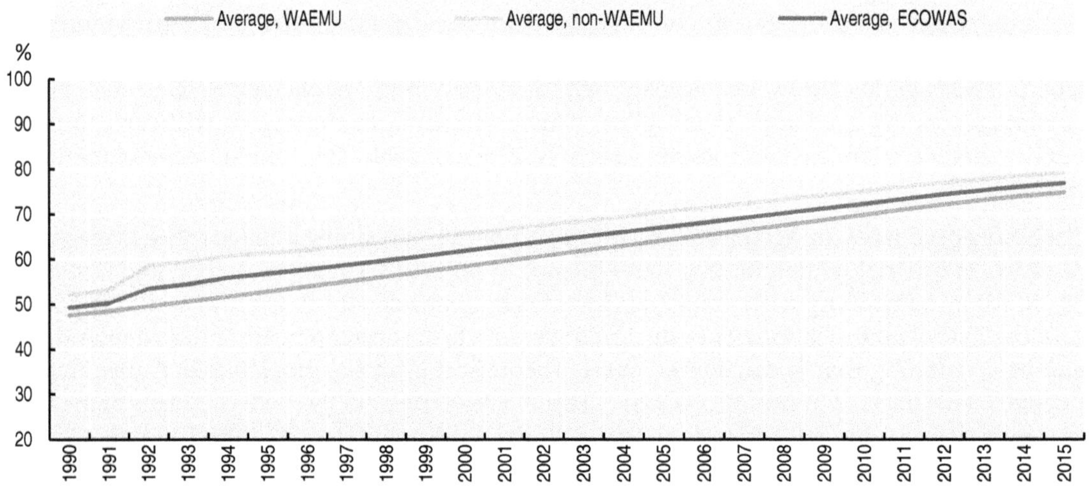

Source: Constructed from World Bank (2017), *World Economic Indicators* database.
StatLink http://dx.doi.org/10.1787/888933784178

Practically all the countries experienced a relative decline in poverty rates over the 1990-2015 period, although the number of poor has increased. According to 2017 World Bank data, extreme poverty – at the threshold of USD 1.90 at purchasing power parity – decreased from 55.4% to 43.8% from 1990 and 2015 (Figure 7.A.3.1). These improvements are primarily due to national poverty reduction strategies and the Heavily Indebted Poor Countries Initiative (HIPC) which benefitted 13 countries (Benin, Burkina Faso, Côte d'Ivoire, Gambia, Ghana, Guinea, Guinea-Bissau, Liberia, Mali, Niger, Senegal, Sierra Leone and Togo). In Burkina Faso for example, since 2000 the rhythm of poverty reduction is identical to that seen in China between 1996 and 2013 (Chapter 1).

However, this relative decline in poverty hides an absolute increase in the number of poor, as well as very high deprivation among the poorest. The number of people living in extreme poverty in West Africa grew from 98.9 million (55.4%) in 1990 to 144.4 million (43.8%) in 2013. This paradoxical increase of rising numbers and falling proportions of poor is due to significant demographic growth, particularly among the poorest. The multidimensional poverty index has remained at 0.4 on average for those countries for which data was available. This level is the highest on the continent along with East Africa. Almost 67% of the population lives in multidimensional poverty and the intensity of deprivation among the poor reaches 56%. Among these privations is the fact that West Africa has the lowest level of education of the continent: only 35% of the population has no primary schooling and in 38% of households, no one is educated (OPHI, 2017).

Inequality is falling overall despite remaining high in the region's largest economies

The Gini index illustrates a broad trend towards falling income inequality. Inequality in West Africa went from 43.2 on average between 1990 and 1995 to 39.6 between 2014 and 2017. However, this overall trend masks deep discrepancies between countries (Table 7.4). Indeed, the fall is most noticeable in the non-WAEMU zone.

Table 7.4. **Income inequality in West Africa (Gini Index, 1990-2017)**

Country	GINI Index		
	First year	Last year	Change
Benin (first year 2003; last, 2015)	38.6	47.8	9.2
Burkina Faso (1994; 2014)	50.8	35.3	-15.5
Cabo Verde (2001; 2007)	52.5	47.2	-5.3
Côte d'Ivoire (1993; 2015)	36.1	41.7	5.6
Gambia (1998; 2003)	48.5	47.3	-1.2
Ghana (1993; 2012)	33	42.2	9.2
Guinea (1994; 2012)	52.6	33.7	-18.9
Guinea-Bissau (1993; 2010)	43.6	50.7	7.1
Liberia (2007; 2014)	36.5	33.2	-3.3
Mali (1994; 2010)	50.4	33	-17.4
Niger (1994; 2014)	41.5	34	-7.5
Nigeria (1993; 2010)	45	44.7	-0.3
Senegal (1994; 2011)	41.4	40.3	-1.1
Sierra Leone (2003; 2011)	40.2	34	-6.2
Togo (2006; 2015)	42.2	43	0.8

Source: Constructed from World Bank (2017), World Development Indicators database.

However, in the richest countries, inequalities remain strong. Between 1993 and 2003, income inequality fell by more than 10 points in Nigeria before starting to rise again between 2004 and 2011, to reach their 1993 levels (UNDP, 2017b). In Ghana, growth-inequality elasticity is positive (0.236 between 1998 and 2014), indicating non-inclusive growth (UNDP, 2017b). Rising revenues (from economic growth) and jobs sometimes coexist with rising inequality and poverty due to unequal distribution of revenue and the dominance of an informal market. At various periods, it has been possible to observe a reduction in poverty that coexists with an increase in equality as in Ghana, Nigeria, Senegal and Togo. In contrast, in Benin, Côte d'Ivoire and Guinea-Bissau, both poverty and inequality have risen at the same time.

The distribution of wealth in West Africa appears to favour the middle or intermediate class. The proportion of revenue held by the 60% of the intermediate population rose by 44.2% to 47.3% between the periods of 1990-95 and 2014-17. This is due to poverty reduction strategies and other Heavily Indebted Poor Countries Initiatives since the start of the 2000s. It is important to continue to invest more in sectors that will result in poverty reduction, to create jobs and ensure social protection to combat vulnerability (Chapter 8).

Inequalities of income and opportunity remain very high between men and women. Half of the countries in the region – Gambia, Liberia, Mali, Mauritania, Niger, Nigeria and Sierra Leone – have a very high level of gender discrimination in their social institutions, according to the Social Institutions and Gender Inequality (SIGI) index, ranging from 0.25 in Côte d'Ivoire to 0.52 in Gambia (Bouchama et al., 2018). Despite efforts to promote female political participation – with the adoption of quotas in six countries – women only accounted for 16% of MPs on average in 2017. These levels vary enormously according to country however, with Senegal counting 43% female MPs, compared with 6% in Nigeria.

These inequalities could be aggravated by certain norms and social practices, among other factors. Despite policies to combat child marriage introduced throughout the region, 30% of girls aged 15-19 years are married (Bouchama et al., 2018: 9). Although legal reforms have been passed, female access to property also remains difficult. In Ghana, only 10% of private land is held by women (Derry, 2016). In Sierra Leone, the 2007 Devolution of Estates Act provides that the land should be equally distributed between men and women, but it is not sufficiently enforced (Corrigan, 2016). Practices that discriminate against women reflect norms connected to the symbolic and economic value attached to arable land. In Burkina Faso, the "mobile" status of women, who live in different households at birth, marriage and widowhood is an impediment to accessing property. The customary right that governs the allocation of arable land in certain communities is also intended to protect agricultural wealth by favouring men (OECD, 2018b).

Policy recommendations

The structural transformation of the region is acknowledged by governments as a primary challenge to sustainable, inclusive growth that creates jobs. In effect, it is crucial to boost the productivity of local activities to create jobs for young people entering the labour market. Accelerating structural transformation will allow the informal sector, which is dominant in the region, to be reabsorbed. At the same time, reforms should provide for the redistribution of wealth and combatting poverty, to correct the effects economic structural transformation has on multiple forms of inequality. Effective systems of social protection need to be created to allocate resources fairly in response to national economic transformation.

The implementation of sectoral policies is not sufficient to bring about the domestic transformation of natural resources. Strategies of structural transformation have focused on natural resource export sectors. Often, special economic areas (like the Lagos Deep Offshore Logistics zone in Nigeria) have also been used to promote export-oriented activities. These strategies have been partly successful, but without enabling a real development of local processing capacities. Furthermore, these policies often tend to create enclaves without building sufficient links between activities and regions that would better harness local dynamism.

Without ignoring these export-focused strategies, development policies could harness regional strengths to promote endogenous and more inclusive growth. Among these strengths is the growth of a middle class, as previously stated. Intermediate cities also support rapid urbanisation and this has made it possible to reduce the distances between producers in rural areas and consumers in urban and peri-urban areas, thus supporting agricultural production and the growth of the agro-food industry. Rapid urbanisation has also resulted in a boom in construction, presenting an important opportunity to develop sustainable cities, particularly by investing in proper infrastructure and collective transportation networks. Another regional strength is the economic integration that connects many countries in the region. These ECOWAS countries have set ambitious convergence criteria that must be implemented and deepened to make integration even more beneficial.

Develop urban-rural links to create jobs

The growth of secondary cities and the promotion of both capital-producing activities and service activities present an opportunity for youth employment in rural and urban areas. Spatial transformation also presents an opportunity to increase productivity in rural and peri-urban areas by meeting urban demand in neighbouring areas. In urban areas, demand for food products is in effect more diverse than in rural areas (Staatz and Hollinger, 2016). To meet this potential, it will be important to continue to push forward the multi-level governance reform agenda. Fiscal decentralisation policies must thus be accompanied by a clarification of national, regional and local government competencies using the subsidiarity principle; citizen participation must be strengthened; and, transparency and accountability must be increased. These priorities are important for boosting regional and local economic development.

Several cross-border corridors in West Africa present opportunities to enhance regional value chains. The Sikasso-Korhogo-Bobo Dioulasso (SKBo) cross-border co-operation programme connects intermediate cities in Mali, Côte d'Ivoire and Burkina Faso in which the economy remains rural. It is directed by regional cultural identity and cross-border exchanges along major trade routes. By focusing on local identity, SKBo contributes to the diversification of agricultural production and the growth of profitability and trade. The programme supports local farmers (of cotton, fresh vegetables, oilseeds, tropical fruit, cashew nuts, citrus fruit, potatoes and mangos) and helps access quality agricultural inputs by supplying fertilisers, animal feed and improved seed (AfDB/OECD/UNDP, 2015). In May 2018, this corridor was given special economic area status by the authorities in the three countries to incentivise agro-industrial and mining companies to set up in the area.

To develop these regional strengths, countries could consider new approaches that will complement other rural-urban policies. Thus, countries could draw up a regional industrial strategy to develop activities that connect rural farmers with urban industrial producers and rural farmers with urban consumers (Allen et al., 2018). For example, to develop the mango sector, Mali adopted targeted actions aimed at: improving training, developing quality certifications, promoting the formalisation of private companies and improving logistics (particularly transportation through rural roads in the Sissako region), packaging and the cold chain, and, creating connections between various links in the value chain. These actions also benefitted cross-border co-operation by helping regions to open up.

Reinforcing the quality of public goods necessary for economic activity will enable constraints on agricultural growth to be lifted. The food economy already accounts for one-third of regional GDP (Allen and Heinrigs, 2016). Despite African Union recommendations regarding the sector, it suffers from a lack of investment. Under the 2003 Maputo Declaration, the Comprehensive Africa Agriculture Development Programme (CAADP) provided for African countries to allocate 10% of their national budget to it. Since then, only Burkina Faso, Guinea, Mali, Niger and Senegal have met this objective several years running, and Ghana has met it in any single year (Wade and Niang, 2014). Electricity generation and access to small agricultural equipment and machinery are other areas for greater development. Furthermore, rural economies are not exclusively dependent on agriculture and productivity is greater in non-agricultural segments. Policies could harness the dynamism of local economies to develop post-harvest activities, such as food processing, logistics or retail. Targeted investments, for example in transportation, warehousing or distribution capacities could prove strategic.

States should co-ordinate to anticipate changes linked to population dynamics, notably equitable access to land. In the absence of firmly established systems, land disputes and conflicts recur in certain zones. Land security could reduce the risk of conflict, encourage productive investment in agriculture and ease the rural exodus of youth. The States of the region should envisage pragmatic solutions to land security by finding a balance between traditional rights and modern law. To this effect, certain countries such as Mozambique, Tanzania, or even Viet Nam have introduced land reforms (OECD, 2016) that could serve as an inspiration.

Modernise the local supply capacities in consumer goods and services

Regional development policies must upgrade the currently predominantly informal provision of goods and services to meet the new demands of the middle class. Urban migration has changed household consumption. As such, households increasingly buy food and goods rather than produce them (Allen and Heinrigs, 2016). Public policies could help microenterprises improve their productivity and revenue with programmes of microfinancing, training and support for innovation.

Local companies could benefit from targeted initiatives to support existing industry groupings to help them regularise their situation. In Ghana, by developing public services (roads, electricity, social services) and facilitating skills and training in the Suame Magazine cluster, local productivity has increased, specifically due to improved access to infrastructure. The Suame Magazine Industrial Development Organization (SMIDO) was created to mitigate against a lack of both support and public social protection mechanisms (AfDB/OECD/UNDP, 2017). In Nigeria, the experience of the regional authorities of Lagos demonstrates that the grouping of informal firms within an organisation is a more effective mechanism towards regularisation than fighting against their creation. Thus, in the Otigba area of Lagos, CAPDAN is an organisation that represents companies in the information and communications technology sector (ICT). It deals with administration and helps collect taxes (Oyelaran-Oyeyinka, 2014).

To increase productivity among informal workers, education policies should promote investment in human capital. At the national level, States should invest in management-level training in small companies and offer certification for skills in the informal sector, as in the case in South Africa, Benin, Ethiopia, Mali and Senegal (AfDB/OECD, 2008). In Ghana for example, self-employed apprentices who have received training at a professional development and training institution earn 49% more than in a salaried position (AfDB/OECD/UNDP, 2017). However, the number of secondary students enrolled in vocational training programmes remains very low in Ghana (1.8%), followed by Senegal (4.5%). Informal apprenticeships are the primary method of skills acquisition in urban areas in West Africa. In Ghana, informal apprenticeships represent up to 90% of basic training and apprentices constitute almost 25% of the active population. To promote dynamic entrepreneurs within the formal economy, it is important that measures are targeted and consistent supporting entrepreneurs throughout their careers. It is also necessary to bear in mind impact assessment at the moment of programme creation. Policies are more effective when entrepreneurial training is integrated into formal education, and an entrepreneurial spirit is awakened in youth via success stories and models they can follow (OECD, 2017a).

It is advisable to offer material and institutional support to talented young entrepreneurs to enable them to develop their activities beyond the start-up stage. Since 2014, local incubators have encouraged the creation of high value-added technological companies (Table 7.5). Like the Kenyan investment in Savannah Valley, West African states could collectively define a digital strategy and create regional competitive hubs. In Nigeria, the start-up ecosystem in Lagos benefitted from the organic growth of small companies. If the region has managed to harness the impressive advances in digital technology, the example of East Africa demonstrates that these technologies could be launched at an even faster pace.

Table 7.5. **Main start-up incubators in West Africa**

Country	Name
Benin	e-TRILABS, Jokkolabs Cotonou
Burkina Faso	Yam Pukri, Jokkolabs Ouagadougou
Côte d'Ivoire	Jokkolabs Abidjan, W Hub, Akendewa
Gambia	Jokkolabs Banjul
Ghana	mFriday, Meltwater Entrepreneurial School of Technology, MEST, gSpace, Kumasi Hive
Liberia	iLab Liberia
Mali	Jokkolabs Bamako
Nigeria	Tony Elumelu Foundation, L5 Lab, Co-creation Hub, Wennovation Hub
Senegal	Jokkolabs Dakar, CTIC Dakar, Africa Living Lab, E-Cover, Synapse
Sierra Leone	AFFORD Sierra Leone
Togo	Woe Lab, Ecohub, Innov'Up, FabLab

Source: AfDB/OECD/UNDP (2017).

Savings and financial flows could be better mobilised to finance local businesses. West Africa has a problematic level of over liquidity, indicating difficulties in accessing credit for entrepreneurs (Doumbia, 2011). Without access to credit and with low skills levels, small companies cannot take advantage of economies of scale (AfDB/OECD/UNDP, 2017). A 2014 survey of 3 000 SMEs and 18 commercial banks in Nigeria revealed that two-thirds of banks reject more than half of SME loan applications (KPMG/EDC, 2014).

States could channel migrant remittances – estimated at USD 27.82 billion in 2016 – towards investment (Table 7.2). This task could be undertaken by investment promotion agencies (OECD, 2017b) or special units devoted to the diaspora as is the case in Ghana. Credit guarantee agencies could combine financial support with an advisory service.

International aid – estimated at USD 12.36 billion (OECD/DAC, 2017) – could better serve investment. The African Guarantee Fund for SMEs, which allocates 54% of its capacity to West Africa (USD 124 million) is a good example of the financial viability of credit. Burkina Faso has an effective service that brings together private capital with donor contributions. Asset-based lending, such as leasing and factoring, could boost company cash flows, whilst permitting the company to free itself from the strict requirements of conventional lending.

The region's economy could improve by modifying the export structure and trade orientation. Regional trade is certainly above the African average, but it remains impacted by the magnitude of informal trade flows (Mitaritonna et al., 2017). In addition, the effect of trade openness on growth is not significant in the ECOWAS zone. It has proven negative for WAEMU and positive for the WAMZ due to the structure of both exports (dominated by raw materials) and imports (dominated by consumables). Another explanatory factor is that regional trade is scarce at 10.5% of all foreign trade, with exports within the region not exceeding 13.6% of the total.

Upgrading local economies involves improving data on jobs and trade. Currently, available statistics are drawn from administrative databases that are often either incomplete or unreliable. As such, they underestimate the respective weight of the informal and agricultural sectors. Statistics pertaining to rural income remain rare. The World Bank's household surveys and its Living Standards Measurement Survey (LSMS), as well as the Food and Agricultural Organisation's (FAO) RIGA database cover a limited number of countries (AfDB/OECD/UNDP, 2015). States could draw on the expertise and financial aid of international organisations to conduct censuses. In addition, giving technical and administrative support to polling and research organisations will help complete national data.

Strengthen measures to improve institutional capacity, the business regulatory framework and appropriate taxation

Improving institutional capacity, the business environment and tax systems will consolidate previous reforms to increase State resources and extend the formal economy. States should continue to create an environment favourable to business, investment and the accumulation of capital to underpin sustainable growth. The fight against corruption, fraud, tax evasion and misappropriation of public funds is an important undertaking that requires institutional capacity, complementarity and co-ordination to be strengthened. For example, illicit financial flows fuel insecurity, violence and conflict in West Africa with the region accounting for 3.6% of global criminal revenue (OECD, 2018a: 70). ECOWAS, States and international organisations should undertake multilateral cross-border interventions to reduce opportunities for criminal economies (OECD, 2018a). Lastly, mobilising domestic tax revenue is becoming easier as the population perceives the benefit of paying taxes in terms of good public services (OECD/ATAF/AUC, 2017).

Temporary tax exemption and complementary measures that could encourage the creation of formal companies need to be set out. Administrative formalities and the tax system must be simplified. This could include for example, the adoption of a one-off tax, committing to the non-retroactivity of taxes as well as introducing points of single contact to simplify administrative procedures. The temporary systemisation of grace periods or tax refunds could encourage informal economy actors to regularise. Good tax policy could contribute to reducing inequalities if it positively affects household wellbeing. Further, complementary measures should be undertaken to encourage regularisation such as the development of systems of social protection or training aimed at improving worker skills, or financial aid to SMEs.

Local investment should reduce tax distortions between large international organisations and local small companies. Tax exemptions granted to multinational organisations do not always promote jobs and represent a loss of income for public resources. The West African States could reconsider a co-ordinated tax policy towards foreign enterprises. Equally, the complexity of tax procedures and the tax burden deter workers from declaring their revenues. A double-pronged approach of simplification and tax relief could increase the proportion of companies created in the formal economy.

The informal sector should be protected from abrupt reforms, as it acts both as a social shock absorber and a reserve of jobs for West Africa. On one hand, it enables the creation of jobs for new entrants to the labour market, and on the other it brings a degree of job security and financial income to those who are vulnerable on the formal labour market, particularly women and the young.

Strengthening the social security system and incorporating the informal sector could break the vicious cycle of job insecurity and inequality. In effect, combatting job insecurity and its intendent difficulties of accessing both productive resources and basic social services requires social protection mechanisms (Chapter 8) that promote decent jobs and improve productivity. Broadly, a social stability pact in West Africa should accompany the existing WAEMU zone economic stability pact and investigations are underway to extend this throughout ECOWAS. Social programmes could also focus on the most vulnerable. In Niger, the programme of social connections introduced in 2002 that subsidises the connection of poor households to the water networks in deprived urban areas, has proven effective: in just one and a half years, access rates have attained the goal set out in the five-year plan.

By supporting mobile banking, States could encourage companies to adopt formal financial practices. In 2016, ECOWAS adopted a mobile banking development strategy to reinforce financial inclusiveness to 75% of the population by 2021. This instrument could bring a certain material security to traders in the informal sector. If public authorities collaborate with telecommunications companies, it should be possible to introduce a form of tax or social security contribution connected to each transaction. Such a system could be both a source of public revenue and a more effective traceability system than self-declaration.

Annex 7.A1. Economic zones in West Africa

Box 7.A1.1. ECOWAS Economic Areas

In addition to the archipelago of Cabo Verde, ECOWAS is comprised of two economic areas. In 1994, the West African Economic and Monetary Union (WAEMU) succeeded WAMU (founded in 1962). It is comprised of eight states (Benin, Burkina Faso, Côte d'Ivoire, Guinea-Bissau, Mali, Niger, Senegal and Togo) linked by the use of a common currency, the CFA franc (XOF). In 1999, a convergence, stability, growth and solidarity pact was adopted, limiting the annual inflation rate to 3%. In 2000, six additional countries (Gambia, Ghana, Guinea, Liberia, Nigeria and Sierra Leone) joined together in a new entity called the West African Monetary Zone (WAMZ). Between 2015 and 2017, they represented approximately 83% of ECOWAS. The creation of a single monetary zone is envisaged, but the introduction of a single currency scheduled for 2015 was postponed to 2020. In 1976, Cabo Verde joined ECOWAS and in December 2000, Mauritania withdrew. In June 2017, Morocco expressed its intention to join the organisation, which, once achieved could have an impact on all of the region's indicators. The drivers of the region are currently Nigeria, Ghana (7.5% of total regional GDP), and Côte d'Ivoire (6%, Figure 7.A1.1).

Figure 7.A1.1. **Share of countries in West African GDP, 2000-18**

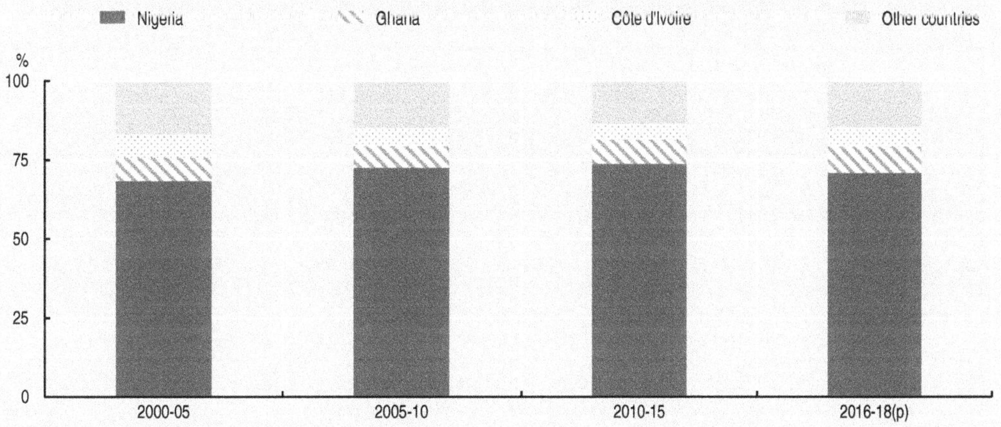

Note: (p) = projections.
Source: Authors' calculations based on IMF (2018) *World Development Indicators* database.
StatLink http://dx.doi.org/10.1787/888933784197

Annex 7.A2. Dynamics and determinants of growth

Figure 7.A2.1. Sectoral analysis of growth in ECOWAS, 1990-2015

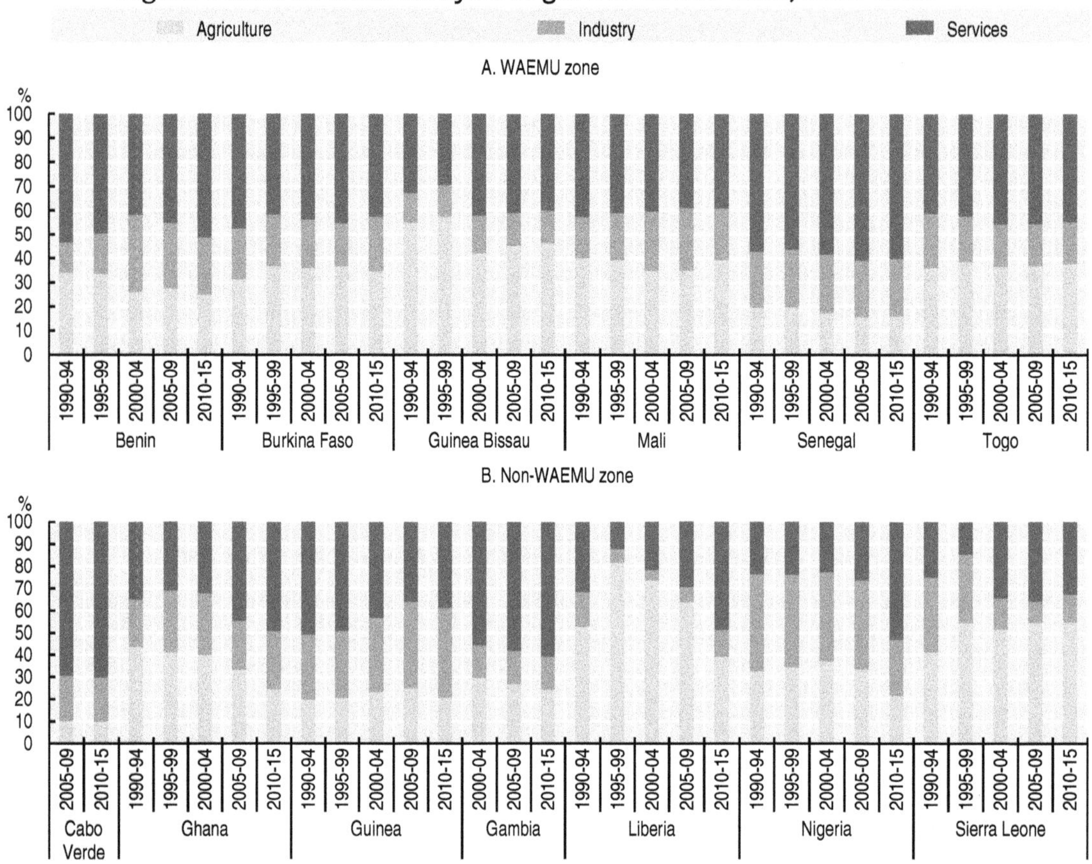

Notes: Data unavailable for Côte d'Ivoire and partial data for Cabo Verde (2005-15) and Gambia (2000-15).
Source: World Development Indicators database (World Bank, 2017).
StatLink http://dx.doi.org/10.1787/888933784216

Annex 7.A3. Dynamics and determinants of inequality

Figure 7.A3.1. Revenue distribution in West Africa

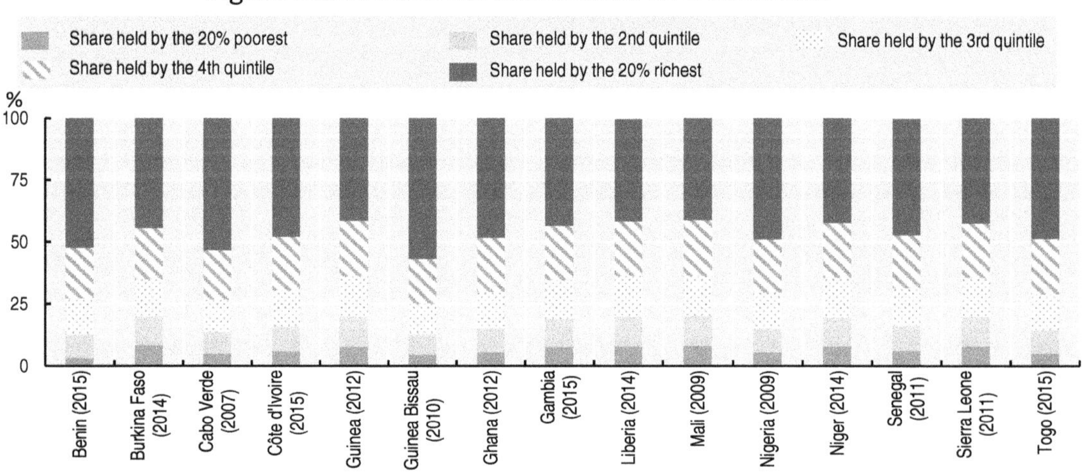

Source: Authors' calculations based on World Bank (2017) World Development Indicators database.
StatLink http://dx.doi.org/10.1787/888933784235

Table 7.A3.1. **Inequality of opportunity in West Africa (averages 2008-17)**

	Benin	Burkina Faso	Cabo Verde	Côte d'Ivoire	Gambia	Ghana	Guinea	Guinea-Bissau	Mali	Liberia	Niger	Nigeria	Senegal	Sierra Leone	Togo
Education indicators															
Primary school completion rate, total (% of revelant age group)	73.5	54.3	89.7	56.3	71.2	91.8	59.5	64.3	54	61.6	48.3	72.4	58.7	63	74.4
Primary school completion rate, girls (% of revelant age group)	66.1	53.5	89.6	49.7	73	91.6	51.7	56.8	48.7	56.4	41.9	67.1	61	61.5	66.3
Secondary school enrolment (net %)	37.7	18.6	69.1	27.5		48.4	25		26.1	14.8	9.9			30.5	
Secondary school enrolment, girls (net %)	11.7	8.8	63			33.3	13.2	6			5.4		15.7		15.3
Health indicators															
Infant mortality (per 1 000 live births)	68.4	61.5	20.9	74.1	46.4	47	65.9	67.3	75.6	60.4	58.5	76.2	39.7	98.4	56.2
Life expectancy at birth, total (years)	59.8	58.2	72.2	51.5	60.1	61.5	57.8	55.8	56.1	60.5	58	51.7	65.2	49.5	58.5
Living conditions indicators (percentage of population)															
Access to electricity	36.1	16.4	83.5	59.7	42.8	69.5	27.9	11.4	28.8	8.3	14.2	53.7	57.3	14.8	39.4
Access to basic water services (rural areas)	57.4	42.6	72.1	54.8	67.3	62.6	52.4	50.8	57.4	57.2	34.2	48.7	58.3	41.3	41.3
Access to basic water services (urban areas)	76.4	77.8	91.7	89.5	87.2	86.2	86	82.3	87.4	79.6	88.5	80.1	90.5	72.5	86.9
Access to basic sanitation	13	19.4	61	28.1	44.5	13.6	19.2	18.9	28.5	11.2	16	33.4	46	13.5	13.2
Technological indicators (per 100 people)															
Access to fixed-line telephone	1.5	0.8	13.3	1.3	2.9	1	0.1	0.1	0.8	0.2	0.5	0.4	2.3	0.3	1.2
Access to mobile telephone	77.1	54.4	87.6	86.2	100.1	94.4	56.1	53.9	85.1	53.3	30.9	65.6	78.7	46.5	49.9

Source: Compiled by authors based on World Bank (2017) *World Development Indicators* database.

References

AfDB (2011), *The Middle of the Pyramid: Dynamics of the Middle Class in Africa – Market Brief*, African Development Bank, Abidjan, https://www.afdb.org/fr/documents/document/market-brief-the-middle-of-the-pyramid-dynamics-of-the-middle-class-in-africa-23582/.

AfDB/OECD/UNDP (2017), *African Economic Outlook 2017: Entrepreneurship and Industrialisation*, OECD Publishing, Paris, https://doi.org/10.1787/aeo-2017-en.

AfDB/OECD/UNDP (2016), *African Economic Outlook 2016: Sustainable Cities and Structural Transformation*, OECD Publishing, Paris,https://doi.org/10.1787/aeo-2016-en.

AfDB/OECD/UNDP(2015), *African Economic Outlook 2015: Regional Development and Spatial Inclusion*, OECD Publishing, Paris,https://doi.org/10.1787/aeo-2015-en.

AfDB/OECD/UNDP(2012), *African Economic Outlook: 2012: Promoting Youth Employment*, OECD Publishing, Paris, https://doi.org/10.1787/aeo-2012-en.

AfDB/OECD (2008), *African Economic Outlook*: 2008, OECD Publishing, Paris,https://doi.org/10.1787/aeo-2008-en.

Allen, T., P. Heinrigs and I. Heo (2018), "Agriculture, food and jobs in West Africa", *West African Papers*, N° 14, OECD Publishing, Paris, https://www.oecd-ilibrary.org/agriculture-and-food/agriculture-food-and-jobs-in-west-africa_dc152bc0-en.

Allen, T. and P. Heinrigs (2016), "Emerging opportunities in the West African Food Economy", *West African Papers*, N° 1, OECD Publishing, Paris, https://www.oecd-ilibrary.org/development/west-african-papers_24142026.

ANSD (2015), *Rapport global du recensement général des entreprises*, Agence nationale de statistique et de la démographie, Ministère de l'Économie, des Finances et du Plan du Sénégal, Dakar, http://www.ansd.sn/index.php?option=com_rapports&view#.

Bouchama, N. et al. (2018), "Gender inequality in West African social institutions", *West African Papers*, N° 13, OECD Publishing, Paris, https://www.oecd-ilibrary.org/development/gender-inequality-in-west-african-social-institutions_fe5ea0ca-en.

Corrigan, T. (2016), "Space, soil and status: Insights from the APRM into the governance of land in Africa", *SAIIA Occasional Paper* N° 229, South African Institute of International Affairs, Johannesburg, www.saiia.org.za/occasional-papers/1032-space-soil-and-status-insights-from-the-aprm-into-the-governance-of-land-in-africa.

Derry, I. (2016), "Access to and Control Over Land as gendered: Contextualising Women's Access and Ownership Rights of Land in Rural Ghana", *Africanus Journal of Development Studies*, 45 (2) pp. 28-48.

Doumbia, S. (2011), "Surliquidité bancaire et sous-financement de l'économie", *Revue Tiers Monde*, (1), pp. 151-170.

ECOWAS (2016), *ECOWAS Convergence Report 2016*, ECOWAS Commission, Abuja, http://www.ecowas.int/wp-content/uploads/2017/11/2016-Convergence-report_Clean-final-final.pdf.

ILO (2012), *Croissance, emploi et politiques pour l'emploi au Mali*, Employment Policy Department, International Labour Organization, Genève, http://www.ilo.org/emppolicy/pubs/WCMS_244833/lang--fr/index.htm.

IMF (2018), *World Economic Outlook*, database updated April 2018, International Monetary Fund, Washington D.C., https://www.imf.org/external/pubs/ft/weo/2018/01/weodata/index.aspx (consulted in May 2018).

IMF (2017a), *Update - World Economic Outlook: Seeking Sustainable Growth*, International Monetary Fund, Washington D.C., http://www.imf.org/en/Publications/WEO/Issues/2016/12/27/A-Shifting-Global-Economic-Landscape.

IMF (2017b), *Sub-Saharan Africa: Regional Economic Outlook: Fiscal Adjustment and Economic Diversification*, International Monetary Fund, Washington, D.C., https://www.imf.org/en/Publications/REO/SSA/Issues/2017/10/19/sreo1017.

IMF (2017c), *Sub-Saharan Africa: Regional Economic Outlook: Restarting the Growth Engine*, International Monetary Fund, Washington, D.C., https://www.imf.org/en/Publications/REO/SSA/Issues/2017/05/03/sreo0517.

IMF (2016), "Sub Saharan African Migration: Patterns and Spillovers ", *Spillover Notes*, Issue 9, International Monetary Fund, Washington, D.C., http://www.imf.org/en/Publications/SPROLLs/Spillover-Notes.

Kouakou, C. and A. Koba (2015), "Youth employment in Côte d'Ivoire: A diagnostic study", International Development Research Centre (IDRC) research report, Ottawa, https://www.africaportal.org/publications/lemplois-des-jeunes-en-côte-divoire-une-étude-diagnostique-youth-employment-in-ivory-coast-a-diagnostic-study/.

KPMG/EDC (2014), *Strengthening Access to Finance for Micro, Small and Medium Enterprises (MSMEs) in Nigeria*, KPMG et Enterprise Development Center, http://edc.edu.ng/wp-content/uploads/2017/02/MSME-Banking-Study-2014.pdf.

Ministère de l'Économie et des Finances du Sénégal (2011), *Rapport National de la Compétitivité du Sénégal*, Ministère de l'Économie et des Finances du Sénégal, Dakar, http://www.cepod.gouv.sn/?q=node/65.

Mitaritonna, C., S. Bensassi, and J. Jarreau (2017), "Regional Integration and Informal Trade in Africa: Evidence from Benin's Borders", *CEPII Working Paper*, N° 2017-21 – December 2017, http://www.cepii.fr/CEPII/en/publications/wp/abstract.asp?NoDoc=10990.

Nordman, C. and L. Pasquier-Doumer (2015), "Transitions in a West African labour market: The role of family networks", *Journal of Behavioral and Experimental Economics*, vol. 54, pp. 74-85, https://doi.org/10.1016/j.socec.2014.11.008.

OECD (2018a), *Illicit Financial Flows: The Economy of Illicit Trade in West Africa*, OECD Publishing, Paris,https://doi.org/10.1787/9789264268418-en.

OECD (2018b), *Étude Pays SIGI Burkina Faso*, OECD, Paris, https://www.genderindex.org/burkina-faso-country-study/.

OECD (2017a), *Unlocking the Potential of Youth Entrepreneurship in Developing Countries: From subsistence to performance*, Development Centre Studies, OECD Publications, Paris, https://doi.org/10.1787/9789264277830-en.

OECD (2017b), *Suivi de la mise en œuvre des réformes vers l'émergence de la Côte d'Ivoire – Rapport d'avancement n°2, OECD Development Pathways*, OECD Publications, Paris, http://www.oecd.org/development/mdcr/countries/cotedivoire/.

OECD (2016), *Examen multidimensionnel de la Côte d'Ivoire: Volume 2. Analyse approfondie et recommandations*, OECD Development Pathways, OECD Publicshing, Paris, http://dx.doi.org/10.1787/9789264251670-fr.

OECD (2013), *Settlement, Market and Food Security, West African Studies*, OECD Publishing, Paris, http://dx.doi.org/10.1787/9789264187443-en.

OECD/ATAF/AUC (2017), *Revenue Statistics in Africa 2017*, OECD Publishing, Paris, http://dx.doi.org/10.1787/9789264280854-en-fr.

OECD-DAC (2017), *International Development Statistics* (database), OECD Development Assistance Committee, www.oecd.org/dac/stats/idsonline.htm.

OPHI (2017), *Global Multidimensional Poverty Index Winter 2017/2018* (database), Oxford Poverty & Human Development Intitiative, Oxford, http://ophi.org.uk/multidimensional-poverty-index/global-mpi-2017/.

Oyelaran-Oyeyinka, O. (2014), "Industrialization pathways to human development: Industrial clusters, institutions and multidimensional poverty in Nigeria", report presented at the *First Annual Bank Conference on Africa: Harnessing Africa's Growth for Faster Poverty Reduction*, Paris School of Economics and World Bank, 23-24 June 2014.

Staatz, J. and F. Hollinger (2016), "West African Food Systems and Changing Consumer Demands", *West African Papers*, N° 4, OECD Publishing, Paris, http://dx.doi.org/10.1787/b165522b-en.

UNCTAD (2015), *Economic development in Africa Report 2015: Unlocking the potential of Africa's services trade for growth and development*, United Nations Conference for Trade and Development, Geneva, http://unctad.org/en/PublicationsLibrary/aldcafrica2015_en.pdf.

UNDP (2017a), *Human Development Report 2016: Human Development for Everyone*, United Nations Development Programme, New York, http://hdr.undp.org/en.

UNDP (2017b), *Income Inequality Trends in Sub-Saharan Africa: Divergence, determinants and consequences*, United Nations Development Programme, New York, http://www.africa.undp.org/content/rba/fr/home/library/reports/income-inequality-trends-in-sub-saharan-africa--divergence--dete.html.

UNDP (2013), "Cadre institutionnel et réglementaire du marché du travail" in *National Human Development Report 2013: Jobs, structural change and human development in Côte d'Ivoire*, United Nations Development Programme, New York, http://www.ci.undp.org/content/cote_divoire/fr/home/library/poverty/rndh_2013.html.

UNDESA (2018), *World Population Prospects: The 2018 Revision*, United Nations Department for Economic and Social Affairs, New York, https://esa.un.org/unpd/wpp/.

UNDESA (2017), *World Population Prospects: The 2017 Revision*, United Nations Department for Economic and Social Affairs, New York, https://esa.un.org/unpd/wpp/.

UNECA (2015), *Socioeconomic Profile of West Africa in 2015 and Prospects for 2016*, United Nations Economic Commission for Africa, Niamey, https://www.uneca.org/sites/default/files/PublicationFiles/reg_econprofile_2015_ice18_fre_def_def_23_11_2015.pdf.

Wade I. and A. Niang (2014), "L'engagement de Maputo: le mot d'ordre a-t-il été respecté ?", Passerelles, Volume 15, n° 3, International Centre for Trade and Sustainable Development, Geneva, https://www.ictsd.org/bridges-news/passerelles/issue-archive/la-s%C3%A9curit%C3%A9-alimentaire-et-le-commerce-en-afrique.

World Bank (2017), *World Development Indicators* (base de données des indicateurs du developpement dans le monde), http://databank.worldbank.org/data/reports.aspx?source=world-development-indicators (consulted in January 2018).

World Bank (2014), *The Economic Impact of the 2014 Ebola Epidemic: Short and Medium Term Estimates for West Africa*, Washington D.C., World Bank, https://doi.org/10.1596/978-1-4648-0438-0.

Chapter8

Policyrecommendations

This chapter proposes ten policy actions to address growth,jobcreationandinequalitiesinAfrica.These recommendations rest on three pillars: sustainable economic development, social development and institutional development. To sustain economic development, African governments should consider betterinvestments,diversifyingexports,rural-urban linkages and green growth. Measures to achieve social development relate to education and skills, social protection, and health coverage. To improve institutional development, governments should address their engagements with Africa's global partners, regional integration, domestic revenues, economic and political governance, as well as their owninstitutionalandstatisticalcapacities.Thepolicy recommendations are divided into specific actions to meet the objectives of Agenda 2063 and of the sustainabledevelopmentagenda.Theyassesshowto improvestatisticsandbettermeasurepolicyimpact.

IN BRIEF

Africa's development agenda calls for implementing development strategies with a context-specific, multifaceted and holistic approach. Actors at all levels can contribute: pan-African institutions, regional communities, national, subnational and local governments, the local private sector, African citizens, and international partners. Generating quality data is key to monitor, evaluate and adjust countries' development policies. To achieve inclusive and sustainable development, strategies should go beyond simply spurring economic growth: they must also target social and institutional development.

Policies for **sustainable economic development** should aim at boosting the domestic private sector, which forms the basis for diversifying products and export baskets. This requires building on local comparative advantages, strengthening linkages between foreign investment and local economies, and improving the efficiency of public investment and institutions. Reforming land ownership, planning and management and developing sustainable intermediary cities will strengthen the linkages between rural and urban economies. "Greening" economic activities will help countries grow, create jobs and eradicate poverty while using natural resources responsibly.

Countries can promote **social development** through universal access to and improved quality of education and technical and vocational skills training. Seeking greater synergies with the private sector would align skills with labour market needs. Social development also rests on expanded, inclusive and financially sustainable social protection and health systems.

Institutional development is necessary to implement strong policies for inclusive growth. Policy makers should respect regional integration commitments. Reforming the tax administration can mobilise domestic revenue. Better global partnerships can strengthen capacity, and help reduce illicit financial flows and other harmful practices. Finally, implementing this African reform agenda requires enhancing government capacity, accountability, transparency and co-ordination, as well as promoting good corporate governance.

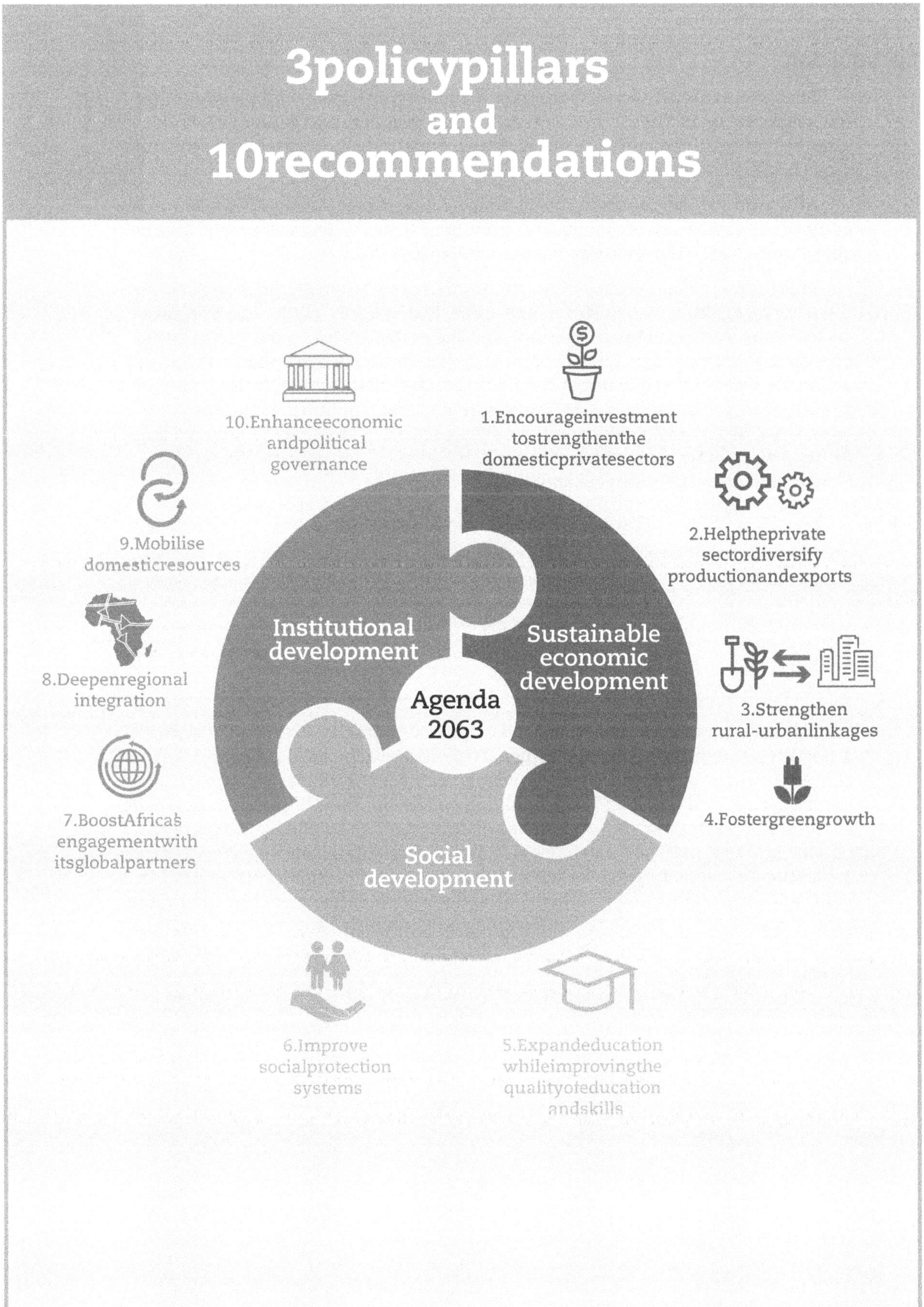
3policypillars
and
10recommendations
10.Enhanceeconomic andpolitical governance
1.Encourageinvestment tostrengthenthe domesticprivatesectors
9.Mobilise domesticresources
2.Helptheprivate sectordiversify productionandexports
Institutional development
Sustainable economic development
Agenda 2063
8.Deepenregional integration
3.Strengthen rural-urbanlinkages
4.Fostergreengrowth
7.BoostAfrica's engagementwith itsglobalpartners
Social development
6.Improve socialprotection systems
5.Expandeducation whileimprovingthe qualityofeducation andskills

Introduction

The patterns of growth, job creation and inequality in Africa are complex and differ from region to region. The continental trend is one of resilient but jobless growth with a slight reduction in inequality. In some regions, inequality has increased with economic growth, while in others inequality has receded.

African governments will need much stronger policies to meet Agenda 2063's aspiration of "a prosperous Africa based on inclusive growth and sustainable development" and the objectives of its First Ten-Year Implementation Plan 2013-2023.

This chapter proposes ten policy actions for improving growth, creating jobs and reducing inequalities. While far from exhaustive, this list of policy actions addresses key issues for most African countries (see Table 8.1). They fall under three pillars: sustainable economic development, social development and institutional development. These policy actions derive from the challenges posed by the Megatrends presented in Chapter 2 and from the main goals of Agenda 2063. They also relate to the five dimensions of the 2030 Agenda for Sustainable Development: people, prosperity, planet, partnership and peace. Annex 8.A1 provides an overview of the links between the ten policy actions and the Megatrends, Agenda 2063 targets, and SDGs.

Table 8.1. **Ten policy actions for Africa**

Sustainable economic development	Social development	Institutional development
1. Encourage domestic investment	5. Expand and improve education	7. Boost Africa's global partnerships
2. Diversify exports	6. Develop social protection systems, including labour and health	8. Deepen regional integration
3. Strengthen rural-urban linkages		9. Mobilise domestic revenue
4. Foster green growth		10. Enhance economic and political governance

Inclusive growth requires strong development strategies. These will necessarily differ between countries. Policies must be participative, place-based, multi-sectoral, and carried out with a holistic and co-ordinated approach. All stakeholders must participate in monitoring, evaluating and reformulating policies for their implementation to be successful. Stakeholder roles and responsibilities need to be clearly integrated into national strategies to ensure coherence, effective implementation and revision after their evaluation. Implementing policies adequately requires that the right level of government intervene, in co-ordination with other levels and development partners. This follows the principles of value addition and subsidiarity included in the African Union's Agenda 2063 Ten Year Implementation Plan. Development strategies must move forward with Africa's integration agenda.

PILLAR I: SUSTAINABLE ECONOMIC DEVELOPMENT

Action 1: Encourage investment for domestic private sector development

Context:

- Public investment is often inefficient, and private investment remains low. Between 2009 and 2016, private investment averaged only 15% of gross domestic product (GDP).
- Interest rates and risk premiums are often too high to enable firms to borrow and invest effectively (AfDB/OECD/UNDP, 2017; UNCTAD, 2014).
- Limited access to financing opportunities, marketing infrastructure and reliable demand make it difficult for even the most productive informal firms to keep up profitability levels or to innovate.
- Foreign direct investment (FDI) inflows do not result in strong linkages or knowledge transfer to local firms.
- Public investment plays a vital role in Africa. In 2016, 42% of the financing for infrastructure projects in Africa came from governments (ICA, 2017).

Proposed actions:

Simplify investment for domestic firms:

- improve the business environment
- provide public goods to business clusters
- facilitate the extension of credit by reducing borrowing costs and promoting financial intermediation services.

Ensure consistency between FDI promotion strategies and the capacity of local firms:

- enhance local firms' capacity to meet requirements of foreign investors
- guide foreign investment to benefit local firms' productivity, technology and know-how.

Leverage domestic savings and remittances to increase domestic investment:

- promote long-term savings while expanding the variety of savings instruments
- attract diaspora savings with dedicated institutions and investment projects.

Increase the efficiency of public investment:

- improve public procurement rules to reward and promote competitiveness
- tailor investments to local institutional capacity and project types.

Simplify investment for domestic firms

Improve the business environment to enable firms to invest more.

The investment climate should be good for all firms – foreign and domestic, large and small (see for example the OECD's *Policy Framework for Investment* [OECD, 2015a]). International co-operation initiatives such as the G20's Compact with Africa can help countries improve the instruments and funding conditions for private investment.

- Ensuring the reliability of the overall investment policy framework is essential to encourage both domestic and foreign investors. This can notably be done through predictable business laws and stable taxation systems. Predictable, transparent and fairer taxes are often more important for investors than fiscal holidays or other incentives (see for example Action 9). Priorities should include the following:

- setting up reliable regulations and institutions, including by strengthening the legal and regulatory frameworks to reduce uncertainty
- establishing investor protection and dispute resolution mechanisms (for both local and foreign investors)
- standardising contracts, such as clauses and provisions of public-private partnerships (PPPs) (AfDB/IMF/WBG, 2017).

• Conducting comprehensive surveys on a regular basis can help inform policy makers about the challenges and needs of domestic firms in upgrading their production and products. Adding special modules on employers and own-account workers to labour force surveys (such as those done in the 1-2-3 surveys [see Cling et al., 2014]) can provide such comprehensive information at low cost.

Use public investment to provide public goods to business clusters.

• Governments should invest in energy and transport infrastructure, provide other policy support (such as skills training), facilitate export and import procedures, and promote linkages between business clusters and the surrounding local economies. South Africa's government funded firms to join industrial associations, leading to the organic development of business clusters (Morris and Barnes, 2006). Similarly, Morocco successfully used the existing infrastructure in Tangier-Med to develop a competitive automotive and aeronautics cluster by involving multinationals, local firms, as well as central and local levels of government.

Facilitate the extension of credit by reducing borrowing costs and promoting financial intermediation services.

• In East Africa, innovations such as M-Pesa (mobile money transfer) offer access to online platforms and e-services. These have paved the way for new mobile-based financial intermediation (e.g. micro-insurance, savings accounts), opening up market niches. This has had a positive impact on micro-enterprises' profitability, trade volumes and survival rates (Oosthuizen et al., 2016). Evidence shows that as firms increase in size, they benefit more from the advantages of joining the formal sector, such as access to credit (see Gelb et al. 2009, Amin and Islam, 2015).

• Development finance institutions (DFIs) can invest in micro-finance institutions that lend to small and medium-sized enterprises (SMEs), in addition to commercial banks. For example, Norfund and others support a private equity fund, *Fundo de Investimento Privado Angola*, by providing up to USD 8 million for individual investments in SMEs, particularly for project expansion, privatisation and start-ups. DFIs should try to crowd in private capital to increase the availability of commercial credit (see for example OECD, 2018a).

Ensure consistency between FDI promotion strategies and the capacity of local firms

FDI flows have a more durable impact on growth and productivity when foreign firms can contribute to the local private sector's development.

Enhance local firms' capacity to meet the needs and requirements of foreign investors.

• Direct financial support or technology transfers can help improve firms' production techniques, management and marketing practices. Domestic firms can learn to comply with international trade standards and product specifications and adapt their production processes to global demand. Official development assistance (ODA) and development partners can promote high quality products by supporting quality label initiatives.

Guide foreign investment to benefit local firms' productivity, technology and know-how.

- National and local authorities can work together to attract FDI, as shown by the Tangiers' logistics and automotive cluster in Morocco (see Chapter 6). There, local firms are slowly moving up the supply chain by collaborating with lead firms, with tailored support from the local and national governments.
- Spill-over effects are broader when local firms can freely use available technologies or acquire technologies through licensing agreements with lead firms. For example, productivity spill-overs from participating in global value chains (GVCs) appear stronger through joint ventures than through fully foreign-owned firms (Farole, 2016).

Leverage domestic savings and remittances to increase domestic investment

Promote long-term savings while expanding the variety of savings instruments.

- Increasing domestic investment rests on increasing the propensity to save and on expanding market solutions. Policy makers and financial institutions should work towards locking in those savings in longer-term assets and utilise them to provide more credit without adding pressure to balance sheets.
- In countries with deep capital markets, SMEs and young companies can be listed on stock exchanges, following the example of the Johannesburg Stock Exchange's platform for SMEs. Rwanda has recently waived the USD 23000 listing fee for SMEs and will subsidise the cost of hiring transaction advisors, brokerage services and legal services (Esiara, 2018).

Attract diaspora savings with dedicated institutions and investment projects.

- Morocco's policies to handle investment issues for its diaspora have largely been successful. This is especially the case for housing investments (see OECD, 2017a). Likewise, Ghana has a new dedicated unit to handle investment issues for its diaspora (UNIDO, 2013). Mauritius has set up a Diaspora Scheme to make it easier for diaspora to return and invest in the country. Ethiopia and Nigeria created diaspora-indexed bonds, but underwriting remained limited.

Increase the efficiency of public investment

Improve procurement rules to reward and promote competitiveness.

- Governments should improve their contract awarding procedures and their criteria to reward competitiveness and efficiency, rather than merely rewarding low costs. They should also better prepare public investment projects and enhance transparency, monitoring and evaluation mechanisms.

Tailor investment modes to local institutional capacity and project types.

- Public-private partnerships can increase the efficiency of the design and implementation of projects, thus creating substantial savings. However, PPPs require careful public involvement and expertise. The PPP model used in Morocco's solar power station in Ouarzazate provides a good example of ways to engage key players (see Climate Policy Initiative, 2012).
- Governments can opt for modes of governance for infrastructure projects other than PPPs. These can range from direct delivery, where governments fully manage all aspects of a project, to procurement for specific phases and operations, to privatisation, where governments only retain their regulatory role. More complex project governance requires empowering regulators and ensuring that an independent judiciary can handle disputes (Kappel, Pfeiffer and Reisen, 2017).

Action 2: Help the private sector to diversify production and exports

Context:

- Africa's exports mostly concentrate in natural resources and agricultural commodities.
- Intermediate and capital goods represent 49% of Africa's imports, compared to 55% in Latin America and the Caribbean and 64% in developing Asia.
- Most export promotion activities in the region have met with limitations.

Proposed actions:

Design export strategies that are consistent with the country's potential:

- base export strategies on comparative advantages
- regularly assess the government's approach as comparative advantages evolve over time
- facilitate trade.

Facilitate access to intermediate and capital goods:

- reduce import barriers for essential intermediate and capital inputs that are not produced locally
- apply the correct tariff rates to lower the cost of imported inputs.

Empower public agencies to diversify exports:

- provide export and investment promotion agencies with adequate funding and governance structures
- assign export promotion agencies with focused objectives.

Africa can benefit more from global integration by diversifying its product and export baskets (see Chapter 1). Economic diversification requires a system-wide approach, with strategies for a long-term vision of the future shared by both public and private stakeholders. These strategies need to define development priorities that are specific to the local contexts (OECD, 2013). For example, the Southern African Development Community (SADC) Industrialisation Strategy rests on the principle of both public and private involvement. One aim of the Strategy is to move away from commodity exports and increase the share of intermediate products to 60% of total manufactured exports.

Design export strategies that are consistent with the country's potential

Base export strategies on comparative advantages.

- African countries that have comparative advantages can specialise in specific stages in global value chains. For example, Ethiopia has developed an apparel and textile export sector by investing in skills and infrastructure and developing domestic value chain linkages between cotton, textile and apparel firms.
- Mauritius developed globally competitive businesses in the sugar, tuna and textile sectors, and South Africa has done so in the automotive and agro-processing sectors. These countries built on their pool of capable workers, geographical endowment and preferential access to key markets. Botswana and Ghana, on the other hand, have focused on upgrading in the value chains of existing exports, namely diamonds and fresh fruit respectively.

- **Regularly assess strategies as comparative advantages evolve over time.**
  - Re-assessing industrial strategies helps to progressively upgrade industrial capabilities and respond to inevitable changes in a country's comparative advantages and in global economic conditions. For example, Mauritius first supported the sugar, tuna and textile products industries for the European Union market before expanding to logistics, financial services and blue economy activities (in particular tourism).

- **Facilitate trade between Africa and other continents.**
  - To facilitate trade, governments should improve logistics and customs performance, trade infrastructure and the quality of electricity supply (see Lopez Gonzalez, Kowalski and Achard, 2015). Several development partners provide capacity building for countries to improve the quality of export products to meet international standards, especially in food safety and pesticides.

Facilitate access to intermediate and capital goods

- **Reduce barriers to imports for essential intermediate and capital inputs that are not produced locally.**
  - Lowering tariffs on intermediate inputs and capital goods that are essential for industrialisation but not available locally can enhance African producers' competitiveness. African governments can also facilitate these strategic imports by reducing delays in granting import licenses and in gaining access to these inputs.

- **Apply the correct tariff rates to lower the cost of imported inputs.**
  - Applying the correct tariff rates according to products' end use could make manufacturing firms more competitive. In the East African Community, nearly 400 products that are typically inputs for manufacturing are misclassified in the higher tariff band intended for final consumption products (Frazer, 2017). An agreed international classification, such as the broad economic category can serve for reclassifying products.

Empower public agencies to diversify exports

- **Provide export and investment promotion agencies with adequate funding and governance structures**
  - Export and investment promotion agencies can play a strong role in a system-wide approach to transforming production. Their scope can cover many activities: providing financial assistance (credit, insurance), generating market intelligence, building a national image and branding, promoting FDI in strategic sectors, providing investors' aftercare, and expanding overseas presence.
  - The returns on funding for export promotion agencies (EPAs) are large. In Africa, the marginal return to a 1% increase in EPAs' budgets can boost export growth by 0.05% (Botswana) to 0.14% (Uganda) (ITC, 2016).

- **Assign EPAs objectives that are focused and aligned with industrial objectives and national economic development priorities.**
  - Global experience suggests that EPAs support export diversification better than increases in export volumes. EPAs are also better at improving the performance of established exporters than at encouraging non-exporters to start exporting.
  - Private sector representation on EPA boards can ensure greater influence on strategic decision-making (ITC, 2016). Charging the private firms fees for EPA services can ensure that EPAs' activities are aligned with private companies' interests and that they provide quality services. However, service fees must be moderate to include SME clients.

Action 3: Strengthen linkages between rural and urban economies

Context:

- Urbanisation can play an important role in Africa's economic transformation (see Chapter 2, Megatrend 4). Although the patterns and rates of urbanisation differ by country, at least 50% of Africans are expected to reside in urban areas by 2035.
- In most sub-Saharan African countries, land is still regulated under customary law. Only about 10% of rural land in sub-Saharan Africa is registered. In Malawi, over 90% of the land is governed by customary law (Byamugisha, 2013).
- Many local government authorities lack cadastral systems or land title records, making it difficult to collect land-based revenue or to certify transfers of ownership. According to a 2015 survey, only 20 countries raise local taxes on landholdings (AfDB/OECD/UNDP, 2015).
- Investment in urban infrastructure in sub-Saharan Africa has remained constant at less than 20% of GDP since 1960 (compared to 42% in East Asian developing countries) (Lall, Henderson and Venables, 2017).
- African urbanisation is hampered by overcrowding, low access to public goods and lack of connectivity. Although levels vary by country, almost 62% of the African urban population live in slums. They suffer from shortages of water, sanitation services, power and affordable transportation. The latter limits their links to jobs and commercial activities.

Proposed actions:

Reform land ownership and management:

- simplify regulations on land ownership and use, particularly for women
- improve land information and management systems by adopting low-cost and scalable technological solutions
- manage urban land and public goods provision through participatory approaches.

Upgrade urban infrastructure and services:

- invest in infrastructure and services that are affordable, inclusive, sustainable and tailored to local needs
- invest in public transport networks to reduce spatial segregation and inequality
- couple investment in urban areas with enabling environments in rural areas.

Strengthen rural-urban linkages through sustainable intermediary cities:

- develop intermediary cities to enhance productivity of rural areas and strengthen rural-urban linkages.

Reform land ownership and management

- **Simplify regulations on land ownership and use to increase productivity, investment and reduce inequalities (recognising customary laws and aiming for gender equality)**
  - In addition to introducing legal frameworks, governments must ensure that laws are enforced and reforms properly implemented to avoid exacerbating inequalities. Civil society and development partners can help governments in this respect (see OECD, 2016a).
  - In Ethiopia and Rwanda, certifying ownership of agricultural land increased land productivity and the propensity to invest (Byamugisha, 2013). Ethiopia's low-cost

land titling programme of 2003, mainly conducted by sub-regional committees, distributed 20 million land titles. The programme enabled more women to access land (Quisumbing and Kumar, 2014:407).

- **Improve land information and management systems by adopting low-cost and scalable technological solutions.**
  - Excessively centralised land administration can restrict access to services for rural and low-income populations, thus limiting their legal protection. Zambia is attempting to decentralise land administration procedures for this reason (Corrigan, 2016). Namibia established communal land registration and the Communal Land Boards in 2002; by 2014, 160 000 plots had been surveyed and 82 000 land rights registered in communal areas (GIZ, 2013; Kasita, 2011).
  - In Burkina Faso, a project using very high spatial resolution satellite images produced detailed territorial mapping. Similar projects are taking place in other countries.

- **Manage urban land and public goods provision through participatory approaches.**
  - Land planning and reforms should aim to reduce spatial, income and gender inequalities. Governments should provide formal and affordable housing and dedicate enough land for transportation infrastructure linking peri-urban areas, where most informal settlements are located (Locke and Henley, 2016).
  - Urban planning should also avoid strict top-down approaches and encourage citizen participation in policy making. For example, a programme in five Ugandan intermediary cities benefited from citizens' involvement which led to settlement upgrading and secured the tenure of thousands of informal settlers (AfDB/OECD/UNDP, 2016).
  - As availability of urban land and opportunities for its development increase, mechanisms for land value capture can help recoup investments by both the state and private developers (Berrisford, 2013).

Upgrade urban infrastructure and services

- **Invest in infrastructure and services that are affordable, inclusive, sustainable and tailored to local needs.** Providing public goods and adequate infrastructure can strengthen agglomeration dynamics in cities and improve economies of scale.
  - Urban infrastructure plans should be inclusive and avoid exacerbating gender inequality. For example, plans should reduce distances to water sources and ensure streets are well lit to prevent sexual assault of girls and women and other forms of violence.
  - At least 45% of urban areas should be dedicated to public spaces such as roads and green areas (public spaces in African cities represent around 20%) (UN Habitat, 2013).

- **Invest in public transport networks to reduce spatial segregation and inequality.**
  - Setting up affordable transportation systems can facilitate job searching for poor urban dwellers and decrease spatial segregation, especially in urban areas. The light rail system in Addis Ababa connects the industrial suburbs to the city centre; providing affordable transportation services has increased the intensity of job searches and reduced the likelihood of people accepting temporary and informal work. The Bus Rapid Transit System in Lagos stabilised transportation prices and reduced them by 30% (AfDB/OECD/UNDP, 2016).

Couple investment in urban areas with enabling environments in rural areas.

- Regional and national governments can engage and co-ordinate with local administrations to implement place-based policies that transcend urban administrative boundaries. New tools based on geographic information systems (e.g. Africapolis) can help analyse how urban development affects rural areas and can determine the functional boundaries of cities. Policies and investment in favour of urban areas should take into account the surrounding environment and promote virtuous interactions between rural areas and cities.

Strengthen rural-urban linkages through sustainable intermediary cities

Develop intermediary cities to enhance the productivity of rural areas and strengthen rural-urban linkages.

- Intermediary cities can expand public services to rural areas and develop labour-intensive industries such as agro-processing and textiles, as well as service sectors such as tourism.
- In West Africa, rural areas with closer proximity to intermediary cities tend to have more diversified economies, larger working populations and higher income from non-farm activities (Christiaensen and Todo, 2014; Moriconi-Ebrard, Harre and Heinrigs, 2016). Urbanisation together with rising incomes and populations has led to an increase in West Africa's food economy, accounting for 36% of the region's GDP (SWAC, 2016).
- Formal employment creation in intermediary cities attracts higher migration flows from rural areas, helping reduce rural poverty. Longitudinal studies from Kagera (Tanzania) showed that migration from rural areas to intermediary cities reduced the poverty headcount by 24% and raised income by 77% (Christiaensen, De Weerdt and Kanbur, 2017; Christiaensen et al., 2018).
- Governments should link intermediary cities to metropoles for a sustainable and equitable urban system. Well-linked intermediary cities can help alleviate pressures that megacities face for housing, infrastructure, transportation and service provision. They can absorb the administrative capacities of outlying areas and serve as new centres for social transformation (Otiso, 2005).

Action 4: Foster green growth

Context:

- African countries contribute less than 4% to global gas emissions, but 27 of the 33 countries most at risk from climate change are in Africa (see Megatrend 5, Chapter 2).
- With current trends, urban waste in sub-Saharan Africa is estimated to rise by 161% between 2000 and 2025. Africa is not yet prepared for this. It currently has the lowest levels of waste collection services of any region (Brahmbhatt et al., 2017).
- Mortality from air pollution in African cities has increased in recent years, representing an equivalent cost of USD 447 billion in 2013, a third of the continent's GDP (Roy, 2016).
- Population growth and inappropriate land use practices are increasing deforestation, land degradation, damage to ecosystems and water scarcity. The agricultural sector accounts for the livelihood of two-thirds of the population, and most traditional livelihoods depend on environmental services (UNECA, 2016a; Brahmbhatt, Haddaoui and Page, 2017).

Proposed actions:

Promote the circular economy:

- re-use resources and manage waste efficiently to create value, develop new economic activities, cut costs and reduce pollution.

"Green" existing economic activities:

- promote environmentally-friendly and sustainable farming and tourism as value-added activities
- introduce standards and regulations to limit pollution and preserve people's health and the environment.

Green growth can facilitate Africa's structural transformation and should be integrated into productive strategies. Adopting environmentally-friendly strategies and enhancing the productivity and reuse of natural resources can spur sustainable and inclusive growth (UNECA, 2016a).

Promote the circular economy

- **Re-use resources and manage waste efficiently to create value, develop new economic activities, cut costs and reduce pollution.**
  - Farms in Morocco use olive by-products to meet 60% of their energy needs through biomass, saving almost USD 4 million on energy costs between 2009 and 2015.[1]
  - The Recycling and Economic Development Initiative of South Africa increased collection rates for scrap tires from 3% to 70% in 18 months, leading to the creation of small and mid-size processing and recycling companies. South Africa expects to reap an aggregate benefit of USD 6 million by 2020.
  - Rwanda invested USD 1 million in its e-waste facility, with the potential to recycle 7 000 tonnes of plastic per year, as well as metals and electronic materials.[2]

"Green" existing economic activities

- **Promote environmentally-friendly and sustainable farming and tourism as value-added activities without sacrificing yields or productivity.**
  - In Mali and Senegal, farmers using sustainable fertilisers have raised their crops' net worth by 61%, increasing income and savings. Uganda has decreased its use of artificial fertilisers from 9 kg/ha to 1 kg/ha, consequently increasing its export revenues of organic farm products by 600% (UNDP, 2014).
  - Since its creation in 1989, Madagascar's shrimp farming industry in the Western Indian Ocean has become one of the country's leading export sectors by integrating environmentally-friendly methods and community development activities. Its methods are now expanding to Mozambique and Tanzania (UNECA, 2016b).
  - Mauritius is making eco-tourism the main pillar of its tourism industry. The country expects to earn USD 5 million in revenue with an estimated 1.2 million tourists by 2020.[3]

- **Introduce standards and regulations to limit pollution, thus preserving human health and the environment.**
  - Since 2003, 27 African countries have established vehicle emission standards (e.g. limiting the age of imported vehicles) and set fuel parameters to phase out lead. However, most of those countries need to implement stronger monitoring and enforcement mechanisms (AfDB/OECD/UNDP, 2016).
  - Green growth also implies improving energy and water services. Egypt's current investment in water saving devices is expected to reduce household water use by 10-15% (UNEP, 2015). The Upper Tana-Nairobi Water Fund in Kenya aims to improve water management, to increase water availability and revenues and to reduce maintenance costs for generating electricity (TNC, 2015).
  - In the medium term, countries should aim to introduce full-fledged green growth strategies. Tools and indicators for such strategies could be drawn from OECD work on the topic (OECD, 2017b). Adopting sectoral approaches could be a first step. For example, South Africa has introduced policy instruments such as carbon taxing and energy efficiency requirements for new buildings and for reporting greenhouse gases (AfDB/OECD, 2013).

PILLAR II: SOCIAL DEVELOPMENT

Action 5: Expand education while improving the quality of education and skills

Context:

- Many Africans remain excluded from basic education. Approximately 34 million children of primary school age (6-11 years) are out of school. Of these, 45% never enter school, 37% enter late and 17% drop out (UNESCO, 2015a).
- Only 6% of the African population were enrolled in tertiary education in 2015. A young person is four times more likely to reach higher-education in East Asia and the Pacific than in Africa (Van Fleet, 2012).
- Quality education remains a key challenge for Africa's job market. In sub-Saharan Africa, 61.4% of young workers do not have the level of education to work productively on the job (ILO, 2015).
- Across sub-Saharan Africa, girls receive on average about 9 years of schooling compared to 10 years for boys. Females face higher dropout rates for secondary and tertiary education. [4]
- Rural children face greater learning disadvantages: 5.9% of urban children were unable to meet basic learning levels compared to 29.1% in rural areas (Van Fleet, 2012).
- Over 10% of secondary school students in Africa are enrolled in technical and vocational education and training (TVET), yet TVET programmes receive on average 2-6% of educational budgets (AfDB/OECD/UNDP, 2017).
- In sub-Saharan Africa, only 7% of students in higher education enrol in science, technology, engineering and mathematics (STEM).
- Expenditure on education in sub-Saharan Africa represented 16.8% of total government expenditure between 2000 and 2013, which is higher than the global average of 14.1%.

Proposed actions:

Push for universal access to education, especially for females:

- reduce the cost for families to send children to school
- invest in education systems (e.g. infrastructure and teachers) and aim for gender parity.

Promote specialised education in strategic sectors:

- advance formal and specialised education in agriculture
- promote enrolment in STEM subjects and invest in scientific research
- increase focus on management and entrepreneurial education.

Improve technical and vocational education and training:

- promote and increase financing of TVET education
- introduce innovative curricular elements (e.g. entrepreneurship).

Bring educational institutions closer to job markets and private firms:

- involve the private sector in the design and delivery of education curricula and introduce on-the-job training requirements and industrial placements
- conduct regular consultations between educational institutions, the public sector and the private sector to better tailor curricula and policies.

Quality education, in particular promoting skills in science, technology and innovation, is one of the most important pillars for sustainable development and growth. African governments can take several actions to improve access to and the quality of education, matching education to labour market needs.

Push for universal access to education, especially for females

Reduce the cost for families to send children to school.

- Recent randomised experiments show that cash transfers (both conditional and unconditional) are effective in increasing school attendance and the re-enrolment of dropouts. This is the case particularly for girls and for all children in marginalised communities.[5] In Uganda, making primary education free increased enrolment and reduced the dropout rate, most notably for girls and children in rural areas (Deininger, 2003; Grogan, 2009; Nishimura et al., 2009).

Invest in education systems and aim for gender parity to improve educational outcomes.

- Countries that have managed to improve overall school enrolment, education levels and gender parity rates have all used a mix of policies. These included waiving school fees, expanding pre-primary schooling, investing more in school infrastructure, increasing recruitment and improving training, particularly of female teachers.
- Countries should look beyond enrolment statistics and ensure grade progression. South Africa managed to solve the problem of limited school progression by gathering granular data at class and age levels and subsequently introducing norms on age-grade schooling and expanding pre-primary schooling (Bashir et al., 2018).
- In Benin, the government abolished school fees for all girls in public primary schools in rural areas in 2000 (Benin Ministry of Education and Scientific Research, 1999).

It combined this measure with community mobilisation strategies to increase demand for girls' education. As a result, the ratio of female-to-male students increased from 0.64 in 1999 to 0.89 in 2012. For further details on solutions for educationpoliciesinAfricaandotherdevelopingcountries,seeUNESCO(2015b).

Promotespecialisededucationinstrategicsectors

Advanceformalandspecialisededucationinagriculture.

- Investingintertiaryagriculturaleducationcouldincreasethenumberofknowledge brokers, trainers and teachers. Using new technologies and online courses to complement formal education could also prove useful in promoting agricultural studies. Currently, only 2% of university students are enrolled in agricultural programmesdespitetheagriculturalsectoraccountingfor32%ofAfrica'sGDPand employingtwo-thirdsofitsworkforce(WorldBank,2014).

PromoteenrolmentinSTEMsubjectsandinvestinscientificresearch.

- Improvinghighereducation'scapacitytoproduceSTEMresearchwouldenhancea country'sabilitytobetterharnessitscomparativeadvantages.Itwouldalsobetter equiptheyouthtodeveloptheskillsneededtocompeteintoday'slabourmarkets (WorldBankandElsevier,2014).

Increasefocusonmanagementandentrepreneurialeducation.

- Many African entrepreneurs lack the necessary management skills to succeed. Possibleactionstoimprovebusinesseducationcouldincludethefollowing:
  - increasethenumberofhigh-qualitybusinessschoolsinAfrica,whichiscurrently verylow,andthequalityofstudents'learningoutcomes(Naudé,2017)
  - establishpermanentendowmentsorfundsforuniversitiesorbusinessschools, possiblyincludinggrantsfromdevelopmentpartners(America,2013).

Improvetechnicalandvocationaleducationandtraining

PromoteandincreasefinancingofTVETeducation.

- ImprovingtheperceptionofTVETinsocietygoeshand-in-handwithbetterTVET programmes.Governmentscouldencourageenrolmentbyincreasingbothfunding totheTVETsectorandthenumberofscholarshipsallocatedtostudentspursuing these studies. Employers could provide opportunities for industrial placements andinternshipsforTVETtrainees.

Introduceinnovativecurricularelements(e.g.entrepreneurship)

- Adopting innovations can help train people and build skills outside of the typical TVET framework. Malawi has introduced entrepreneurial education by adopting technical, entrepreneurial and vocational education and training (TEVET) programmes and recognising the importance of informal training (e.g. traditional apprenticeships), especially for disadvantaged youth (OECD, 2018d). Othercountrieswheretraditionalapprenticeshipsarewidespread(e.g.Benin,Côte d'IvoireandGhana),couldformaliseorrecognisethisformofprofessionaltraining. InGhana,forexample,apprenticeshipsrepresentupto90%ofbasicskillstraining (AtchoarenaandDelluc,2002).TEVETcoursesalsorequirestronglinkageswiththe privatesectortoenhancetheirqualityandrespondtolabourmarketneeds.

Bring educational institutions closer to job markets and private firms

- **Involve the private sector in the design and delivery of education curricula and introduce on-the-job training requirements and industrial placements.**
  - To close the skills gap, governments should bring educational institutions closer to job markets by favouring on-the-job training. The private sector can contribute to the design and delivery of training programmes by offering internships and on-the-job training, by financing training institutions and by advising on curriculum reforms (Bughin et al., 2016).
  - Increasing private sector engagement can help develop more demand-driven training programmes, for instance in activities such as business, commerce, and information and communications technology (ICT) (AfDB/OECD, 2008). Aligning TVET with domestic labour market needs is important to avoid fostering emigration (OECD, 2017c).

- **Conduct regular consultations between educational institutions, the public sector and the private sector to better tailor curricula and policies.**
  - Partnerships can improve the quality of public training programmes and address the skill needs of enterprises. Public-private partnerships could lower the cost of training,[6] inform TVET providers of which skills are in demand and provide employers with skilled workers.

Action 6: Increase the coverage of social protection systems, including labour and health

Context:

- SDG Target 1.3 calls on countries to provide "nationally appropriate social protection systems and measures for all, including [social protection] floors, and by 2030 achieve substantial coverage of the poor and vulnerable".
- Poverty rates in Africa have declined significantly since 1990, yet over 35% of the population live on less than USD 1.90 a day. About 45% of the population earn USD 1.90-5.50 a day and are vulnerable to falling back into extreme poverty.
- Health expenditure grew from an average 5.1% of GDP in 2000 to 6.2% in 2015. However, in 2015, only Madagascar and Swaziland surpassed the threshold of 15% of government spending prescribed by the 2001 Abuja Agreement. Eighteen African countries now spend less than the minimum required for essential health services, as per the 2001 WHO Commission on Macroeconomics and Health's recommendation.
- Scaling up social protection systems is the main challenge for policy makers in this area. Today more than 45 African countries implement unconditional in-kind transfers and public works programmes, reaching approximately 20% of the continent's total population (World Bank, 2018). The number of countries implementing a cash transfer programme has more than doubled since 2010.
- Resources for social safety nets represent over 3% of GDP in Lesotho, Mauritius, Namibia and South Africa but much less in other countries. Social safety nets cover only 24% of sub-Saharan Africa's population and 29% of the poorest quintile (World Bank, 2018).

Proposed actions:

Establish social protection floors:

- target the poorest populations in order to reduce income inequalities, and ensure that social protection systems cover an individual's entire life
- cater for recipients with low economic and social status as well as those of retirement age.

Make social protection systems financially sustainable

- in the short term, optimise the fiscal revenue allocated to social protection and rely on external financial assistance if necessary
- in the medium term, design social security/protection financing mechanisms that are self-sustaining and that do not burden the poor
- build the statistical capacity to inform policy making on social protection.

Social protection is vital to eradicate poverty, increase economic resilience and facilitate human development. Agenda 2063 highlights social protection as a crucial instrument to ensure that no citizen is without access to basic income and essential health care. The African Union's Social Policy Framework for Africa encourages member states to adopt minimum social protection policies such as essential health care, social insurance and social welfare. African Union targets for 2023 include providing the following:

- social protection to at least 30% of vulnerable populations including people with disabilities, seniors and children
- social security to everyone who works in the formal sector
- social security to at least 20% of the informal sector and rural labour.

Establish social protection floors

Target the poorest populations in order to reduce income inequalities, and ensure social protection systems cover an individual's entire life.

- African governments need to establish an integrated framework for social assistance, social insurance and labour market policies to address current and long-term challenges. Central governments also need to facilitate co-ordination and develop centralised administrative systems, budgets and strategies. Supporting this framework requires investing in statistical and administrative capacity by:
  - enhancing civil registration
  - carrying out regular population censuses and household surveys
  - establishing single registries and unified management information systems
  - building rigorous monitoring and evaluation mechanisms.
- Gender aspects also need to be incorporated to increase access to social protection for women and girls, who often constitute a disproportionate share of the poor. This includes promoting females' access to health and education services as well as supporting them when they are out of the labour force caring for dependents (OECD, 2017d).
- The few African countries that have completed their demographic transition (e.g. Mauritius, Seychelles and Tunisia) are now confronted with a large portion

of the population reaching retirement age. Low labour force participation may worsen existing inequalities, particularly since the cost of care for the elderly falls disproportionately on the poorer members of society (OECD, 2017e).

- **Cater for recipients with low economic and social status as well as those of retirement age.**
  - Varying social protection programmes can increase their impact and target different status groups. South Africa's public works scheme complements other existing welfare programmes. While work is short-term and wages are below formal sector salaries, participation in the scheme counts towards unemployment insurance and other benefits (AfDB/OECD/UNDP, 2016). Ethiopia and Tanzania have safety net programmes that target the poorest through public works for those who can work and through direct support for those who cannot. In Ethiopia, people enrolled in the Productive Safety Net Programme are more likely to take part in health programmes.

Make social protection systems financially sustainable

- **In the short term optimise the fiscal revenue allocated to social protection and rely on external financial assistance if necessary.**

Financing strategies need to combine improvements to the tax system (see Action 9) with reforms on the expenditure side that optimise existing social or pro-poor spending. Natural resource rents can provide a portion of the revenue mix, yet they are not available to all countries and their volatility poses a risk to sustainable long-term financing. Removing fuel and food subsidies (without hurting the poor) could free up significant resources for social protection systems. Removing fuel subsidies in five Eastern African countries could save between 0.6% and 2.1% of GDP (OECD, 2017d).

- **In the medium and long term design social security/protection financing mechanisms that are self-sustaining and that do not burden the poor.**
  - Establishing social protection floors requires African governments to raise annual spending on social protection from today's average of about 1.5% of GDP to 5%, as stated in Agenda 2063. To reach this objective, governments should consider the following:
    - increasing domestic resource mobilisation and investing part of that additional revenue in social protection
    - managing social protection programmes sustainably (on both revenue and expenditure sides, while taking stock of demographic projections).

- **Build the statistical capacity to inform policy making on social protection.**
  - Employing new tools such as the Commitment to Equity analysis can help governments understand the impact of the fiscal system on the final income of different groups in the society.[7]
  - Capacity building and increased information sharing across relevant government bodies can develop the institutional capacity to forecast long-term social protection financing needs.

PILLAR III: INSTITUTIONAL DEVELOPMENT

Action 7: Boost Africa's engagement with its global partners

Context:

- Africa's engagement with development partners is receiving new impetus. The process of *shifting wealth*, or the increasing wealth created by developing countries has brought considerable attention to the roles of more recent partners for Africa's development such as Brazil, China and India.
- Africa's partnerships have generated mixed results and can benefit from enhanced co-ordination.

Proposed actions:

Strengthen global co-operation:

- open up to new partners (e.g. private sector and philanthropy) and strengthen existing initiatives such as the G20's Compact with Africa.

Improve existing African partnerships and co-operation:

- streamline relations and improve co-ordination between African bodies and institutions.

Strengthen global co-operation

Open up to new development partners (e.g. private sector and philanthropy)

- New donors have emphasised economic co-operation involving a wide range of activities such as resource-for-infrastructure swaps and FDI in agriculture, in natural resources and in manufacturing. China played a key role in the creation of two new multilateral development banks (MDBs): the New Development Bank and the Asian Infrastructure Investment Bank. The country pledged significant financing to the two MDBs, whose combined loan portfolios are estimated at USD 230 billion (Reisen, 2015).
- The Africa Global Partnership Platform was launched in 2015 to promote high-level dialogue on and partnerships for Africa's interest and priorities, but follow-up has been weak. New actors will need to be involved, including the private sector and civil society. Philanthropic groups and corporate social responsibility programmes are now emerging as important sources of development finance. Between 2013 and 2015, Africa received USD 6.6 billion from philanthropic foundations (OECD, 2018b), which offer a new business-like approach.

Improve existing African partnerships and co-operation

Streamline relations and improve co-ordination between African bodies and institutions.

- The African Union should strengthen its role in monitoring the impact of partnerships with continental and regional agencies in close partnership with the NEPAD, the African Union's development agency.
- The African Development Bank, as the executing agency for the Programme for Infrastructure Development in Africa, established an infrastructure fund, Africa50. It is leading efforts to leverage private investments for high-impact infrastructure projects.

Action 8: Deepen regional integration

Context:

- On 21 March 2018 in Kigali (Rwanda), the heads of 44 African countries signed the Continental Free Trade Area (CFTA) Agreement. Fully liberalising trade in goods could boost Africa's GDP by 1% and total employment by 1.2%. Intra-African trade could grow by 33% and Africa's total trade deficit could be halved (UNCTAD, 2018).
- Forty African countries have multiple memberships to Regional Economic Communities (RECs) recognised by the Abuja Treaty. This has created duplication and unclear mandates.
- High trade costs persist among African countries despite their longstanding integration into RECs. Ten years after the signing of the regional agreement, the East African Community is the only bloc where trading costs had fallen (de Melo, Nouar and Solleder, 2017). Only SADC has managed to maintain a positive trend in intra-regional trade, pushing it beyond 5% of GDP.
- Intra-African merchandise exports make up less than 19% of the total, compared to 63% in Europe (EU-28) and 58% in Asia.
- Informal cross-border trade represents 30-40% of total trade within SADC. Around 70% of informal cross-border traders in Africa are women (Afrika and Ajumbo, 2012; FAO, 2017).
- Over the period 2011-14, only about 20% of trade finance went to intra-African trade.
- Borders remain difficult to cross for capital, services and people. Only ten countries currently waive visa requirements or issue visas on arrival to all African citizens. Restrictions still hamper trade in services. National governments often take too long to implement regional commitments (UNCTAD, 2015). Moreover, the scope of services negotiations in some RECs remains limited.

Proposed actions:

Improve the co-ordination and governance of RECs and rationalise memberships:

- encourage REC secretariats to co-ordinate and align policies to deepen continental integration
- prioritise REC engagements to resolve the issue of overlapping memberships
- increase policy commitment, co-ordination and harmonisation.

Facilitate trade in goods:

- operationalise the African Continental Free Trade Area
- remove non-tariff barriers to trade
- invest in infrastructure and simplify customs procedures
- expand financing for intra-regional trade
- remove constraints for small-scale cross-border traders.

Deepen regional integration to include the free movement of people, capital and services:

- remove visa requirements and restrictions on labour movement
- facilitate cross-border capital movements to reduce costs of payments and business operations
- further liberalise service sectors and enhance their trade.

The African Union's Agenda 2063 calls for a united continent where people, goods, services and capital cross borders freely. Achieving this will substantially increase continental trade and investment flows. Investments in ICT and transport infrastructure coupled with trade facilitation measures are expected to push the share of intra-African trade to 50% of the continent's total trade by the year 2045, more than three times the current level (AUC, 2015). Such regional integration is also key for connecting African firms to GVCs, which require competitiveness through economies of scale (Ahmad and Primi, 2017).

Improve the co-ordination and governance of Regional Economic Communities and rationalise memberships

- **Encourage REC secretariats to co-ordinate between themselves and align policies to strengthen continental integration.**
  - Reviving the NEPAD's African Peer Review Mechanism and encouraging all African countries to sign up could strengthen peer learning and policy dialogue among African countries. Today, 37 countries participate on a volunteer basis. Other organisations conducting peer reviews, such as the OECD, could share their experiences.

- **Prioritise REC engagements to resolve the issue of overlapping memberships.**
  - The pursuit of multiple regional trade agreements discourages states from seeking deeper integration and decreases intra-regional trade (Chacha, 2014). African RECs need both the power to legally enforce their policies and stronger dispute resolution mechanisms (de Melo, Nouar and Solleder, 2017). Additionally, RECs and their member states need to clarify whether the recent mega-regional agreements (e.g. the Tripartite Free Trade Area and CFTA) supersede the legal provisions of regional agreements.

- **Within RECs, countries need greater policy commitment, co-ordination and harmonisation.**
  - SADC countries are working together to promote regional industrialisation and value chain upgrading. The 2017 SADC Industrialisation Strategy Action Plan looks at investment and industrialisation potential for specific products while taking into account comparative advantages at regional level.
  - East African Community countries market the Community as a single tourist destination, since launching the East African Tourist Visa in 2015. The private sector-led East Africa Tourism Platform is promoting a co-ordinated approach to enhance the region's competitiveness in travel and tourism (Dihel and Goswami, 2016).

Facilitate trade in goods

- **Operationalise the African Continental Free Trade Area.**
  - Signatory countries commit to reducing tariffs and non-tariff barriers to trade. Removing tariffs will result in sizeable long-run gains for the vast majority of the countries, in spite of significant short-run adjustment costs. As regional economic communities move from free trade areas to common markets, common external tariffs will solve the issue of different rules of origin across RECs. Countries can also follow the BIAT Action Plan[8] to prioritise the policy reforms required to derive the full benefits of the CFTA (AU/UNECA, 2012).

- **Remove non-tariff barriers to trade.**
  - Policy makers can reduce market entry costs for firms by harmonising standards and regulations (e.g. different rules of origins, for instance between SADC and the Common Market for Eastern and Southern Africa [COMESA]). Mutual recognition agreements between standards bureaus and national certification agencies can avoid costly duplication of procedures for firms.
  - Various RECs can target different non-tariff barriers to trade:
    - North African countries can build on their current GVC integration with European Union (EU) countries to upgrade to branding, retailing, and research and development processes for Africa-focused value chains.
    - The South African apparel sector benefited from a customs union arrangement (i.e. SACU) for offshore production to Lesotho and Swaziland. Mauritian firms invested in Madagascar, another SADC country, to then access the South African market (Fessehaie, 2018).

- **Invest in infrastructure and simplify customs procedures.**
  - The East African Community's Single Customs Territory (SCT) shows how RECs can co-ordinate the removal of non-tariff barriers. The SCT streamlined border crossings, eliminating both unnecessary checks and clearing procedures (NCTTCA, 2017). Here are two of the many results:
    - Transit times between Mombasa and Kigali were halved, from 11.4 to 5.7 days.
    - Road freight costs from Mombasa to Kigali decreased by over 30%, from USD 4 350 in 2015 to USD 3 300 in 2017.
  - Electronic Single Windows and one-stop border posts can significantly reduce the time and cost of trading. The Uganda ESW simplifies submission and processing of trade information, reducing time for administrative procedures and transaction costs by 30%.

- **Expand financing for intra-regional trade and make financing more affordable.**
  - Focusing export credit and trade finance on regional trade could reduce transaction costs and information asymmetries for African lenders. SMEs could also benefit from scaled-up financial solutions, such as asset-based lending or credit-guarantee schemes as well as capacity building initiatives to help them meet quality standards (AfDB/OECD/UNDP, 2017).

- **Remove constraints for small-scale cross-border traders.**
  - Policies supporting small-scale traders can vary from building infrastructure to reducing bureaucracy, while enabling informal businesses to enter the formal economy. For instance, building cross-border marketplaces can increase the safety of women travelling long distances with their merchandise. Simplified procedures such as the COMESA Simplified Trade Regime reduce paperwork and encourage formal economic activity along border regions.

Deepen regional integration to include the free movement of people, capital and services

- **Remove visa requirements and restrictions on the movement of people.**
  - Only ten countries waive visa requirements or issue visas on arrival for all African citizens (AfDB/AU, 2017), and only half of the AU members have signed the CFTA Agreement on the free movement of people. Though implementing this policy

requires a serious commitment from signatory countries, the free movement of people could play a central role in unleashing the continent's economic potential (ICTSD, 2018). A joint OECD-ILO study found that immigrants in four African countries made a positive – albeit limited – net fiscal contribution (OECD/ILO, 2018).

- Within RECs under common market arrangements, countries should allow people to cross borders as freely as their own citizens, with no additional procedures. For example, Kenya, Rwanda and Uganda allow their citizens to travel between their countries with only their national ID cards.

▶ **Facilitate cross-border capital movements to reduce costs of payments and business operations.**

- Strengthening the cross-border use of banking and non-banking services can enable firms to serve regional markets at lower costs. Countries should promote the cross-border use of payment instruments. Through the banking sector, the East African Payment System reduced the time and cost of transactions thanks to direct currency exchange. Other such payment services include mobile money (e.g. Orange Money in West Africa), whose costs have fallen thanks to the removal of cross-border and roaming fees.

▶ **Further liberalise services sectors and enhance their trade.**

- Countries can benefit from further liberalising services sectors. The scope of services negotiations in some RECs remains limited. The launch of the Single African Air Transport Market in January 2018 is a step forward.
- Encouraging cross-border services such as education and health could help establish regional centres of excellence. Several programmes promote exchanges of African students and practitioners to enhance learning opportunities. These include the Intra-African Exchange Program established by the Association for the Development of Education in Africa and the EU-AU Intra-Africa Academic Mobility Scheme.

Action 9: Mobilise domestic resources

Context:

- Achieving Agenda 2063 or reaching the Sustainable Development Goals may require increasing annual public spending by up to 30% in low-income countries (Baum et al., 2017). However, foreign aid and other non-tax revenues such as resource rents can fluctuate wildly and unpredictably (OECD/ATAF/AUC, 2017).
- To strengthen tax systems, policy makers should be mindful of the size of the informal sector, which reaches 38% of GDP in sub-Saharan Africa, and adapt their policies (OECD/ATAF/AUC, 2017). For example, it is generally more difficult to collect reliable statistics from informal businesses and effectively apply regulations to them.
- Aid for public sector policy and administrative management has been falling. It accounted for less than 2% of the total aid allocated to Africa in 2015.
- African governments are currently experiencing reduced non-tax revenues. ODA averaged 10% less in 2015 than in 2013 (though low-income countries saw the amount decrease by only 1%). Revenues from oil exports from African countries are a third of their peak in 2011.

Proposed actions:

Design tax systems that broaden the tax base and promote compliance:

- increase the transparency of tax systems and improve communication with taxpayers
- design a tax system that reduces the burden and costs of complying.

Invest in making tax administrations more effective and efficient:

- simplify tax administrations and procedures

Co-operate at the international level to improve tax systems:

- co-ordinate tax policies and systems at REC and continental levels
- join international fora and efforts to stem practices such as base erosion and profit shifting, tax arbitrage, and illicit financial flows
- collaborate with international partners to improve revenue statistics.

African countries will need to invest heavily in order to meet their development needs. Agenda 2063, the Addis Ababa Action Agenda of the Third International Conference on Financing for Development and the SDG Target 17.1 all stress that increased taxation is pivotal to foster sustainable development finance.

Design tax systems that broaden the tax base and promote compliance

Increase the transparency of tax systems and improve communication with taxpayers.

- Better communication to help taxpayers understand the link between tax payments and government expenditure can increase public acceptance and encourage tax compliance. Some countries go further, explicitly linking certain taxes to specific programmes, for example by instituting taxes whose revenues pay directly into special funds for emergency policy responses, health coverage programmes or large investments. Rwanda raises taxes that go to the national road maintenance fund, while Uganda has an infrastructure levy to finance the construction of a standard gauge railway.
- Increasing communication and proximity between government officials and citizens can have a major impact on tax revenues. Decentralising tax collection in Rwanda showed that greater geographic proximity can improve the flow of information as well as tax compliance (AfDB/OECD/UNDP, 2017). The Ethiopian Revenue Authority increased tax collections by 32% when reminding taxpayers of their duty to pay taxes and increased them by 38% when threatening taxpayers with an audit (Shimeles, Gurara and Woldeyes, 2017).

Design a tax system that reduces the burden and costs of complying.

- By "unbundling" policies, for example separating business registration from taxation (Jütting and Laiglesia, 2009), governments can make entering the formal sector more attractive. Business licenses could be offered for free, and in exchange businesses could obtain social protections or incentives. This could be a first step towards improving firms' performances and enabling tax compliance over the medium term.
- Flat taxes may be useful where compliance costs are high due to small business size or high informality. Côte d'Ivoire, for example, charges a flat rate to individuals

on their business income when it is below a certain threshold. This can increase compliance by simplifying payment for small businesses (OECD, 2016b, 2015b). However, these taxes can have unintended consequences such as providing an incentive for businesses to remain under the threshold.

- Requiring small businesses to retain the part of their employees' salary which will be paid as personal income tax (i.e. "withholding taxes") could reduce the cost of compliance for employees and increase revenues.

Invest in making tax administrations more effective and efficient

Simplify tax administrations and procedures.

- Removing inefficient tax exemptions can increase revenues while reducing administrative burdens and removing harmful distortions. Morocco increased VAT revenues by introducing reforms to expand the tax base and to simplify taxation rules, reducing both exemptions and VAT rates. As a result, between 2004 and 2013, VAT revenue as a share of GDP increased by 2.8 percentage points, constituting more than half of the total tax revenue growth over the period (OECD/ATAF/AUC, 2017).
- E-filing can increase compliance by saving time for taxpayers, as well as reduce calculation errors and make the paperwork easier to fill out. South Africa's introduction of e-filing in 2001 reduced tax compliance costs by 22.4% (Coolidge and Yilmaz, 2014).
- One common approach is the creation of a separate office to handle high-income taxpayers. Despite requiring more resources, these are usually cost-effective. Rwanda increased the compliance rate of high-income taxpayers by up to 97% after strengthening its compliance enforcement mechanism and establishing a separate Small and Medium Taxpayers Office (AfDB/OECD/UNDP, 2017:34).

Co-operate at the international level to improve tax systems

Co-ordinate tax policies and systems at REC and continental levels.

- Some RECs, such as the Economic Community of West African States, have harmonised import tariffs and VAT rules across member countries, while allowing some variation in the rates. The Southern African Customs Union (SACU) went a step further, modernising its full revenue sharing formula by including customs excise duties and a development component, which are administered by the SACU Customs Union Commission. This has made tax collection more efficient and served as a forum in which to work collectively on the problem of development finance in the region.

Join international fora and efforts to stem practices such as base erosion and profit shifting (BEPS), tax arbitrage, and illicit financial flows.

- Twenty-one African countries currently participate in the Inclusive Framework on BEPS. In developing countries, BEPS mainly results from abusive and inappropriate transfer pricing, as well as excessive interest payments, abuse of tax treaties and of the definition of permanent establishment. The OECD, together with other international organisations and the African Tax Administration Forum (ATAF) is conducting tailored country-level capacity building programmes in 17 African countries to support BEPS transfer pricing and VAT standards.

- Twenty African countries and two African international organisations (ATAF and the Centre de rencontres et d'études des dirigeants des administrations fiscales [CREDAF]) are participating in the OECD Global Forum on VAT. They participate in the development of global VAT standards (the International VAT/GST Guidelines) and share policy analysis, experiences and best practices.
- Governments should work together to strengthen border controls, track down illegal funds, and remove significant differences in tax rates in order to reduce incentives for cross-border arbitrage and smuggling. In West Africa, the most significant net losses due to illicit financial flows were attributed to natural resource revenues invested outside the region. To stem these flows, national governments can engage with international initiatives and fora such as the Joint AfDB-OECD Initiative to Support Business Integrity and Anti-Bribery Efforts in Africa (OECD, 2018c).

Collaborate with international partners to improve the quality and comparability of revenue statistics.

- African governments can benefit from making their revenue statistics comparable and available for international comparison. Making information on tax systems easily accessible to a wider range of experts would increase transparency while improving policy making and international co-operation. The Revenue Statistics in Africa project has created a single comprehensive dataset of detailed statistics on African countries' revenues. The project, now in its third year, is a partnership of the African Union, the African Tax Administration Forum and the OECD. The dataset will soon feature 21 countries and is aligned with an international classification standard, allowing for data comparisons at a detailed level with countries around the world.

Action 10: Enhance economic and political governance

Context:

- Most African countries continue to face key challenges in meeting citizens' expectations on policy-making processes and public service delivery. Over 22% of protests in Africa between 2014 and 2016 were motivated by such unmet expectations.
- Government accountability remains low according to the Mo Ibrahim Index of African Governance. Progress has been marginal since 2008 and is losing momentum.
- The lack of statistics in Africa reflects low institutional capacity and may prevent governments from clearly understanding their countries. For example, seven countries in Africa have not carried out population censuses in over ten years (CEPED, 2016).
- Many countries have gone through political and administrative decentralisation since the 1990s, notably by organising local elections and transferring more power to sub-national governments. However, fiscal decentralisation often lags behind political decentralisation.

Proposedactions:

Increase accountability and transparency of policy-making processes and redistributivepolicies:

- makeuseofdigitalsolutionsforopendataandfreedomofinformationinitiatives aswellasforgovernmentservices.

Promotegoodcorporategovernanceandastablebusinessenvironment:

- establishnationalregulatoryframeworksandinitiativesoncorporategovernance toenhanceprivatesectorcapacity
- enhancethetransparencyandcompetitivenessofstate-ownedenterprises.

Continuallyinvestinupgradinginstitutionalcapacity:

- undertakesystematiccapacity-buildingprogrammestoacquirenewsetsofskills, managerialapproachesandinstitutionalculture
- implementthedecisionoftheAUHeadsofStateandGovernmenttoallocate0.15% ofthenationalbudgeteachyeartostatisticalactivities.

Ensurereformsareimplementedattheappropriatelevelofgovernment:

- adoptthesubsidiarityprinciple,wheretherightlevelofgovernmentintervenesfor specificpolicies,inco-ordinationwithotherlevelsofgovernment
- bringfiscaldecentralisationonaparwithpoliticalandadministrativedevolution.

Increase accountability and transparency of policy-making processes and redistributivepolicies

Make useofdigital solutions foropen data andfreedom ofinformation initiatives as wellasforgovernmentservices.

- Cabo Verde's citizen information centre, *Casa do Cidadao*, provides a single portal to access administrative services. This initiative has reduced time for procedures, facilitatedcitizens'interactionwithgovernmentandmadeinformationmoreaccurate.
- The Kenya Open Data Initiative (KODI), launched in 2011, gives free access to governmentdatasetsandpromotestransparentgovernance.Today,31ministries contributedata.

Promotegoodcorporategovernanceandastablebusinessenvironment

Establish regulatory frameworks and initiatives on corporate governance to enhance privatesectorcapacity.

- Forpubliclylistedcompanies,governmentsshouldsetandenforceaccountingand auditingstandards.Kenya'sPrivateSectorCorporateGovernanceTrustworkswith the private sector and government to build institutional capacity and establish goodgovernancepractices(Gatamah,2002).

Enhancethetransparencyandcompetitivenessofstate-ownedenterprises.

- Governments can increase transparency and improve governance of state-ownedenterprisesbylimitingconflictsofinterest,designingeffectiveregulatory frameworks, treating other shareholders and investors equitably, and following internationalstandardsoncorporateethicsandstakeholderrelations(SOENetwork for Southern Africa, 2014). More generally, countries should consider aligning nationalregulationstoglobalbestpracticesandprinciples.Forfurtherdetails,see *OECDGuidelinesonCorporateGovernanceofState-OwnedEnterprises* (OECD,2015c).

Continually invest in upgrading institutional capability

- **Undertake systematic capacity-building programmes to acquire new sets of skills, managerial approaches and institutional culture at all government levels.**
  - South Africa's eThekwini Municipality established the Municipal Institute of Learning (MILE) to build capacity for local government. Since 2009, MILE has trained 3 600 local government practitioners from different African countries.
  - The International Monetary Fund, together with a number of other donors, has set up six African Regional Technical Assistance Centers. The centres aim to build local capacity for economic and financial management. They provide assistance with a team of resident experts and organise in-country workshops, professional training and regional courses.

- **Dedicate greater resources to building Africa's statistical capacity**
  - Implement the decision of the Heads of State and Government to allocate 0.15% of national budgets each year to statistical activities, as recalled at the 4th Conference of African Ministers responsible for Civil Registration and Vital Statistics in Nouakchott, December 2017. South Africa has met this target by allocating to statistics 0.19% of its 2018 budget.
  - Strong monitoring and evaluation frameworks are needed to track progress in implementing Agenda 2063. Support to the update and review of the Strategy for the Harmonisation of Statistics in Africa (SHaSA) by all stakeholders can help national statistical agencies to develop harmonised indicators, definitions, measurement and verification processes for all the targets under Agenda 2063.
  - Countries should follow up on commitments to operationalise the Pan African Institute of Statistics by 2023, as set out in Agenda 2063.

Ensure reforms are implemented at the appropriate level of government

- **Adopt the principle of subsidiarity, where the right level of government intervenes for specific policies, in co-ordination with other levels of government.**
  - Many African governments need to expand their multi-level governance agenda. In 2014, the African Union adopted the African Charter on Values and Principles of Decentralisation, Local Governance and Local Development. Despite the consensus on the matter among African governments, at the time of writing only 13 African countries have signed the charter (AU, 2018).
  - Multi-level governance dynamics are country-specific. Finding the right balance between the different levels of government requires trial and error (AfDB/OECD/UNDP, 2016).

- **Bring fiscal decentralisation on a par with political and administrative devolution.**
  - Effective reforms in fiscal decentralisation can enable local governments to boost resources and invest in the necessary infrastructure and services. Such reforms include national transfers, automatic sharing of revenues from natural resources, land value capture, increased capacity of local tax administration and the promotion of private finance (AfDB/OECD/UNDP, 2016). Efforts to improve local government transparency and institutional capacity must accompany fiscal decentralisation.
  - Participatory budgets can improve tax legitimacy for subnational governments, as shown by the YTAX system software in Senegal.

Annex 8.A1. Links between each policy action and megatrends, Agenda 2063 goals and SDGs

Policy Action	Related Agenda 2063 Goals	Related Sustainable Development Goals	Megatrends addressed
Action 1: Encourage investment for domestic private sector development	**Goal 4.** Transformed economies and jobs **Goal 12.** Capable institutions and transformative leadership in place at all levels **Goal 20.** Africa takes full responsibility for financing its development	**SDG 8.** Promote sustained, inclusive and sustainable economic growth, full and productive employment and decent work for all **SDG 9.** Build resilient infrastructure, promote inclusive and sustainable industrialization and foster innovation **SDG 12.** Ensure sustainable consumption and production patterns **SDG 17.** Strengthen the means of implementation and revitalize the global partnership for sustainable development	1. "Shifting wealth" 2. The new production revolution (Industry 4.0) 4. Africa's urban transition
Action 2: Help the private sector to diversify production and exports	**Goal 4.** Transformed economies and jobs **Goal 5.** Modern agriculture for increased productivity and production	**SDG 8.** Promote sustained, inclusive and sustainable economic growth, full and productive employment and decent work for all **SDG 9.** Build resilient infrastructure, promote inclusive and sustainable industrialization and foster innovation **SDG 17.** Strengthen the means of implementation and revitalize the global partnership for sustainable development	1. "Shifting wealth" 2. The new production revolution (Industry 4.0) 4. Africa's urban transition
Action 3: Strengthen linkages between rural and urban economies	**Goal 1.** High standard of living, quality of life and well-being for all **Goal 10.** World class infrastructure criss-crosses Africa	**SDG 1.** End poverty in all its forms everywhere **SDG 8.** Promote sustained, inclusive and sustainable economic growth, full and productive employment and decent work for all **SDG 10.** Reduce inequality within and among countries **SDG 11.** Make cities and human settlements inclusive, safe, resilient and sustainable	3. Africa's demographic dividends 4. Africa's urban transition
Action 4: Foster green growth	**Goal 5.** Modern agriculture for increased productivity and production **Goal 6.** Blue/ocean economy **Goal 7.** Environmentally sustainable and climate-resilient economies and communities	**SDG 1.** End poverty in all its forms everywhere **SDG 7.** Ensure access to affordable, reliable, sustainable and modern energy for all **SDG 8.** Promote sustained, inclusive and sustainable economic growth, full and productive employment and decent work for all **SDG 13.** Take urgent action to combat climate change and its impacts **SDG 14.** Conserve and sustainably use the oceans, seas and marine resources for sustainable development **SDG 15.** Protect, restore and promote sustainable use of terrestrial ecosystems, sustainably manage forests, combat desertification, and halt and reverse land degradation and halt biodiversity loss	5. Climate change and the transition to a green economy
Action 5: Expand education while improving the quality of education and skills	**Goal 2.** Well-educated citizens and skills revolution underpinned by science, technology and innovation **Goal 17.** Full gender equality in all spheres of life **Goal 18.** Engaged and empowered youth and children	**SDG 4.** Ensure inclusive and equitable quality education and promote lifelong learning opportunities for all **SDG 5.** Achieve gender equality and empower all women and girls **SDG 12.** Ensure sustainable consumption and production patterns	2. The new production revolution (Industry 4.0) 3. Africa's demographic dividends
Action 6: Increase the coverage of social protection systems, including labour and health	**Goal 1.** High standard of living, quality of life and well-being for all **Goal 3.** Healthy and well-nourished citizens	**SDG 1.** End poverty in all its forms everywhere **SDG 3.** Ensure healthy lives and promote well-being for all at all ages **SDG 10.** Reduce inequality within and among countries	3. Africa's demographic dividends
Action 7: Boost Africa's engagement with its global partners	**Goal 19.** Africa as a major partner in global affairs and peaceful co-existence **Goal 20.** Africa takes full responsibility for financing her development	**SDG 10.** Reduce inequality within and among countries **SDG 17.** Strengthen the means of implementation and revitalize the global partnership for sustainable development	1. "Shifting wealth"

Policy Action	Related Agenda 2063 Goals	Related Sustainable Development Goals	Megatrends addressed
Action 8: Deepen regional integration	**Goal 4.** Transformed economies and job creation **Goal 8.** United Africa (federal or confederate) **Goal 9.** Key continental financial and monetary institutions established and functional **Goal 10.** World class infrastructure criss-crosses Africa	**SDG 9.** Build resilient infrastructure, promote inclusive and sustainable industrialization and foster innovation **SDG 10.** Reduce inequality within and among countries **SDG 11.** Make cities and human settlements inclusive, safe, resilient and sustainable **SDG 17.** Strengthen the means of implementation and revitalize the global partnership for sustainable development	1. "Shifting wealth" 3. Africa's demographic dividends 4. Africa's urban transition
Action 9: Mobilise domestic resources	**Goal 20.** Africa takes full responsibility for financing its development	**SDG 8.** Promote sustained, inclusive and sustainable economic growth, full and productive employment and decent work for all **SDG 17.** Strengthen the means of implementation and revitalize the global partnership for sustainable development	2. The new production revolution (Industry 4.0) 3. Africa's demographic dividends 4. Africa's urban transition
Action 10: Enhance economic and political governance	**Goal 8.** United Africa (federal or confederate) **Goal 11.** Democratic values, practices, universal principles of human rights, justice and the rule of law entrenched **Goal 12.** Capable institutions and transformative leadership in place at all levels	**SDG 8.** Promote sustained, inclusive and sustainable economic growth, full and productive employment and decent work for all **SDG 16.** Promote peaceful and inclusive societies for sustainable development, provide access to justice for all and build effective, accountable and inclusive institutions at all levels **SDG 17.** Strengthen the means of implementation and revitalize the global partnership for sustainable development	2. The new production revolution (Industry 4.0) 4. Africa's urban transition

Notes

1. Adaptation of www.aaainitiative.org/circular-economy (accessed 31 January 2018).
2. www.fonerwa.org/ (accessed 31 January 2018).
3. www.travelmauritius.net/eco-tourism.html (accessed 31 January 2018).
4. See https://tellmaps.com/uis/gender/#!/tellmap/1152163451.
5. See for example https://www.poverty-action.org/sites/default/files/publications/evaluations of cash transfer programs in african settings policy memo.pdf.
6. www.adeanet.org/adeapmp/sites/default/files/activities/tvsd and ppp policy brief v1.pdf.
7. The Commitment to Equity (CEQ) project is led by Nora Lustig since 2008 and is an initiative of the Center for Inter-American Policy and Research (CIPR) and the Department of Economics, Tulane University, the Center for Global Development and the Inter-American Dialogue. The CEQ project is housed in the Commitment to Equity Institute at Tulane. See www.commitmentoequity.org.
8. The Action Plan for Boosting Intra-Africa Trade (BIAT), endorsed by Africa's head of states in January 2012, identifies seven clusters: trade policy, trade facilitation, productive capacity, trade-related infrastructure, trade finance, trade information and factor market integration.

References

AfDB/AU (2017), *Africa Visa Openness Report 2017*, African Development Bank and African Union, Abidjan, www.afdb.org/fileadmin/uploads/afdb/Documents/Publications/2017 Africa Visa Openness Report - Final.pdf.

AfDB/IMF/WBG (2017), *The G20 Compact with Africa: A joint Report*, African Development Bank, International Monetary Fund and World Bank Group, Baden, www.compactwithafrica.org/content/dam/Compact%20with%20Africa/2017-03-30-g20-compact-with-africa-report.pdf.

AfDB/OECD (2013), *Enabling Green Growth in Africa*, joint report from the workshop on "Green Growth in Africa" held in Lusaka, Zambia, African Development Bank and OECD, www.oecd.org/dac/environment-development/AfDB-OECD%20Enabling%20green%20growth%20in%20Africa%20workshop%20report.pdf.

AfDB/OECD (2008), *African Economic Outlook 2008*, OECD Publishing, Paris, http://dx.doi.org/10.1787/aeo-2008-en.

AfDB/OECD/UNDP (2017), *African Economic Outlook 2017: Entrepreneurship and Industrialisation*, OECD Publishing, Paris, http://dx.doi.org/10.1787/aeo-2017-en.

AfDB/OECD/UNDP (2016), *African Economic Outlook 2016: Sustainable Cities and Structural Transformation*, OECD Publishing, Paris, http://dx.doi.org/10.1787/aeo-2016-en.

AfDB/OECD/UNDP (2015), *African Economic Outlook 2015: Regional Development and Spatial Inclusion*, OECD Publishing, Paris, http://dx.doi.org/10.1787/aeo-2015-en.

Afrika, J.-G. K. and G. Ajumbo (2012), "Informal cross border trade in Africa: Implications and policy recommendations", *Africa Economic Brief*, Vol. 3/10, African Development Bank, Abidjan, https://www.afdb.org/fileadmin/uploads/afdb/Documents/Publications/Economic%20Brief%20-%20Informal%20Cross%20Border%20Trade%20in%20Africa%20Implications%20and%20Policy%20Recommendations%20-%20Volume%203.pdf.

Ahmad, N. and A. Primi (2017), "From domestic to regional to global: Factory Africa and factory Latin America?", in *Global Value Chain Development Report 2017: Measuring and Analyzing the Impact of GVCs on Economic Development*, World Bank, Washington, DC, http://documents.worldbank.org/curated/en/440081499424129960/Measuring-and-analyzing-the-impact-of-GVCs-on-economic-development.

America, R. (2013), "Economic development with limited supplies of management. What to do about it: The case of Africa", *Challenge*, Vol. 56/1, pp. 61-71, https://doi.org/10.2753/0577-5132560103.

Amin, M. and A. Islam (2015), "Are large informal firms more productive than the small informal firms? Evidence from firm-level surveys in Africa", *World Development*, Vol. 74, pp. 374–385, https://doi.org/10.1016/j.worlddev.2015.05.008.

Atchoarena, D. and A. Delluc (2002), *Revisiting Technical and Vocational Education in Sub-Saharan Africa: An Update on Trends, Innovations and Challenges*, report for the World Bank, International Institute for Educational Planning/UNESCO, Paris, http://unesdoc.unesco.org/images/0012/001293/129354e.pdf.

AU (2018), *List of Countries Which Have Signed, Ratified/Acceded to the African Charter on Values and Principles of Decentralisation, Local Governance and Local Development*, African Union, Addis Ababa, https://au.int/sites/default/files/treaties/7802-sl-african charter on the values and principles of decentralisation local .pdf(accessed 3 May 2018).

AU/UNECA (2012), *Boosting Intra African Trade*, African Union Commission and United Nations Economic Commission for Africa, Addis Ababa, www.uneca.org/sites/default/files/uploaded-documents/ATPC/issues affecting intra-african trade proposed action plan for biat and framework for the fast tracking en.pdf.

AUC (2015), *Agenda 2063: The Africa We Want,* African Union Commission, Addis Ababa, https://au.int/en/Agenda2063/popular version.

Bashir, S. et al. (2018), *Facing Forward: Schooling for Learning in Africa*, World Bank, Washington, DC, https://openknowledge.worldbank.org/handle/10986/29377.

Baum, A. et al. (2017), "Can they do it all? Fiscal space in low-income countries", *IMF Working Paper,* No. 17/110, International Monetary Fund, Washington, DC, www.imf.org/en/Publications/WP/Issues/2017/05/05/Can-They-Do-It-All-Fiscal-Space-in-Low-Income-Countries-44889.

Benin Ministry of Education and Scientific Research (1999), *Education pour tous: Bilan à l'an 2000*, http://unesdoc.unesco.org/images/0021/002193/219306f.pdf.

Berrisford, S. (2013), "Getting land governance right in sub-Saharan cities: More than land administration", in M. Napier et al., *Trading Places: Accessing Land in African Cities*, Urban LandMark, Pretoria.

Brahmbhatt, M., C. Haddaoui and J. Page (2017), "Green industrialisation and entrepreneurship in Africa", *Contributing Paper for African Economic Outlook 2017: Entrepreneurship and Industrialisation, New Climate Economy*, London and Washington, DC, http://newclimateeconomy.report/workingpapers/wp-content/uploads/sites/5/2017/10/Green-Industrialisation-and-Entrepreneurship-in-Africa.pdf.

Bughin, J. et al. (2016), *Lions on The Move II: Realizing the Potential of Africa's Economies*, McKinsey Global Institute, McKinsey & Company, https://www.mckinsey.com/featured-insights/middle-east-and-africa/lions-on-the-move-realizing-the-potential-of-africas-economies.

Byamugisha, F. (2013), *Securing Africa's Land for Shared Prosperity: A Program to Scale Up Reforms and Investments*, World Bank, Washington, DC, http://documents.worldbank.org/curated/en/732661468191967924/pdf/780850PUB0EPI00LIC00pubdate05024013.pdf.

CEPED (2016), *Inventaire des recensements et enquêtes démographiques en Afrique*, Centre Population et Développement, Université Paris Descartes, Paris, www.ceped.org/ireda/spip.php?article66&lang=fr.

Chacha, M. (2014), "Regional integration and the challenge of overlapping memberships on trade", *Journal of International Relations and Development*, Vol. 17/4, pp. 522-544, https://link.springer.com/article/10.1057%2Fjird.2013.13.

Christiaensen L. et al. (2018), "Migrants, towns, poverty and jobs: Insights from Tanzania", *Policy Research Working Paper*, No. 8340, World Bank Group, Washington, DC, http://documents.worldbank.org/curated/en/613771518633294230/pdf/WPS8340.pdf.

Christiaensen L., J. De Weerdt and R. Kanbur (2017), "Where to create jobs to reduce poverty: Cities or towns?", *Working Paper C-40300-TZA-1*, International Growth Centre, www.theigc.org/wp-content/uploads/2017/05/Christiaensen-et-al-2017-working-paper.pdf.

Christiaensen, L. and Y. Todo, (2014), "Poverty reduction during the rural-urban transformation: The role of the missing middle", *Policy Research Working Paper*, No. 6445, https://openknowledge.worldbank.org/bitstream/handle/10986/15587/wps6445.pdf.

Climate Policy Initiative (2012), "San Giorgio group case study: Ouarzazate I concentrated solar power – Morocco", report prepared by the Climate Policy Initiative for the San Giorgio Group, https://climatepolicyinitiative.org/publication/san-giorgio-group-case-study-ouarzazate-i-csp/.

Cling, J.-P. et al. (2014), *The Informal Economy in Developing Countries*, Routledge, London/New York.

Coolidge, J. and F. Yilmaz (2014), "Does e-filing reduce tax compliance costs in developing countries?", *Investment Climate in Practice*, No. 21, https://openknowledge.worldbank.org/handle/10986/20428.

Corrigan, T. (2016), "Space, soil and status: Insights from the APRM into the governance of land in Africa", *SAIIA Occasional Paper*, No. 229, South African Institute of International Affairs, Johannesburg, www.saiia.org.za/occasional-papers/1032-space-soil-and-status-insights-from-the-aprm-into-the-governance-of-land-in-africa.

De Melo, J., M. Nouar and J.-M. Solleder (2017), "Integration along the Abuja road map – A progress report", *FERDI Working Paper,* No. 191, www.ferdi.fr/fr/publication/p191-integration-along-abuja-road-map.

Deininger, K. (2003), "Does cost of schooling affect enrollment by the poor? Universal primary education in Uganda", *Economics of Education Review*, Vol. 22/3, pp. 291-305, http://citeseerx.ist.psu.edu/viewdoc/download?doi=10.1.1.629.4081&rep=rep1&type=pdf.

Dihel N. and A.G. Goswami (2016), *The Unexplored Potential of Trade in Services in Africa: From Hair Stylists and Teachers to Accountants and Doctors*, World Bank, Washington, DC, http://hdl.handle.net/10986/24968.

Esiara, K. (2018), "Rwanda bourse rolls out an SME segment", *The East African*, 1 April 2018, www.theeastafrican.co.ke/business/Rwanda-bourse-rolls-out-an-SME-segment/2560-4367674-1sqqf8/index.html.

FAO (2017), *Formalization of Informal Trade in Africa Trends, Experiences and Socio-economic impacts*, Food and Agriculture Organization, Accra, www.fao.org/3/a-i7101e.pdf.

Farole, T. (2016), *Factory Southern Africa?: SACU in Global Value Chains - Summary Report (English)*, World Bank Group, Washington, DC, http://documents.worldbank.org/curated/en/973351468195001238/pdf/102850-WP-P149486-Box394847B-PUBLIC-Factory-Southern-Africa-FINAL-PUBLISH-002.pdf.

Fessehaie, J. (2018), "How can the CFTA help Africa respond to its economic transformation imperative?", *Bridges Africa*, Vol. 7/1, International Centre for Trade and Sustainable Development, Geneva, www.ictsd.org/bridges-news/bridges-africa/news/how-can-the-cfta-help-africa-respond-to-its-economic-transformation.

Frazer, G. (2017), "Examining the impact of the common external tariff of the East African Community in Uganda", *International Growth Centre Policy Paper.*

Gatamah, K. (2002), *Launching Corporate Governance in Africa with an Emphasis on Kenya*, Centre for International Private Enterprise, Washington, DC, www.cipe.org/sites/default/files/publication-docs/gatamah.pdf.

Gelb, A. et al. (2009), "To formalize or not to formalize? Comparisons of microenterprise data from Southern and East Africa", *Center for Global Development Working Paper*, No. 175, Washington, DC, www.cgdev.org/content/publications/detail/1422458.

GIZ (2013), *Support to Land Reform Project in Namibia*, German Federal Ministry for Economic Cooperation and Development (BMZ), www.giz.de/projektdaten/projects.action?request locale=en EN&pn=201322767.

Grogan, L. (2009), "Universal primary education and school entry in Uganda", *Journal of African Economies*, Vol. 18/2, https://doi.org/10.1093/jae/ejn015.

ICA (2017), *Infrastructure Financing Trends in Africa 2016*, Infrastructure Consortium for Africa, Abidjan, www.icafrica.org/fileadmin/documents/IFT 2016/Infrastructure Financing Trends 2016.pdf.

ICTSD (2018), "African leaders prep for summit on continental trade deal", *Bridges Africa*, Vol. 22/4, International Centre for Trade and Sustainable Development, Geneva, www.ictsd.org/bridges-news/bridges/news/african-leaders-prep-for-summit-on-continental-trade-deal.

ILO (2015), *Global Employment Trends for Youth 2015: Scaling Up Investments in Decent Jobs for Youth*, International Labour Office, Geneva, www.ilo.org/wcmsp5/groups/public/---dgreports/---dcomm/---publ/documents/publication/wcms 412015.pdf.

ITC (2016), *Investing in Trade Promotion Generates Revenue - A Study of Trade Promotion Organizations*, International Trade Centre, Geneva, www.intracen.org/uploadedFiles/intracenorg/Content/Publications/160204-Investing%20in%20trade%20promotion low-res.pdf.

Jütting, J. and J. de Laiglesia (2009), *Is Informal Normal?: Towards More and Better Jobs in Developing Countries*, OECD Publishing, Paris, http://dx.doi.org/10.1787/9789264059245-en.

Kappel, R., B. Pfeiffer and H. Reisen (2017), "Compact with Africa: Fostering private long-term investment in Africa", *Discussion paper 13/2017*, German Development Institute (DIE), Bonn, www.die-gdi.de/discussion-paper/article/compact-with-africa-fostering-private-long-term-investment-in-africa/.

Kasita, M. (2011), "Establishing communal land registration in Namibia: The process, benefits and challenges", Annual World Bank Conference on Land and Poverty 2011, Washington, DC, http://siteresources.worldbank.org/INTIE/Resources/475495-1302790806106/EstablishingKasitaPres4.pdf.

Khan, M. (2009), *Governance, Growth and Poverty Reduction*, United Nations Department of Economic and Social Affairs, New York, http://dag.un.org/handle/11176/377014.

Lall S.V., J.V. Henderson and A.J. Venables, (2017), *Africa's Cities: Opening Doors to the World*, World Bank Group, Washington, DC, https://openknowledge.worldbank.org/handle/10986/25896.

Locke, A. and G. Henley (2016), *Urbanisation and Land Property Rights: The Need to Refocus Attention*, Overseas Development Institute, London, www.odi.org/sites/odi.org.uk/files/odi-assets/publications-opinion-files/10309.pdf.

Lopez Gonzalez, J., P. Kowalski and P. Achard (2015), "Trade, global value chains and wage-income inequality", *OECD Trade Policy Papers*, No. 182, OECD Publishing, Paris, http://dx.doi.org/10.1787/5js009mzrqd4-en.

Moriconi-Ebrard, F., D. Harre and P. Heinrigs (2016), *Urbanisation Dynamics in West Africa 1950–2010: Africapolis I, 2015 Update*, West African Studies, OECD Publishing, Paris, http://dx.doi.org/10.1787/9789264252233-en.

Morris, M. and J. Barnes (2006), "Regional development and cluster management: Lessons from South Africa", in *Development on the Ground: Clusters, Networks and Regions in Emerging Economies*, University of Cape Town, pp. 278-298, https://open.uct.ac.za/bitstream/item/22614/ Morris Regional 2006.pdf?sequence=1.

Naudé, W. (2017), "Entrepreneurship, education and the Fourth Industrial Revolution in Africa" *Discussion Paper Series*, No. 108555, Institute of Labor Economics, Bonn, http://ftp.iza.org/dp10855.pdf.

NCTTCA (2017), *Northern Corridor Transport Observatory Report: Trade and Transport Facilitation, 10th* Issue, Northern Corridor Transit and Transport Coordination Authority, http://top.ttcanc.org/download doc.php?docid=150410290402214866.

Nishimura, M. et al., (2009), "A comparative analysis of universal primary education policy in Ghana, Kenya, Malawi and Uganda", *Journal of International Cooperation in Education,* Vol. 12/1, pp. 143-158, http://home.hiroshima-u.ac.jp/cice/wp-content/uploads/2014/03/12-1-10.pdf.

OECD (2018a), *Making Blended Finance Work for the Sustainable Development Goals*, OECD Publishing, Paris, http://dx.doi.org/10.1787/9789264288768-en.

OECD (2018b), *Private Philanthropy for Development*, The Development Dimension, OECD Publishing, Paris, http://dx.doi.org/10.1787/9789264085190-en.

OECD (2018c), *Illicit Financial Flows: The Economy of Illicit Trade in West Africa,* OECD Publishing, Paris, http://dx.doi.org/10.1787/9789264268418-en.

OECD (2018d), "Youth well-being policy review of Malawi", EU-OECD Youth Inclusion Project, Paris, www.oecd.org/dev/inclusivesocietiesanddevelopment/Youth-well-being-policy-review-Malawi.pdf.

OECD (2017a), *Examen multidimensionnel du Maroc: Volume 1. Évaluation initiale*, OECD Development Pathways, OECD Publishing, Paris, http://dx.doi.org/10.1787/9789264274945-fr.

OECD (2017b), *Green Growth Indicators 2017*, OECD Green Growth Studies, OECD Publishing, Paris, http://dx.doi.org/10.1787/9789264268586-en.

OECD (2017c), *Interrelations between Public Policies, Migration and Development*, OECD Publishing, Paris, http://dx.doi.org/10.1787/9789264265615-en.

OECD (2017d), *Social Protection in East Africa: Harnessing the Future*, OECD Publishing, Paris, http://dx.doi.org/10.1787/9789264274228-en.

OECD (2017e), *Preventing Ageing Unequally*, OECD Publishing, Paris, http://dx.doi.org/10.1787/9789264279087-en.

OECD (2016a), *Sub-Saharan SIGI Regional Report*, OECD Publishing, Paris, www.genderindex.org/wp-content/uploads/files/docs/Brochure SIGI SSA web.pdf.

OECD (2016b), *Multi-dimensional Review of Côte d'Ivoire: Volume 3. From Analysis to Action*, OECD Development Pathways, OECD Publishing, Paris, http://dx.doi.org/10.1787/9789264258501-en.

OECD (2015a), *Policy Framework for Investment 2015 Edition,* OECD Publishing, Paris, http://dx.doi.org/10.1787/9789264208667 cn.

OECD (2015b), *Taxation of SMEs in OECD and G20 Countries*, OECD Tax Policy Study, No. 23, OECD Publishing, Paris, http://dx.doi.org/10.1787/9789264243507-en.

OECD (2015c), *OECD Guidelines on Corporate Governance of State-Owned Enterprises, 2015 Edition*, OECD Publishing, Paris, http://dx.doi.org/10.1787/9789264244160-en.

OECD (2013), *Perspectives on Global Development 2013: Industrial Policies in a Changing World*, OECD Publishing, Paris, http://dx.doi.org/10.1787/persp glob dev-2013-en.

OECD/ATAF/AUC (2017), *Revenue Statistics in Africa 2017*, OECD Publishing, Paris, http://dx.doi.org/10.1787/9789264280854-en-fr.

OECD/ILO (2018), *How Immigrants Contribute to Developing Countries' Economies*, International Labour Organization, Geneva, and OECD Publishing, Paris, http://dx.doi.org/10.1787/9789264288737-en.

Oosthuizen, M. et al., (2016), "Informality and inclusive growth in sub-Saharan Africa", *ELLA Regional Evidence Papers*, authored by the Development Policy Research Unit, University of Cape Town, http://bit.ly/REPDpru.

Otiso, K.M. (2005), "Kenya's secondary cities growth strategy at crossroads: Which way forward?" *GeoJournal*, No. 62, pp. 117-128, https://link.springer.com/content/pdf/10.1007%2Fs10708-005-8180-z.pdf.

Quisumbing, R.A. and N.Kumar, (2014), *Land Rights Knowledge and Conservation in Rural Ethiopia, Mind the Gender Gap*, International Food Policy Research Institute, www.gender-gap.net/sites/default/files/documents/ifpridp01386.pdf.

Reisen, H. (2015), "Will the AIIB and the NDB help reform multilateral development banking?", *Global Policy*, Vol. 6/3, pp. 297-304, https://doi.org/10.1111/1758-5899.12250.

Roy, R. (2016), "The cost of air pollution In Africa", *OECD Development Centre Working Paper*, Paris, www.oecd.org/officialdocuments/publicdisplaydocumentpdf/?cote=DEV/DOC/WKP%282016%295&docLanguage=En.

Shimeles A., D.Z. Gurara and F. Woldeyes, (2017), "Taxman's dilemma: Coercion or persuasion? evidence from a randomized field experiment in Ethiopia", *American Economic Review*, Vol. 107/5, pp. 420-424, www.aeaweb.org/articles?id=10.1257/aer.p20171141.

SOE Network for Southern Africa (2014), *Guidelines on the Governance of State-Owned Enterprises for Southern Africa*, OECD-Southern Africa Network on the Governance of State-Owned Enterprises, www.oecd.org/daf/ca/SOE-Guidelines-Southern-Africa.pdf.

SWAC (2016), *Transformations in the Food Economy and Implications for Policy Making*, The Sahel and West Africa Club Secretariat, Abuja, Nigeria, www.oecd.org/swac/topics/handout-transformations-food-economy-ENG.pdf.

TNC (2015), *Upper Tana-Nairobi Water Fund Business Case. Version 2*, The Nature Conservancy, Nairobi, www.nature.org/ourinitiatives/regions/africa/upper-tana-nairobi-water-fund-business-case.pdf.

UN-Habitat (2013), *Streets as Public Spaces and Drivers of Urban Prosperity*, UN-Habitat, Nairobi, https://unhabitat.org/books/streets-as-public-spaces-and-drivers-of-urban-prosperity/.

UNCTAD (2018), *African Continental Free Trade Area: Challenges and Opportunities of Tariff Reductions*, United Nations Conference on Trade and Development, Geneva, http://unctad.org/en/PublicationsLibrary/ser-rp-2017d15_en.pdf.

UNCTAD (2015), *Economic Development in Africa Report 2015: Unlocking the Potential of Africa's Services Trade for Growth and Development*, United Nations Conference on Trade and Development, Geneva, http://unctad.org/en/PublicationsLibrary/aldcafrica2015_en.pdf.

UNCTAD (2014), *Economic Development in Africa: Catalysing Investment for Transformative Growth in Africa*, United Nations Conference on Trade and Development, http://unctad.org/meetings/en/SessionalDocuments/tdb61d4_en.pdf.

UNDP (2014), *Inclusive Green Growth in Africa: Rationale, Challenges and Opportunities*, United Nations Development Programme, South Africa, www.za.undp.org/content/dam/south_africa/docs/mdgs/Inclusive%20Green%20Growth%20in%20Africa-Rationale%20Challenges%20and%20Opportunities1.pdf.

UNECA (2016a), *Greening Africa's Industrialisation, Economic Report on Africa*, United Nations Economic Commission for Africa, Addis Ababa, www.uneca.org/publications/economic-report-africa-2016.

UNECA (2016b), *Africa's Blue Economy: A Policy Handbook*, United Nations Economic Commission for Africa, Addis Ababa, www.uneca.org/sites/default/files/PublicationFiles/blueeco-policy-handbook_en.pdf.

UNEP (2015), *Green Economy: Building Inclusive Green Economies in Africa, Experience and Lessons Learned 2010-2015*, United Nations Environment Programme, www.greengrowthknowledge.org/sites/default/files/downloads/resource/Building_Inclusive_Green_Economies_In_Africa_UNEP.pdf.

UNESCO (2015a), *Children out-of-School, or in School but Still Not Learning?*, United Nations Educational, Scientific and Cultural Organisation, Paris, http://uis.unesco.org/sites/default/files/documents/children-out-of-school-or-in-school-but-still-not-learning-en.pdf.

UNESCO (2015b), *Gender and EFA 2000-2015: Achievements and Challenges*, United Nations Educational, Scientific and Cultural Organisation, Paris, http://unesdoc.unesco.org/images/0023/002348/234809E.pdf.

UNIDO (2013), *Africa Investor Report 2013-Executive Summary*, United Nations Industrial Development Organization, Vienna, www.unido.org/sites/default/files/2014-09/Executive_Summary_AIS_2013_Report_xiamen_2014_0.pdf.

VanFleet J.W. (2012), *Africa Learning Barometer*, Centre for Universal Education, Brookings Institution, https://www.brookings.edu/wp-content/uploads/2012/09/Africa-Learning-BarometerFINAL.pdf.

World Bank (2018), *The State of Social Safety Nets 2018*, World Bank, Washington, DC, https://openknowledge.worldbank.org/bitstream/handle/10986/29115/9781464812545.pdf?sequence=5&isAllowed=y.

World Bank (2014), Human Capital for Agriculture in Africa, World Bank, Washington, DC, http://documents.worldbank.org/curated/en/685101468009998164/Human-capital-for-agriculture-in-Africa.

World Bank/Elsevier (2014), *A Decade of Development in sub-Saharan African Science, Technology, Engineering & Mathematics Research*, World Bank, Washington, DC, http://documents.worldbank.org/curated/en/237371468204551128/pdf/910160WP0P126900disclose09026020140.pdf.

Statistical annex

Data used in this first edition of *Africa's Development Dynamics* has been compiled and presented in tables on the Development Centre's website (www.oecd.org/development/africa-s-development-dynamics-2018-9789264302501-en.htm) along with some additional social and economic indicators that add context to the report's analysis. Figures are presented on a national basis for African countries for which data is available. The following are the names of the tables available for download in Excel format:

Table 1	Indicators of growth, employment and inequality	Table 10	Export diversification
Table 2	Annual GDP growth	Table 11	Global and regional trade
Table 3	Sectoral breakdown of the economy	Table 12	External financial inflows
Table 4	Growth decomposition by expenditure	Table 13	Population projections
Table 5	Public finances	Table 14	Subjective well-being
Table 6	Indicators of inequality and poverty	Table 15	Basic health indicators
Table 7	Gender indicators	Table 16	Basic education indicators
Table 8	Labour force characteristics	Table 17	Infrastructure
Table 9	Trade by manufacturing intensity	Table 18	Ecological sustainability

In addition to country-level data, statistics are used to calculate aggregates for the following groups:

- The five African Union regions (as defined by the Abuja Treaty)
- Africa, Asia, Latin America and Caribbean, and the World
- **Resource-rich countries**
  Countries that obtain a significant fraction of their GDP from underground natural-resource extraction are referred to as "resource-rich". These resource endowments can have major implications for economic, political, and social development. Countries defined as resource-rich in this report were identified as those for whom over 10% of GDP came from underground natural resources for at least 5 of the previous 10 years.
- **Income level**
  The World Bank divides the countries of the world into four categories based on GNI per capita in 2016, using their Atlas Method:[1] low-income countries, lower middle-income countries, upper middle-income countries, and high-income countries.
- **Geographic access**
  The report provides a breakdown between countries that are landlocked, countries that have a portion of coastline, and island nations. Gaining access to world trade can be complicated by a country's access to the ocean or lack thereof, while island nations have been shown to have different development patterns than other coastal nations. In addition to this three way breakdown of countries, this report provides data on countries deemed "Landlocked Developing Countries (LLDC)" and "Small Island Developing States (SIDS)" by the UN Office of the High Representative for the Least Developed Countries, Landlocked Developing Countries and Small Island Developing States (UN-OHRLLS).[2]
- **Least Developed Countries**[3]
  In addition to defining countries as LLDC and SIDS, the UN-OHRLLS also classifies some countries as "Least Developed Countries (LDC)" as of 1 July 2018. This categorisation of countries was officially established in 1971, by the UN General Assembly, and represents countries that face low levels of socio-economic

development.CountriesaredesignatedasLDCcountriesbasedonincomecriteria, thehealthandeducationoftheirpopulations,andtheireconomicvulnerability.

Thesetablespresentthemostrecentyearofdata,butacompletedatasetcontaining datagoingbackasfaras2000isalsoavailablefordownload.

Notes

1. Please see http://datahelpdesk.worldbank.org/knowledgebase/articles/378832-what-is-the-world-bank-atlas-method.
2. Pleaseseehttp://unohrlls.orgformoreinformation.
3. Pleaseseehttp://unohrlls.org/about-ldcs/criteria-for-ldcs/.

African Union Commission, PO Box 3243, Roosevelt Street (Old Airport Area), W21K19, Addis Ababa, Ethiopia
ISBN 978-92-95104-14-3
OECD PUBLISHING, 2, rue André-Pascal, 75775 PARIS CEDEX 16
(41 2018 22 1 P) ISBN 978-92-64-30249-5 – 2018

www.ingramcontent.com/pod-product-compliance
Ingram Content Group UK Ltd.
Pitfield, Milton Keynes, MK11 3LW, UK
UKHW051459290926
15471UKWH00008B/1302